The History of the Riverside Church
in the City of New York

RELIGION, RACE, AND ETHNICITY
General Editor: Peter J. Paris

THE HISTORY OF THE
Riverside Church
IN THE CITY OF NEW YORK

*Peter J. Paris, John Wesley Cook, James Hudnut-Beumler,
Lawrence H. Mamiya, Leonora Tubbs Tisdale,
and Judith Weisenfeld*

WITH A FOREWORD BY

Martin E. Marty

New York University Press

NEW YORK AND LONDON

NEW YORK UNIVERSITY PRESS
New York and London
www.nyupress.org

Library of Congress Cataloging-in-Publication Data
The history of the Riverside Church in the city of New York /
Peter J. Paris . . . [et al.].
p. cm. — (Religion, race, and ethnicity)
Includes bibliographical references and index.
ISBN 0–8147–6713–3 (cloth : alk. paper)
1. Riverside Church (New York, N.Y.)—History.   2. New York (N.Y.)—
Church history.   I. Paris, Peter J., 1933–   II. Series.
BX6480.N5H57   2004
280'.4'097471—dc22   2003022055

New York University Press books are printed on acid-free paper,
and their binding materials are chosen for strength and durability.

Manufactured in the United States of America
10 9 8 7 6 5 4 3 2 1

Contents

A Time Line

1925   Harry Emerson Fosdick becomes pastor of Park Avenue
Baptist Church.

1927   The cornerstone is laid for a new church building on
Riverside Drive.

1928   Fire destroys Riverside's Tower.

1930   First service is held at Riverside in September.

1931   The Riverside Church is dedicated in February.

1946   Dr. Harry Emerson Fosdick retires.

1947   Dr. Robert James McCracken is called to be the senior minister.

1956   The Church Council is formed.

1959   The South Wing is dedicated.
Rev. Pablo Cotto is appointed to lead the "Hispano" ministry.
Rev. Robert Polk, Riverside's first African American minister,
is appointed.
Riverside begins broadcasting on its FM radio station, WRVR.
Riverside hosts the dedication of the Interchurch Center.
Rev. Phyllis Taylor becomes the first woman ordained at Riverside.

1960   Dr. Martin Luther King Jr. preaches for the first time at Riverside.

1961   Stone Gymnasium is dedicated.

1962   WRVR broadcasts a series of six documentary programs on the
civil rights struggle in Birmingham, Alabama.

1967   Dr. Martin Luther King Jr. delivers his anti–Vietnam War speech.
Rev. Carl Flemister is the first African American minister to be
elected to board of deacons.
Dr. McCracken retires.

1968   Rev. Cynthia Wedel becomes the first woman to preach in
      the nave.
      Dr. Ernest T. Campbell is called to be Riverside's senior minister.

1969   A memorial service is held for Dr. Fosdick.
      The Black Christian Caucus is organized.
      James Forman interrupts the communion service to deliver his
      Black Manifesto.

1970   The Riverside Fund for Social Justice is established.

1973   A vigil for those who died in the Vietnam War is held.

1975   Rev. Evelyn Neuman becomes the first woman appointed to
      the collegium.

1976   Dr. Campbell resigns.
      The church sells the WRVR radio station.
      Rev. Jitsuo Morikawa is called to be the interim senior minister.

1977   Dr. William Sloane Coffin Jr. is called to be the senior minister.

1978   The first in a series of disarmament conferences is held.
      Maranatha is approved as an official organization.

1981   Riverside Church celebrates its fiftieth anniversary.

1985   Riverside adopts its Statement of Affirmation of Gays
      and Lesbians.

1987   Dr. Coffin resigns.

      Rev. George Hill is called to be the interim senior minister.

1989   Dr. James A. Forbes Jr. is installed as Riverside's first African
      American senior minister.

1990   Riverside hosts a welcoming celebration service for
      Nelson Mandela.

1991   A unicameral governance system is established.
      Dr. Forbes welcomes James Forman back to Riverside.

1998   The "Space for Grace" begins.

2000   The Jubilee Fund is established.

2002   The "Americans in Healing Service" is held on September 16.

Foreword

Martin E. Marty

A book on modern Italian church architecture assembled after the post–World War II building boom includes an image that informs our understanding of the Riverside Church and serves as an entering point to this book.

On one page are schematic drawings, in the proper scale, showing how medieval cathedrals towered over the one- and two-story huts and shops of French villages.

Next to them is a drawing of St. Patrick's Cathedral in New York City, rendered on the same scale, which matches the French cathedrals in height.

On the opposite page, the authors and editors show what happens in the modern metropolis in the era of skyscrapers, using an aerial photo of St. Patrick's, taken in such a way that all of Rockefeller Center and the other tall buildings surround and dwarf it, or at least put it into context.

A caption, badly translated, describes what occurred: In a modern city, a sacred place cannot tower over the temples of commerce. This means that the church must have a reference that is more "substantive" than "dimensional."

In the case of Riverside Church, there is less reason to hurry past the dimensional indicators than there is with respect to St. Patrick's. It still towers. The pioneers and planners knew what they were doing by placing it on Morningside Heights, where it is a landmark visible for many miles. One of the chapters in this book details the decisions that went into placing and making this neo-Gothic cathedral. The church building creates awe among those who come to worship or to sightsee, even as it casts long shadows over the Heights and does more than almost any other building to suggest that New York City has a churchscape.

All the other chapters in this book deal with the "substantive" aspects of Riverside Church, although the authors insist that the two do not contradict but complement each other. As a product of modern Protestantism, interior architecture could be captured in a phrase by Le Corbusier: it was and is to be a "machine for preaching." Riverside trusts the word and words and marks the epochs of its history by the comings and goings of the people who serve as preachers, and their guests.

How does neo-Gothic work as a machine for preaching? As once a preacher there and often a speaker in another Rockefeller-endowed place of worship, the Rockefeller Chapel at the University of Chicago, and having endured hours of rehearsal with mikes and sound systems and minutes of coaching about the pace and tone of preaching, I sometimes agree with Peter Taylor Forsyth. He said that Gothic architecture was an invention of the devil to keep people from hearing the gospel.

Hearing the gospel, however, has continued, and those who make up the congregation at Riverside bring high expectations that, through the years, have been met more often than not. (Riverside is a *very* easy church and congregation from which to walk away; it knows little about the boundaries of fundamentalism, the nemesis of its first pastor, Harry Emerson Fosdick.)

At certain times during Riverside Church's life, some half-generations of people have mistrusted or downgraded the spoken word. Occasionally Riverside has been dismissed as "touchy-feely" or favored by those who speak of communication "beyond words." Yet Riverside's leaders have noted that all the major movements of our time—civil rights, the search for racial equality, sexual revolutions, feminism, the environmental movement, protests against war—have been inspired by skillful rhetoricians.

At the same time, as this book makes clear, much of Riverside's substance does go "beyond words." As St. Francis commanded: "Preach the gospel. Use words if necessary." The awe of the nave inspires preachers, as does the music so well chronicled here. Most of all, the "social activism"— or, more simply, the "social action" of its leaders and congregations—tells New York and the nation that Riverside relates substantively. Trying to keep track of all the efforts at outreach undertaken by Riverside and described in this book is not easy.

Those of us who have occasionally visited and always kept an eye on Riverside see it as exemplary, an example, or, in medieval Latin terms, an *exemplum*. A medieval dictionary reminds us that an *exemplum* (*eximere*, to "cut out") may be a "clearing in the woods." The mobile, ever changing, cultural and social scene in a metropolis and our nation looks for and is moved by such *exempla*.

A clearing in the woods does three things. First, it defines where the woods ends and something else starts. Second, the clearing is where the light falls. Third, it is where cultivation takes place. It may seem strange to speak of Riverside Church, on its almost treeless heights, as a "clearing in the woods." But the chapters in this book reveal it and its people as definers of fundamentalism versus modernism, conservatism versus liberalism, closedness versus openness, and exclusivism versus expansiveness. On all these occasions, the users of words and the doers of deeds illuminate those places where most of us have been stumbling in dark woods. In regard to cultivation: simply read on, particularly those chapters on the church's public role.

Great cathedral-like buildings have facades, and facades cover up all kinds of things. But the Riverside Church is secure enough to invite historians to go behind the facade and uncover the stories behind the stories. Now and then conflicts there became national news: the May 4, 1969, incident with the Black Manifesto is an example. That the old Men's Club had become a fossilized version of the initiating and support group from the founders' era was no secret, but the degree of infighting there will be news to readers. Similarly, conflicts among head pastors and executives, board members and staffers, must be revealed.

From our earliest glimpses of congregations, those addressed in the letters of the apostle Paul, Christians have had a harder time getting along with one another than in grasping what the gospel is supposed to mean and do. But most congregations' fights occur in highly creedal groups, in which definitions are sharp, light and darkness are in bold contrast, and two or more sets of people have a book that in their minds puts borders around the cultivation.

But Riverside Church has had none of that. Leader after leader has been bemused, bewildered, and sometimes defeated by the task of discerning what the polity was, who had the power, and how the elements fit together. Sometimes it must have looked like an athletic field with no nets and no boundaries. At many times, the god Proteus, who could take any shape he wished, could almost have been the icon for Riverside Church.

Even so, Riverside Church has endured, thrived, responded to and inaugurated changes, adapted, adjusted, anticipated, written new scenarios, attracted new groups of people, and turned out to be exemplary also for places with a smaller endowment, less fiscal strain at cutback time, less famous preachers, and less daunting human and social environments.

When he was cardinal of Krakow, Pope John Paul II wrote that the church has a special interiority and a specific openness. It is easier to find that interiority in Eastern Orthodoxy than in liberal Protestantism. When Bill Coffin preached the Bible straight—a very dangerous thing to do—some members thought he was too traditional. When Jim Forbes uses his Pentecostal background and fire to address people hungry for "spirituality" and get right to the soul, some people wonder what all this will do to social activism. The answer: it fires activity.

To describe how this interiority works, as it has for Howard Thurman and Dorothy Day and so many more, I always reach back to the French Catholic socialist and journalist of a century ago, Charles Pegúy, who asserted: "Everything begins in mysticism and ends in politics."

Riverside's mysticism—embodied in many circles of prayer, dances, retreats, and individual seeking—is not ordinary mystical mysticism, but it brings action. Moreover, Riverside's politics is not confined to Democratic versus Republican versus liberal or socialist or libertarian—well, maybe leave out libertarian—but it contains everything that goes by the name of the *polis*, the human city and its needs. Those who act in the city without attending to soul and spirit and heart tend to be Sunday soldiers who disappear as the figurative week goes on. Those who are mystical in the ways of those who abandon the world may be serving God in their own way, but often they are serving only their own aesthetic and psychological interests. Such interests are fine, many Riverside leaders of worship would say, but to what do they connect?

Riverside, the *exemplum*, that strong yet fragile place, the towerer that in the end does not dominate but tries to serve "from below," is revealed as a place of paradoxes in the stories in this book. For those moved by biblical faith, this means what Riverside intends to do and, at its best, achieves and squares with, or at least deserves to be measured by, the biblical stories of very human prophets who are transparent to the divine and a divine-human child of God and his sisters and brothers in the *polis* we call New York, America, the world, in a new millennium.

Acknowledgments

As the authors of this book, we wish to acknowledge our indebtedness to all those who willingly rendered their services to us in producing this work. First, we wish to thank Riverside Church's senior pastor, the Rev. Dr. James A. Forbes, Jr., for his enthusiastic support throughout the process.

The idea for this project emerged from conversations between Dr. Forbes and his beloved friend and colleague, the late Professor James Melvin Washington of Union Theological Seminary. Sadly, Professor Washington's life ended before their dream was realized.

We also are grateful for the encouragement and support of the Riverside History Project Committee and especially its members, Ruth Britton, Richard Butler, Betty Davis, Robert O'Meally, Dr. Katherine Wilcox, and George Younger (who died before the project was completed). Special thanks also go to Dr. William B. Kennedy, who read drafts of our chapters and spent a day with us giving very helpful suggestions. Most important, we deeply appreciate the admirable work of Dr. Sheila Gillams, who, as project director, provided for all our administrative needs.

In addition to Dr. Forbes, we are grateful for the pleasure and insights gained from interviews with former senior ministers Drs. William Sloane Coffin and Ernest T. Campbell, as well as very informative conversations with Drs. Eugene Laubach and Paul Sherry. Our appreciation is extended to the following for granting interviews: Susan Blaine, Rev. Keith Boyer, Rev. Mariah Britton, Pee Wee Dance of the Rap Writers Workshop, Rev. Kanyere Eaton, Rev. Fanny Erickson, Ernie Lorch, Jewel Miguel, Martha Rolon, Corinne O. Nelson, Rev. Sally Norris, Tinoa Rodgers, Heru Shango, Elza Sharpe, Jeffrey Slade, Dr. Timothy Smith, Dr. Brenda Stiers, Rev. Bernahu Wedneh of the Ethiopian Orthodox Tewahedo Church of Our Savior, and Heyward Wong of the Chinese Christian Fellowship.

Since most of our research was done at the archives of the Riverside Church, we are most indebted to the excellent archival knowledge, skills, and commitment of Mr. Victor Jordan, whose dedicated helpfulness was greater than words can express. The Riverside Church has a precious treasure in his full-time voluntary work. Early in the project we were well assisted by the excellent work of the church's then part-time archivist, Tanya Elder. In addition, the editor of this book wishes to thank his research assistant, Christopher S. G. Rogers, for his helpful work in the archives and the Social Ethics Seminar for its critical review of his chapter.

Finally, we deeply appreciate the interest and encouragement we have received from the editors at New York University Press: Eric Zinner, Jennifer Hammer, Nicholas Taylor, and Despina Papazoglou Gimbel. Also, special thanks go to Margaret B. Yamashita for her excellent work in copyediting this book.

Introduction

Peter J. Paris

The Riverside Church is often thought of as a Protestant cathedral, a national institution, a megachurch, and a multicultural congregation that continues to nurture a distinctively liberal theological tradition. Housed in a magnificent building on the Upper West Side of New York City, this church has consistently proclaimed a gospel that is both prophetic and pastoral. The former has been enabled by the church's resolve to give the senior minister complete freedom to preach as he sees fit. The church's pastoral ministry has been supported by well-trained personnel and relevant programs.

The Riverside Church is the world's most prominent institutionalization of Protestant liberalism. Most important, it is a church that was built in the midst of the fundamentalist-modernist debate over the infallible inspiration of the Bible, a debate that engulfed the Protestant churches from the early 1920s until the present day. This church emerged out of the mutual vision of John D. Rockefeller Jr. and Harry Emerson Fosdick, a collaborative venture between one of America's greatest philanthropists and its most renowned liberal preacher.

For more than seven decades, the Riverside Church has developed a progressive ministry to the universities, colleges, and racial/ethnic communities in the Morningside Heights area of New York City. In its early years, the church concentrated on developing an effective campus ministry to the neighborhood's academic institutions. Later, in response to the demographical changes in the area that were intensified by the turbulent events of the 1960s, Riverside turned more of its attention to the area's racial and ethnic issues.

Riverside Church's magnificent architecture, sizable endowment, liberal theology, progressive thought, exceptional preaching, and courageous practices have marked its uniqueness and importance from the beginning of its history to the present day. In deference to its founders, all succeeding generations of members have envisioned the Riverside Church as the premier model of Protestant liberalism in the United States. The chapter by James Hudnut-Beumler in this book is a historical analysis of this church's place in the history of Protestant liberalism. Similarly, the other authors describe how the church's traditions have changed over the years.

This church's self-understanding has always been guided by its efforts to institutionalize a liberal form of Protestantism that would not be limited by the dictates of doctrine, race, or denominational loyalty. Accordingly, the Riverside Church publicly declared itself to be "interdenominational, international, and interracial" and immediately began to introduce those aims in the formation and expansion of alliances and partnerships across denominational and racial lines. In its endeavor to become genuinely interdenominational, Riverside has welcomed new members from a variety of denominations by allowing them to retain their membership in their previous denominations. In addition, the church has made several attempts to form official alliances with a number of denominations. These efforts, however, succeeded only with the American Baptist Convention and the United Church of Christ. Nonetheless, Riverside's interdenominational character, coupled with its vigorous opposition to biblical fundamentalism, soon established its place in the vanguard of Protestant liberalism.

Although Riverside's liberal beliefs concerning membership, theology, and the Bible were prominent at the beginning of its history, issues of church governance, racial equality, and sexual inclusiveness eventually caused considerable internal conflict and trauma beginning in the late 1960s. It is interesting that in each of these congregational conflicts, the church grounded its moral and theological arguments in the liberal tradition that it has always embraced. Foremost among the marks of that tradition are freedom of thought and expression, as well as the inclusiveness of all peoples regardless of belief, race, or national origin.

Although this church has always embraced the principle of racial inclusiveness, sizable numbers of African Americans, Hispanics, and others did not begin joining the church until the late 1960s. The chapters in this book by Judith Weisenfeld, Lawrence Mamiya, and Peter Paris identify and discuss some of the dilemmas and contradictions between the church's tolerant spirit and its internal practices. For the most part, the congregation has tried to resolve conflicts through study, discussion, debate, position papers, prayer, and meditation.

As several of the chapters in this book attest, Riverside's liberal tradition has always promoted a spirit of toleration that has permeated the church's life and mission and, most important, is reflected in the changes in the current composition of the congregation. All the senior ministers then and now have affirmed this principle of toleration with respect to theological understandings and beliefs while advocating social justice for racial and ethnic minorities. In fact, the steadily changing racial and ethnic diversity of the church's present membership reflects its institutional practice catching up with its public rhetoric.

In the 1920s, the church's aim to be interdenominational, interracial, and international was augmented in the second half of the twentieth century by various social and theological movements demanding equal rights for African Americans, women, Native and ethnic Americans, and gays, lesbians, and bisexuals. Although the church's teaching on some of these issues was in the forefront of popular opinion, concerned constituencies among some of the church's diverse groups often highlighted various ambiguities in the church's practices which, in turn, specified certain injustices in its midst.

That the Riverside Church has been viewed widely as a public space open to all the peoples of the city has been made evident in many and various ways. For example, most people in the city and elsewhere assume that this church is the proper place to host major public celebratory events, and the following dignitaries have been honored at the church: Fidel Castro, Daniel Ortega, Olaf Palme, Archbishop Desmond Tutu, Martin Luther King Jr., Oliver Tambo, Nelson Mandela, and Coretta Scott King, to mention only a few. Furthermore, no one was surprised to learn that in the aftermath of the September 11, 2001, terrorist attack on the World Trade Center and the Pentagon, the Public Broadcasting Corporation decided to film a documentary entitled "America in Healing at the Riverside Church." It was a special service of mourning in which Christian, Jewish, Muslim, and Buddhist clergy and laity united in proclaiming messages of comfort and hope to a grieving city. An overflow audience of thousands witnessed this memorable interreligious event.

The Riverside Church's superb architecture and outstanding preaching have always been its two most prominent visible features and were viewed by its chief benefactor as a fitting contribution to the glorification of God. John Wesley Cook and Leonora Tubbs Tisdale analyze and assess the meaning, relevance, and impact of the church's architectural achievement and its practice of preaching.

The true meaning of the church's life and mission is in neither the grandeur of its aesthetic form nor the eloquence of its preaching alone but in the substance of its combined activities, as set forth in its 1992 mission statement: "To serve God through word and witness; by treating all human beings as sisters and brothers; and by fostering responsible stewardship of all God's creation." More specifically, this same mission statement embraces the church's present tradition of Protestant liberalism by affirming the following:

> The Riverside Church commits itself to welcoming all persons, celebrating the diversity found in a congregation broadly inclusive of persons from different backgrounds of race, religion, culture, ethnicity, gender, age and sexual orientation. Members are called to a spiritual quality of life individually and collectively and to personal and social transformation that witness to God's saving purposes for all creation. Therefore, the Riverside Church pledges itself to action, reflection and education for peace and justice, the realization of the vision of the heavenly banquet where all are loved and blessed.

This mission statement represents the consensus of the congregation concerning its ongoing life and mission. The church's capacity to change its structure, programs, and membership while maintaining its identity is commensurate with its liberal ethos of openness and inclusiveness of all peoples in the city, the nation, and the world at large.

Methods and Procedures Used in This Book

In the area of religion, this book belongs to the nascent genre of congregational studies, a field that is rapidly gaining ascendancy in contemporary church scholarship. Because congregations are complex, it is fitting that this book is both interdisciplinary and collaborative.

In 1996 the Riverside Historical Committee proposed that a group of scholars be authorized to write a critical history of the church as it approached its diamond jubilee anniversary. The committee's objectives were as follows: "to chronicle significant moments in the life of the congregation, to investigate and interpret Riverside's cultural impact as a leading liberal Protestant institution, and to provide scholars and church people with introspective examinations of the shifting fortunes of religious progressivism in the twentieth century."[1] Clearly, the historical committee hoped that this history would help the church set its goals for the opening decade of the twenty-first century. "Through this project, we seek to reexamine the Riverside experience and present members and scholars alike with perspectives on the intersections of theology, wealth, race, and politics in this and other mainline congregations."[2]

After accepting the invitation to serve as the senior editor of this project and after consulting with the Historical Committee, I assembled a team of religious scholars. Each had demonstrated that he or she had the knowledge, skills, and experience needed for the successful completion of this project. Most important, each one readily accepted the challenge to work with the others for three years exploring the church's archives, interviewing persons, submitting progress reports twice a year to both one another and the Historical Committee, and preparing the chapters for this book.

We all accepted that we had to learn the church's history from the time its cornerstone was laid in 1927 until today. As time went on, we gradually became familiar enough with the church's history that we were able to engage one another intelligibly and critically on the broad range of subjects that comprises this book. Such an approach enabled each of our academic perspectives to be enriched by those of our colleagues, and we hope that our readers will discern our collegiality in the cross-referencing of the chapters.

In sum, this book demonstrates how different methodological perspectives can be used to enhance the quality of the entire story. After we had written drafts of our chapters, we exchanged them with one another for a critical review, to detect any misperceptions, redundancies, and oversights. Of course, we addressed each of them.

Many helpful suggestions were made by William B. Kennedy, professor emeritus at Union Theological Seminary and an adviser to this project, who read the chapters and met for a day with the authors.

One problem with a collaborative work like this is losing internal coherence, which each of us tried to avoid. Thus, we agreed that each chapter in this book should be able to be read both independently of the others and together with them as a part of a larger whole. Each chapter offers one perspective of the common subject matter, namely, the Riverside Church. I also should note that none of the chapters contradicts any of the others.

Rather, like a patched quilt, each harmonizes with the whole and therein is found the richness of the project.

New challenges continue to confront this progressive church in the heart of the nation's most spectacular city: the challenge of preserving its openness to other peoples and their cultures despite the numerical dominance of one particular racial or ethnic group in its membership; the challenge of attracting and retaining larger numbers of young people; the challenge of bringing justice and empowerment to the poor of the city, nation, and world; and the challenge of enabling conflicting spiritualities to thrive in a public church that has long been committed to being international, interracial, and interdenominational.

NOTES

1. See "A Proposal for a Research Project at the Riverside Church in the City of New York," 1.

2. Ibid., 2.

The Riverside Church and the Development of Twentieth-Century American Protestantism

James Hudnut-Beumler

We could tell the story of modern American Protestantism through the lens of the Riverside Church, for few of its major themes have not been manifested in the life of this one church. In fact, Riverside has not been merely a reflector of these larger events. Rather, it often has had a leading hand in crafting the way that liberal American Protestants thought, worshiped, and responded to their times. Riverside was founded in 1930 by John D. Rockefeller Jr., the greatest philanthropist of his age, and members of the Park Avenue Baptist Church as a preaching venue for Riverside's first senior minister, Harry Emerson Fosdick, for many years the best-known minister in the United States. The succession of senior ministers through the rest of the century—Robert J. McCracken, Ernest T. Campbell, William Sloane Coffin Jr., and James A. Forbes Jr.—has maintained the church's reputation as a place to hear great preaching. At the same time, innovations in education and public witness have made Riverside beyond the pulpit a leading institution in American Protestantism. Even Protestantism itself changed dramatically over the twentieth century, with three major themes emerging from viewing the Riverside and liberal Protestant stories in tandem: theological modernism and the Riverside theology, the goal of revising the Christian tradition, and the difficulty of living up to the church's ideals.

Theological Modernism and the Riverside Theology

If Harry Emerson Fosdick and John D. Rockefeller had neither lived nor met, the Riverside Church would never have been built, for the church was a product of the passions of these two men and the people who respected and followed them. To a remarkable degree, their collective vision represented the religious spirit of the age. The Riverside Church began at the peak of what William Hutchison called the "modernist impulse" in American Protestantism.[1] Although they were born into different circumstances— Fosdick was the son of a high-school teacher, and Rockefeller was the son of one of Cleveland's most successful businessmen—they had much in common. Both their families were from the Western Reserve, the region stretching along Lake Erie through western New York to northern Ohio, a flat and fertile region deeply marked by the Second Great Awakening.[2]

Both Rockefeller and Fosdick were the products of homes in which the Bible was the most important—though not the only—book. For both, prayer and religious reflection were regular parts of their daily activities. For Fosdick, religion was both omnipresent and oppressive:

> I was a sensitive boy, deeply religious, and, as I see it now, morbidly consci-
> entious, and the effect upon me of hell-fire-and-brimstone preaching was
> deplorable. I vividly recall weeping at night for fear [of] going to hell, with
> my mystified and baffled mother trying to comfort me. Once, when I was
> nine years old, my father found me so pale that he thought me ill. The fact
> was that I was in agony for fear I had committed the unpardonable Sin, and
> reading that day in the book of Revelation about the horrors of hell, I was
> sick with terror.[3]

Rockefeller remembered his upbringing in religious terms as well. On Friday nights the Rockefeller family held prayer meetings, and at an early age, each was encouraged "to take part like the older people, either in a brief word of prayer or word of personal experience."[4] Biographer Ron Chernow described Sundays with the Rockefellers:

> Sunday was a heavily regimented day, starting with the morning prayers
> and Sunday school then proceeding through an afternoon prayer meeting
> and culminating with evening hymns. If the children had spare time, they
> couldn't read novels or worldly literature but had to restrict themselves to

the Bible and Sunday-school literature. Laura Spelman Rockefeller, in the end was the more conservative of the two parents and led her children in hour-long "home talks," in which she asked each child to choose a "beset-ting sin," and then prayed with that child to the Lord, "asking for guidance and help in combating the sin."[5]

Like countless other late Victorian evangelicals, Fosdick and Rockefeller each carried parts of the old piety with them for the rest of their lives. Nei-ther man drank or smoked. Their respective moves toward a greater open-ness to the world were the product of personal experience but, even more, the outcome of a sweeping turn-of-the-century movement to modernize the Christian faith for a new age.

Theological Modernism

The Protestant modernism that emerged in the late nineteenth century was the complex development of the Enlightenment's impact over more than a century. A key turning point away from the sin-obsessed Protes-tantism that characterized the Fosdick and Rockefeller households was Congregationalist minister Horace Bushnell's insistence in the mid-nine-teenth century that nurture was as important a route to faith and salvation as a radical conversion experience was. Bushnell developed several of the themes that dominated the turn-of-the-century mainstream Protestant mind. He argued for the eminence of God, the importance of continued experiences of growth as a Christian, the need for received doctrines to be updated to speak to contemporary understandings, and the poetic—as opposed to literal—nature of religious language.

After the Civil War, Charles Darwin's evolutionary theory and the find-ings of geologists and paleontologists began to challenge traditional or-thodox understandings of the history of creation and the place of humans within it. Meanwhile, the rapid rise of industrialization after the war, cou-pled with immigration and repeated economic panics and depressions, left some religious leaders wondering how following Jesus could be squared with the squalor of the burgeoning American cities. The development of the telegraph, telephone, artificial light, railroads, and steamships brought progress along with the industrial and mining injuries and the dehuman-izing aspects of female and child employment. It was only too obvious to religious leaders that the old pietism was not sufficient. Indeed, late-nine-teenth-century religious thinkers coined a new term, *social sin*, to describe the evil they experienced. To them, sin was not just the result of individual rejections of the ways of God but something more, the wholesale system of institutions and behaviors at odds with the ways of God. Out of this basic mismatch of modern urban social organization and existing forms of Christian discipleship was born the Social Gospel.

At the same time, what the scientific method did for biology and geology, opening them to new critical insights, it also did for the study of ancient texts and peoples. By the end of the century, biblical scholars were establishing textual variants for biblical passages and, by juxtaposing biblical claims and historically verifiable facts, were calling into question simple and literal readings of the Bible. Through the seminaries and church-sponsored colleges that made up most of American higher education at the time, they exposed would-be ministers and others to their findings. Most of the scholars and ministers who encountered these teachings assimilated them into their personal faith, and it was this accommodation of Christian faith to modern science that made them modernists. A significantly large group of ministers and theologians preferred not, however, to accept modern beliefs when they conflicted with the received tradition of the Christian faith. That is, Protestant modernism stood for the high doctrine of human beings' spirit and capability for the good and intellectual achievement. Modernism also endorsed a highly immanent God, and sin became a soluble problem, not an irrecoverable state. Consequently, modernism generated much talk about the rights of individuals and the value of human progress toward the end of an earthly kingdom of God. Those who opposed modernism argued that with its emphasis on human goodness and social perfectibility, belief in humanity had replaced God as the first article in the creed, for Christian affirmations of faith had always begun with one variation or another of the words "I believe in God the Father Almighty."

Both Rockefeller and Fosdick were modernists in regard to the pivotal place of belief in humanity. On July 8, 1941, in a radio broadcast appeal on behalf of the USO and the National War Fund, Rockefeller gave a statement of his own principles, which was widely reprinted under the title "I Believe":

> I believe in the supreme worth of the individual and in his right to life, liberty, and the pursuit of happiness.
>
> I believe that every right implies a responsibility; every opportunity, an obligation; every possession, a duty.

I believe that the law was made for man and not man for the law; that government is the servant of the people and not their master.

I believe in the dignity of labor, whether with head or hand; that the world owes no man a living but that it owes every man an opportunity to make a living.

I believe that thrift is essential to well-ordered living and that economy is a prime requisite of a sound financial structure, whether in government, business, or personal affairs.

I believe that truth and justice are fundamental to an enduring social state.

I believe in the sacredness of a promise, that a man's word should be as good as his bond; that character—not wealth or power or position—is of supreme worth.

I believe that the rendering of useful service is the common duty of mankind and that only in the purifying fire of sacrifices is the dross of selfishness consumed and the greatness of the human soul set free.

I believe in an all-wise and all-loving God, named by whatever name, and that the individual's highest fulfillment, greatest happiness, and widest usefulness are to be found in living in harmony with His will.

I believe that love alone is the greatest thing in the world; that it alone can overcome hate; that right can and will triumph over might.[6]

Rockefeller's first principle combines individualism and civic humanism. The second quotes Jesus and turns him against contemporary totalitarian governments abroad (and perhaps against totalistic tendencies in government at home). Most of the central four principles are the ideals typical of a Progressive-era businessman. In the next to last principle, Rockefeller describes his own experience as a rich man redeemed from the selfish possibilities of wealth. Finally, only in the last principle is the old religion—man living according to the will of God—present. But alongside the old religion is the new, that God might be known by some other name.

Harry Emerson Fosdick had been arguing since the 1920s that a religion that denigrated the human being was not Jesus's religion. In a remarkable sermon entitled "I Believe in Man," delivered during Fosdick's early career at the First Presbyterian Church, he presented his belief that the missing article in the Apostles and Nicene creeds was a belief in humanity. Fosdick's approach was both a subtle attack on creedalism and a claim that true Christianity was fundamentally pro-humanity. Jesus, Fosdick noted, suffered not for what he said about God—all of which had

FIGURE 1.1 John D. Rockefeller Jr. around the
time of the founding of the Riverside Church.
Used by permission of the Riverside Church Archives.

been said before—but for what he said about man. Healing on the Sabbath, allowing himself to be touched by women, and consorting with sinners all demonstrated Jesus's radical new humanism. Fosdick believed that
modern Christians should demonstrate no less concern for the "father-
hood of God and the brotherhood of man" than Jesus had. In their combined beliefs that the human sphere was the most important locus for religious activity and attention, Rockefeller and Fosdick held views in line
with the developing Protestant modernism, views that ultimately shaped
the approach of the new Riverside Church.

Fundamentalism

Fundamentalism was a broad-based movement reacting to modern trends in theology that centered on the nature of biblical authority and doctrines arising from a reading of the Scriptures. The term *Fundamentalism* itself derives from a series of twelve paperback volumes published between 1910 and 1915. The series, entitled *The Fundamentals*, was intended by Lyman Stewart, a southern California oil millionaire, to be a "testimony to the truth." The editors, starting with A. C. Dixon, a well-known evangelist and pastor of Moody Church in Chicago, gathered together a variety of Bible teachers and seminary professors in hopes that they would be "the best and most loyal teachers in the world." Lyman Stewart and his brother, Milton, financed the printing and distribution of enough copies of *The Fundamentals* so that every missionary, pastor, theological professor and student, YMCA and YWCA secretary, college professor, Sunday school superintendent, and religious editor in the English-speaking world could have a copy. In all, some three million volumes were sent out.[7]

As Fundamentalism evolved in the 1910s and 1920s into a list of five fundamentals that one had to believe in, in order to be a Christian, it became the doctrine of biblical inerrancy and the literal and verbal inspiration of the Scriptures that most rankled moderate Baptists like Fosdick and Rockefeller. The five fundamentals were the inerrancy of Scripture, the virgin birth, substitutionary atonement, miracle-working power, and the bodily resurrection of Christ. Often added to these were a belief in the second coming of Christ and an affirmation of the doctrine of the Trinity. The first time that a list had formed from the diffuse movement of opposition to theological liberalism was in 1910, when the General Assembly of the Presbyterian Church in the United States of America affirmed the five fundamentals as beliefs essential to candidates for ordination into the ministry. This attempt to control what was preached by controlling who became ministers of the gospel was again affirmed by the General Assembly in 1916. The mere existence of these lists as a litmus test of orthodoxy in one of the Protestant denominations helped promote its spread to other churches, not the least of which was the Northern Baptist Convention. Unlike the Presbyterians, Baptists did not require their ministers to subscribe to a particular confession. Although the Northern Baptist Convention was organized to promote cooperation in missionary and educational activities, those convinced of the dangers of liberalism in the church tried to use the convention as a forum for pushing a Fundamentalist agenda.

It is no accident that the two denominations—the Northern Baptists and the Presbyterians—most seriously affected by the Fundamentalist challenges were the two evangelical denominations that most emphasized theology and that ordered their common life with laity and clergy without the presence of bishops. The Methodists and Episcopalians were spared the full brunt of Fundamentalism because of the role of the episcopacy. The Disciples of Christ (Christian Church) were constitutionally resistant to creedalism, and even the Fundamentalist list of essentials smacked of a creed. Congregationalists did not have large assemblies in which this kind of thing was discussed, and they too were constitutionally configured to handle diverging beliefs by allowing different congregations to worship and believe differently.

The Baptists and Presbyterians, however, were ripe for a fight. In the past fifty years, these two denominations had produced most of the American biblical scholars and had sent more of their bright young men to Germany to study the Bible and theology than had all the other American churches combined. Therefore, when the Northern Baptists and Presbyterians opposed the higher criticism and liberal theology, they were objecting to moves made by their own intellectuals. The so-called Fundamentalist controversy was a family fight, all the more painful since no one in such a fight wishes to concede ownership of the family property to others. In this case, the family property at issue were the churches' colleges, seminaries, publishing operations, and pulpits. The Methodists, meanwhile, incorporated another form of liberal religion, the Social Gospel, which could and did apply Jesus's teachings to the problems of turn-of-the-century America without having to accept any of the new biblical criticism. Indeed, an older hermeneutic suggestion that Jesus lived as the Gospels said and actually said what they recorded him as saying—a truly historical Jesus—was essential in order for his sayings to have as powerful a claim on modern lives as the Social Gospel proclaimed. Fundamentalism, therefore, is best seen as a movement to arrest a broad range of trends in contemporary late-nineteenth- and early-twentieth-century Protestantism.[8]

Fosdick's Response to Fundamentalism

Into the midst of this controversy strode Harry Emerson Fosdick, a Northern Baptist minister preaching to a Presbyterian congregation. Fosdick had abandoned the pre-Fundamentalist conservative faith of his youth. Furthermore, he had been educated at Union Theological Seminary in New York City shortly after the seminary declared its independence from the Presbyterian Church in order to retain Charles Augustus Briggs, a biblical professor of decidedly moderate views who nevertheless embraced the higher criticism. Much like his teachers at Union, Fosdick had arrived at a personal state of theological equilibrium in which critical study of the Bible could not shake his faith but could only contribute to it. New scientific discoveries or evolutionary theories could not disturb Fosdick's conviction that the gospel was true and relevant to modern life.

Before World War II, it was common in American cities for congregations to move their place of worship every generation or so as residential and commercial patterns changed. It was such a change that brought Fosdick to the pulpit of a Presbyterian church, when the members of the Madison Square Presbyterian Church at Madison Avenue and Twenty-fourth Street and the University Place and First Presbyterian Churches decided to combine their operations at the site of the old First Presbyterian Church on Fifth Avenue between Eleventh and Twelfth Streets. All the pastors of the former churches were of retirement age and resigned so that a new minister could be appointed. In the meantime, they invited Fosdick, then a full-time professor of preaching at Union Theological Seminary, to preach at the Sunday services. In January 1919, the church's designated committee recommended to the congregation that Rev. George Alexander, one of the three pastors of the former churches, be elected pastor and Dr. Fosdick be elected associate minister and preacher. This arrangement meant that Fosdick would retain his Union professorship and Alexander would not have the responsibility of weekly preaching. Although Fosdick never formally became a Presbyterian minister, he was permitted to serve as preacher at the First Presbyterian Church from 1918 until 1925.[9]

Although Harry Emerson Fosdick is often thought of as a pastoral preacher and even described his preaching style as "pastoral care on a mass scale," he often talked about the religious dimensions of political and social problems. Fosdick was concerned about alcoholism but opposed Prohibition. Rare among white preachers of the 1920s, he used his pulpit to oppose lynching, the Ku Klux Klan, and the assertions of "Nordic superiority" that eventually constricted the free flow of immigrants to a trickle following the enactment of the McCarran-Walters Immigration Act in 1924. In the labor unrest of the late 1920s, he tried to refocus the view of business from one in which both labor and capitalist sought individual

gain to one in which business was seen as "an absolutely essential social
service to the whole community, in which everyone has a part—the man
that puts his money in, the man who puts his labor in, the whole com-
monwealth depends on the finished product."[10] *Traditionalism* and *orthodoxy* were words that usually figured negatively in Fosdick's preaching,
whereas *progressive Christianity* were the words under which he offered his
positive assessments. It was in the context of the traditionalisms and false
new orthodoxies, as Fosdick saw them, that he preached a sermon that
spread his name and fame in infamy throughout American Protestantism.
The sermon was "Shall the Fundamentalists Win?"

"Shall the Fundamentalists Win?" is remembered as a kind of gauntlet,
a liberal manifesto that was in turn taken up by enraged and insulted conservative Christians. In fact, Fosdick was more conciliatory than polemic
in his approach to this issue. The sermon itself draws on the fifth chapter
of Acts, in which Gamaliel speaks to his fellow members of the Sanhedrin:
"Refrain from these men and let them alone: for if this counsel or this
work be of men, then it will be overthrown: but if it is of God He will not
be able to overthrow them; lest haply ye be found even to be fighting
against God." Fosdick's purpose in using the example of Gamaliel was to
suggest that more conservative Christians would do well to apply his principle of tolerance to progressive Christians, with the assurance that if they
were not of God they would die out. He went on to make clear that not all
conservatives were Fundamentalists. For conservatives could have the lib-
erality of spirit, "but the fundamentalist program is essentially illiberal
and intolerant." The essential problematic of the age, he claimed, was that
there was a great mass of new knowledge about both the physical universe
and human history, including ancient human history. Then Fosdick
launched into his principal apologetic:

> Now, there are multitudes of reverent Christians who have been unable to
> keep this new knowledge in one compartment of their minds and the
> Christian faith in another. They have been sure that all truth comes from
> one God and is His revelation. Not, therefore, from irreverence or caprice or
> destructive zeal, but for the sake of intellectual and spiritual integrity, that
> they might really love the Lord their God not only with all their heart and
> soul and strength, but with all their mind, they have been trying to see this
> new knowledge in terms of the Christian faith and to see the Christian faith
> in terms of this new knowledge.[11]

Fosdick compared the liberal camp with those people of a former age who reconciled Galileo's discoveries of planetary motion and relationship to older beliefs. Likewise, the people in this generation were trying to reconcile the new knowledge and the old faith, and the Fundamentalists were trying to shut against them the doors of Christian fellowship. "Shall they," Fosdick asked, "be allowed to succeed?"

"Shall the Fundamentalists Win?" was probably applauded by all who heard Fosdick deliver it. Many were reported to be moved by its good sense and its perfect statement of the issues to mainstream Christians and Protestants in the early 1920s. One of these was Ivy Lee, the father of professional public relations. Indeed, Lee was so convinced of its good sense that he personally arranged to have the sermon printed as a pamphlet. In just a few months, thousands of the pamphlets were in circulation and were quickly reaching readers who did not applaud its content. The very success of Fosdick's case made him a bête noire for the Fundamentalists, and the Presbyterian Church's General Assembly was pushed by leading conservative ministers, including Clarence McCartney, an arch-Fundamentalist from Pittsburgh, to force the New York City Presbytery to force the First Presbyterian Church into conforming to the church's polity by prohibiting them from having a non-Presbyterian regularly preaching the gospel. Fosdick was given a choice: to become a Presbyterian or to leave the pulpit of First Church. Many of his followers urged him to join the Presbytery of New York, but Fosdick declined, believing that the next move would be his being tried for heresy. Even though New York City Presbytery was controlled by liberals, the prospect of a heresy trial for preaching no more than he considered to be the truth was anathema to Fosdick. So, too, was subscribing to a fixed historical creed like the Westminster Confession of Faith, another requirement that would have been forced on him. Denominations, he was starting to believe, were more trouble than they were worth and an anachronism. "The tragedy of Protestantism has been this, that any time anybody got a new idea in doctrine or ecclesiastical polity, he went out, if he had power enough, and founded a new denomination to represent it." Better an ecumenical spirit of inclusion, Fosdick thought, than to continue the Protestant pattern of propagating the church through organic division.

In his farewell sermon to the congregation of First Presbyterian Church, delivered on March 1, 1925, Fosdick tried to describe what the seven years at First Presbyterian Church with a Baptist preacher who welcomed all who wished to follow Jesus Christ meant to him. He labeled his time with them an experiment:

> These are the things we have stood for: tolerance, an inclusive church, the
> right to think religion through in modern terms, the social application of
> the application of the principles of Jesus, the abiding verities and experi-
> ences of the Gospel. And these are right. I am not sorry we tried this exper-
> iment. It was worth trying. We have lifted a standard that no one will put
> down. We have stated an issue that not man nor denomination is strong
> enough to brush aside. The future belongs to those things we have been
> standing for.[12]

The church that Fosdick said he represented remained just a vision of the future when he and First Presbyterian Church closed their mutual ministry. Fosdick's ecumenical and inclusive experiment belonged to a church named Riverside that was not yet born. This was the progressive, inclusive theology that New Yorkers flocked to hear. Fosdick's genius was preaching the gospel of progressive revelation, rooted in the Bible but not limited to the formulations of the Bible's time or constrained by the creeds of Reformers or modern theologians.

Since 1912, the Fifth Avenue Baptist Church in Manhattan had chosen to stay on its minister's modernist side. Dr. Cornelius L. Woelfkin was preparing to retire, and the church's lay leaders, first among them John D. Rockefeller Jr., were beginning to look for a minister who would be a strong advocate of the liberal position. From the start they knew whom they wanted to be their minister. It was a man whom they had seriously considered during the pastoral search that led to Dr. Woelfkin's calling. At that time, some of the Fifth Avenue Baptist church leaders had felt that Harry Emerson Fosdick, then pastor of the First Baptist Church in Montclair, New Jersey, was excellent but perhaps too young. Now, thirteen years later, Fosdick had emerged as one of the nation's most prominent preachers.

Through his association with wartime relief efforts and his less happy experiences with the Interchurch World Movement of the early 1920s, Rockefeller had formed a theological vision of his own. In World War I he had seen what Christians and their churches working together could do to improve the life, spirit, living conditions, and moral welfare of millions of people. After the war he developed a permanent distaste for petty denominationalism and denominational territorialism.

In Fosdick, Rockefeller saw more than just a great preacher. He also saw an ecumenical compatriot; someone who could represent his theological worldview to the American people, someone who would not spend time articulating what it meant to be a Baptist or a Presbyterian or a Methodist but, rather, just a Christian in the modern age. Fosdick was already known for his antidenominationalist positions, and when Rockefeller first approached him about becoming his minister, Fosdick declined. Not once but twice, Fosdick refused to consider Rockefeller's offer, raising objections that were eventually met in a pattern of offer, refusal, and finally agreement, which, though perhaps improved by Fosdick's retelling, itself has almost a biblical flavor.

When Rockefeller first asked Fosdick to become the pastor of Fifth Avenue—by that time relocated on and renamed the Park Avenue Baptist Church—Fosdick declined, saying he could not conduct a ministry in a church that required baptism by immersion for full membership. Rockefeller went back to the lay leaders of the church and was able to counter that the baptism requirement could be changed. Now Fosdick explained that he did not want to be merely a private chaplain to a fairly small group of extremely wealthy people in Manhattan's most affluent residential neighborhood. To this, Rockefeller responded that a new, larger church could be built in Morningside Heights that would allow Fosdick to reach a larger, more metropolitan audience, drawn from a wide variety of denominations. Still Fosdick refused. Exasperated, Rockefeller asked, "Why?" "Because," Fosdick said, "you are too wealthy, and I do not want to be known as the pastor of the richest man in the country." Rockefeller replied, "I like your frankness, but do you think that more people will criticize you on account of my wealth than will criticize me on account of your theology?" Having thus won over Fosdick, Rockefeller began assembling the resources that would allow the building of a great interdenominational church on the Upper West Side.

In December 1930 the first officers of Riverside Church, formally constituted, were elected, and in February 193l the church was dedicated in an interdenominational ceremony. The week after the first Sunday service was held on October 5, 1930, *The Christian Century* carried an article on the opening, assessing it as "an event of arresting importance in American church life." The article went on to indicate that public interest in Fosdick's career had reached a point "equaled in American pulpit history only in the public interests in Henry Ward Beecher after the Civil War, and, close after him, by that in Phillips Brooks." Without a doubt Fosdick was indeed the kind of major preaching personality whose association with a huge new costly Gothic church situated high on the banks of the Hudson River was in itself a news story. Fosdick already was a best-selling author who attracted multiple-capacity crowds to his Sunday morning services. His sermons were studied by thousands of his ministerial contemporaries and theological student preachers in training, and he achieved even greater national fame as the National Broadcasting Corporation's national radio preacher of the airwaves.[13]

But *The Christian Century* also recognized that the opening of the Riverside Church signaled even more than a great preacher's obtaining a new, larger venue. While the *Century*'s self-appointed architectural critic held that the Riverside Church came to "strike no new note" and complained that in its faithful replication of the Gothic ideal what it tried to say "has been said before, and in many respects better," he also acknowledged that the new house of worship represented a spiritual project as well.

> This project is one of the most fateful, and it is one of the most daring, ever undertaken by a Protestant congregation. It is an attempt to bring the gospel in an impressive and convincing way to those who have dismissed it as of no importance. That multiplied thousands of city dwellers have so dismissed it is depressingly clear. . . . Even of those who are still to be found in city congregations, great numbers are there on account of the operation of conservative survival values rather than because of vital conviction.

The author then explained that the location of Riverside, next to the educational institutions on Morningside Heights, was an attempt to take the Christian gospel to the very place in American society in which it was held in lowest esteem: higher education: "Paul faced no more skeptical, no more aloof audience on Mars Hill than Dr. Fosdick faces on the heights of the American metropolis."

In this way, even at its beginning, the Riverside Church was a surrogate for organized Protestantism in the twentieth century. Not ten days after its opening, it was held up as the most important attempt to bring the Christian gospel to modern urban America. This representative role constituted a challenge to both Riverside and Fosdick. True, the church would certainly succeed in drawing great crowds every time Fosdick preached, but the true test, the *Century* maintained, was whether he could shape his crowds into a true church. Moreover, whether the message would get through was also a challenge:

> Can the Christian gospel be so interpreted to that questioning, individualistic, indifferent and religiously irresponsible population concentrated around Columbia University in such a way as to draw them together in an organic fellowship? A congregation of transients, of curiosity seekers, or even of those who keep up their churchgoing habits without seriously questioning their worth, may be gratifying to the deacons of Riverside, but it will mean very little to the cause of religion in America.

The *Century's* editors wished Fosdick and the Riverside Church well. Riverside was on its way to becoming, at least in the hearts and minds of ordinary people throughout the United States, the national cathedral of mainstream Protestantism.

For their part, Fosdick, Rockefeller, and the members of the newly dedicated church conceded nothing. A hymn that Fosdick composed for the dedication sounded the great themes of progressive modern Christianity: the evils of war, the perfectibility of the church, selfishness as sin, and fear and doubt as the enemies of salvation. But inside each verse was the strong steel of Christian conviction. The hymn ends with the recognition that God's purposes and human courage were the basis for the new church's hope:

> Save us from weak resignation
> To the evils we deplore;
> Let the search for Thy salvation
> Be our glory evermore.
> Grant us wisdom,
> Grant us courage,
> Serving Thee whom we adore.[14]

The entire hymn, later named "God of Grace and God of Glory," became not only the signature hymn of Riverside Church but also an anthem of liberal Protestant mainstream churches. It is loved and sung in churches today and is included in countless hymnals. Like much else in Riverside's early days, it struck the right balance between faithful reliance on God and a determination to make human progress in this lifetime.

Indeed, the hymn's balance between lofty aims and concrete action, between what the longtime Riverside associate minister Eugene Laubach later termed "holiness and hustle," captures the enduring legacy of theological modernism for Riverside and mainstream Protestantism more generally.[15] It lives as a faith orientation because it is grounded in God but oriented toward progress in the world. The Riverside theology continues to be contentious, however, because it seeks no definite end but only the progressive goals that its members and ministers have brought to it over time. Generations of Riversiders have come to the church hoping to extend the Christian tradition to meet new duties and convictions.

A Home in the City

As much as the Riverside Church can sometimes appear to be a message church for the liberal wing of American Protestantism, for particular individuals it has always been their church home. As such, it has functioned as a characteristic Protestant mainstream congregation in quite another way. Its men's Bible class, for instance, continued the practice of having a lay-led gathering of men listen to a prepared lesson sandwiched between the opening and closing hymns and prayers, which would have been familiar to the churchgoers of any Baptist, Methodist, or Presbyterian church of the era, and many others besides. Indeed, the absence of such a group, or others for married women and for youth, would have been instantly noted.

When the groups within the church's fellowship gathered each Sunday, they lived out a pattern that dated back more than a century. For the most committed, going to church meant being with other men or women or youths in a setting of kindred souls. The Protestants' Sunday school class had an informal, yet definite, code of behavior. Members could share their personal and business successes and setbacks, but in the context of asking for prayers or offering thanksgiving. They were not to ask for help in too concrete a way. For example, in John D. Rockefeller Sr.'s church in Cleveland, the young business associate who tried to talk business at the end of the class before church was firmly turned aside. The association among the men and among the women in such churches might, and often did, have implications for their lives outside the church. Men got a sense of another man's strength of character and force of personality, or "vitality" as they would have put it. Their wives, meanwhile, often had something to add or remove from the picture if the man in question had a wife whom they knew to be "delightful," "long suffering," or "the salt of the earth." In these associations, a young man might find a way up in the business world or be introduced to a future spouse.

Riverside Church, like many other Protestant churches in early-twentieth-century American cities, filled the spaces in times outside the worship hour in ways that consciously or unconsciously replicated the social world of the village or small town where Protestant churches were most often found. As James Lewis observed, in the early 1900s American Protestants were not certain they were at home in the city.[16] The city, with its diversity of tongues and mores, its density and grit, and its pockets of great wealth and poverty, did not seem a safe place for the churchgoing youth of the hinterlands. The advantages and opportunities of New York, Chicago, and other great cities attracted the young and ambitious, as they did the immigrants from Europe—indeed, the cities were growing too fast to survive without regional immigration.

But whereas immigrants were quick to form institutions outside the church—unions, "vereins," burial societies, insurance pools, and bands, all along ethnic lines—native-born Protestants tended to develop their socially supportive institutions within their congregations. Unlike some churches and immigrant groups, Protestants and their leaders had an almost one-to-one correspondence in regard to ethnicity. These were, in short, their churches led by pastors of their people. Thus, although the city's Anglo-American Protestants trusted the market to provide insurance and jobs, they depended on the church to replace the missing features of small-town life that populated their nonmarket social world. Book and study groups, athletic contests, plays, readings, and other performances all became features of urban church life in a way they had not been part of rural and village church life.

At one level, Riverside was an "institutional" church—a large membership church with comprehensive programs—which was increasingly common in American cities after the Civil War. But Riverside's ability to blur the line between members and adherents again and again throughout its history set it apart from most other mainstream institutional churches. This ability ensured that many of the activities offered under the church's auspices would survive years of little support or attention from the paid ministers and staff of the church. This ability also, however, created fiefdoms and constituencies that periodically led to conflicts without resolution. Many of the people who found their way into Riverside's many groups and fellowships were women. New York, and especially Manhattan, from 1900 onward displayed a voracious demand for secretaries, book-keepers, and telephone operators.

Unlike a half-century earlier, these jobs were widely open to women. Business colleges and vocational technical high schools prepared women for these careers outside the home while at the same time more and more economic activities moved from farms and households to larger-scale institutions. The modern corporations, the general and specialty manufacturers of the new cities, and even Morningside Heights's educational institutions required clerical labor. From the 1930s through the 1950s, a growing number of women in New York City pursued better-paying careers as doctors, professors, and lawyers, in addition to social workers and teachers. Barnard College, founded in 1889, was the city's first private college to award a liberal arts degree to women, and it was the source of many high-achieving women in the professions. Women and girls came to the city to fill its economic labor needs and to live an exciting and cosmopolitan life. But life for a single woman in the first half of the twentieth century was not easy. Gender role expectations made it socially unacceptable for women of good character to go to some places alone. At night, going to restaurants, plays, and other diversions required a male escort or female companions. There were, as always, men who preyed on women in the city, and security was a constant concern. Despite the social and practical constraints on women, their friendships needed outlets.

Riverside was much like any other Baptist church of the era in having a women's association that met during weekdays for fellowship, service, and Bible study. Riverside was distinctive, however, for having a fellowship exclusively for women who had careers. The Business and Professional Women's Group was founded in 1930. As Riverside's ministers thought about the programs that might fill up the tower of the church then being built, they determined not to impose programs on the community but allow the community to offer ideas for programs that might engage people associated with the church. A member of Fosdick's staff, Myra Vance, told him that a group of women, about a dozen in all, thought that a business and professional women's club would be worthwhile and that they would like to start one.

Fosdick thought this was a "harmless idea" and perhaps even a promising one and gave Vance permission to proceed. The club quickly grew. Mary L. Stockwell looked back in 1990 over the nearly fifty years she had been a member of the B & Ps:

We served a real need. In a large impersonal city where the employed single woman might easily get lost, the Bs and Ps provided a social situation that was pleasant and comfortable and in many instances led to long-lasting, close friendships. I especially remember one member who left New York to take a better position, in Atlanta—but who after a year or two returned to New York and the Bs and Ps because all the "out of office" life revolved around couples and the single woman was stranded.[17]

The club's social activities included monthly dinners and special holiday banquets, along with groups interested in books, antiques, cooking, eating out, going to the theater, drama, poetry, sewing, tours and trails, opera, ballet, philharmonic performances, and service. Not only were nighttime activities offered to women in the club, but at least from the 1940s through the 1960s, club members cooperatively leased cabins and cottages for weekend and vacation retreats. Weeks at the beach or weekends at the lodge helped cement relationships between the women and their loyalty to the church, although at its peak membership of more than five hundred in the 1950s, perhaps only three-fifths of the B & P club members were also members of the church. Through this group, therefore, Riverside served a broader community than did its membership alone and demonstrated an attitude characteristic of liberal Protestant churches in the middle of the twentieth century. That is, the church's programs were conceived as services to others and not as rewards for, or enticements to, membership. The church itself existed to serve its community, and boundaries between the church's own membership and the world were relatively porous.

The B & Ps were by no means the only group to attract people from the surrounding community to Riverside. Four other programs—the Guild, the Navy Midshipmen's School, the arts and crafts program, and religious education—also illustrate the kind of church that Riverside, from its earliest years, tried to be.

The Guild was one of the activities that began with the building's opening in the fall of 1930. At its inception Harry Emerson Fosdick described its ideal as

a fellowship of young people, bound together, not by unanimity of opinion, but by community of purpose who wish to discuss real problems, enjoy worthwhile recreations, use beauty as a means of worship, find avenues of practical service, and, in effect, make the most of themselves for the sake of

B. & P. PRESIDENTS. (LEFT TO RIGHT)

1930-1932 Mrs. Marguerite Smith Gullans
1932-1933 Mrs. Mary Gleason Fowle
1933-1934 Mrs. Marjorie Brown Kehrbach
1934-1935 Miss Mildred E. Adams
1935-1936 Miss Eva N. Edwards
1936-1937 Miss Dorothy J. Livermore
1937-1938 Mrs. Erma Z. Luetscher
1938-1939 Miss Laura N. Vossler

FIGURE 1.2 The presidents' table at the Business and Professional Women's Group in 1939. The group provided an important outlet for New York women who worked during the day, often choosing careers that differentiated them from the married women who attended the daytime meetings of the Women's Association. *Used by permission of the Riverside Church Archives.*

others. Like the Riverside Church, of which it is a part, it is free from questions of theological subscription and sectarian partisanship. The religion for which it stands delights in variety of form and opinion, is inclusive, not exclusive, and to all who are sincerely interested in high-minded living it extends open-doored hospitality.

As a youth and young adult league, the Guild was designed as a place where liberal Christians might not be lost to the church but might also find one another. The Guild functioned as a social club, a place where college students and people new to the city might meet a good crowd of people and even find someone to marry. Its purpose was to mitigate the domination of life in New York by work and commerce. Photos of Guild activities in the 1940s and 1950s looked like ones from college yearbooks and their depictions of fraternity and sorority life. A promotional brochure for the Guild asked, "Who are you? It's easy to guess—you are probably from out of town—a student, or perhaps in business or following your chosen profession. Who are we? Well—6 months, 2 years, or 5 years ago we were newcomers too. We are also out-of-staters and native New Yorkers; students and professional people" (see figure 1.3). The Guild promised these newcomers that they might make lifelong friends or discover dormant talents, but its most important benefit was "the spiritual satisfaction that this is the way we are supposed to live—under the guidance of our religious convictions."[18]

Sometimes Riverside sought simply to open its doors to a community need and soon found itself more deeply involved. During World War II the church opened its facilities to a Sunday evening vespers service for the

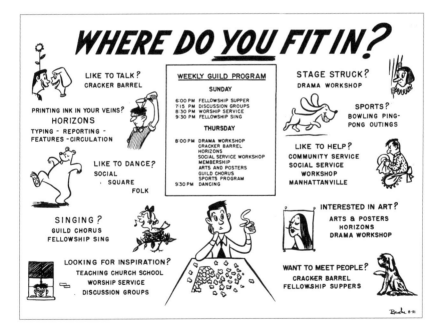

FIGURE 1.3 A 1951 promotional brochure offered young adult New Yorkers a chance to meet people and "live under the guidance of our religious convictions." Drawing by Brooks. *Used by permission of the Riverside Church Archives.*

Midshipmen's School. The first mention of the midshipmen's presence at Riverside appeared in the *Church Monthly* for June 1942:

> The midshipmen marched to the church from their quarters, about one-half of them coming from the USS *Prairie State* at West 138th Street and the Hudson River, and one-half of them from the dormitories on the campus of Columbia University. They have their own organist, their own choir, re-cruited from the ranks of the midshipmen, and their [own] chaplain, Rev. C. Leslie Glenn.[19]

The article explained that Riverside was chosen because of its location between the two centers of the school's activities and noted that

> the Riverside Church has no responsibility in connection with the service other than to make its facilities available. We do find great satisfaction in the presence here for their service of worship of these many hundreds of men, and want them to know that the congregation as well as the ministers and officers give them a cordial welcome.

With each passing month, the relationship between the midshipmen and the church became closer. The chaplain's assistant, Grover J. Oberle, him-self had been the organist and choir master of St. John's Church in Wash-ington, D.C., and the choirs of midshipmen he led met to sing glee club and church music at the church.[20]

At the end of 1942, Riverside hosted a chaplain's Christmas dinner for the men of the U.S. Naval Reserve Midshipmen's School, in Riverside's as-sembly hall. Dr. Fosdick attended as a special guest of honor. So too did Robert Wamsley, chairman of Riverside's War Service Committee. Wams-ley persuaded the Riversiders to become active in humanitarian support for the war effort. More than six hundred people took physician-led classes in first aid and gave and helped receive blood and plasma, a rela-tively new practice at the time. Others initiated a group-training course in the care of children, designed to qualify the trainees to supervise large numbers of children should the need arise during the war. Scores of River-side women acted as greeters to welcome the men in uniform, both at Riverside Church affairs and in entertainment centers throughout the city. Some fifty of the committee's women, "with a sprinkling of male helpers," planned the social and recreational needs of the school's two thousand navy trainees. Indeed, Riverside became the recreational and social center for the Midshipmen's School, and navy men often filled the building for choir practice, bowling, or a workout in Stone Gym. The most important of these activities were the Saturday night socials. The church wondered whether the socials would be successful, given that Saturday night was the only night that midshipmen had free. Nevertheless, Saturday night at Riverside became a great success for lonely officers in New York. In fact, after each commencement of a midshipmen's class, twenty or more midshipmen were married in Christ Chapel before shipping out.[21]

Although Fosdick was a confirmed pacifist, he and Norris Tibbetts, a former service chaplain himself and minister to men at Riverside, excelled at anticipating and meeting servicemen's pastoral needs. Fosdick sent a personally addressed letter to the wife, mother, or sister, or perhaps minister, of the five thousand men who had signed the army and navy register in the Riverside narthex. The replies to these letters were filled with deeply felt gratitude for the church's ministry. To Riverside men in uniform, the minister sent "constant assurance of members' prayers for their welfare and for their safe return." Christmas packages were also sent, containing, among other things, copies of Fosdick's "The Three Meanings" and a little book entitled *Words of Jesus* that had been introduced by Dr. Fosdick.[22]

Long before the midshipmen turned up at Riverside, women, children, and the poor were being encouraged to express themselves through arts and crafts activities. Historically, Protestantism had reserved little room for the arts apart from music and some forms of architecture. Yet in the beautiful setting of the Gothic Riverside Church, the Baptists who, like Fosdick and Rockefeller, had discovered the possibilities of "using beauty as a means to worship," now embraced the arts. People whose parents never went, for religious reasons, to the theater now had a theater right in their church. Not only that, but their theater hosted programs of modern dance. Up in the Tower, meanwhile, people were painting murals, staging plays and puppet shows, and encouraging children to express themselves. Sometimes the artistic product conveyed the church's religious sensibility, as, for example, in one of the large canvases the arts and crafts program produced in the 1930s featuring Dr. Fosdick in the center of the painting and representations of foreign and domestic mission partners around him. At other times it was the process of making art that accomplished religious objectives, as when art brought together children from different races. The more practical arts of sewing were used to provide women with a means of earning a living during the Depression when the middle-class women of the church (shown with hats in figure 1.4) set up a sewing employment room, called the Sewing Guild in the Tower for working-class women.[23]

The arts also figured prominently in religious education at Riverside. The Primary Department had a drama program featuring the usual Sunday school bathrobe-clothed magi, but it also encouraged more progressive and imaginative renderings of biblical favorites such as the south-of-the border dramatization of the good Samaritan shown in figure 1.5.

Such dramatic license was encouraged as children were challenged over the three-hour Sunday school period to discover truths for themselves. Teachers did not follow set curricula; they crafted their own lessons. At a time when most church schools were still stressing memorization of Bible verses, Riverside was challenging young learners to "build churches" by determining what a church needed in order to be a church, a lesson shown in figure 1.6.[24]

Riverside classes for children featured experimental lessons and multiple centers of learning and focus within the room. In an experiment in

FIGURE 1.4 Women's Association members try out the sewing room and equipment set up in the 1930s to provide unemployed women with skills and employment opportunities. *Used by permission of the Riverside Church Archives.*

FIGURE 1.5 Dramatization with a twist in the Primary Department: The Mexican Good Samaritan. *Used by permission of the Riverside Church Archives.*

progressive education by Riverside's minister of education, Ivar Hellstrom, the children were not required to face forward or to sit at tables. Hellstrom confessed in a *Church Monthly* article that the most difficult question visitors asked was, "How do you get to the Sunday school?" He noted that in response to this seemingly innocent question,

> [The visitor] is directed to the Church School Office to secure written permission to visit, or to the elevators, the mention of which brings a smile as though they were an incongruous bit of church equipment. He explains that he wishes to see the Church School, meaning probably a general assembly for worship or opening exercises. This is unfortunately not as simple as might be imagined for such gatherings are held, in a half dozen departments widely separated. A bit confused at learning this, the visitor then proposes that he just wander around and see what he can, only to discover that

FIGURE 1.6 Progressive education comes to Sunday school. Children in this 1930s class worked on designing a church—facilities, worship, and program—of their own from scratch. Photograph by Frank Ehrenford. *Used by permission of the Riverside Church Archives.*

general visiting is taboo, that visiting particular groups is limited and should have been arranged for in advance, and that, if he wishes to visit in the elementary grades, he is expected to forego [*sic*] the privilege of the morning service, including Doctor Fosdick's sermon. Fortunately, there are a Men's Class, a Women's Class, and special classes for students and parents—six groups offering worth-while programs in which a visitor can be sure of a welcome without conditions or special arrangement.[25]

People neither casually visited nor dropped their children off to Sunday school at Riverside in the 1930s through the 1950s. Children were enrolled just as if they were in private schools, and their parents attended parenting classes and made sure all members of the family regularly attended. Otherwise they would lose a place that might have taken years on a waiting list to obtain.[26]

What parents and children who were admitted into the Sunday school received was a religious education, not indoctrination in the Christian faith. Above all, what they got was Sophia Fahs. Sophia Blanche Lyon Fahs was born in China in 1878, the daughter of Presbyterian missionaries. Educated at the turn of the century as a missionary child at the College of Wooster, she joined the Student Volunteer Movement and pledged herself to the "evangelization of the world in this generation." Her first assignment after graduating from college was on the University of Chicago campus, where she met the philosopher and educational theorist John Dewey. Soon her religious ardor and understanding of how children learned (for she had five of her own between 1905 and 1914) turned into a progressive ideal for religious education that insisted that children not be exposed to other people's ideas about God until they had developed their own. Most radically for her time, Fahs believed that "other people's ideas about religion" included the stories of the Bible. Edith Fisher Hunter described the transformation of Sophia Fahs's educational philosophy:

> As she hammered out her increasingly liberal theology and its implications for religious education, she found herself drawing less exclusively on the Judeo-Christian tradition and more on the natural sciences, on the religion of primitive people, and on other world religions. She had discovered that primitive people developed their religious ideas as they reacted to the natural world around them. What if today's children were allowed to express freely their reactions to the same primary phenomena—birth and death, sun and moon and stars, dreams, shadows, wind and rain? Should not children's inescapable confrontations with and reflection on these realities be the beginning of their religious education rather than Bible stories about people of long ago and far away?[27]

In 1930 Riverside Church hired Fahs to continue her progressive approach in its new Junior Department. Even though she retired from her Riverside Church duties in 1943, Fahs had already begun a new career in 1937 as the developer of children's curricula for the Unitarian denomination. The series of lessons that she produced for the Unitarians from the late 1930s until 1965 drew directly on her Riverside lessons and ranged from everyday miracles like sun, light, and water; death as a new beginning; deceit and deception; and an appreciation of Hindu beliefs. From this list it might appear that Fahs had no use for the Bible in religious education. On the contrary, she held the Bible in great estimation but believed exposure to it was educationally and developmentally appropriate only for secondary students who were ready to read and interpret history.

Like members of the Guild, the B & Ps, and even the navy midshipmen who talked with Dr. Fosdick before shipping out to war, people who passed through the Riverside Church's religious education program were marked by the experience. They created a home in the city at Riverside, and their heightened sense of belonging became part of what made the church both a model institutional church and effective.

The Quest to Revise the Christian Tradition

Fosdick's progressive ecumenical vision attracted people who wanted to extend and revise forms of traditional Protestantism that were quite different from the evangelical Baptist faith they had inherited. Harry Emerson Fosdick tried to detach the Bible from its unsupportable supernatural moorings and reattach it to modern and intelligible phenomena such as personality and progress. Robert James McCracken, who succeeded Fosdick as Riverside's senior minister in 1946, wanted a congregation that was also a teaching post, a place where people of all ages who were serious about faith could examine it and explore their doubts. More effectively than any Riverside minister before or since, McCracken used the church's teaching office to examine a progressive theology with church members. Ernest Campbell, who followed McCracken in 1968, hoped to prove that one could think and still be a Christian. In fact, he hoped to prove that one could be a better evangelical Christian than he was when growing up at Broadway Presbyterian and later at Bob Jones University. For William Sloane Coffin, who served as senior minister from 1977 to 1987, the main question was whether it was possible to be part of the social, political, and economic establishment and still be progressive on matters of faith and discipleship. James Forbes, who became senior minister in 1989, sees himself in dialogue with the Pentecostal, Revivalist, and Wesleyan traditions. For Forbes, progress at Riverside consists of extending the work of the Holy Spirit to both people whose experience of God has been limited by traditional holiness mores and those who have no great sense of a living God at all. Both Forbes and Coffin led their fellow Riversiders to become what they hoped to be. Part of the success of the Riverside preachers is that each articulated a leading progressive sentiment in the Protestantism of their day. The postwar generation wanted to learn from McCracken;

the 1960s demanded relevant religion; and people in the 1990s wanted spirituality.

Educational trends in American Protestantism changed even more dramatically than did the emphases in preaching. Here again, Riverside educators like Ivar and Helga Hellstrom reflected and shaped their times. By concentrating on religious education, the Hellstroms tried to separate the formation of youth from the moralism of the Victorian era in which they had grown up. For Sophia Fahs, a religious education was preparation for a Christian education and a much better place to start than the evangelical culture of certainty in which she had been raised as a missionary child. By contrast, J. Gordon Chamberlain, Riverside's minister of Christian religious education in the 1950s, turned to neoorthodoxy as a way to reemphasize the role of the Bible as containing timeless truths without going back to literal interpretations. For him, neoorthodoxy represented liberation not only from conservative fundamentalism but also from a Deweyan emphasis on the individual child in isolation from a community's commitments to a faith. For Eugene Laubach, coming to work at Riverside Church while completing a doctoral degree at Union, the liberative goal was to develop quality lessons taught by people who were new to Riverside and who cared about growing numbers of children in the program, without foreclosing theological options, as Chamberlain had wanted to do. As a Methodist, Laubach was committed to turning no child away and thus became the perfect minister for a time when a waiting list to get into the religious school was thought inappropriate.

Coming to Riverside

From the very beginning, Union Theological Seminary was the Riverside Church's closest institutional neighbor. Even though Harry Emerson Fosdick was a faculty member at Union, his preaching and worship at Riverside were not always universally welcomed by Union's faculty. Perhaps because so many Union students served internships through the congregation or perhaps because so many faculty families attended Riverside, Union theologian Reinhold Niebuhr took the unusual step of trying to diminish Fosdick's reputation, in an article entitled "How Adventurous Is Dr. Fosdick?"[28] Subtle and overt criticisms notwithstanding, Union students continued to flock to Riverside. Indeed, part of Union's attraction was the degree to which Riverside, just next door, represented Union's progressive Protestantism at prayer. Protestant denominational leaders who worked at another of Riverside's neighbors, the Interchurch Center located south of Riverside, greatly contributed to the church's leadership from the late 1950s until the late 1980s. The 1956 "Riverside Church Survey Report" noted that the opening of the Interchurch Center in the summer of 1958 should bring with it new opportunities for service and influence. The seventeen-story office building designed to house up to three thousand church executives and clerical employees was scheduled to open with nearly complete or complete staffs of the National Council of Churches, the United Presbyterian Church, the Reformed Church in America, the Board of Missions of the Methodist Church, and foreign mission boards of the American Baptist Convention and the same denomination's Ministers and Missionaries Benefit Board. As the American office of the World Council of Churches, the Interchurch Center would also serve as a hub for Christian visitors from all over the world. The report's writers anticipated that

> members of this group will greatly enrich the spiritual and intellectual life of the Church and the neighborhood. Nationally known specialists on work with students, migrants, racial and cultural minorities, religious education, and international relations will be literally at our doorstep. Television, radio, and film activities of the National Council and these other bodies will center here. Important research projects will also be directed from this headquarters building.[29]

To a remarkable degree, this optimistic assessment of the opportunities implied by the creation of the Interchurch Center, also financed by John D. Rockefeller Jr., came true. Here, because their denominations had brought them to the neighborhood, ordained and lay ministers from more than twenty denominations worshiped and contributed to Riverside's programs. Fosdick's ecumenical vision in the 1930s of a congregation of Christians drawn from diverse denominational backgrounds was being realized through the Interchurch Center. Because of the association of its employees at the center with the greater church, Riverside became more closely involved with that era's movements for social justice and change. A visitor to Riverside from the mid-1970s onward was confronted with numerous display tables encouraging awareness and involvement (see figure 1.7).

As it grew, Riverside became more racially diverse. From the end of World War II, Riverside embraced inclusionary ideals. An early attempt at

FIGURE 1.7: A typical Sunday morning in the
early 1970s in the Cloister Lounge, with displays
informing worshipers of ways to become engaged
in social causes, such as this table promoting addiction awareness. *Photograph by Bill Anderson.*
Used by permission of the Riverside Church Archives.

a multicultural orientation was the postwar Christmas service including
infants representing the white, Native American, Chinese, and black families in the church (see figure 1.8). Yet this declaration of ideals only slowly
transformed the actual fellowship of the church. The principal engine for
making Riverside more inclusive was the change in its membership, accel-
erated by the building of the Interchurch Center and the demographic
changes in the Morningside Heights and Harlem neighborhoods. At the
very moment in the late 1950s and early 1960s that Riverside began attracting religious professionals from its Interchurch Center, it also began
attracting a larger number of African American members. One indication
of the growing African American presence is the fact that in 1969 James

Forman chose Riverside as a forum for presenting his demands for reparations for slavery, as will be discussed later in this book, because Riverside, virtually alone among affluent establishment churches, had enough black members, he believed, to obtain a respectful hearing. Nearly a decade earlier, Riverside member Ted Britton had broken the color line of the previously all-white board of ushers, and later he became the first black member of the board of trustees. Most significantly, it was the ushers' board itself that decided it would be unfair to start an African American usher where new ushers traditionally started, out of sight in the upper balcony. As a result, the ushers began the process of dismantling those features that subtly excluded others.

From the early 1960s onward, black and white Riversiders worshiped, learned, and served side by side in a church that modeled the diversity of New York far more effectively than did most city congregations, which were race- and class-specific enclaves. Like many churches in mainstream American Protestant denominations, Riverside in the 1970s and 1980s was caught up in the issues of the day, such as opposing the war in Vietnam, advocating nuclear disarmament, and providing sanctuary for oppressed refugees from Central America. Unlike many of those denominations, however, the advocates for the progressive side of those issues at Riverside had few opponents outside the increasingly few and embittered members of the Men's Class. For both Riverside and the denominations, however, it was issues regarding human sexuality that proved to be the most contentious from the mid-1980s onward.

Because of the open-mindedness of its clergy and its many other commitments to justice for the oppressed, Riverside began to attract significant numbers of gays and lesbians. Riverside's official stance was not one of deliberate openness and affirmation, however, but a matter of receptivity to differences as a matter of good liberal form. In this respect Riverside was not unlike hundreds of liberal arts colleges and universities at which the presence of gay and lesbian students and faculty was tacitly acknowledged as part of the community's culture, without their acceptance being a matter of policy. In the early 1980s, this situation changed, with perhaps the strongest force for change being the AIDS crisis.

Conservative Christians, most notably evangelist Jerry Falwell, were quick to identify AIDS as God's punishment of gay men for the sin of homosexuality. Even before the modes of disease transmission were fully known, those churches that had welcomed gays were on the defensive. Nothing irritated Bill Coffin so much as the smug self-righteousness of re-

FIGURE 1.8: Babies of four different races who assisted in the children's Christmas service in 1948. *Left to right*: Native American, Okuata Dorsey (Little Owl); white, John Manwring; black, Robert Taylor; and Chinese, Webster Waugh. *Used by permission of the Riverside Church Archives.*

ligious leaders, particular those in the New Christian Right. Coffin preached often on the topic of hypocrisy and also delivered a sermon, "On Homosexuality," in which he made clear his own welcoming views of gays and lesbians. His other sermons were filled with comments on these questions as well, including this remark about religion and the AIDS crisis: "Doctors don't know much about AIDS. You can be sure that Jerry Falwell knows even less."[30]

In the context of the AIDS crisis and Riverside's open discussion of the issue, it became clear that Coffin, among many others in the congregation, did not believe that there was anything wrong with being gay. A study document entitled "Statement of Openness, Inclusion and Affirmation of Gay/Lesbian Persons" was also making its way through the congregation.

While Bill Coffin was away preaching at Duke University Chapel, Channing Phillips, the church's executive minister, announced his disagreement with Coffin and his colleagues over homosexuality. In his sermon Phillips stated that there was good news and bad news. The bad news, he said, was that homosexuality was a sin and was contrary to the parable of human sexuality given in Genesis that man should cleave to woman.

> The point is that the gospel does meddle with our lives! If we take Jesus' words seriously, not just that adultery is sin, or that lust is adultery; the point is that as far as the biblical understanding of human sexuality is concerned, any and all deviation from the parable given in Genesis and referenced by Jesus, whether within heterosexual or homosexual relationships, is sin, is contrary to the will of God. And no theological or exegetical sleight of hand can erase that "word of the Lord."[31]

The good news, Phillips continued, was that God forgives, just as Jesus forgave the woman caught in adultery. Yet even here was something less than acceptance, for Phillips noted that "after saying 'neither do I condemn thee,' [Jesus] goes back to the inescapable parable from Genesis, and says to each of us, whatever our sexual orientation, 'Go and sin no more.'"

Phillips, a black Christian minister, had articulated what many African American members themselves had been taught and believed: that homosexuality was a sin. Whit Hutchinson, a young white United Methodist minister and ethics Ph.D. candidate at Union, vehemently disagreed with the witness of the morning. After the sermon, Hutchinson stood up and said that he disagreed with what he had heard that morning and invited those who disagreed with him to gather around the communion table in the chancel during the last hymn. For the Reverend Joan Kavanaugh, another clergy member of the staff present that morning, this was a *causa confessionis*, and so she, too, gathered with those who disagreed. Many black parishioners were incensed by this unprecedented rejection of a preacher's words. Back in the pulpit the next week, Bill Coffin declared, "We really have a divided church here—or is it a church? If we still have a church we will not back away either from one another or from the issue."[32] This was a very painful time to be a Riversider, since gay identity and the integrity of a black church witness were repeatedly set against each other. So too were the authority of the Bible and the Fosdickian liberal tradition. Eugene Laubach thought about it this way:

He [Phillips] could have walked out of the pulpit, and they could have just said, "Listen to that crank." Except that with his Bible bit, he undermined everything that this Church stood for, every single piece of Fosdick history was imperiled with somebody who says, "It isn't me saying it, it's the Bible that says it and therefore you ought to obey it." And so on. You know, this is risky stuff. It isn't homosexual stuff. It's where's your authority?[33]

A great deal was at stake for all kinds of Riverside members and ministers. The church wrestled with its witness as it had never before in its history wrestled with a theological issue. After hours of meetings, lay leaders from across the divided congregation arrived at an affirmation with which all parties present could agree and presented a revised version of the "Statement of Openness, Inclusion and Affirmation of Gay/Lesbian Persons" to the church's membership for adoption four Sundays after Phillips's sermon. The key compromise that made the statement a viable expression for a wide variety of members was the inclusion of the following sentence: "We reaffirm the traditional family and we further recognize and embrace single persons, Lesbian/Gay relationships, extended families-all families of support that are founded on the principles of love and justice." In classic liberal Protestant fashion and in tradition with Riverside's ethic, inclusivity premised on hoped-for love and justice won the day.

Church politics at Riverside could be complicated. One minister might disagree with the sentiments expressed by another; affinity groups (beginning with the Black Caucus) took positions; and those groups and others (especially Open and Affirming, a group focused on accepting homosexuals in the church) lined up supporters in the official power structure of the councils and the board of deacons. Then chaos worked its magic until natural leaders emerged to help the people recover a sense of a church that could survive. Finally, the congregation was asked to bless their efforts, and a new stasis was achieved. Indeed, the whole process resulting in an affirmation—a previously unparalleled instance of participatory democracy combined with the very kind of group statements so loathed by Fosdick from his battles with the Fundamentalists—proved so satisfying that it was used again to create the church's Mission Statement in 1992:

> The Riverside Church seeks to be a community of faith. Its members are united in the worship of God known in Jesus, the Christ, through the inspiration of the Holy Spirit. The mission of the Riverside Church is to serve

God through word and witness; to treat all human beings as sisters and brothers; and to foster responsible stewardship of all God's creation.

The Riverside Church commits itself to welcoming all persons, celebrating the diversity found in a congregation broadly inclusive of persons from different backgrounds of race, economic class, religion, culture, ethnicity, gender, age, and sexual orientation. Members are called to an individual and collective quality of life that leads to personal, spiritual, and social transformation, witnessing to God's saving purposes for all creation.

Therefore, the Riverside Church pledges itself to education, reflection, and action for peace and justice, the realization of the vision of the heavenly banquet where all are loved and blessed.[34]

The Mission Statement also sounded theological tones not heard before at Riverside. Joining the familiar religious rhetoric of peace and justice were spiritual concerns and concerns about personal transformation. In the 1990s in American Protestantism, mission statements and spirituality were in fashion. At Riverside these enthusiasms took a distinctive shape. Not only was the Holy Spirit named, but also God was said to have "saving purposes for all creation." The norm of inclusivity was just as prominent in this document as it was in any in the church's history. But now it was also articulated in the Johannine image of the beloved community and the eschatological promise of the heavenly banquet. These last were important innovations reflective of the times and also indicative of the larger number of African American leaders at Riverside. By the late 1980s the liberal conviction that men (and women) of goodwill could work things out to achieve justice in this world had largely dissipated. Without abandoning the struggle for justice, a greater interest in spirituality and realities beyond the realm of politics and economics emerged. Meanwhile, leaders in the black church had never believed that all of God's purposes would be fulfilled in their lifetimes. But believing that these purposes and promises were real, they maintained a theology of hope. It is this theological emphasis that James Forbes brought to his work at Riverside. The Mission Statement represented not only the outcome of a new mass politics at Riverside but also a theology that was articulated by and for the current members, in keeping with the theology they heard from the pulpit. Until that time, meaning at Riverside had been created by listening to preaching and/or joining a group of people with shared values. These ways of being religious have, of course, continued to operate at Riverside, but they have been joined by the increasingly common practice of defining one's fellowship by means of congregational confessions, affirmations, and statements of mission or belief. Fosdick's Riverside was a place where any thing could be said from the pulpit. Campbell's and Coffin's Riverside was a church where a thousand flowers might bloom but unity of mind was not desired. By contrast, late-twentieth- and early-twenty-first-century Riverside under Forbes has returned to the root meaning of religion, "to bind"— and to be bound by common values, commitments, and beliefs in a world that was more secular than any the earlier Riverside ministers had ever faced.

The Difficulty of Living up to the Church's Ideals

The Riverside Church began its life with trustees, as required by New York state law; with deacons, as required by Baptist custom; and with a charismatic minister in the person of Harry Emerson Fosdick to lead them all. Like other large urban Protestant churches, Riverside was an institutional church, whose facilities and programs far outstripped the Sundays- and Wednesdays-only operations of earlier models of church life. This growth in activity forced one of the key questions in twentieth-century Protestant church life: who is going to run the church? Riverside began its life in 1930 with the customary pattern in place. Fosdick and his associates ran the church's affairs and received a striking amount of deference from lay leaders in their exercise of power. Yet as early as 1937, the board of trustees believed that the structures of governance and direction brought over from Park Avenue were not up to the task of guiding the new ministries and activities sponsored by Riverside. The trustees authorized its president to appoint a special committee to oversee the church's policies, programs, and activities. In 1939 the church adopted a framework for organizing the church's work into general, standing, and special committees, plus a coordinating committee to tie together the deacons, the trustees, and the ministerial collegium.[35]

Until James Forbes helped the deacons and trustees understand the value of merging into a unicameral body in 1989/90, the senior ministers after Fosdick had little direct input into the way the church was structured and in deciding how it was to be led. Indeed, in the 1956 "Riverside Church Survey Report," the picture that emerges is one of ambivalence about the role of the clergy in the church's administration. On the one hand, the ministers are valued for their spiritual leadership, but on the other hand, they are not to administer the church. This ambivalence is seen in this passage from the Report:

> The ministry of Dr. Harry Emerson Fosdick, succeeded by that of Dr. Robert James McCracken, has given Riverside a continuing spiritual leadership unique in ecclesiastical history. Members and congregation can only be grateful for them and determine to devise ways and means by which Riverside can best help its ministers present their message. To that end we offer the following recommendations . . . that the preaching minister should be relieved, so far as possible, of other demands on his time so that he can concentrate on giving his message the widest possible outreach. (p. 15)

For all the concern that the clergy be free of worldly concerns, leadership issues surfaced again and again in the church's history. The 1956 "Riverside Church Survey Report," for instance, stated that "careful exploration be made of means for closer coordination in the functions of the music personnel of the Church, and for closer contacts between the music personnel and the music programs of major organized groups within the Church." A member of the survey's committee conducted confidential interviews with the staff and discovered that most felt that from a personnel point of view, no one was in charge. Other concerns pertained to the program staffs' and ministers' conducting their own programs with little relation to the official boards.

The overall thrust of the 1956 reorganization was to create six major councils, responsible to the deacons and trustees, and to relate the Collegium to those boards through the Joint Committee and at points through the work of the councils themselves.[36] Such a structure worked reasonably well for Jim McCracken personally, accustomed as he was to the ministry of the pulpit. But preaching was one of the few things that the ministers and staff of the church did without the collaboration of others, and the effect of the new organization was to create fiefdoms ruled by some clergy and staff, supported by lay members of councils, and unresponsive to direction from either the senior minister or the boards. One administrator, Carroll Fitch, was hired under the new plan and served as perhaps the most effective lay church administrator the church had ever had. But the ministerial leadership and authority and lay leadership and authority continued to be exercised without clear relation to one another.

By the time Eugene Laubach joined the ministerial staff in 1961, the ideals of the 1956 reorganization had already fallen apart in the chaos of real-life contingencies. In the late 1980s, Laubach remembered:

> In 1961, if I had known what I was going to get into when I arrived, I would not have taken the job even after making my own job description. Because what I really hadn't analyzed very well was what kind of a collegium I was going to be working with. And in 1961, it was a devastated collegium.[37]

Illness and staff incompatibility made the situation worse. Riverside, like many other churches, had not found a way to face clergy and staff problems. As Laubach recalled, "Riverside suffers, as other churches suffer from the fact that it doesn't know how appropriately to get rid of anybody. When it has somebody, they tend to hang in for life, or have a big blow-up with one or the other of the clergy." Part of the reason that clergy members of the staff were able to continue was that there was no external authority to arbitrate problems. In a 1988 interview, Ernest Campbell compared his experience at Riverside unfavorably with his prior experience in Presbyterian churches, at which at least the presbytery could help arbitrate disputes: "We had no court of appeal. I used to say flippantly the only thing we had at Riverside was God and that wasn't enough."[38]

By the early 1960s, the Collegium no longer included all the ministers at Riverside. Other ordained clergy worked at the church, including Robert Polk, Phyllis Taylor, and Pablo Cotto of the Hispanic ministry. Laubach recalled the low morale produced by having two classes of ministers:

> They began to have this double standard, described very aptly in a devastating moment when Pablo Cotto, the Hispanic minister, was introduced to a Men's Class banquet and the toastmaster stood up and said, "You all know that at Riverside there are big ministers and there are little ministers. And tonight we're going to present you with one of the little ministers."[39]

To deal with ministerial disparity issues, the Collegium was eliminated from 1963 to 1967, but Ernest Campbell brought it back in the late 1960s to suit his sense that the clergy ought to be in charge of the church. He was also given the title of senior minister, which replaced the title of preaching minister with which he began his work. But Campbell soon found that the new title changed little:

> That became in the long run, an ominous sort of a switch, because I was actually given responsibility for everything, but I had authority over nothing. ... To me, that was tantamount to let's say having responsibility to keep a street clean, but having no authority to stop people who were dropping refuse on the street.[40]

Where the authority had actually gone was to the councils, which bit by bit became the structures that supported particular ministers and ministries. Senior ministers from Campbell to Forbes have found themselves confronting powerful interest groups when they have tried to deal with colleagues resistant to playing as part of a team. Campbell recalled how in his experience the politics worked:

> I would try to get at the matter in a reconciliatory way, whether it be substance of curriculum or whatever, and one would find then that the people who were doing Christian Ed had more than allegiance to their council. That council would form a very strong bond and at the next meeting of deacons, anything you would try to do through that council would be overcome by the council appealing to the whole board. So, in other words, you had a series of mini-kingdoms, each of which operated under the rubric of a council.[41]

Frustrations over administrative leadership matters like these eventually drove Campbell to resign unexpectedly.

Campbell was a strong leader whose previous ministries had offered challenges he had been able to overcome by force of personality and clarity of moral vision. Or so it seemed. For Campbell's leadership style to be effective at Riverside, he perhaps would have needed the powerful place at the table to which he had become accustomed in his Presbyterian churches in York, Pennsylvania, and Ann Arbor, Michigan. Instead, he found himself again and again trying to run the church without the authority to do so. In fairness to Campbell, the issues he faced were unlike those that had confronted Fosdick and McCracken. Increasingly, Riverside's most important issues had internal dimensions. After the mid-1960s the church no longer looked down from its lofty position on Morningside Heights and asked what it should do about the city. Instead, the church began to grapple with what it should do with the city within Riverside. Managing the staffs and councils that had taken on a life of their own in the later McCracken years became much more challenging in the late 1960s than knowing what to preach. Campbell's preaching never failed him, but his style of leadership increasingly did. Eugene Laubach's conciliatory style was more successful in getting the council and staffs (by this time there were several staffs and not a single group of professionals working together on a common agenda) to work toward common ends. But Ernest Campbell was not about to play the part of a political "fixer." Throughout the early 1970s, therefore, the boards, various councils, and various staff members and Ernie Campbell found themselves in constant low-intensity conflict. When Campbell resigned, it came as a complete surprise to most parishioners, but for Campbell it was a final act of refusal to accept the humiliation of working as a pastor in the highly charged political environment of Riverside's councils and boards.

When William Sloane Coffin came to be senior minister, he was told by the interim minister, Jitsuo Morikawa, "You cannot be a strong enough leader here. They desperately need strong leaders here." Coming from an academic setting, Coffin had a strong stomach for dissent and even took a certain delight in creative chaos. But Riverside in 1977 seemed to have much more dissent and chaos than even he expected. Ten years later he recalled,

> I asked Laubach shortly after I got here when I was being driven out of my mind by lack of structure; I said, "How come this place is so chaotic?" He said, "Because it's Baptist. Because there's no organization. There's too much organization." It's a very good answer. There's not a nice Presbyterian structure, Anglican structure, Methodist structure. There's no kind of structure. So there's much too much structure. Two boards? That's crazy. And then there's no clear understanding of what's staff and what's board. And there's no very clear understanding of what kind of respect and authority is due an ordained person.[42]

Not surprisingly, clerical authority and the changing dynamics of lay power proved to be the moving targets of Riverside's organizational life in the second half of its history.

From Deference to Politicization

If Riverside was an organizational mess by the early 1970s, for reasons unique to its own history, it was also illustrative of factors working to change relations between the clergy and laity and among the laity themselves throughout American Protestantism in the second half of the twentieth century. These factors included declining social deference to "elites," an assertion of the value of popular democracy, and reduced respect for the "office" of minister.

When Riverside began, the deacons and trustees were handpicked by the clergy in consultation with lay elites. In the early years, the board of trustees met for one hour a month on the fifty-fourth floor of the Rockefeller Center Building. Fosdick and, later, McCracken attended. The trustees met, their committees reported, they divided work among themselves, they gave the staff things to do, they read reports, and they left. The trustees came from business settings where they were empowered to make decisions for others, and they did not hesitate to do so in the context of Riverside Church. In this respect they were not unlike the local lay leaders of a hundred thousand other Protestant churches in America. But by the early 1960s, an ideology of participation was taking hold. At first during the McCracken and Campbell years at Riverside, the move toward greater inclusion took the form of symbolic actions. In a series of photographs of the board of ushers from various years, one can see the tremendous change in its racial, ethnic, and gender makeup. These sorts of changes continued in the Coffin era as women were added to the ministerial and professional staffs and preached more frequently. The ideal of fuller lay participation also took the form of election of trustees and deacons in the mid-1960s. Still, however, the nomination of a slate for these elections came from a closed process, controlled by clergy and lay elites in the congregation. Meanwhile, church members were finding their voices in other places, including protest politics.

The campus and antiwar protests of 1968 and 1969 deeply affected all institutions on Morningside Heights. Increasingly Riversiders themselves took to the streets, protesting policies in the name of God. The relative novelty of the protest approach is more apparent when comparing the actions of William Sloane Coffin and his generation of leaders with those of Harry Emerson Fosdick and Robert James McCracken. To be sure, Coffin, as Yale's chaplain, helped pioneer the use of the post–civil rights movement's domestic protest in the antiwar movement, but something else had changed as well: the way things were was no longer perceived as basically "all right." Even with Ernest T. Campbell, it seemed that whatever was wrong with the world could be solved with a healthy dose of real religion rightly understood and a good conversation among people of goodwill. Knowledge and understanding, it was thought in the pre-Vietnam era, would bring about social transformation. For liberal Protestants, the lesson of the war was that governmental policies could be diametrically opposed to the teaching of the gospel and that religious leaders were nearly powerless to change this state of affairs through moral suasion. The National Radio Pulpit and conversations with the rich and powerful were no longer useful tools. So Coffin and those like him turned to the streets, to the people, to the means of protest to block unjust uses of power. The liberal religious agenda in the 1970s and 1980s, therefore, was a prophetic critique of society. This critique could be found in the pages of *Christianity & Crisis* (which was published right in the Morningside Heights neighborhood and presented the Niebuhrian view of politics as power), *The Christian Century*, and even *Sojourners*, an evangelical magazine associated with countercultural evangelicals Jim Wallis and Ron Sider. The only people in the Protestant mainstream who still prayed for the president each week in church in a supportive way were the Episcopalians, and their *Book of Common Prayer*'s liturgy required it. In most liberal congregations, any mention of the president of the United States in a public prayer was liable to sound much like a plea from the ancient Hebrews to soften Pharaoh's hardened heart. Then, as now, what God's people sought most was liberation.

In the course of engaging the political world, Riverside and many other churches created a political awareness in its members about the church itself. First, groups and caucuses began fielding candidates for the deacons and council chairs, and at that point, politics hit the internal workings of the boards. Eugene Laubach remembered:

At the same time that this populism was moving the elections process, it was moving in the deacons. And you had people like Lou Gropp, who dies now to think that he once said it, but once said very specifically, "There are three power centers in this church: the deacons, the trustees, and the collegium. I'm going to make the deacons the power center in this church. And the way we're going to do it is cut you guys out." And he did it. He absolutely did it. He arranged, as chair of the board of deacons, that the collegium would make a report, and except for that, we were not to speak on any issue unless we were invited to do so. And he made that stick.[43]

And so the shift from clergy to lay authority continued. Throughout Coffin's time at Riverside, deacons meetings were so unpleasant for the clergy that he rarely attended.

The 1989 reorganization of church governance into a single church council, five commissions, two committees of the church, and seven committees of the council was designed to bring budgets, programming, and mission under one authoritative roof. Soon, however, the senior minister, James Forbes, found himself in a dispute with the executive minister, David Dyson, and running afoul of the same "mini-kingdom" powers that had developed thirty years earlier. At that time, Ernest Campbell's opponents had fought him sub rosa. Now, Forbes saw the fight taken outside the church to the newspapers by a group calling itself "Riversiders for Riverside," a controversy described elsewhere in this book. For all his efforts to lead the church from somewhere in addition to the pulpit, Forbes found his goodwill returned with opposition. Some of this opposition was related to race, but some came from a decline of ministerial authority, which had diminished over forty years more widely than Riverside alone.

Like many churches in the mainstream, Riverside was a hard place to be in ministry in the 1990s. Jim Forbes still carries the sting of his early confrontations. "I wish," he declared, looking back, "that I was not so helpful to the Holy Spirit in bringing about reconciliation."[44] The cost of helping Riverside be the body of Christ was often, too often, paid disproportionately by its clergy. Why did they continue to put up with the difficulties of leading in a time after the eclipse of leadership? Perhaps mostly because this form of Christian community at the turn of the new millennium still beats the alternatives. Gene Laubach commented, "I've sent three children out from this church who try in vain to repeat it. I know the Riverside theology exists because, in spite of all the crap that you experience here, there is also something that is so powerful that you want to repeat this when you get away."[45]

Just what is the Riverside theology? A theology of culture. To some outside critics there is little to tie the influential church of America's richest Depression-era family to the predominantly black church of today except for a great building and a name. But such critics who trade on surface appearances miss not only the genius of Riverside Church but also how it has carried the spirit of liberal Protestantism into the new century far more consistently than have most other institutions of the old mainstream establishment. Riverside's enduring theology of culture might be summed up with a question: "Is anything secular?" For three-quarters of a century Riversiders have, by their actions and words, answered that question with a resounding "no." In successive religious climates of fear of being characterized as "not Christian," or a later fear of decline, other liberal Protestant institutions have chosen to avoid dealing with fundamentalism, poverty, race, sexuality, nuclear defense, immigration, and other faiths. Riverside has rarely failed to embrace a new issue or group of people in American culture. This is not to suggest that everything is acceptable to the Riverside theology. Things may be imperfect, corrupt, unjust, unpleasant, or simply unaesthetic, and the prophetic preaching of the Riverside pulpit testifies to the church's values at critical points. Yet the fact remains that the God of Riverside Church has always been assumed to encompass enough of all realities to allow their discussion without fear. The slogan on the church's website also testifies to the enduring faith in God met in culture by answering the question "Who We Are" with the "THE THREE "I"s. . . .We are an interdenominational, interracial, and international congregation." At Riverside, the liberal ideal of inclusion still lives.

The Riverside Church set out to be an exemplary church and to live by progressive ideals. What have seventy years wrought? Enormous service to be sure, but an honest narration of the church's history must include disappointment on the part of many as Riverside has struggled to meet its own high expectations. In this way, too, Riverside has mirrored liberal Protestantism at large, for throughout the twentieth century, the church has labored to be both a beloved community and a prophetic voice to the world. Riverside has done far better than most liberal Protestant entities in living up to a theological mandate begun in the Progressive era and constantly enlarged ever since. Nevertheless, some of the very ideals—democracy, participation, inclusion, acceptance of difference—that Riverside and others have embraced entailed extraordinary effort and risk. If the mainstream Protestant decline is about not being fully willing to pay the costs of one's theological commitments, then Riverside's history is more hopeful: a narrative about living somewhat gracefully with those same costs in an unredeemed world.

NOTES

1. William R. Hutchison, *The Modernist Impulse in American Protestantism* (Cambridge, Mass.: Harvard University Press, 1976).

2. Harry Emerson Fosdick, *The Living of These Days* (New York, Harper Bros., 1956), 21.

3. Ibid., 35.

4. Ronald Chernow, *Titan: The Life of John D. Rockefeller* (New York: Vintage Books, 1999), 125.

5. Ibid., 126.

6. John D. Rockefeller Jr., "I Believe," a radio broadcast appeal on behalf of the USO and the National War Fund, July 8, 1941. This statement of principles was widely reprinted and in 1960 was permanently inscribed in stone at Rockefeller Center as a tribute to him.

7. George M. Marsden, *Fundamentalism in American Culture: The Shaping of 20th-Century Evangelicalism, 1870–1925* (New York: Oxford University Press, 1980), 118–19.

8. Bradley J. Longfield, "For Church and Country: The Fundamentalist-Modernist Conflict in the Presbyterian Church," *Journal of Presbyterian History* 78 (spring 2000): 36–37.

9. John B. Macnab, "Fosdick at First Church," in *A Preaching Ministry: 20-1 Sermons Preached by Harry Emerson Fosdick at the First Presbyterian Church in the City of New York, 1918–1925* (New York: First Presbyterian Church in the City of New York, 2000), 22.

10. Fosdick, sermon manuscript, March 9, 1919, 6, quoted in Macnab, "Fosdick at First Church," 32.

11. Fosdick, "Shall the Fundamentalists Win?" in *A Preaching Ministry*, 191.

12. Fosdick, "Farewell," *Church Tower* 2 (March 1925): 22.

13. "Dr. Fosdick Accepts the Challenge," *The Christian Century*, October 15, 1930, 1239.

14. Processional Hymn created for the Dedication, *The Church Monthly*, October 1930, 233.

15. Eugene Laubach, "Holiness and Hustle," sermon, 1964.

16. James W. Lewis, *At Home in the City* (Knoxville: University of Tennessee Press, 1992), 3–5.

17. "Riverside Business and Professional Women's Club Historical Committee, in Celebration of Our 60th Year, 1990 Supplement," n.p.

18. Guild box, archives cage.

19. *Church Monthly*, June 1942, 160.

20. *Church Monthly*, November 1942, 34–35.

21. *Church Monthly*, February, September, and November 1943.

22. *Church Monthly*, November 1943.

23. Photos located in archives, Guild folder, drawer 5, and Arts and Crafts folder.

24. Ninth-floor archives, "Budget drama photos Primary Department 1930s, men's class 1930s, McCracken, ministers, bell ringers"; *Church Monthly*, December 1945, 3.

25. C. Ivar Hellstrom, "Our Venture in Religious Education," *Church Monthly*, February 1933, 70.

26. Interview with Eugene Laubach, March 16, 1988; interview with George Younger, February 19, 1989.

27. Edith Fisher Hunter, "Sophia Lyon Fahs: Liberal Religious Educator, 1876–1978" (http://www.harvardsquarelibrary.org/unitarians/fahs.html).

28. Reinhold Niebuhr, "How Adventurous Is Dr. Fosdick?" *The Christian Century*, January 6, 1927, 17–18.

29. "Riverside Church Survey Report," 1956, 50.

30. For examples of William Sloane Coffin's preaching against religious hypocrisy and the tendency of Christians to single out sexuality as the locus of evil, see "Neither Do I Condemn You," sermon delivered on July 15, 1979, and May 1, 1983; "On Homosexuality," sermon delivered on July 12, 1981; and "Judge Not That You Be Not Judged," sermon delivered on January 27, 1980. See interview with Robert T. Handy and George David Smith by WSC, November 23, 1987.

31. Channing E. Phillips, "On Human Sexuality," sermon delivered on May 5, 1985.

32. Interview with William Sloane Coffin, June 8, 2000.

33. Interview with Eugene Laubach by me, March 16, 1988.

34. Statement of Mission of the Riverside Church in the City of New York, approved by the Religious Society, May 17, 1992.

35. "Riverside Church Survey Report," 1956, 63–64.

36. "Riverside Church Survey Report," 1956, 71–72.

37. Interview with Laubach.

38. Interview with Ernest T. Campbell by me, March 14, 1988.

39. Interview with Laubach.

40. Interview with Campbell.

41. Ibid.

42. Interview with Coffin.

43. Interview with Laubach.

44. Interview with James Forbes by me, June 9, 2000.

45. Interview with Laubach.

2

Preachers for All Seasons
The Legacy of Riverside's Free Pulpit

Leonora Tubbs Tisdale

For many people in the United States and elsewhere, the terms *Riverside Church* and *excellence in preaching* are synonymous. While other Protestant churches may be able to name an outstanding preacher or two in their past, the Riverside Church was founded for the preaching ministry of Harry Emerson Fosdick and has insisted throughout its history that pulpit eloquence and excellence be major criteria in the selection of its senior ministers. Fosdick's name still may loom large over the pulpit of Riverside, but each of his four successors—Robert James McCracken, Ernest T. Campbell, William Sloane Coffin Jr., and James A. Forbes Jr.—has contributed to Riverside's reputation as a church where intelligent, challenging, relevant, socially aware proclamation of the gospel is the norm.

Moreover, throughout its history the Riverside pulpit has hosted some of the greatest preachers and leaders of the nation and world, adding to its aura as a place where the gospel and the real world meet in a highly visible way. It was from the Riverside pulpit that in 1967 Martin Luther King Jr. first publicly voiced his opposition to the Vietnam War. It was from the Riverside pulpit that Nelson Mandela, after spending long years in prison for his antiapartheid activities in South Africa, first addressed U.S. church leaders in 1991 after his release from prison. And it was from the Riverside pulpit that speakers as diverse as Cesar Chavez, Jesse Jackson, Dom Helder Camara, Desmond Tutu, Joan Brown Campbell, Gardner Taylor, Reinhold Niebuhr, K. H. Ting, Andrew Young, and Marian Wright Edelman talked to the church and nation about issues that were near and dear to their hearts.

FIGURE 2.1: The nave pulpit. The Riverside Church's strong commitment to prophetic preaching is symbolized by the five large prophetic figures—Anna, Amos, Isaiah, Hosea, and Miriam—that are carved into the limestone of the supporting column beneath the pulpit and by the fifteen additional prophets that occupy niches in the pulpit rail. *Used by permission of the Riverside Church Archives.*

People may have been lulled to sleep by sermons they have heard from other pulpits, but such has not been the norm at Riverside. Indeed, Riverside's preachers have often served as spiritual gadflies for the nation's corporate conscience, taking on the critical issues of the day and challenging people of faith to rethink and re-view them through the lens of Bible and theology. From Fosdick's preaching of pacifism before and during World War II, McCracken's outspokenness against racism, and Campbell's case for reparations to Coffin's persistent advocacy for a nuclear arms freeze and Forbes's deep concern for the poor in a time of economic prosperity, these men have not shied away from preaching a relevant and prophetic gospel even when it was costly to do so. In this regard, they have been "preachers for all seasons," crafting through their sermons a contextual and public theology that, at its best, pressed church and nation beyond the confines of self-interest and individualism and toward a concern for the common good of all, especially the marginalized and dispossessed. Consequently, many liberal Christians across the nation have viewed Riverside Church as a "beacon on the hill" giving hope, encouragement, and a theological vision for a more open and inclusive church and society.

It would be a mistake, however, to think that the only witness from the Riverside pulpit has been a prophetic one. Riverside preachers have also been pastors, and their sermons have exhibited a concern for the personal and existential questions that haunt worshipers in every age. Fosdick judged the efficacy of his sermons by the number of people who wanted to see him in his study for pastoral care in the week following his proclamation. Coffin, widely known for his prophetic voice on disarmament issues, gave a sermon following his teenaged son's death in a car accident that has since become one of his best-loved, offering hope and comfort to many facing similar tragedies in their own lives. Forbes has been concerned that the congregation's activism also be undergirded by a life rich in prayer and spirituality. Although none of the Riverside preachers has shrunk from addressing the corporate and public concerns of their day, each of them has also had a concern for individual and personal dimensions of the faith and has served as a pastor to the Riverside flock even while ministering to a larger city, nation, and world.

Indeed, one of the tensions that every Riverside pastor has had to face is being, on the one hand, the preacher to a local congregation—the membership of the Riverside Church—and, on the other hand, the preacher to a bigger world. From the outset, visitors have come to Riverside Church by the hundreds, and people across the nation have felt that Riverside was, in some sense, their church too. Certainly the radio ministries of Riverside's early pastors, the Riverside sermon subscription service, the church's long-term social outreach programs, and its insistence on having an ecumenical, international, and interracial membership have helped heighten the sense that the Riverside Church was not only a local congregation with members, officers, and an internal life of its own but also a national cathedral for American Protestantism and, on a grander scale, "the people's church." Each of the Riverside preachers has had to live with this tension, balancing local concerns with the larger concerns of the city, nation, and world and keeping a finger not only on the pulse of a particular congregation but also on the heartbeat of a bigger church and society.

Consequently, the Riverside preachers have needed to be contextual theologians of the highest order. Well trained in Bible and theology, this pulpit has also required that they be sensitive, intelligent, and well-read "exegetes" of a larger church and culture, adept at engaging in a gospel-cultural dialogue capable of expanding the hearts and visions of the broader American public.

The legacy of the five senior ministers who occupied Riverside's pulpit in the twentieth century and, now, the twenty-first, is that while each brought his own gifts and personalities to his preaching ministry, all also shared certain traits. Among them are the following:

- A commitment to reflect theologically on the problems and issues facing city, church, nation, and world.
- A willingness to challenge the status quo in light of larger gospel realities.
- A belief in a God whose love embraces all races and nations and whose church is bigger than any one denomination's vision of it.
- A concern for the societal and individual dimensions of the gospel, the prophetic, and the pastoral.
- A wide-ranging knowledge of the Bible and an engagement of biblical themes in proclamation.
- A sensitivity to the changing times and situations in which they lived and an openness to altering their preaching and its emphases, if necessary, in order to address more adequately the shifts in church and culture.
- A willingness to enter into a dialogue through preaching with the intellectual forces of their times (whether science, technology, economics, politics, or literature and the arts) and to become better educated themselves in order to engage the intellectual currents of their day.
- An ability to bring their gifts as artists to bear in sermonic language, forms, and rhetoric that have the capacity to delight their listeners as well as to instruct, convict, and move them.
- An appreciation for the larger liturgical context in which preaching occurs and a sensitivity to the ways in which music, prayer, art, and architecture can also draw people into the presence of God.

It is these common commitments, as well as their skills and gifts in proclaiming the Christian message, that have set apart the Riverside preachers. They have guided not only the Riverside Church itself but also a larger American church and public, toward a faith that is "seriously imaginable" for contemporary people, that is not afraid to tackle the toughest issues of our day, and that seeks to have a transformative and prophetic witness in public life. Consequently, most of these preachers have also had critics who accused them of everything from heresy to apostasy. Their contextual gospel has not been universally loved by a larger church and world—or even by the Riverside members themselves.

Nonetheless, it is to the credit of the Riverside Church that its pulpit has always been a free and sacred space in which preachers, unfettered by congregational or denominational restraints, have been able to interpret the word of God for today's world. Riverside's membership has consistently called strong and capable preachers who have not hesitated to exercise the freedoms granted them there. Even in the 1960s and 1970s, when preaching in the United States was attacked for being too authoritarian or too passive in an age of egalitarianism, Riverside never wavered from its commitment to a strong preaching and worship ministry. The church has consistently affirmed that the service given to God in worship and in the public sphere go hand in hand and that activism in the streets is always strengthened by active engagement with God in the sanctuary.

Each of the first five Riverside preachers contributed to the church his own personality, gifts, life experience, preaching style, theology, and faith commitments in interpreting the various seasons of church and nation. Each as well helped shape a trajectory of preaching and worship that is unique to Riverside. Thus, as we focus on the individual contribution of the Riverside preachers, we also ask: What can be said about the proclamation and worship that have shaped the Riverside Church, its vision, and its ministries in the past? What have been its major strengths and weaknesses? And what can we learn from an overview that will help the church as it continues ministering in the future?

Harry Emerson Fosdick (1925–1946)

When surveying the homiletical landscape of the United States in the first half of the twentieth century, no pulpit giant's shadow looms larger than that of Harry Emerson Fosdick. Fosdick, whose reputation and influence

FIGURE 2.2: Dr. Harry Emerson Fosdick. *Photo-graph by Lilo Kaskell Photo. Used by permission of the Riverside Church Archives and Lilo Kaskell Photo.*

extended far beyond New York City and the Riverside Church, preached a message that reached millions through his printed sermons, published books (almost fifty in all), and radio broadcasts. What set Fosdick apart from some of the other well-known national evangelical preachers was his commitment to a liberal theology that made the Christian faith intelligible to contemporary people. Eschewing fundamentalism, biblical literalism, and a conservatism that refused to engage the intellectual forces of his time, Fosdick insisted that the Christian faith was reasonable and that it was possible to embrace it without checking one's intellect at the door.

Fosdick's preaching, thoughtful as it was, was not simply an intellectual reflection on relevant topics. He also brought to his proclamation a love for people, a pastoral sensitivity to his listeners' problems, a deep faith in God, and an evangelical desire to convince modern people that embracing the Christian faith would not only improve the well-being of their own lives but could also strengthen the moral and spiritual fiber of their church, nation, and world. Robert Moats Miller, whose 1985 biography of Fosdick remains the best to date, called him an "evangelical liberal" and quoted Fosdick responding to a critical interviewer: "I may be a liberal, but I'm evangelical, too." *The Christian Century* agreed with that assessment, saying of Fosdick, "He has stood within the evangelical tradition and preached the great doctrines of God and Christ and grace and regeneration with a consistency and power which no conservative theologian could excel."[1]

It was this blend of a liberal intellect, an evangelical passion for preaching the Christian message, a pastoral love for people, an ecumenical vision for the church, and a prophetic witness for pacifism in a time of war that caused people either to love and admire Fosdick or to vilify him and deem him "heretical." But even those who strongly differed with Fosdick's theology or pacifist stance also had enormous respect for his intellect, courage, compassion, and the persistent faithfulness of his witness. Rabbi Stephen S. Wise is said to have commented that Fosdick was "the least hated and best loved heretic that ever lived."[2] Although theologians will long argue whether or not the gospel that Fosdick preached was "heretical," there is no question that thousands of Americans were drawn to it—and to the man himself—because of his thoughtful and compassionate preaching. By daring to ask the tough questions of faith in light of modern knowledge and the tough questions of how to live in a modern world in light of Christian faith, Fosdick earned a place as one of the foremost Christian apologists of the modern era.

Early Life Influences on Fosdick's Preaching

Fosdick's strong commitment to preaching a gospel that moved beyond legalism, literalism, and authoritarianism was fueled by two struggles of faith in his own early life. The first was his theological battle with the hell-fire-and-damnation kind of God he heard preached in his childhood years, and the second was the psychological torment he suffered as a young adult student at Union Theological Seminary in New York.

Fosdick was born in 1878 in Buffalo, New York. In his autobiography he recounts that as a boy he was reared by democratic and open-minded parents who exuded an uplifting and thoughtful Christianity that was "natural, practical [and] livable."[3] Both his father Frank, a high-school teacher and principal, and his mother Amie, a homemaker, were people of faith and intellect and early devotees of such forward-looking ecumenical endeavors as the Chautauqua movement in western New York State. They reared Harry and his twin younger siblings, Raymond and Edith, in the Christian faith and taught them to think for themselves.

But also during his youth Fosdick regularly heard the preaching of itinerant evangelists who described in detail a fearsome God dangling unworthy sinners over the yawning gates of hell if they refused to forgo such sins as dancing, card playing, and theatergoing. Fosdick struggled with this frightening image of God throughout his youth and recalled that the main source of his unhappiness in an otherwise happy childhood was his religion. He lived in constant terror of the God that many evangelists and churches then proclaimed and longed to experience God in a different way.

During his years as a college student at Colgate University, Fosdick finally rebelled against the bibliolatry and fundamentalist theology of his childhood and began a theological struggle that, for him, was "mental rather than moral," with the stakes being "the intellectual credibility of Christian faith." Under the tutelage of Colgate professors who were both devoutly Christian and intellectually well respected in their fields, Fosdick began to embrace the liberal theology that characterized his preaching in the years to come.[4]

The second struggle that shaped Fosdick's preaching occurred while he was a student at Union Theological Seminary in New York in the early 1900s. During his first year as a seminarian—while he was studying theology at Union, philosophy at Columbia University, and helping run the mission at Mariners' Temple in the slums of the Bowery—Fosdick had an emotional breakdown. After months of treatment in a sanitarium in Elmira, New York, and many more months of convalescence at home, he was able to emerge from his depression and return to his studies at Union. During this time, as he himself readily acknowledged, all the techniques he had previously used for self-preservation "petered completely out," and he had to rely on God and prayer to see him through. This experience

> was one of the most important factors in my preparation for the ministry. For the first time in my life, I faced, at my wit's end, a situation too much for me to handle. I went down into the depths where self-confidence becomes ludicrous. . . . I learned to pray, not because I had adequately argued out prayer's rationality, but because I desperately needed help from a Power

greater than my own. I learned that God, much more than a theological proposition, is an immediately available Resource . . . a spiritual Presence in living communion with whom we can find sustaining strength.[5]

His breakdown and his own encounter with God in the midst of it gave Fosdick great empathy for others undergoing psychological struggles and helped shape his understanding of preaching as "group counseling on a grand scale." "People," he said, "come to church on Sunday with every kind of personal difficulty and problem flesh is heir to. A sermon was meant to meet such needs; it should be personal counseling on a group scale."[6] Consequently, Fosdick's own preaching throughout his life sought to give hope and encouragement to those battling such personal demons as depression, loneliness, low self-esteem, and an inability to accept forgiveness. Above all, he wanted to bring his listeners closer to the God in whose presence they could find sustaining strength.

It was at Union that Fosdick first began to hear the call to preach and to discern that his particular vocation was to be "an interpreter in modern, popular, understandable terms, of the best that I could find in the Christian tradition."[7] In 1903, his senior year, Fosdick was offered a student assistantship at the Madison Avenue Baptist Church, and in November of that year he was ordained at the Madison Avenue Church.

The following spring Fosdick graduated from Union Theological Seminary *summa cum laude* and shortly thereafter was called to be the pastor of First Baptist church of Montclair, New Jersey. He and Florence Allen Whitney were married in August of the same year and had two children, Elinor and Dorothy. Fosdick served the Montclair Church for eleven years before being called in 1918 to be assistant pastor and chief preacher of the First Presbyterian Church in New York City.

A "Project Method" Preacher Is Born

As early as when he was at Montclair, Fosdick's fame as a preacher began to spread. Before long he was much in demand on the college chapel circuit, preaching at universities such as Harvard and Princeton and actually gaining an attentive hearing from student audiences more accustomed to reading the newspaper through the compulsory morning chapel hour. In order to gain such a hearing, however, Fosdick discovered that he needed to toss out most of what he had learned about preaching in seminary and depart from the expository style that was commonplace among preachers of his day. Rather than beginning a sermon with a lengthy exposition of a particular biblical text and then applying the text to the lives of his listeners,[8] Fosdick preferred to begin a sermon with an extensive examination of a real-life problem facing people and then address the problem from the standpoint of the Christian faith. "Every sermon," he maintained, "should have for its main business the head-on constructive meeting of some problem which was puzzling minds, burdening consciences, distracting lives, and no sermon which so met a real human difficulty, with light to throw on it and help to win a victory over it, could possibly be futile."[9] Fosdick called his mode of preaching the "project method" and found that it allowed him to address a variety of topics that were on the hearts and minds of his worshipers, topics that were not simply individual but also social, economic, political, and international.[10]

But Fosdick believed that a sermon should not simply become a lecture. Indeed, he felt that much of the liberal preaching of his day suffered from being an intellectual exercise that "[did] nothing to anyone." Rather, he maintained that

> the preacher's business is not merely to discuss repentance but to persuade people to repent; not merely to debate the meaning and possibility of Christian faith, but to produce faith in the lives of his listeners; not merely to talk about the available power of God to bring victory over trouble and temptation, but to send people out from their worship on Sunday with victory in their possession. A preacher's task is *to create in his congregation the thing he is talking about.*[11]

In order to design sermons that were not only intellectually appealing but also capable of transforming his listeners, Fosdick turned to the field of psychological counseling and the sermons of popular pulpit giants such as Phillips Brooks, who had been widely heralded for his preaching at Trinity Church, Boston. Fosdick concluded that "while we modern preachers talk about psychology much more than our predecessors, we commonly use it a good deal less."[12] He was well read in the latest psychological theories,[13] devoted three afternoons a week to pastoral counseling while serving as the minister of the Riverside Church, and delivered sermons that moved the mind as well as the heart and will.

Fosdick's preaching was based on hard work and disciplined study. During his Riverside years, Fosdick spent his mornings studying and preparing sermons. He read books on topics from science to Shakespeare, often reading three or four volumes at a time. He also took notes on what he read, keeping notebooks in which he organized quotations, anecdotes, and clippings alphabetically by author and by subject matter with cross-references!

Within four years of Fosdick's graduation, Union called him back to serve on its faculty as an instructor of homiletics. He eventually became the Morris K. Jessup Professor of Practical Theology at Union and continued teaching courses in preaching there until he retired as Riverside's pastor in 1946. Although he never wrote a textbook on preaching, his teaching of the subject influenced hundreds of seminarians who studied with him at Union. On the anniversary of his one-hundredth birthday, Riverside Church established the "Harry Emerson Fosdick Preaching Colloquium" to honor his memory and preaching legacy.

World War I and the Fundamentalist/Modernist Controversy

In 1918 two events occurred that altered the future direction of Fosdick's ministry. The first was that Fosdick, who until then had been highly supportive of the United States' involvement in World War I , was invited by the British Ministry of Information and the YMCA to speak to the American troops stationed in Europe. For four months he toured Britain, Scotland, France, and Belgium, talking to the soldiers and giving sermons in local churches. Largely as a result of that tour and the atrocities of war that he witnessed at first hand, Fosdick became a pacifist, a stance he maintained throughout World War II and until his death. The tour also heightened his determination to preach a Christian message different from the "egocentric, save-one's-own-soul . . . caricature of Christianity"[14] that many of the soldiers he met heard back home.

The second major event occurred after his return home, when Fosdick was asked to preach for four Sundays at the First Presbyterian Church on Fifth Avenue in New York City and subsequently became that congregation's permanent guest preacher. In May 1922 Fosdick delivered a sermon entitled "Shall the Fundamentalists Win?" that placed him at the center of a theological storm. While it is clear from both his autobiography and the sermon itself that Fosdick intended his message to be somewhat conciliatory (he made a strong plea for a church inclusive enough to accept both liberals and conservatives), the sermon described his "modernist" position, including his view that the virgin birth was no longer accepted as historic fact and his lack of belief in the inerrancy of the Scriptures. The sermon was published in pamphlet form and widely distributed to ministers and churches around the country, catapulting Fosdick into the center of the fundamentalist-modernist storm and resulting in his being viewed as either a hero or a villain by the many church folk who read it. Fosdick eventually resigned his post at First Presbyterian Church, at which time John D. Rockefeller Jr. persuaded him to become pastor of the Park Avenue Baptist Church, the congregation that eventually became the Riverside Church.

The Early Years at Park Avenue

On May 22, 1925, the members of Park Avenue Baptist Church voted to call Harry Emerson Fosdick to be their pastor. Six days later Dr. Cornelius Woelfkin, the outgoing pastor, announced Fosdick's acceptance:

> Dr. Fosdick comes to us following the adoption by our Church, at his suggestion, of the principle of inclusive membership. By inclusive membership Dr. Fosdick means that the Church will receive persons into its communion upon proper letters from churches of any Evangelical Denomination; and that following the Baptist principle of individual freedom and responsibility, the Church will not insist upon the rite of immersion on the part of those who cannot see their way clear to this act.[15]

The day after Fosdick's first sermon in his new church, a front-page headline in the *New York Herald Tribune* read: "Fosdick Opens His 'Thrilling Adventure' in 'Free' Pulpit." With his own profession of faith in an ecumenical and inclusive gospel, Fosdick set the course for the thrilling adventure that became the Riverside Church. With the courage and conviction that were hallmarks of his preaching throughout his twenty-one-year pastorate at Riverside, Fosdick used his pulpit to forge a vision of church that captured the imaginations of those who longed for a church where love of God and love of neighbor were focal and the church was not torn apart by endless debates over creeds and doctrines.

Fosdick preached his first sermon as minister of Park Avenue Church on Sunday, October 3, 1926. A crowd of more than fourteen hundred people packed both the sanctuary and an auditorium, which had been equipped with amplifiers to handle the overflow. Those who could not get in returned home to listen to the service broadcast on the radio. In his sermon Fosdick urged his congregation not to be easy on him as their pastor but to hold him to high standards in his preaching. He, in turn, pledged that he would not be easy on them. "I shall proclaim no diluted Christianity harmonious with popular prejudices," he stated, "but just as piercing and penetrating a gospel as I can compass, which I hope will disturb your consciences, as it disturbs mine, about the quality of life which we live in business, in society, in the nation and in private character."[16]

For three years the congregation continued to worship in the Park Avenue building while a new church building was being constructed on land that Rockefeller had bought overlooking the Hudson River on Riverside Drive. When a fire unexpectedly delayed the construction, the congregation worshiped for an additional year at Temple Beth-El (at Fifth Avenue and Seventy-sixty Street) before moving into its new Riverside sanctuary on October 5, 1930.[17]

Fosdick's sermons during those early years at Park Avenue addressed issues as diverse as "Religion's Indebtedness to Science" (in which he both extolled science for its ability to offer Christians a new view of the universe and new honesty in dealing with facts and criticized it for being bereft of faith and spirit), "Christianity's Supreme Rival" (identified as the current "dogma of nationalism" that "rips our one God into tribal gods, tramples on the sacred heritage of a free conscience, and makes of our Christianity an idle myth instead of a program of serious social action"), and "Christ and the Inferiority Complex" (in which he called on people to overcome their sense of inferiority by identifying themselves with a cause greater than themselves). From the outset, his sermons blended concern for the individual with concern for the national and global in a fluid and seamless manner.

Worship at Riverside: A Sanctuary "Fitted for Worship"

Fosdick's awareness of the importance of worshiping God through proclamation of the Word and also in the beauty of architecture, ritual, and holiness played a critical role in the design of the liturgical space and in the worship life for the church on Riverside Drive. When the Riverside Church was being designed, Rockefeller asked Fosdick if he wanted the sanctuary to be primarily an auditorium for preaching. Fosdick replied that what he wanted instead was "a sanctuary primarily fitted for worship."

> We had the unique opportunity to build all at once not only a center of social service but a cathedral, where one could preach to be sure, but where

not the pulpit but the high altar would be central and where beauty of proportion and perspective, of symbolism and color would speak to the soul
even when the voice of man was silent.[18]

Liturgically, the music and other service elements also were designed to
bring before God the best offerings of the human spirit and to assist worshipers in giving praise to the God that is the source of all beauty. From
the outset Riverside's worship was enriched not only by Fosdick's sermons
(which served as the focal point and "culmination" of each service) but
also by the majestic organ preludes and postludes, the anthems sung by a
highly trained choir, Fosdick's eloquent pastoral prayers, and the regular
singing of "Old Hundredth" (otherwise known as the "Doxology"). A
writer for the *New York Herald Tribune* who attended the opening worship
service in the new Riverside Church on October 6, 1930, captured some of
the grandeur of worshiping at Riverside:

> The audience included, besides almost the full membership of the church,
> persons of every walk of life, every nationality, race, faith, denomination
> and creed. Hindus, Mohametans, Chinese and Japanese, some in their na-
> tive dress who had come from International House, just across a small park
> from the church, were present. Workmen who had built the church—ma-
> sons, plumbers, stone cutters, electricians, wood carvers—sat in special re-
> served seats in the nave. . . .
> The service began with a processional and ended with a recessional, the
> opening lines of the processional being chanted in a cloister outside the
> nave. The choir, vested in blue caps and blue and white robes, entered the
> nave through the northwest door, followed by the three ministers of the
> church, Dr. Fosdick, the Rev. Dr. Eugene C. Carder and the Rev. C. Ivar Hell-
> strom, also in robes.
> As the crescendo of the hymn reached its highest vocal point the chancel
> was flooded with light. Eight red lights, placed just above the eight chande-
> liers hanging in the nave, were turned on. A bright sun came out at just that
> moment, shining through the stained glass windows upon the choir. The
> red curtains in the chancel and back of the black chancel screen, the gor-
> geous rose window at the very rear of the nave, the white offertory steps
> that might have been an altar except for the absence of a cross—all this cre-
> ated a spectacle brilliant with color and beauty that could hardly be
> matched in a city renowned for its beautiful churches.[19]

The *Herald Tribune* journalist also included in her article the quotation that appeared on the bulletin cover at Riverside that first Sunday morning in the new sanctuary:

> On me nor priest nor presbyter nor pope,
> Bishop nor dean may stamp a party name;
> But Jesus, with his largely human scope,
> The service of my human life may claim.
> Let prideful priests do battle about creeds.
> The church is mine that does most Christ-like deeds.

The quotation reflected the spirit of the first service of worship in the new Riverside sanctuary and Fosdick's liberal theology, and the tradition of having a quotation on the bulletin cover (rather than, for example, a picture of the church) continued throughout Fosdick's tenure as minister at Riverside. The quotations came from a wide variety of literary, theological, and scholarly sources, signaling to worshipers Riverside's commitment to an open engagement with the intellectual forces of their day.

The Sunday morning worship service itself followed basically the same order throughout Fosdick's tenure at Riverside: Prelude, Processional Hymn, Call to Worship, Sanctus (sung), Invocation and the Lord's Prayer, Old Hundredth (Doxology) sung by the congregation, Scripture Lesson, Anthem (sung by choir), Prayer (prayed by Fosdick, with a response sung by the choir), Offertory (sung by the choir), Hymn, Sermon, Prayer, Recessional Hymn, and Benediction.

The congregation used a hymnal entitled *Hymns for the Living Age*,[20] and hymns written by Fosdick himself—including "God of Grace and God of Glory," the hymn he wrote for the church's dedication on February 8, 1931—were taped to the back pages. Harold Vincent Milligan, who had been the organist and choir director at Park Avenue Baptist,[21] served in the same capacity when the congregation moved into its new building on Riverside Drive, and the choir, which originally numbered seventeen, grew to more than forty-five within the first few years in the new sanctuary.

While the Sunday morning services may have been glorious at Riverside during the Fosdick years, gaining admission to them was not easy. Visitors flocked to the church by the thousands, making it difficult for the members to get in. Consequently, members were given tickets enabling them to enter the church nave early on Sundays, until 10:45 A.M., at which time the doors were opened to visitors. Visitors and members alike were greeted by the board of ushers, a group of men dressed in cutaway coats, striped trousers, wing collars, and gray gloves, who viewed their mission as being that of "making any visitor to the church feel comfortably at home and contributing to the spiritual dignity to the service."[22]

Other Worship Services

The Sunday morning service was certainly the most widely attended service at Riverside, but it was not the only worship service held at the church during the Fosdick era. On the first Sunday afternoon of each month, a Communion service was conducted in the nave, which also included the reception of new members and baptism by those who desired it. On second, third, and fourth Sunday afternoons, the church hosted a "Ministry of Music" service, which included prayers, readings, and choral anthems. On Sunday evenings the Riverside Guild, the church's young adult fellowship, regularly sponsored worship services that included dramatic readings or plays.

Weddings and funerals also were part of the worship life at Riverside. In the first year in the new building on Riverside Drive, seventy-five couples—most of whom were not church members—were married in the church's nave or in Christ Chapel. During World War II the number of weddings increased dramatically, with 255 marriages recorded in the church's registry in 1942 and 336 in 1943.[23] The church's "Necrology" record during the sixteen years of Fosdick's ministry at the Riverside location lists the deaths of almost six hundred people who were members or friends of the Riverside congregation.

Preaching as Pastoral Counseling

In contemporary homiletical theory, Harry Emerson Fosdick is frequently referred to as the homiletician who saw preaching's primary task as "pastoral counseling on a group scale." An early advocate for incorporating the findings of modern psychological theory into his pastoral counseling, preaching, and writing, Fosdick always showed a special sensitivity to people's existential needs. His Riverside sermons are peppered with such titles as "Handling Life's Second Bests," "The Curse of Cynicism, "The Power of the Tongue," "The Conquest of Fear," and "When Life Goes All to Pieces."

In like manner, Fosdick's Wednesday evening lecture series at Riverside often combined Christian beliefs with contemporary psychological themes and issues, creating an "apology" for the Christian faith that made it believable for his modernist listeners. Many of those lectures were included in daily devotional books that became national and even international best-sellers, such as *The Meaning of Faith*, *The Meaning of Service*, and *The Meaning of Prayer* (Fosdick's all-time best-seller).

Fosdick's preaching, teaching, and writing caught the imagination of millions of people in the United States and around the world because he was, first and foremost, empathetic. Even though his pulpit was physically located at Riverside, his true parish was the larger nation, which he regularly addressed through his widely distributed printed sermons, books, and Sunday afternoon National Vespers broadcasts. His sermons were especially directed to people who wanted to ask tough questions of the Christian faith or who wrestled with how to make sense of the gospel in light of a modern worldview. Fosdick himself was amazingly prescient at identifying the issues and concerns of his time and at addressing them honestly and not defensively.

Fosdick preached out of a belief that the gospel of Christ had the power to lift, encourage, and inspire people. Although he did not deny that sin was a real force in the contemporary world, he did share liberal theology's optimism regarding the basic goodness of humanity and its confidence in the ability of people to transform social institutions.

Fosdick's first sermon in the Riverside sanctuary, entitled "What Matters in Religion," reflects his liberal theological spirit and his pastoral concern for his listeners. He began by reminding the congregation—on a day when they were certainly impressed with the grandeur of their new surroundings—that Christianity began in a carpenter's shop and that "the natural affiliations of the Gospel of Jesus are with lowly places and humble men." He went on to give witness to his belief that Jesus, who "was one of history's first great humanists, . . . cared only to see personality lifted up into abundant life." Reaffirming his own ecumenical and anticreedal stance, Fosdick asserted, "Nothing matters in Christianity, however long the tradition or accumulated the sanctities—not creedal codes or denominational partisanships or ritual regularities—nothing except those things that create abundant spiritual life." For Fosdick, people's abundant spiritual life also strengthened the moral fiber of the nation and the world. "Without [such qualities] no life can be beautiful and no civilization secure. They are radiance to the souls and foundations to the societies of men."

Fosdick's first sermon at Riverside emphasized Christ's ability to bring abundant life to personality—a common theme overall in his preaching—and showed the connections he frequently made between the personal and the societal dimensions of the gospel. An abundant life for individuals also creates a more abundant life for society at large as the moral fiber of the nation is strengthened and the best ideals of humanity are upheld. Consequently, Fosdick's faith was one in which the pastoral and the prophetic, the personal and the societal, were connected. "Group pastoral counseling" for him was comprehensive, embracing the ecclesial, national, and global issues affecting people's lives.

Fosdick did not seem to try to balance the number of sermons he gave on pastoral or personal themes with those he preached on public issues. Instead, his faith frequently pressed him to address both in the same sermon. For him, the personal and public dimensions of the gospel were two sides of the same coin. Indeed, the strength of many of his sermons is the way they move from the personal (and more readily palatable) implications of the gospel to the societal (and more prophetically stretching) implications. Notable, too, was Fosdick's pastoral care for those who viewed critical issues differently than he did, a characteristic of his ministry seen most clearly in his own preaching and position regarding war and peace.

Preaching on War, Economic Depression, and Denominationalism

Even before the outbreak of World War II, Fosdick was known for his antiwar sermons, often delivered on occasions—such as Memorial Day—when the nation remembered or glorified war.[24] His most famous antiwar sermon, "The Unknown Soldier," was delivered on November 12, 1933, a day celebrating the international establishment of the Tomb of the Unknown Soldier to honor those who died in the Great War. In it Fosdick publicly repented his own prowar stance during World War I and recounted the horrors and follies of war that he had personally witnessed while ministering to troops on the front lines. For sheer rhetorical power and eloquence, the sermon is unrivaled in the case it makes for pacifism.[25] Fosdick continued his pacifist stance throughout World War II, denouncing one of the most popular wars of all time as immoral and inhumane and encouraging conscientious objection to it on moral grounds.

But even as Fosdick offered assistance to those who refused to serve in the war, he also offered hospitality to service men and women who worshiped at Riverside during the war. A notice that ran in the bulletin of the Riverside Church throughout the war years welcomed any military personnel who were worshiping with the congregation, encouraged them to sign a guest register designed especially for them, and informed them of Dr. Fosdick's willingness to write a personal note to anyone they desired back home, informing that person of their visit to Riverside. The Navy Midshipmen's Training School, headquartered in New York City, also held a regular worship service in the Riverside sanctuary on Sunday afternoons. In addition, Fosdick tried to protect Japanese students in New York who were ostracized after the bombing of Pearl Harbor.[26]

Although he was extremely outspoken in his Christian opposition to war, Fosdick was less outspoken when confronting economic issues, especially the severe economic depression that was engulfing the nation during the years when the Riverside sanctuary was completed and first occupied. His sermons at this time are not devoid of economic concerns, but they do reveal a reticence to come down as hard on economic evils as he did on the evils of war, fundamentalism, or denominationalism. We cannot help but wonder whether the prosperity of his own congregation, as well as his close personal friendship with Rockefeller, sometimes reined in Fosdick's "free pulpit" in subtle ways of which he himself was not always aware.[27]

On the whole, however, Fosdick was far bolder in addressing personal and public issues than were most ministers of his era. His sermons also reveal a remarkable ability to shift his position when a new strategy was needed. For example, Fosdick, the man best known for his willingness to engage modernism from the pulpit, later—when confronted with such realities as the rise of the Third Reich in Germany—preached a sermon entitled "The Church Must Go Beyond Modernism." In it, he criticized the modernist church for its preoccupation with intellectualism ("the deepest experiences of man's soul . . . cannot be approached head-first"), its sentimentalism ("Underline this: <u>Sin is real</u>"), its watering down of the reality of God ("We have at times gotten so low down that we talked as though the highest complement that could be paid Almighty God was that a few scientists believed in him"), and its overly facile accommodation to the morality of its generation ("It is not in Germany alone that the church stands in danger of being enslaved by society. There the enslavement is outward, deliberate, explicit, organized. Here it is secret, quiet, pervasive, insidious"). Fosdick concluded the sermon by asserting that while the future of the church rested in the hands of modernists, "we must go beyond modernism! . . . What Christ does to modern culture is to challenge it."

Subsequent sermons find Fosdick tackling topics such as "Keeping Faith in Persuasion in a World of Coercion," "Why Is God Silent While Evil Rages?" and "A Time to Stress Unity" (a sermon preached in 1945, following the conclusion of World War II, and the most requested sermon Fosdick ever preached on the National Vespers program).

To a church and nation whose vision was frequently distorted by religious fundamentalism, denominational separatism, and nationalistic militarism, Fosdick's preaching brought a new vision. In large part, Riverside became the church it did because of Harry Emerson Fosdick, who deeply believed in a God of love and peace, a gospel of grace, a church that is ecumenical, and a nation whose concern must extend beyond its own immediate self-interest and welfare. For twenty-one years Fosdick regularly preached such a gospel at Riverside, and his vision continues to shape the identity and character of the church that, for many, became "a beacon on the hill" through his preaching ministry.

Robert James McCracken (1946–1967)

When Robert James McCracken, a Scottish-born professor of systematic theology, was called by the Riverside congregation in 1946 to become its second pastor, he must have accepted with considerable trepidation. He was following not only a pastor who had been much beloved by the Riverside congregation but also a preacher and author whose reputation—both nationally and internationally—was legendary. It is a tribute to McCracken—as well as to Fosdick and the congregation of the Riverside Church—that the transition from the first pastor to the second appears to have been fairly smooth and that McCracken himself enjoyed a tenure at Riverside that was as long as Fosdick's own (twenty-one years).

One of the reasons for the smooth transition was the fact that the two men respected each other and that Fosdick himself blessed and prepared the way for McCracken. At his retirement reception, held just a few months before McCracken's arrival, Fosdick expressed his gratitude to the Riverside congregation for his long years as their pastor, and he also turned toward the future:

FIGURE 2.3: Dr. Robert James McCracken. *Used by permission of the Riverside Church Archives.*

Stand by this church. Give to my successor the same support that you have given me. He is a young man, just turning forty.[28] Help him grow. Pull out of him by your spirit and attitude and loyalty all the best that is there, and may God of all grace, through you, make these next twenty years better than the last.[29]

The transition was smooth also because both men held preaching in the highest regard, and McCracken—like his predecessor—knew that excellence in the pulpit of Riverside was not an option but a requirement. Fosdick, who was named pastor emeritus at the same time that McCracken was called, was invited by McCracken to charge the new pastor at his installation service. In his charge Fosdick tried to put McCracken at ease in his new preaching context, assuring him that most New Yorkers "came from the 'sticks'" and were "plain, ordinary human beings, who need the Christian Gospel to help them live."[30] But his charge also culminated with words about preaching:

> Welcome to this church. It is a seven-day-a-week affair with more things going on here than you can possibly keep track of. Don't try to. Most of all we want your message in the pulpit, born out of long hours of study, meditation and prayer. Guard your morning privacy as a sacred trust!
>
> We have called you because we believe you are a great Christian with a message for this generation. That you will wisely counsel with us in practical affairs, and be endlessly helpful in personal consultations, we take for granted. But what most of all we want from you is that on Sunday morning you should come into this pulpit here like Moses with the word of God emerging from his communion on the mountain, who wist [sic] not that his face shone.[31]

The participants McCracken invited to take part in his installation service symbolized his own commitment to keeping Riverside the "interracial, international, and ecumenical" church that Fosdick had founded it to be. Methodist Bishop G. Bromley Oxnam, president of the Federal Council of Churches of Christ in America (which later became the National Council of Churches of Christ), gave the sermon for the service, and representatives of various races and denominations took part.

A Scottish Theologian in the Riverside Pulpit

Unlike Fosdick, who had grown up in the northeastern United States and was already well acquainted with New York City before becoming Riverside's first pastor, McCracken was an outsider to both the United States and New York City when he became Riverside's second minister. Jim McCracken was born in Motherwell, Scotland, on March 28, 1904, where he was reared in a rather strict and austere Christian home. He attended the University of Glasgow, where he received both his master of arts and his bachelor of divinity degrees, and was ordained to the Baptist ministry in 1928. The following year he married Maud Orr Ibbetson, also from Motherwell. They had two sons: James Desmond McCracken and Richard Norman McCracken.

McCracken spent the early years of his ministry as a pastor to two Scottish congregations. From 1928 to 1932 he served as minister of the Marshall Street Baptist Church in Edinburgh, and in 1932 he was called to become minister of the Dennistoun Baptist Church in Glasgow, where he served until 1937. It was not long before McCracken's scholarly gifts as a theologian were recognized, and he was encouraged to teach in seminaries of the Baptist Church. In 1933 he was appointed a lecturer in systematic theology at the Baptist Theological College of Scotland in Glasgow, and four years later he became an associate professor of Christian theology and philosophy of religion at McMaster University in Hamilton, Ontario. When he was offered the position at Riverside, McCracken was a professor and head of the religion department at McMaster.

Although the transition from Fosdick to McCracken appears to have gone smoothly, it could not have been easy for McCracken. Eugene Laubach, a longtime ministerial colleague of McCracken's on the Riverside staff, said that for years McCracken had a recurring nightmare of the nave at Riverside "being deserted week after week, and echoing with the emptiness."[32]

But the nave was not deserted during the McCracken era. People were drawn to him on both Sunday mornings when he preached in the Riverside nave and on Sunday afternoons and evenings when many tuned in to hear his sermons broadcast over the radio. His Scottish brogue, his warm and engaging personality, his probing theological mind, and his proclamation on relevant issues such as racism, McCarthyism, space exploration, and the Korean War continued to attract members to Riverside.

"Life Situation" Preaching

Before taking the position at Riverside, Jim McCracken, by his own admission, had been primarily an "expository" preacher. In his sermons, he ordinarily moved from the exposition of a biblical text to a theological analysis of the text to an application of its meaning to the lives of his congregation. Then, early in his tenure at Riverside, McCracken switched his preaching method and style and became what he himself called a "life-situation" preacher.

In his Stone Lectures at Princeton Theological Seminary (published in 1956 as *The Making of a Sermon*), McCracken described his preaching style:

Seeking to avoid the remoteness and irrelevance, not to say unreality, which are the bane of much biblical exposition, [life-situation preaching] starts with people where they are, which was what Jesus did over and over again. The point of departure is a live issue of some kind. It may be personal or social; it may be theological or ethical. Whatever it is, the preacher makes it his business to get at the core of the problem, and that done, he goes on to work out the solution with the biblical revelation, and the mind and spirit of Christ, as the constant points of reference and direction.[33]

In adopting this approach, McCracken placed himself in the preaching tradition of Fosdick, whom he deemed to be its "greatest exponent."[34] Although McCracken did not believe a life-situation approach to be the only legitimate way to preach, he adapted it to align more closely with the type of preaching to which the Riverside congregation had grown accustomed, rather than requiring the congregation to accommodate to an expository preaching mode.

There were, however, noticeable differences between his preaching and that of his predecessor. On the whole, McCracken's preaching had a more overtly "theological" focus than did Fosdick's, and it often wrestled with doctrinal—as well as more broadly construed "life situational"—topics. In a 1963 series of sermons entitled "Aspects of the Teaching of Jesus," McCracken dealt with Jesus's teaching on five doctrinal themes: God, Humanity, Christ, Sin, and Forgiveness. Other sermons' titles were questions, signaling their theological themes: "What Is Meant by the Will of God?" "In What Kind of God Do You Believe?" "How Do You Think of Death?" and "Can Human Nature Be Changed?"[35] Or they dealt with denominational or ecumenical doctrinal concerns, such as "The Dogma of the Assumption of Mary," "The Reformation and the Bible," and "Where Protestants Differ from Roman Catholics and Why."

In his Stone lectures, McCracken's first advice to pastors was "Take heed unto thyself." That is, preach in a way that is honest and genuine to who you are. But his second piece of advice was "and [take heed] unto the doctrine."[36]

We shall do well to beware of what has aptly been called "suburban" preaching, the type of preaching that is always out on the circumference of Christian truth. We shall likewise beware of flitting from text to text in the Bible according as casual interest, or idle fancy, or last minute desperation move[s] us. It is our God-given duty to preach regularly and systematically about the basic and perennial themes—the Incarnation and the Atonement, man's exceeding sinfulness and God's exceeding grace, the life of faith and the life everlasting. These are weighty and profound themes.[37]

McCracken urged preachers to "traverse the entire ground of Christian truth, and to do it systematically, periodically and comprehensively." He encouraged following "the main outline of the Christian Year—Advent, Christmas, Lent, Good Friday, Easter, Whitsunday [the name for Pentecost in certain parts of the English-speaking world], and Trinity. It protects us from aimless, haphazard, random utterance, from putting a congregation completely at the mercy of our homiletical inclinations and predilections."[38]

While McCracken shared Fosdick's liberal approach to most social issues, his sermons were generally more theologically "orthodox" in tone than Fosdick's. For example, McCracken frequently referred to the Trinity (language that Fosdick avoided) and stressed God's salvific work in Jesus Christ and humanity's need of forgiveness.[39] For McCracken, cross and resurrection were at the very center of the faith, and many of his sermons dealt with issues related to death and resurrection.[40]

McCracken's preaching also placed more emphasis on personal morality than Fosdick's did. Two of McCracken's most popular sermon series at Riverside were on the seven deadly sins and the seven cardinal virtues. He also preached sermons with titles that revealed his own concern about the breakdown in the nation's personal morality: "Wanted: A New Moral Sense," "Can We Do as We Please?" and "Why the Breakdown in Moral Standards?" as well as a number of sermons on specific moral issues such as gambling, temperance, and sex, and an entire series on the Ten Commandments.

McCracken was not at all sympathetic to the "new morality" that was sweeping the nation, and he repeatedly warned against the dangers that can occur when personal moral fiber is weakened. His strict moral code in the pulpit reflected the moral standards to which he held himself personally accountable. According to Eugene Laubach, McCracken

had very definite and very firm standards of right and wrong. He was gracious but never permissive. He was an effective counselor but never a nondirective one. The faith was too real for him to accept that all options were of equal value. He would be quite frank with you about what his feelings really were and then quite supportive in his personal support as you did what you had to do.

Jim was also a man to whom doing the expedient thing came hard. He always wanted to do the *right* thing. He knew intellectually that there was often no clear distinction between what was *right* and what was *best*, but emotionally he always felt that the two ought to be separate. This particular brand of integrity must have been hard for him to live with. Indeed, it caused him a good deal of personal anguish and, occasionally, some sharp differences with his friends and colleagues. Whenever there was pressure to compromise the standards he had set for himself, he would always be pulled back by his fundamental commitment to God.[41]

In addition to the differences, there were many similarities between McCracken's and Fosdick's emphases in preaching. Like Fosdick, Mc-Cracken's deepest desire as a preacher was to tell people about the love of God. A critical moment for him in ministry came one Sunday, early in his pastorate in Scotland, when a parishioner met him at the church door after he had preached a rather arid sermon, saying, "Tell us about the love of God. More than anything else that is what people need to hear about."[42] McCracken took the advice to heart and tried to let people know that God loved them. Consequently, many of his sermons (like Fosdick's) dealt with pastoral concerns and giving encouragement and hope to the disheartened.

McCracken, also like his predecessor, had a pastor's heart. Laubach recalled:

> He had a deep pastoral concern for people in trouble. Day by day he wrote notes of personal concern and pastoral sympathy to people in all kinds of distress and sorrow. He must have written thousands of them in his ministry, many of them by his own hand and with personal warmth and support. He was quick to hear about and congratulate achievement. He knew how to rejoice with those who rejoiced and weep with those who wept. His was a deep ministry of compassion and concern."[43]

And like Fosdick, McCracken was a liberal in regard to most of the social issues of his day. In his preaching, especially on racial issues, he addressed the issues of his time boldly and unapologetically. McCracken was a prophet as well, challenging the church to live more fully in the faith it professed.

Preaching about Racism, the Cold War, and McCarthyism

If Fosdick is best remembered for his pacifism during one of the most popular wars of modern times, McCracken is probably best remembered for his unequivocal declaration that "racism is a sin" during the turbulent period before, during, and after the 1954 *Brown* v. *Board of Education* ruling by the U.S. Supreme Court. He frequently preached on racial issues during his years as Riverside's pastor.

In February 1954, McCracken gave a sermon entitled "Discrimination, the Shame of Sunday Morning." It began with the assertion that "there is more Jim Crowism in America at 11:00 on Sunday morning than at any time" and proceeded to castigate the church for lagging even further behind than other national institutions (education, politics, housing, the courts) in addressing the race problem. Asserting that "all men are God's children; all without exception are the objects of His love and care," McCracken stated: "We might as well face the facts. We are not taking seriously the practical implications of the Christian Gospel. . . . Thousands upon thousands of church members in their attitude to the race question are fundamentally non-Christian."[44]

McCracken called for "a change of sentiment and disposition so thoroughgoing that it could fairly be called a conversion."

> The creed and the deed must match. The profession has to validate itself in practice. Real social action is required. Freedom from bias and prejudice? Yes. Concern for justice and the establishment of equal standards? Yes. Friendship between whites and Negroes? Yes. But we cannot stop there. Both at the denominational and local levels there ought to be racial integration in the Christian Church. We must learn to work and worship together.[45]

Race was not the only theme McCracken spoke of during his years at Riverside. When the Communist "threat" to U.S. security loomed large, the cold war escalated, and Senator Joseph McCarthy ruined the names and futures of countless Americans by labeling them "Communist sympathizers," McCracken regularly addressed such issues from the pulpit.

As early as October 1948 he delivered a sermon entitled "The Christian Attitude to Communism," in which he called Communism a "heresy" because "it acknowledges no transcendental standards or values." He also asserted that "there can be no compromise as between Christianity and

Communism. They represent diametrically opposed ways of looking at the world and of transforming the world." But in that same sermon he also stated, "Nevertheless the Christian attitude to Communism should not be an arrogant attitude." Christianity, he reminded his listeners, has its own sins and shortcomings, including self-absorption, denominationalism, and "failing to emphasize . . . that building up military might is not the only way of preventing war." Consequently, "the Christian attitude should be an attitude free from malice and hate. There should be no place in it for hysteria or bigotry, the temper which precipitates panicky, ill-advised actions."[46]

Toward the end of his tenure at Riverside, in January 1966, Mc-Cracken—responding to a request of the church's Council on Christian Social Relations—preached a sermon entitled "The War in Vietnam." After detailing the case both for and against U.S. engagement in the war, Mc-Cracken urged the congregation to read and reflect on a statement issued by the General Board of the National Council of Churches. It declares that "war in this nuclear age settles hardly anything and may destroy everything" and that "unilateral action by the US in Southeast Asia will not lead to peace."[47] But McCracken seemed to be discussing the topic rather reluctantly (after he was requested by a church council to do so), because for him the issues were far more ambiguous than, say, race relations.

McCracken's life-situation preaching also addressed such popular topics as the television quiz show scandal of the 1950s, the FCC television hearings of the early 1960s, and the escalating space race. In addition, certain events that occurred during his tenure reflected his particular interests and advocacy. At McCracken's urging, for instance, the congregation became dually aligned denominationally, associating with not only the Baptists but also the Congregationalists (now the United Church of Christ). In 1959 the Interchurch Center was built and dedicated at 475 Riverside Drive—right across the street from the church—marking a new era in interdenominational cooperation among American churches.[48] During McCracken's tenure the South Wing of the Riverside Church was built and dedicated, expanding the church's opportunities for outreach and service in the community. McCracken also spoke at the 1959 worship service during which Riverside ordained its first woman minister, Phyllis Taylor, who was appointed to do pastoral work and serve as a liaison officer with various church organizations (the Women's Society, the Business and Professional Women's Club, the Social Committee, and the Couples' Club).

Like Fosdick, McCracken largely shied away from addressing economic matters related to the distribution of wealth, tending instead to focus on the personal use of money. His sermons also seemed to lose some of their bite in the latter years of his Riverside ministry, becoming a bit more cautious in tone. (In fairness to McCracken, however, these were years in which he was not in good health and in which he also spent a great deal of time caring for his wife, who was very ill.)

Nonetheless, McCracken's lively, intelligent, thought-provoking, pastoral, and prophetic topical preaching placed him in the strong preaching legacy established by Fosdick and also helped establish him as a much beloved and admired Riverside preacher in his own right. At his memorial service, Eugene Laubach noted that McCracken's expression of hope on his installation day that the ties uniting him and the Riverside congregation "in affection, in worship, in Christian action will grow stronger and stronger" had indeed come to pass.

> We came to know him and respect him and love him. We were inspired by the steadiness of his faith, warmed by the winsomeness of his charm, challenged by the steadfastness of his integrity. Part of his greatness was that he could draw others unto himself and on to Christ.[49]

Worship during the McCracken Years

In many ways, the most notable aspect of worship during the McCracken years is that the order for the Sunday morning worship service in the nave did not undergo any major observable changes. Consequently, for the first forty-two years that the church occupied its building on Riverside Drive, Sunday morning worship followed basically the same pattern, and the bulletins continued to have covers with quotations from a variety of sources. The tradition of excellence in classical instrumental and choral music also was maintained, with Virgil Fox becoming Riverside's organist in 1946 and Richard W. Weagly serving as choir director.

The minutes of the Worship Council do show, however, some subtle—and significant—changes in worship practices. The church first began holding two (instead of one) worship services on Easter during the McCracken years, and other special services, such as an Ash Wednesday service and a Christmas service of lessons and carols, became regular features of Riverside's church year observance. The Riverside organ was renovated, and the church adopted a new hymnal, *The Pilgrim Hymnal.* The Lord's Supper (which had previously been celebrated on Sunday afternoons in a separate service) became a regular monthly part of Sunday morning worship services. Women, newly elected as deacons, began serving the communion elements for the first time. And a Hispanic congregation, under the leadership of Pablo Cotto, worshiped on Sunday mornings in the chapel while the traditional service took place in the nave.

McCracken also pressed for other changes. As early as 1958 he began urging the church to secure a permanent or portable baptismal font for the nave (since the church had only a baptistry).[50] Although a portable font was finally obtained toward the end of his tenure, McCracken never was able to realize his dream of incorporating baptisms into the Sunday morning worship service in the nave.

The dress of the Ushers Guild was another matter of concern during McCracken's era. Even though he and the board of deacons encouraged the ushers to change their dress—partly because cutaways were outdated and partly because they depicted an image of wealth and affluence to visitors—the ushers resisted making the change, and they were still wearing cutaways in 1967 when McCracken resigned.

Finally, during the latter years of McCracken's tenure, the Worship Council began struggling with whether the Sunday morning worship service at Riverside needed to become either more liturgical (in keeping with the liturgical renewal movements of the times) or more contemporary (incorporating drama, the visual arts, and dance). It was not, however, until the summer after McCracken's resignation that experimentation in the worship service, under the leadership of Rev. Eugene Laubach, began in earnest. Even though Riverside may have been a liberal church in regard to theological and sociopolitical issues, the congregation was far more conservative in regard to its worship practices.

Ernest T. Campbell (1968–1976)

When Ernest T. Campbell was installed as Riverside's third senior minister on September 29, 1968, he brought with him a number of "firsts." Campbell was the first senior pastor to have been born and raised in New York City and, even more specifically, in Morningside Heights (where he attended public school and played in the local parks). Campbell was the first senior minister who was not Baptist (he was Presbyterian). Campbell was

FIGURE 2.4: Dr. Ernest T. Campbell. *Used by permission of the Riverside Church Archives.*

the first preaching minister who had grown up relatively poor (having been raised by working-class, Irish immigrant parents). And he was the first Riverside pastor who had been raised as a fundamentalist (having had a fundamentalist pastor throughout his youth and having attended Bob Jones University). In many ways Campbell—at least in terms of life experience—represented significant "discontinuities" with the legacy of either Fosdick or McCracken.

Yet Campbell also shared some traits with his predecessors. Like Fosdick, Campbell rejected fundamentalism for a modernist approach to the Bible and the Christian faith. Like McCracken, Campbell was fairly orthodox theologically, having been influenced by the biblical theology movement of his era. And like both his predecessors, Campbell came to

Riverside with a reputation for excellent preaching. By appointing Campbell, Riverside signaled its commitment to continuing its reputation of preaching excellence, even when the efficacy of preaching itself was being questioned.

Campbell's Early Life Influences

"Ernie" Campbell grew up in the home of Irish immigrants who arrived in New York in 1920, three years before he was born on August 14, 1923. In the early years his family lived in the Manhattanville area of New York, in what he describes as "a very, very modest tenement." Later they moved to Morningside Heights, where he attended the local public schools. His father drove trolley cars for the Third Avenue Railroad Company, and his mother "ran the household on slim dollars and did a great job of it." Campbell remembers that money was tight while he was growing up and that he often was sent out in the morning before school to buy day-old bread for the family.[51]

Campbell's parents had been Presbyterians before immigrating from Northern Ireland and raised Ernie and his brother in the Christian faith. Each weekday morning before the two went off to school, their mother would read a psalm and say a prayer with them. She called this "the reading." The entire family attended a local Presbyterian church each Sunday morning: the Morningside Presbyterian Church during Ernie's elementary years and, after its demise, the Broadway Presbyterian Church during his teenage years.

The Broadway Church represented what Campbell later called "a respectable kind of fundamentalism," drawing people from all over the greater metropolitan New York area. The pastor, who had attended Princeton Theological Seminary and sided with Gresham Machen (a fundamentalist) in the fundamentalist-modernist controversy, was antagonistic to Fosdick and espoused a premillennial fundamentalism that, as Campbell put it, "had no social vision." Campbell became a member of the church and joined the young collegians' group, traveling with them to hospitals and missions where the group led worship and offered testimonies and Campbell accompanied the hymn singing at the piano. One evening when he was asked to give his own testimony at the Jerry McAuley Mission, Campbell began to sense the tug toward ministry. He recalls: "I was extremely shy, and blushed easily. I felt some awkwardness, but also a strange fulfillment. . . . I found that words came with some facility."[52]

Campbell loved sports, especially basketball and baseball, and remembered that he used to pass right by Riverside Church on his way to play pickup ball games in Riverside Park. He attended the High School of Commerce in New York, thinking he might go into finance and become a bank credit officer. After graduation he continued studying finance at New York University while working at a part-time job at the Guaranty Trust Company.

The tug toward ministry grew stronger, however, and Campbell eventually ended up attending Bob Jones University, a conservative, fundamentalist school then located in Cleveland, Tennessee. The reasons for his attendance at Bob Jones were two. First, Bob Jones Jr. preached during the summers at the Broadway Presbyterian Church, and Campbell was drawn to his smooth, polished style. Second, Bob Jones was the only school his parents could afford (with tuition of about $600 per year). Despite the school's fundamentalist theological approach, which he later rejected, Campbell did gain something of value at Bob Jones, including a strong grounding in biblical content, an appreciation for excellence in the performing arts, and some lifelong friendships.

After graduating from Bob Jones, Campbell attended Princeton Theological Seminary, an event that he calls "the turning point of my life."[53] There, his biblical and theological assumptions were challenged when he encountered professors who did not accept the fundamentalist assumptions on which he had been reared. He also met a number of students who had a strong passion for social justice and worked in urban ministries in various contexts. Campbell completed two degrees at Princeton, including a master's degree with a thesis on the Book of Amos, and also served for three of his seminary years as the pastor of two small Pennsylvania churches.

In 1949 Ernie Campbell was ordained by Lehigh Presbytery and became the pastor of the Stroudsburg (Pennsylvania) Presbyterian Church. After serving in the Stroudsburg Church and later at the York (Pennsylvania) Presbyterian Church, he was called in 1962 to become the senior minister of the Second Presbyterian Church of Ann Arbor, Michigan. From the Ann Arbor congregation, he was called to the Riverside Church.

By the time Campbell arrived at Riverside, his reputation as a preacher and lecturer of note was already well established. He had already preached in many of the large New York City churches, had preached for ten years at the Massanetta (Virginia) Bible Conference, had led a Lenten lecture series at Riverside, and had broadcast sermons nationally on *The Protestant*

Hour radio program. He also had a record of involvement in social issues, having fought for Ann Arbor's Fair Housing Ordinance, received the American Civil Liberties Union "Man of the Year" Award in 1960 for his work in civil rights, and brought together a priest and a rabbi to form a three-faith panel that successfully mediated a long-term labor strike in York, Pennsylvania. In addition, Campbell had served on various denominational and ecumenical committees, demonstrating his commitment to the church's larger ecumenical movement.

Preaching in a Season of Social Upheaval

Campbell served as pastor of the Riverside Church during a tumultuous time in the life of the nation and the church, and his ministry—including his preaching ministry—was greatly shaped by those issues. The Vietnam War was raging, and the nation remained seriously divided over the United States' escalating involvement in it. Racism continued unabated in America's cities and towns, and anger over its injustice gave way to inflammatory confrontations between protestors and police and to riots in many major cities. College campuses were in turmoil, as students opposed investment policies related to the war, staged sit-ins, and demanded greater justice for women and racial and ethnic minorities. Youth questioned the traditional trappings of authority in the wake of the Kent State killings and the Watergate break-in, and many openly defied the traditional trappings of morality by experimenting with drugs and sex. The recent deaths of national leaders such as Martin Luther King Jr. and Robert Kennedy shook the nation, leaving it grieving and deeply wounded.

In the Protestant churches of America, too, this was a time of great turmoil as members lined up on opposite sides of the social issues and debated at length whether the church's mission should focus primarily on evangelism (and personal salvation) or on social justice (with an emphasis on justice, equality, and peace). Worship, too, became a hot topic, as youth pressed the church to abandon some of its more formal and traditional liturgical styles for worship that was freer, more relevant, more participatory, and more expressive of the age. Preaching itself came under attack as being irrelevant, overly authoritarian, and outmoded in an age in which activism appeared to be the wave of the future.

It was not an easy time in which to minister anywhere, including the Riverside Church. Only six months into Campbell's ministry at Riverside—on May 4, 1969—James Forman, spokesman for the Black Economic Development Conference, interrupted the morning worship in order to present his "Black Manifesto" (see chap. 5). It demanded that the country's churches and synagogues—and the Riverside Church in particular—pay $500 million in "reparations" to African Americans for past economic injustices. The funds were to be used for various projects directed by and for blacks. This event, which received a great deal of national publicity, sparked a debate and controversy over the wisdom of reparations, which were highly divisive at Riverside and elsewhere.

Ten weeks after the incident, Campbell preached a sermon entitled "The Case for Reparations."[54] To argue the case for reparations, he used the Zacchaeus story from the New Testament, in which Jesus forgives and extends God's grace to a tax collector who responds by making restitution to those he has defrauded.

> There were two elements in the reclamation of Zacchaeus: *Generosity* ("Half of my goods I give to the poor"), and *Justice* ("If I have defrauded any one of anything, I restore it fourfold"). To put it differently, Zacchaeus made reparation. Let us not fear the term. The principle is as old as the book of Exodus, and as new as contemporary jurisprudence.[55]

At Campbell's urging, the church established "The Riverside Fund for Social Justice," a fund that supported Manhattan-based organizations trying to enable the powerless of society to achieve power (rather than funneling funds into Forman's organization). But the controversy surrounding Foreman's visit and Campbell's response continued to haunt the new pastor.

"The Case for Reparations" was not the only controversial sermon Campbell preached during his Riverside years. In May 1972, following President Richard M. Nixon's resumption of bombing in North Vietnam, Campbell gave a sermon entitled "The Urge to Win and the Need for Peace." In it he openly admitted that he (unlike Fosdick) was a "selective pacifist" and not an "absolute pacifist." Acknowledging that "for post-Hiroshima mankind there may well be no such thing as a 'just war,'" he proceeded to make his case against the United States' involvement in Vietnam, not so much on biblical and theological grounds, as he did in "The Case for Reparations," but on historical, political, military, and economic grounds.

In December of the same year Campbell gave a sermon entitled "An Open Letter to Billy Graham." In this sermon, written in the form of a letter addressed to Graham and actually sent to him by telegram the Friday before he delivered it, Campbell castigated Graham for refusing to join other religious leaders in urging President Nixon to stop bombing North Vietnam. Although the letter did not begin in a confrontational tone, noting their mutual friends and the fact that they had met on at least one occasion, it quickly became so as Campbell called on Graham to account publicly for refusing to use his friendship and influence with President Nixon to help end the war. "The President," he told Graham, "needs a Micaiah not a Zedekiah, a prophet, not a mere house chaplain."[56] Although Graham never directly responded, when asked about the letter, he is reported to have said in a subsequent press interview that he saw himself as a New Testament evangelist, not an Old Testament prophet.[57]

In May 1973, Campbell addressed the Watergate issue for the first time, in a sermon entitled "Watergate, under God, and All That!"[58] Using as his biblical text the story of Ezra reading the law to the postexilic Israelites at the Water Gate (2 Chron. 26), Campbell reflected "on the meaning of Watergate from the point of view of biblical religion."

1. "Watergate speaks loudly to man's need for exposure to views other than his own." (The president and his closest advisers cut themselves off from larger perceptions of reality at their own peril.)
2. "Watergate speaks loudly to the selfishness in us all" ("The [Watergate figures] got caught up in the same ferocity of ambition, the same quest for material abundance that all of us, to one degree or another, are mixed up with.")
3. "Watergate speaks loudly to the need for an improved public attitude towards politics and politicians." ("In the main we have gotten the kind of government that we deserve. . . . The public sector ought to be a matter of concern for every Christian and a matter of vocation for many of us.")

Campbell concluded the sermon on a note of hope for the good that might emerge from the Watergate scandal: hope for legislative reform, hope for amnesty for those who would not or could not participate in the fighting in Indochina, and hope that the nation would repent.

In February 1974, Campbell preached a sermon on homosexuality that can only be called remarkable in light of its early candor in dealing openly and sensitively with a topic that most preachers avoided for at least another decade or two. Entitled "Overheard in Room 738," the sermon recounts an imaginary conversation among Bill (a cosmopolitan schoolteacher who ends up hospitalized in a small town after a skiing accident and who represents a "liberal" position on homosexuality), Chris (his blue-collar, small-town, "conservative" hospital roommate), and Chaplain Carter (a hospital chaplain who visits the two men in their room and offers his own [liberal] biblical and theological perspective). Through the three men, Campbell stated the arguments on opposing sides of the issue and ultimately made the case for greater tolerance of gays and lesbians, even opening the door to blessing same-sex unions.[59]

Campbell clearly believed that a part of his mission at Riverside was to move the church beyond "social service" toward a greater emphasis on " social action."

> God has brought us to the kingdom at a time when people by the millions have grievances they wish to see resolved. With unsettling frequency this church is being overturned to abandon its abstemious neutrality and take a side. We are being pushed to declare where our fundamental loyalties lie. . . . To stand back and remain noncommittal would be to discredit faith and betray the gospel.[60]

More Overtly Biblical Preaching

In fairness to the overall scope of Campbell's preaching, however, we should note that these prophetic sermons on public issues were only one portion of his regular Sunday message. On the whole, Campbell's sermons—like those of his predecessors—addressed a variety of biblical, theological, and liturgical themes and included many sermons more oriented toward evangelism, pastoral care, or issues of personal piety. Indeed, one of Campbell's main themes at Riverside was that the gospel did not have to take an either/or approach to social action and evangelism but could be "related *both* to the world *and* to men and women in it."[61]

Campbell also deviated from the usual pattern of Riverside preaching, or at least stretched and expanded it. For example, Campbell's sermons generally dealt more overtly and extensively with particular biblical texts than did those of his more topically oriented predecessors.[62] Sometimes he began his sermon with a reference to the day's biblical text and then expounded on its meaning for certain life issues (as in his sermon about Zacchaeus and reparations). On other occasions he began with a topic and then considered how a text related to that topic (as in the Watergate sermon). In some sermons he used many different texts from Scripture to build the case he wanted to make (as in "The Silence of the New Testament,"[63] a sermon in which he argued—on the basis of many Old and New Testament texts—that the church must get involved in the messy business of politics).

In an interview, Campbell candidly stated his preference for more textually based preaching. The contrast with Fosdick's and McCracken's homiletical practice is striking:

> I don't think a homily can be good if the text is exegetically false. I believe in textual preaching. You'll probably see the contrast with some of the others from Riverside.
>
> The weakest kind of preaching is topical preaching. The signal is when you hear/read the words "It seems to me."[64]

Campbell's was not a verse-by-verse expository style or extended narrative style. Indeed, on balance his sermons still devoted more time to life issues than to the particular biblical texts used to address them. But his preaching did represent a definitive shift at Riverside toward sermons with a more overtly biblical content and toward the sermon's greater biblical teaching function as a whole.

It was not just in his use of the Scriptures that Campbell broke or stretched the mold of his predecessors. His sermons also were more creative, innovative, and diverse than those of Fosdick or McCracken, both of whom varied their sermonic *themes* but made only minor variations in their sermonic *forms*. In contrast, Campbell's sermons changed form from week to week. Sometimes he gave three-point sermons (far more of these than his predecessors). On other occasions he used a problem-resolution approach. But he also would try something entirely new, pushing the boundaries with a sermon that was structured like an open letter (as in the Billy Graham sermon), that recounted an imaginary conversation in a hospital room (as in the homosexuality sermon), or that followed an inductive "not only this, not only this, but also this" mode (as in a sermon entitled "Experience, Expectation, and Surprise," in which he talked about how God often moves beyond our previous experience and expectations to engage us in surprising ways).[65]

In many ways it was natural that Campbell should be the first Riverside preacher to experiment with sermon form. He came along at a time when the people in the pews—especially young people—were clamoring for more creativity in the pulpit and when homiletical scholars were pressing preachers to move beyond three-point deductive sermon forms—forms that started with a general theme and then fleshed it out—and to embrace more inductive and narrative sermon forms. Yet Campbell's sermons also display his own gifts as a creative writer, as well as his belief that sometimes people can "overhear" prophetic words (by listening in on a conversation or reading a letter addressed to someone else) better than they can hear them directly.[66]

The Challenges of Liturgical Renewal and Contemporary Worship

Early in his tenure at Riverside, Ernest Campbell began pressing for changes in the Sunday morning order of worship. Specifically he wanted a corporate prayer of confession in each service, moving the Scripture reading closer to the sermon, ending the sermon with some sort of subjective commitment by the congregation (as with an appropriate dedicatory hymn), and having the offering follow the sermon as part of the congregation's response to the Word proclaimed. He also questioned why Riverside had an altar in its sanctuary, arguing that a communion *table* would be far more appropriate to Riverside's Protestant identity.

Although Campbell's proposed changes reflected the liturgical renewal in many Protestant denominations, others at Riverside were pressing for changes that would "contemporize" the morning worship service and make it more accessible to a new generation. Young people, especially, were critical of Riverside's worship, arguing that it was too stiff and formal, lacked warmth and welcome, and failed to engage them or their concerns.[67]

In March 1970 Campbell delivered a sermon entitled "Have We Outgrown Worship?" and several forums were held after the Sunday morning service to give the broader community an opportunity to express its views. Attendance at the first forum was double what the Worship Council had expected, and at the second, representatives from five different constituencies—the Black Christian Caucus, the Hispanic American ministry, the Youth Department, long-term members, and the newer young adult members—were invited to present their perspectives. As a result of these conversations and the divisions among the constituencies regarding their worship preferences and needs, the council began to make a number of changes, including adding a more contemporary service early on Sunday mornings.

The church also began incorporating some of Campbell's liturgical suggestions into the 11 A.M. Sunday service. In 1972 a time for announcements was added to the beginning of the service as a way of showing greater warmth and welcome to visitors, and the service order was changed to include a corporate prayer of confession after the opening acts of praise. A table was eventually brought in to celebrate Communion, and the altar was no longer used for this purpose. Bulletins also began appearing without the familiar cover quotations, and baptism and the reception of new members came to be a regular part of the Sunday morning service.

While worship changes came slowly at Riverside, they did begin during the late 1960s and early 1970s as the congregation responded to the changing world and church. The door was finally opened to a larger congregational dialogue about the nature, theology, and practice of worship, and the changes made also opened the way for more changes in the future.

Internally, though, not all was harmonious at Riverside. Growing conflicts between Campbell and the church boards over administrative and other matters eventually led to his resignation as Riverside's senior minister. The June 23 minutes of the Worship Council read as follows:

> To the shock and dismay of the council, Dr. Campbell announced his resignation as preaching minister of the Riverside Church; July 4, 1976 will be his last Sunday of service. He expressed his unhappiness in leaving, but found that what he came to Riverside Church to do is different from what he is required to do now.

In a press release issued by the church regarding his departure, Campbell—who had the shortest tenure of any Riverside pastor to date (seven and a half years) and who resigned at age fifty-two with no other call on the horizon—stated:

> This decision does not represent a loss of faith in Jesus Christ, a lessening of love for the people of Riverside, or a lack of confidence in the future of New York City. It rises from the fact that my job as constituted under the staff reorganization plan does not provide me with sufficient joy and satisfaction to justify the pressures and demands.[68]

The son of Irish immigrants preached his last sermon at Riverside on July 4, 1976, the Sunday on which the nation of his birth celebrated its bicentennial.

William Sloane Coffin Jr. (1977–1987)

When the Riverside Church called William Sloane Coffin to become its fourth senior minister in 1977, the congregation also announced its own commitment to become more the "activist" congregation that Campbell had urged it to be, or at least to be guided by someone who had a proven track record as an outspoken (and often controversial) activist. Coffin, who had served as chaplain and pastor of the chapel at Yale University from 1958 to 1976, was already nationally well known for his activist stands, including his outspoken opposition to the Vietnam War. In 1968 Coffin and Dr. Benjamin Spock were arrested for aiding and abetting draft resisters, after receiving draft cards from students protesting U.S. military involvement in Southeast Asia. Although the charges against them were later dropped, this incident, along with others, helped catapult Coffin to national prominence as an outspoken critic of the war.

The draft card incident was only the latest in a long history of public actions that Coffin had taken on behalf of peace and civil rights causes. In the summer of 1960 he led a group of college students to Guinea on an Operation Crossroads Africa Project. In 1961 Coffin was named by Sargent Shriver of the Kennedy administration to be one of the initial advisers to the newly formed Peace Corps. That summer he organized and became the first director of the Peace Corps Field Training Center in Puerto Rico. During the same year Coffin was one of seven "Freedom Riders" arrested and convicted in Montgomery, Alabama, while protesting segregation laws that conflicted with decisions by the U.S. Supreme Court. (The Supreme Court later overturned the convictions.) In 1964 Coffin toured Asia, visiting and lecturing in universities in northern and central India. Throughout the late 1960s and early 1970s he was actively involved in the antiwar movement. Along with John Bennett of the Union Theological Seminary and Abraham Heschel of the Jewish Theological Seminary, Coffin served as one of the founders of Clergy and Laity Concerned for Vietnam, an antiwar advocacy group of Jewish and Christian religious leaders.

In 1962 *Life* magazine named Coffin one of one hundred American men under the age of forty years who were deemed outstanding leaders of the "takeover generation." There was no mistaking the type of senior minister Riverside Church was getting. William Sloane Coffin was a well-educated, outspoken, provocative, liberal activist under whose preaching and

FIGURE 2.5: Dr. William Sloane Coffin Jr. *Used by permission of the Riverside Church Archives.*

worship leadership the church would surely be pushed to become more activist as well.

Coffin also was a deeply committed and, in some senses, highly traditional Christian, who believed in the Trinity, was committed to Sunday morning worship as the heart of the church's life, and loved the traditional liturgy and music that had long been a part of Riverside's heritage. (Coffin himself had studied at the Yale School of Music and had trained to become a classical pianist in Paris before the outbreak of World War II.)

When Coffin took over the pulpit at Riverside at the age of fifty-three, he brought with him a past that was as fascinating as the man himself. Because of that past, he also brought an awareness and knowledge of the world and global politics that informed what he said from the Riverside pulpit as well as the actions he continued to take in the larger global arena.

Not the Usual Path to Ministry

William Sloane Coffin Jr. was born in 1924 into an affluent family in New York City. The second of three children, his father worked in the upscale family furniture business (W. & J. Sloane) and also served as president of the Metropolitan Museum. His uncle, Henry Sloane Coffin, was the president of Union Theological Seminary in New York. The family divided their time between their winter home, "a penthouse apartment comprising both the fifteenth and the sixteenth floor of a brand new building on East Sixty-eighth Street in Manhattan," and their summer home in Oyster Bay on Long Island.[69]

When Bill Coffin was nine, his father died and the family moved to Carmel, California. There Coffin attended public school and immersed himself in music (piano) and athletics. Several years later he returned east to preparatory school and in 1938 went to Paris to study harmony with Nadia Boulanger, with the goal of becoming a concert pianist.

When war broke out in Europe, Coffin's plans to pursue a piano career were interrupted, and he returned to the United States. He graduated from the Phillips Academy in Andover, Massachusetts, in 1942 and then enrolled in the Yale Music School. Coffin enlisted in the army a year later, serving in Europe as an infantry officer during the last years of World War II. Because of his excellent language skills (he was fluent in both French and Russian), Coffin also served as a liaison officer to the French army. For two years after the war, he was assigned as a liaison officer to the Russian army in Czechoslovakia and Germany.

> Like many other 18-year-old Americans in 1943, I was an enthusiastic member of the military. Already it had become clear that not since God created the earth had any group been responsible for as much suffering and for as many deaths as the Nazi Party of Germany. . . . Never did it occur to me that fighting fire with fire would produce more ashes than anything else. . . . But by war's end . . . I had heard enough to convince me that on occasion Stalin could make Hitler look like a Boy Scout. I had had an important experience. Four years in the service had ended my boyhood innocence. I had lifted my head out from under five feet of sand. All I knew for sure was that human life was not as pure as I had thought, and that in the sullied stream of human life our only option is not innocence but what we might call holiness. Although I didn't know it, I was ready for a religious experience.[70]

In 1947 Coffin returned to the United States and completed his B.A. in government at Yale University. He was drawn to the writings of the French existentialists Sartre and Camus but found their answers ultimately lacked weight.

> By contrast theologians like Richard and Reinhold Niebuhr and Paul Tillich seemed in touch with a deeper reality. They too knew what hell was all about, but in the depths of it they found a heaven that made more sense out of everything, much as light gives meaning to darkness.[71]

While he was a senior in college, anticipating a career in diplomacy and already having been accepted by the Central Intelligence Agency, Coffin attended a conference on ministry at the Union Theological Seminary in New York. Moved by such speakers as Reinhold Niebuhr and James Muilenberg and by the work of George Webber in East Harlem, Coffin was "converted to the possibility of becoming a minister."[72] He sent a letter of apology and turned down the CIA and entered Union instead.

Again, however, Coffin's career plans were interrupted by war. In 1950, after the outbreak of the Korean War, Coffin did join the CIA and worked in Germany for three years, training Russians opposed to the Soviet government for operations inside the Soviet Union. After returning to the United States, he resumed his seminary education, this time at the Yale Divinity School, from which he graduated in 1956.

If Coffin's preordination years set him apart from his three predecessors at Riverside (Riverside had never before had a former CIA operative in its pulpit!), so too did his postordination years. Rather than following the usual Riverside career path of graduating from seminary, followed by distinguished service as a pastor in several local congregations, Coffin was the first (and only) Riverside minister whose entire ministerial career had been spent in student chaplaincy. He served first at the Phillips Academy and Williams College and then, for eighteen years, as chaplain and pastor of the chapel at Yale University.

At Yale Coffin gained a reputation not only as an activist but also as a passionate, intelligent, provocative, and eloquent preacher, whose sermons—like his public actions—always challenged the status quo.

Preaching for Structural Change

If the courage and conviction of Harry Emerson Fosdick as a preacher began with his strong belief in God's love for individuals and then moved outward to embrace national and global concerns, it is probably fair to say that for William Sloane Coffin the reverse was true. Because he believed God "so loved the world," Coffin also believed that the church should love the whole world. Consequently, his preaching challenged the church to move beyond nationalism, militarism, racism, sexism, heterosexism—whatever was blocking human ability to love the world—and to work for the kinds of structural changes that would make the world a more habitable place for all creatures.

Early in his tenure at Riverside, Coffin articulated the theological foundation of his activism in a sermon entitled "A World Fit for Children":

> As Christians we don't believe in a Gospel of private salvation. Salvation is a package deal, including everyone and everything, politics and economics, the past, the present, and particularly the future. . . .
>
> Let us declare our INTERDEPENDENCE with all people. Let us dare to see pragmatically that the survival unit in our anguished time is no longer an individual nation or an individual anything. The survival unit in our time is the whole human race plus its environment. . . .
>
> We all belong to each other; that's the way God made us. Christ died to keep us that way. So our sin is that we are always trying to put asunder what God himself has joined together. I am not my brother's keeper, I am my brother's brother. . . . God cares for all, as if all were but one.[73]

Coffin's sermons during his ten years as Riverside's pastor covered the world's social, political, and economic concerns. He seemed unafraid to tackle any public issue, no matter how controversial or complex, and his sermons are remarkably consistent in their intelligence, breadth of knowledge, and in-depth analysis.

Many of the sermons he preached have one-word titles, like "Abortion," "Iran," "Homosexuality," or "AIDS," showing his willingness to devote his entire sermon to one of the moral and ethical issues confronting the nation and world. Other titles clearly reveal Coffin's own (often controversial) position on a public issue: "And Pray for the Iranians, Too" (preached just before Coffin, at the invitation of the Iranian government, traveled with two other U.S. clergy to Tehran to celebrate Christmas with the

Americans held hostage there) and "It's a Sin to Build a Nuclear Weapon" (given first at the World Council of Churches Hearing on Nuclear Weapons and Disarmament in Amsterdam and also on the following Sunday at Riverside).

Still other sermons signal Coffin's willingness to use a recent event in national, congregational, or even his own personal life as an occasion for moral, theological, and ethical reflection. For example, in February 1979, on the Sunday immediately following the Riverside funeral service of former New York governor and Republican presidential candidate Nelson Rockefeller, Coffin delivered a sermon entitled "After Rocky's Funeral." After opening with the contrasting observations of two people who had witnessed the funeral service—one a nun who saw the service on television and thought it was so beautiful that she came to the church to pray and the other a theological student who felt that Riverside had been "raped" by its use for a service that included no prayer of confession or penitence for the crimes of the Vietnam War and included among its eulogizers Henry Kissinger—Coffin proceeded to talk about Christ's ministry of reconciliation. Encouraging his parishioners to recognize that we all share in the frailty of life, that "this is God's world" and that "at best, we are guests. Even the Rockefellers are guests in this world," Coffin encouraged his listeners to follow God's example in allowing their generosity to others to outstrip their judgment.[74]

Coffin also used his own international travels to encourage greater tolerance and perspective in his congregation. In "A Message from Christians in Cuba," a sermon Coffin preached on a Sunday immediately preceding the celebration of U.S. Independence Day 1979 and following his own return from a visit to Cuba, he challenged Riversiders to recognize that the Cuban revolution of 1959 had had some benefits in regard to the social services many Cubans now received and to see that Cubans were looking to rich American churches to be both more faithful and also more outspoken in their advocacy for lifting the economic embargo against Cuba.

The following December, just before Coffin went to Iran, he used his Sunday morning sermon to encourage greater willingness by Americans to at least listen to the Iranian point of view. While stating that he would be pleading for the return of all hostages during his visit, he also noted,

> We scream about the hostages, but few Americans heard the scream of tortured Iranians. . . . I must confess to a little apprehension that we Americans are better talkers than listeners, especially when it comes to listening to peo-

ple of countries smaller than our own, countries that have been unimpressed by our greater power, countries that have thwarted our national will. The descendants of Thomas Jefferson tend to make like George the Third. Two hundred years after our own revolution we don't listen easily to revolutionaries. Pray, then, that your pastor who understands the problem may overcome it. Pray that the preacher may recognize that is more blessed to listen than to speak.[75]

In a sermon Coffin gave the following Sunday—entitled "Report from Tehran"—Coffin provided a very moving report of his own experience of leading worship with sixteen of the American hostages (four at a time) on Christmas Day: reading the Christmas story aloud in their presence, praying with them and their guards (with all holding hands together in a circle) "that the Christ Child might find hearts wide enough to lodge in" and "that rather than rally around any flag we would be able to gather around the Holy child, as members of one family," and delivering to them messages and greetings from home. But he also recounted his conversations with Iranians as he argued for the hostages' release and tried to understand the situation from their point of view. Again he encouraged an alternative path to the hard-line approach most Americans at the time favored:

> If we want to get our fellow Americans back soon I think we should forget about any "hard line." It will only stifle resistance. I think we should, first of all, follow a path of reciprocal gestures. It wouldn't be difficult for somebody in the government to say, "We appreciate the gestures made to our people in allowing three clergy to celebrate Christmas services with the hostages. And we would like to reciprocate. We have decided not to deport any more students. Let them stay in their studies. . . . Such gestures would help cool the situation."
>
> Beyond that, we have to think realistically, biblically, if you will. We have to face the fact that "the sins of the fathers are visited upon the children." We cannot pretend that history began yesterday, that life is not consequential, that we do not have to pay for our sins. Somewhere, somehow, the just grievances of the Iranians have to be heard.[76]

Probably more than any preacher before him, Coffin's thematic emphases in his sermons tilt toward the global, the ethical, and the communal dimensions of the gospel. Certainly his most common sermon themes during his Riverside years were international peacemaking and nuclear disarmament. (Indeed, some of his critics have charged that he had only one theme during his pastorate, although his sermons prove the contrary.)

In March 1978, three months after Coffin became Riverside's pastor, Church World Service shipped ten thousand metric tons of wheat—most of it donated by American farmers— to schools and hospitals in Vietnam as a gesture of reconciliation. Coffin flew to Houston to take part with other religious and political leaders in "blessing the ship" before it left for Vietnam and then returned to the Riverside pulpit the next day to deliver a sermon entitled "A Gesture of Reconciliation." The sermon reflected at length on the action, offering a theological and political rationale for it. The entire morning worship service was centered on a reconciliation theme, with special Mennonite bread from Kansas used for Communion, an offering taken for the wheat shipment, and special instrumental music from Southeast Asia.

Notably (and not accidentally), Coffin chose the anniversary of the hundredth birthday of Harry Emerson Fosdick later that same year to announce through his Sunday sermon a major new disarmament venture, based at Riverside. Structurally, the sermon also displayed Coffin's practice of beginning on grounds that all his listeners could affirm—in this instance, on Fosdick's peacemaking legacy—and then to stretch toward new territory (congregational advocacy for nuclear disarmament). Toward the sermon's end Coffin announced to the congregation that the board of deacons had unanimously endorsed a national disarmament program that would be located at Riverside and that the church had employed one of the best organizers in the country, Cora Weiss, to oversee it.[77] Not promising success in this venture, he nonetheless urged the congregation forward, saying, "We must dream visions larger than our times."

Coffin continued to preach on disarmament themes throughout his tenure at Riverside, either devoting entire sermons to the topic or weaving them into sermons on other texts and themes. But as his sermon titles indicate, disarmament was certainly not Coffin's only goal. In July 1981—in response and opposition to a sermon that Dr. Channing Phillips, one of Riverside's ministers, had preached in Coffin's absence the previous Sunday, calling homosexuality a sin—Coffin offered a sermon simply entitled "Homosexuality," in which he urged Christians to move beyond rejection or a conditional acceptance of homosexual persons to an unconditional acceptance of gays in all avenues of life, including the ordained ministry.[78] Two weeks later he preached a sermon, "Abortion," in which he challenged, on the one hand, the traditional

Roman Catholic view that abortion is murder and, on the other, the view that a woman's right to choose is an absolute right.[79] In April 1984, Coffin gave a sermon urging the Riverside Church to engage in civil disobedience by becoming a "sanctuary" church for illegal Guatemalan refugees.[80] In January 1986 he talked about AIDS, contrasting the loving care the dying receive through hospice programs with the abandonment that many experience dying of AIDS. He concluded the sermon by inviting one of the congregation's own members to give "his own testimony of faith" in living with AIDS.[81]

Coffin's liberal views may have been appreciated by many Riverside members, but they were not applauded by all. Among his most outspoken and habitual critics were members of the men's Bible class, a group that had been an extremely powerful and influential body earlier in Riverside's history but whose numbers, by Coffin's time, were greatly diminished. They attacked Coffin both personally and professionally in print, picketed some of his Sunday morning services, and eventually even called for his resignation. Although the board of deacons denounced their actions in 1988, their actions made life difficult for Coffin (for a fuller discussion of the conflict between Coffin and the Men's Class, see chap. 5).

Like the other Riverside preachers before him, Coffin addressed a broad range of topics, tending to place more emphasis on the societal and corporate dimensions of the gospel and less on the personal and individual. Coffin's most famous sermon, however, "Alex's Death," deals with the most personally existential of all issues: death. He preached it in 1983, only two weeks after the death of his own twenty-four-year-old son, Alexander, in an automobile accident. Coffin used the sermon to wrestle with the existential tragedy of death and with the gospel's hope in facing it. He spent much of his sermon mourning his loss ("When parents die, as did my mother last month, they take with them a large portion of the past. But when children die, they take away the future as well. That is what makes the valley of the shadow of death seem so incredibly dark and unending.") and debunking the myth that such deaths are the "will of God." "God doesn't go around this world with his finger on triggers, his fist around knives, his hands on steering wheels. God is dead set against all unnatural deaths. And Christ spent an inordinate amount of time delivering people from paralysis, insanity, leprosy, and muteness."[82]

But at the end of the sermon, Coffin testified to the hope within him and to the hope at the heart of the gospel and the biblical faith he professed.

And of course I know, even when pain is deep, that God is good. "My God, My God, why has thou forsaken me?" Yes, but at least, "My God, My God" and the psalm only begins that way; it doesn't end that way. As the grief that once seemed unbearable begins to turn now to bearable sorrow, the truths in the "right" biblical passages are beginning, once again to take hold: "Cast thy burden upon the Lord and He shall strengthen thee"; "Weeping may endure for a night, but joy cometh in the morning"; "Lord, by thy favor thou hast made my mountain to stand strong"; "for thou hast delivered my soul from death, mine eyes from tears, and my feet from falling." "In this world ye shall have tribulations, but be of good cheer, I have overcome the world." "The light shines in the darkness, and the darkness has not overcome it."

And finally, I know that when Alex beat me to the grave, the finish line was not Boston Harbor in the middle of the night. If a week ago last Monday a lamp went out, it was because, for him at least, the Dawn had come.[83]

Coffin once said of the preacher's task, "Finally, you preach for yourself but, if you go down deep enough, you touch enough common humanity so that everyone's involved."[84] One of his strengths was that he was able to preach deeply enough to himself that he also touched the common chord of humanity in everyone. While his sermons were, on the whole, the most overtly political of all the Riverside preachers, they also were grounded in a shared humanity that bound Coffin to his hearers.

Truth "on the Slant" with a Turn of Phrase

Like Fosdick and McCracken, Coffin wrote out his sermons before delivering them on Sunday morning.[85] A common saying of the time was that preachers should spend one hour in the study for every minute they spent in the pulpit, and Coffin says he did so. "I spent a lot of time on my sermons. These people wanted good intellectual fare."[86]

With Coffin they certainly got it. His sermons—like Fosdick's—were dialogues with some of the leading intellectual forces of the past and present, and they were filled with the complexity that comes from deep thinking and wide reading. Coffin knew the arguments on both sides of an issue equally well, and it was unwise to engage him in debate without being equally well prepared.

Coffin frequently began preparing his sermons by reflecting on one or more of the assigned common lectionary text(s) for the day, but his sermons generally were more "topical" than "exegetical." He tended to use biblical texts more as starting points for reflection on larger ethical issues or as summaries of his theological stand on a particular matter than as focal points for teaching or explication.

Coffin's sermons also reflected his preference for truth that comes—as he put it—"on the slant." One of the things that made his preaching so engaging was that it also was unpredictable. Coffin delighted in turning platitudes on their head or in making statements that initially seemed outrageous. He approached issues from a variety of angles, did not bore his listeners by stating the obvious, and clearly relished his role as provocateur.

Yet Coffin was also aware that people "want something from the heart that goes through the head" and crafted sermons that not only analyzed issues but also moved people. To that end, Coffin took great care with the creative use of language in his sermons and worked extensively with Richard Sewall, a professor of creative writing at Yale, to ensure that his writing was as good as it could be. Every Sunday morning at 8 A.M., Coffin called Sewall and read his entire sermon to him over the phone. Sewall would then suggest improvements, and Coffin would revise the sermon before the 11 A.M. service.

If Campbell was the most creative Riverside preacher in terms of sermonic form, Coffin was one of Riverside's most poetic preachers. He often quoted poets in his sermons and especially loved Emily Dickinson. Coffin also loved playing with words and writing memorable sentences. He once said, "I've always thought of preaching as speaking the truth and turning a phrase, but there must never be any question where the [real emphasis] is."[87] Coffin was a master at creating a memorable phrase:

"Take yourself lightly, so that, like angels, you may fly."

"It is not because we have value that we are loved, it is because we are loved that we have value."[88]

"God is known devotionally, not dogmatically."[89]

"Imagination comes harder than memory, and faithfulness is more demanding than success."

"The Bible knows nothing of a moral majority . . . it insists that a prophetic minority always has more to say to a nation than any majority."[90]

"It is not enough to resist with confession; we must confess with resistance."[91]

"Like any book the Bible is something of a mirror: if an ass peers in, you can't expect an apostle to peer out!"[92]

The two goals of intelligent, well-crafted proclamation and work to enhance human life were at the heart of Coffin's ten-year preaching ministry at Riverside. When he announced his resignation from Riverside in July 1987 in order to become director of SANE/FREEZE, a new organization committed to issues of disarmament and peacemaking, he moved his pulpit and activism back into an arena he knew well: the messy world of politics, governments, and nations.

Traditional Worship with an Open Door Policy

Although Coffin was liberal (some would even say radical) in his politics, he was far more traditional in his worship preferences. He seemed to relish the relatively "high church" Protestant worship in Riverside's cathedral and viewed the Sunday morning service as being the center of the church's life and ministry.

Well schooled in music, Coffin had a great appreciation for the classical music tradition at Riverside. Under the able direction of Frederick Swann and John C. Walker, the music program continued to flourish during his pastorate, and he occasionally left the pulpit to join the choir for their Sunday morning anthem or to play the piano with an ensemble before the service began. He also helped form the Inspirational Choir, which intentionally incorporated more African American music in its repertoire.

The principal tensions during this period were not the form and style of the Sunday service, as in Campbell's era, but issues of inclusivity. What would be the congregation's position regarding the inclusion of gay and lesbian persons in the church's life, including its worship life? Would the congregation use women—especially ordained women—more fully in its ministerium and its worship leadership? (Until this time, women had been almost completely absent from the Riverside pulpit.) And how would the church deal with the issue of inclusive language in its worship services?

The matter of how or whether the church would become fully open to gays and lesbians was a volatile one, especially in a congregation in which so many homosexual persons were already active long-term members. The tension at Riverside grew during the Coffin years because of a division within the ministerium itself.[93] In 1985 the congregation voted to adopt its Statement of Openness, Inclusion and Affirmation of Gay/Lesbian Persons, pledging to accept into membership lesbians and gays and to expect and encourage them "to share in liturgy, general life, employment and leadership of our congregation."[94]

During Coffin's tenure, Riverside called its second clergy woman to the staff, the first woman on the ministerium to share the preaching duties at Riverside. Rev. Evelyn Newman, an ordained pastor in the United Methodist Church, joined the Riverside staff in 1976 with special expertise in spirituality and mysticism. The worship records indicate that during her four years on the staff, she preached thirteen times in the nave during Sunday morning worship.

Also during these years the church began wrestling in earnest with issues of inclusive language in worship. Coffin, who occasionally referred to God as "she" in his sermons, also used a unique baptismal formula (developed in consultation with faculty at Union Theological Seminary) that used both traditional Trinitarian language and feminine language for God: "I baptize you in the name of the Father, the Son and the Holy Spirit, One God, Mother of us all." Although inclusive language increasingly became normative for Riverside worship services during the Coffin years, it was not until later, during the Forbes era, that the Worship Council finally decided on an official policy on inclusive language.[95]

James A. Forbes Jr. (1989–present)

When the Reverend James Alexander Forbes Jr. was installed as the fifth senior minister of the Riverside Church on the evening of June 1, 1989, the entire service of worship exuded the hope, celebration, pageantry, and joy that surround an inaugural event of great magnitude. More than five hundred clergy and invited guests—including some of the nation's most prominent African American preachers and church leaders—followed colorful banners and preceded Forbes in procession into the nave, as organ and brass played Gigout's "Grand Choeur Dialogue." A multicultural gathering of representatives from ecumenical, denominational, and educational bodies brought greetings and extended their good wishes for the church and its new leader. Choral music was provided by the Riverside Choir and Inspirational Choir as well as the Ebony Ecumenical Ensemble,

FIGURE 2.6: Dr. James A. Forbes Jr. *Photograph by Jonah LaMoitte-Teunissen. Used by permission of the Riverside Church Archives and the photographer.*

founded and directed by Bettye Franks Forbes. Dr. Gardner C. Taylor, pastor of Concord Baptist Church in Brooklyn and "dean" of black preachers in the United States, gave the sermon: "I predict, nay, I prophesy, that [Dr. Forbes's] preaching here will confirm the Riverside pulpit as one of the dramatically influential preaching places in the English-speaking world."

Not only did this service celebrate the installation of Riverside's fifth senior minister, it also signaled to the world the dawning of a new era, in which the cathedral of American liberal Protestantism would now be headed by its first African American pastor. The Riverside Church, long known for championing racial equality from its pulpit, had finally called—by a unanimous vote of its search committee and board of deacons and a nearly unanimous vote of its congregation—a person who, by his very presence, was starting a new era of African American leadership in the congregation and beyond.

In calling James A. Forbes Jr., the church also continued its long tradition of pulpit excellence by appointing a preacher whose reputation was not only well established in New York City, where Forbes had served for thirteen years as professor of preaching at Union Theological Seminary and had spoken from the pulpits of many distinguished churches, but also nationally and internationally. In 1984 *Ebony* magazine named Forbes one of the ten outstanding black preachers in the nation, and in 1996, *Newsweek* magazine, announcing the findings of an extensive survey by Baylor University, named Forbes one of the twelve most effective preachers in the English-speaking world. Forbes appeared to be the perfect choice to head Riverside: one whose charismatic preaching and love for preaching placed him in the tradition of pulpit "greats" at Riverside, and one whose upbringing as an African American in the segregated South and whose record of activism for civil rights causes uniquely equipped him to lead this multicultural community of faith into the future.

Forbes brought more "differences" to the preaching and worship life of Riverside than any senior minister had before him. Because he was an African American (whose history was one of identification and solidarity with an oppressed minority community), a Pentecostal (Forbes grew up and was ordained in the Original United Holy Church International, in which his father was a bishop), and a southerner (as opposed to all four of his Riverside predecessors), Forbes brought an ethos to the preaching and worship life of Riverside that challenged some of its underlying values and assumptions.

Black, Pentecostal, and Southern

In many ways it is no surprise that Jim Forbes became a minister. He was born on September 6, 1935, in Burgaw, North Carolina, into what might be referred to as a "tribe of Levites": his grandfather, grandmother, several uncles, an aunt, and his father all were preachers. The eldest of eight children, Forbes recalls that as a child he used to stand on a coffee table and imitate his father's fiery preaching style. He also remembers seeing his grandfather so dramatically reenact Bible stories in his own sermons that Forbes (then six or seven) was certain that Mary's baby—ripe and ready for birthing under his grandfather's preaching robe—was going to pop right out in the center aisle of the church![96] Much of Forbes's youth was spent "listening to one of these [family] preachers or observing a host of ministers at various conferences, convocations, revivals and assorted district meetings,"[97] and their influence on his own formation as a preacher was profound.

Forbes and his close-knit siblings grew up in the parsonage of Providence Holiness Church in Southeast Raleigh, North Carolina, where his father was pastor. One reporter noted that as a child, James was known for his intelligence, his boxing talent, and his ability to influence other children to do good without seeming like a teacher's pet. A high-school friend also remembers Forbes (who has long loved music) as being one of Raleigh's best whistlers.[98]

The principal influence on Forbes's life during these early years was his Pentecostal upbringing. When *Sojourners* magazine interviewed Forbes later in his life and asked how his Pentecostal background influenced his understanding of ministry and theology, he replied:

> To be Pentecostal means that you have to give evidence that you are willing to let the Holy Spirit come into your life, seize the nerve centers of consent, and provide guidance for your life, both your life of worship and your life in the work-a-day world. The Pentecostal influence on faith that makes a difference in daily life is very strong with me.[99]

After graduating from high school, Forbes enrolled at Howard University in Washington, D.C. During his junior year, when he was majoring in chemistry and planning to become a physician, he heard the call of God to preach. The call for Forbes came through both preaching, when he was listening to a revival sermon, and music, when he, in an effort to flee the "hound of heaven," put on a recording of Tchaikovsky's Fourth Symphony and heard God saying, "Jim Forbes, don't you know I have called you? Jim Forbes, don't you know I have called you?"[100]

Forbes subsequently enrolled at Union Theological Seminary in New York in 1958, despite warnings from some of the bishops of his Holiness Church that he might "lose" the Holy Spirit in an environment steeped in liberalism and biblical criticism. At Union he took courses with well-known theologians like Paul Tillich and Reinhold Niebuhr and later referred to himself as a "Tillichian Pentecostal." "I was at Union when Paul Tillich was giving lectures on his third volume of systematic theology," he recalled. "I didn't understand every word he said, but I got the impression that he brought rational categories that were not incompatible with the experiential dimensions of the Spirit that I had learned about in my early upbringing."[101] Forbes also took every opportunity to listen to the outstanding preachers of his day, including Bishop H. H. Hairton, Mordecai Johnson, Vernon Johns, Howard Thurman, Gardner C. Taylor, Adam Clayton Powell Jr., Samuel Procter, and Martin Luther King Jr.[102]

Forbes spent the first summer after his 1962 graduation from Union at Olin T. Binkley Memorial Baptist Church in Chapel Hill, North Carolina, where he served under the leadership of Dr. Robert J. Seymour. He then served as pastor in three congregations of his own denomination: St. Paul Holy Church in Roxboro, North Carolina; Holy Trinity Church in Wilmington, North Carolina; and St. Johns United Holy Church in Richmond, Virginia. In Richmond he also served for two years as campus minister at Virginia Union University.

In 1976 Forbes was called to the faculty of Union Theological Seminary in New York, where he served as the Brown and Sockman Associate Professor of Preaching from 1976 to 1985 and as the Joe R. Engle Professor of Preaching from 1985 to 1989. His reputation as a charismatic preacher and teacher of preaching spread both nationally and internationally. By the time he was called to be senior minister of the Riverside Church at age fifty-three, Forbes had already delivered the prestigious Lyman Beecher Lectures at Yale University (subsequently published as *The Holy Spirit and Preaching*), had been a featured lecturer and preacher at many preaching conferences in the United States and beyond, and had received honorary doctorates from several colleges and seminaries.

A "Spirituality for Activism"

In many ways, the sermon James Forbes preached on the Sunday in 1989 when Riverside voted to call him, and the color, pageantry, and tone of his installation service, clearly marked a new day for the church's preaching and worship life. Forbes, wearing a red robe symbolic of the Holy Spirit's outpouring at Pentecost, began and ended his sermon with a poem that he himself had written, entitled "Release Your Song." The poem and the sermon called on the congregation in a time of "cosmic malaise" to reclaim the song within them that had been silenced by various internal and external forces and to assert, in freedom, their own individual and corporate songs that could also bring liberation to the world.

Forbes—who sometimes refers to himself as "an evangelical liberal"[103]—addressed both evangelicals and liberals in his candidate sermon at Riverside. In response to more conservative Christians who argued that the church should not be involved in politics, Forbes asserted:

The minister is the one who pronounces judgment on the community when it is failing to fulfill its responsibility to all of it citizens. If the minister's role is seen as political, so be it: We are all political. People who say they are not political mean that they have found great satisfaction or at least are content with the world as it presently exists. The minister tells people how a community and interpersonal relationships would be configured if the plan of God was taken seriously.[104]

Yet even in this initial sermon, we sense Forbes's desire to renew, through his ministry at Riverside, individual and corporate dimensions of the gospel, spirituality, and activism. While claiming Riverside's past history of activism as his own, it was clear that Forbes wanted to deepen the spirituality of activists and also activate evangelicals who had separated their spirituality from political engagement with the world.

Forbes himself speaks of his particular mission at Riverside as giving the congregation a "spirituality for activism." He remembered that before coming to the church he had asked a longtime Riverside member three questions:

1. "How do people get saved at Riverside?" Forbes says that he was really asking about Riverside's doctrine of soteriology. Does the event of Jesus Christ mean anything other in human life than to show people the right way to act? Is joining Riverside Church the same thing as being a disciple of Jesus Christ?
2. "What kinds of teachings exist at Riverside that help trace the spiritual maturity of its members?" For Forbes, from a Wesleyan faith tradition emphasizing a lifelong growth in spirituality, it was important that Christians have some kind of evaluative standards for measuring their own growth in faith.
3. "Where is the Holy Spirit at Riverside?" Forbes sensed that there was not much language of the Spirit used in the life of the church and also not much opportunity for experiencing the free winds of the Spirit.[105]

Forbes's sermons emphasize themes like being born again, prayer, healing, loving enemies, temptation, confession, and encouragement. Although he regularly combines these more "spiritual" and "evangelical" themes with a call to engagement with the larger world (so that in no sense can he be said to advocate otherworldly escapism), it also is clear that his preaching seeks to tilt the scales more toward what he believed had been underemphasized before he arrived at Riverside: the spiritual revitalization and renewal of the Riverside Church for mission and service in the world.

One of Forbes's activist causes during his early tenure as Riverside's pastor was the antiapartheid movement in South Africa. On the Sunday immediately following his installation as Riverside's pastor—a Sunday designated as "Peace Sabbath"— Forbes spoke to the Riverside congregation about his own recent travels in South Africa and strongly encouraged support of U.S. economic sanctions in South Africa. He assured the congregation that South African blacks would rather suffer for a cause than continue to suffer senselessly and that the majority supported sanctions. But he also asked: "How do you talk about truth and love for the Afrikaner at the same time you are talking about divestment and disengagement?"

Forbes's answer was that the church needs to participate in a "new strategy for peace" because of faith in a God who "gives food and drink to enemies of truth, rather than slaying them."[106] The Afrikaners also need love, he argued, because of their increasing rates of hypertension, illness, family murders, and suicide. Invoking the names of antiapartheid leaders such as Frank Chicane, Archbishop Desmond Tutu, and Rev. Alan Boesak, he urged the congregation toward the kind of truth speaking and acting that is grounded in love toward both the oppressed and the oppressor. The following week Forbes and a group of Riversiders traveled to Washington, D.C., to join a national march at the Washington Monument in support of the struggle to end apartheid in South Africa.

Forbes continued to keep his congregation abreast of the latest developments in the antiapartheid movement and remained an outspoken and engaged advocate for the cause throughout his early months as Riverside's pastor. Consequently there was great rejoicing, for both Forbes personally and the Riverside congregation, when Riverside was chosen as the place where Nelson Mandela would make his first address to religious leaders of the United States after his release from prison in February 1990. The worship service brought together an ecumenical gathering of leaders from all over the United States as well as many local church members and politicians and was as joyous and celebrative as any that has been held in the Riverside nave. Forbes participated with Mandela in a service that literally had people dancing and swaying to the beat and rhythms of African drums as they joined in singing freedom hymns.

Another of Forbes's themes has been the growing disparity between the rich and the poor in the United States and the need for churches to try to eradicate poverty. Perhaps more than any other minister before him, Forbes has dared to talk about classism in American society and has called on the Riverside congregation to use all means at its disposal to fight poverty. In a 1995 sermon entitled "Affirmative Action for Rich and Poor," Forbes asked, "Why have we [at Riverside] not taken on the mission of the emancipation of the poor from their plight?" His answer:

> I think we have not moved in that direction because it will be impossible to respond to that mandate without a radical transformation in our lifestyle. . . . We are a part of a capitalistic system which in its ideology has suggested the acceptability of the perpetual impoverishment of some, the obsolescence of some of God's children. And we have been nourished in that ideology . . . we have become beneficiaries of the system.[107]

Based on a gospel vision in which "God has a preference for the poor [because] God views all people on the earth as a part of God's family," Forbes urged the congregation to get involved in uplifting poor people in New York, by taking action both personally and corporately. He also expressed his hope that "this congregation would be as invested in Third World debt as we were in the hope of ever escaping from the clutches of the gnawing hands of abject poverty."[108]

In 1997 Forbes came closer to defining some of the corporate actions the church might take in its fight against poverty, in his sermon "Emancipation from Poverty." Delivered during the weekend of the Martin Luther King Jr. birthday celebration and on the Sunday immediately following Forbes's own participation, at the invitation of President Bill Clinton, in a White House economic summit, the sermon called on Riversiders to get involved in the fight against poverty in the nation. Specifically Forbes suggested starting a job development program at Riverside, joining with corporate America to help train people for jobs, and establishing a watchdog committee to keep an eye on welfare reform.[109] A month later Clinton himself came to Riverside Church for a roundtable discussion on poverty that included national and local religious, business, and social service leaders.

Other themes on which Forbes echoed the liberal tradition of the pulpit he inherited are the war in the Persian Gulf, the motherhood of God, human sexuality, the Rodney King trial verdict, and the need for prophetic (versus Rambo-style) patriotism.[110] But Forbes deals with such themes in a distinctive way.

First, while urging action, Forbes often fails to specify exactly what sort of action the congregation should take. He seems to view his role as more a "motivator" to action or a "suggester" of possible appropriate actions than a prescriber and community organizer.[111]

Second, Forbes consistently uses a compassionate tone toward those who disagree with Riverside's liberal stance even as he defends it. He insists that the love of God is extended not only to the oppressed but also to the perpetrators of oppression, who themselves need God's liberating word.

Third, Forbes's style and manner of preaching differ in a number of respects from that of his predecessors, not only in the way he preaches prophetically, but also in the way he preaches generally.

A Black Pentecostal Challenges
Riverside's Topical Preaching Tradition

Forbes's sermons reveal that he is, to a greater extent than any of his Riverside predecessors, a narrative biblical preacher, who begins his sermon with a biblical text (ordinarily chosen from the *Revised Common Lectionary*) and devotes a major portion of his sermon to a contemporary retelling of it. Forbes says that his first task as a preacher is to "discern a word from the Lord" and that to do so requires intensive listening on his part. A regular part of his own sermon preparation is to read the biblical text over and over before turning to commentaries or word studies to enrich his understanding of it.[112]

Whereas many of Coffin's sermons have one-word titles identifying controversial issues, Forbes's sermon titles more often refer to the biblical story and hint at ways in which the Bible relates to life today. For example, his sermon "Hannah Rose," which he has given on several occasions at Riverside by popular demand, discusses both a particular moment in the biblical story (when Hannah, having been misunderstood and misinterpreted by Eli in the temple, rose and prayed) and the need of the church today to rise and pray when the world gets us down. Likewise, his sermon "Cliques and Caucuses in the Church" deals with the cliques and caucuses Paul speaks of in his letter to the Corinthians and also those at Riverside. Forbes clearly believes that a faith supported by biblical teaching is a faith spiritually equipped for activism in the world, and his sermons both teach the stories of the Bible and also use those same stories to alter this world's status quo.

For Forbes, as for many other African American Christians, the Bible is the primary source of comfort, hope, and empowerment in a world that has too often oppressed and enslaved people of color. In his book *The Heart of Black Preaching*, Cleophus J. LaRue contends that what unites black preaching across the centuries is not so much its form or style but its belief in a God who, when interpreted through the African American experience, is seen to act "mightily on behalf of dispossessed and marginalized people." A belief in this God, an awareness of the sociocultural context of the black experience, and the creation of a sermon that speaks to the common black experience ultimately result in a powerful message that resonates with those in the listening congregation.[113]

In their structure and movement, Forbes's sermons are not always predictable, although many of them follow roughly this pattern: (1) an introductory section, raising some issue, theme, or tension point arising out of the biblical text, contemporary life, or the two in conversation; (2) the main body of the sermon in which Forbes recounts, usually in a highly narrative and contemporized style, the central story or key theological affirmations of the biblical text; and (3) a concluding section in which he fleshes out some of the implications (both personal and corporate) of the passage for our living in the world as Christians. Many of his sermons also reach a celebrative climax at some point, sending listeners away more uplifted, energized, and encouraged than they were when they entered the sanctuary.

Such sermons represent a significant departure from the "problem/resolution" mode of some of Forbes's predecessors (notably Fosdick and Mc-Cracken) and from the extended social analysis common in Coffin's sermons. But Forbes argues that there is good theological and communicative reason to proceed as he does. Namely, the "indicative"—the good news of what God has done for us—always precedes the "imperative"—what we are called to do for God and the world. In other words, people first need to hear the good news of God's actions on their behalf before they can be empowered to live as God's people in the world.

We should also note that before Forbes begins the sermon proper, he spends a lot of time in the pulpit each Sunday making extended comments about events in the life of church, community, or world; introducing visitors and guests; or giving updates on congregational celebrations and concerns. This practice, added to Forbes's habit of using the names of his congregants in his sermons and of preaching more regularly on issues of concern to the congregation's internal life, adds a "small church" feel to worship at Riverside and creates a strong sense of Forbes's own personal engagement with his flock. If Fosdick's intended "congregation" in preaching was the larger nation (with Riversiders viewed as a part of a much larger collective body), during the Forbes era Riverside has most felt like an ordinary, local congregation, gathering for worship with its own pastor speaking to his parishioners from the pulpit. Indeed, one of Forbes' great gifts is his ability to turn the formal cathedral space of Riverside into a warm and hospitable space for members and visitors alike.

The shrinking trajectory of the preaching audience from Fosdick to Forbes is evidence of the disestablishment of American Protestantism during the twentieth century. No longer do reporters from the *New York Times* regularly cover worship services at Riverside, and Forbes's services, unlike Fosdick's, are not broadcast on the radio during the prime afternoon hours but at 5 A.M. on Sunday mornings, to a local listening audience. Even though Riverside is moving into the new technology age with live broadcasts of its Easter service on its Internet website and live broadcasts of its New Year's Eve service on the Odyssey Cable Channel, the congregation on most Sunday mornings is composed of only those gathered in the nave. If Forbes preaches more sermons related to Riverside's own internal life as a congregation, it is because on most Sundays, that is who is listening.

It is not only in the form, content, and intended audience that the preaching of Forbes contrasts with that of previous ministers. The style, tone, and tenor of the sermons are different as well. Forbes stands in the long tradition of African American preachers for whom storytelling, song, and call-and-response patterns between pastor and people (including verbal "Amens") are the norm. He also comes out of a tradition that has long given prominence to the freedom and work of the Holy Spirit in the preaching and worship event itself and that is suspicious of any human attempts to control or to limit the Spirit's manifestation in worship through an overly ordered or scripted sermon or service.

Consequently, Forbes does not write out his sermons before he delivers them. Instead, his sermon files are filled with handwritten notes on small sheets of paper, usually containing a biblical text and a "proposition" for the sermon (a theological statement regarding its central theme), a written-out introduction, an outline of points he wishes to make, and a conclusion. The proclamation is filled out only in the preaching moment itself when Forbes opens himself to the directions in which the winds of the Spirit might wish to blow him and his congregation and allows himself to be caught up in the power of the Spirit in the preaching moment. Whereas most of his predecessors' "inspiration" came in their study, Forbes's inspiration comes at least as often in the preaching moment itself, and he never knows where the winds of the Spirit will blow him on a Sunday morning.

Forbes's sermons are more "embodied" than those of his predecessors. From Fosdick to Coffin, Riverside's preachers seemed content to stay in the high Riverside pulpit, but Forbes is not. It is not uncommon to find him leaving the pulpit on a Sunday morning to preach from the midst of the congregation, engaging people one-on-one, singing, swaying, dancing, and moving his body in ways that help communicate and dramatize his message, just as his grandfather before him did. He expresses his enormous passion for the gospel not only by what he says but also by what he physically does as he preaches. He literally throws his whole self into the endeavor.

Forbes's sermons adopt the cadences, rhythms, and repeated alliterative refrains of African American preaching. Occasionally he literally breaks into song during his sermons, singing a hymn he has written or humming the tune of a piece of music to which he is referring. As the first Riverside pastor to encourage the call-and-response patterns of the African American tradition during his proclamation, it is not unusual for his congregation to express their heartfelt "Amens" or to break into applause when particularly appreciative of something that happens in the sermon or worship (a practice that was a source of tension earlier in Forbes's ministry at Riverside).[114] Clearly Forbes—through his own highly emotive proclamation style—has encouraged Riversiders not only to use their heads in worship but also to engage their emotions and bodies.

Sea Changes in Worship and the Resulting Controversy

Just as preaching has changed during the Forbes era, so also has worship. The music on Sunday morning now includes many more styles, such as jazz, gospel, spirituals, and reggae, and frequently blends the music of many cultures in one service.[115] Visually the service is also more colorful, in the ministers' flowing robes of jewel-tone colors and the sanctuary's complementary paraments. The service, which begins at 10:45 with an informal hymn sing, lasts until well past noon, with Forbes preaching as long as the Spirit moves him.

After several years of discussions with Forbes, in September 1998 the Worship Council of Riverside Church decided to begin a new midweek evening service that is much beloved by those who regularly attend and by Forbes himself. The service, called "Creating a Space for Grace," takes place in an auditorium with folding chairs placed in a semicircle around a lectern, piano, and table. Several hundred people regularly attend, and the congregation includes long-term and newer members of the Riverside Church as well as people from the community who come after work (for more on this service, see chap. 6). The service involves a great deal of lay leadership and allows enough time for testimonies, prayer requests, or the sharing of celebrations (such as births, newfound jobs, and healings). Forbes usually preaches for the service, and it is obvious that in this worshiping environment—reflective of his own Pentecostal and African American heritage—he feels the freest to be himself.

In addition, the church offers a "Morning Light Meditation" service early on Sunday mornings in Christ Chapel. This service of healing, communion, and prayer draws a small but committed congregation of participants who want quieter and more reflective worship.

While many in the congregation have welcomed the changes that Forbes's preaching and worship leadership have brought to Riverside, early in his ministry there was a vocal minority who did not. In 1992/93 a group within the congregation called the "Riversiders for Riverside"— many of whom had been leaders during the Coffin era—publicly opposed Forbes, eventually calling for his resignation (for more on the "Riversiders for Riverside" controversy, see chap. 6). While some of the group's charges against Forbes pertained to his managerial style, they also complained about issues related to his preaching and worship.[116] Although the Riversiders failed in their attempts to pressure Forbes into resigning, the church did lose a number of long-term members in the wake of the controversy. It was a difficult period for all involved and especially for Forbes himself. However, both Forbes and the Riverside congregation weathered the storm, and in recent years there has been not only a more "peaceable" atmosphere at Riverside but also a healthy upturn in budget and membership numbers. When the congregation celebrated Forbes's tenth anniversary as senior minister in a festive service of worship on February 3, 1999, it was apparent that both Forbes and the congregation were grateful for the renewed unity, growth, and bright hope for the future.

The Nation's Spiritual Renewal at a Time of Terrorism and War

Although through the years Forbes has tried to foster a spirituality for activism at Riverside, his greater desire has always been that through Riverside's unique witness and ministry, spiritual renewal and revitalization might also come to the entire nation. Perhaps nothing better prepared the American people to hear his message of hope and encouragement than the tragic events of September 11, 2001.

On the Sunday following terrorist attacks on the World Trade Center and Pentagon, members and visitors packed the 2,500-seat Riverside sanctuary for both the morning worship service and a special afternoon interfaith service called "America in Healing" (for more on this service, see chap. 4). At both services Forbes preached a sermon entitled "Is There a Word from the Lord?" in which he urged his listeners not to succumb to paralyzing fear but to embrace and receive the strength God provides in times of need. Relying on the wisdom of the human body (which God has especially designed to guide people during difficult times), on the power of the Spirit (the breath of God available to members and nonmembers alike), and on the power available in community for healing and transformation, Forbes urged his listeners to "break out and risk living" despite the clouds hanging heavy and gray above them. He concluded his sermon, as he had concluded his candidate sermon at Riverside, with a poem he had written, echoing the celebrative hope that lies at the heart of the Christian faith.

The Guest Preaching Tradition at Riverside

While most congregational histories would be complete without reference to guest preachers, Riverside's would not. Through the years, the pulpit of the Riverside Church has served as a forum for excellence in preaching by its senior ministers and other ministers on the church staff, and it has also played host to preachers and leaders of national and international renown. Indeed, reading the guest preacher list for the Riverside Church is like reading a "Who's Who" list of visionary and eloquent communicators, whose words and witness have stirred and challenged church and nation alike.

During the Fosdick years, the three other ministers on the staff—Eugene Carder, C. Ivar Hellstrom, and Norris L. Tibbetts—each preached at

Riverside several times a year and assisted in the church's various other worship services. The pulpit was most often filled during the summer months by well-known pastors and scholars whom Fosdick invited to preach in his absence.[117] The most frequently invited guest was Frederick W. Norwood, the minister of City Temple in London, who preached twenty-two times between 1938 and 1945. Other favorites of Fosdick were distinguished pastors (including Methodist Harold Bosley, Presbyterian George Buttrick, Congregationalist J. Gordon Gilkey, and Baptist Harold Cooke Phillips), and theologians (such as Reinhold Niebuhr, Henry Sloane Coffin, and Charles W. Gilkey). Although almost all the invited guests were Anglo men, on September 1, 1940, Dr. Mordecai Johnson, the first African American president of Howard University, preached during Riverside's Sunday morning service.[118]

During McCracken's era (1946–1967), the guest preaching list continued to include some of the favorite pastors of the Fosdick era but also expanded to include McCracken's own choices. Joseph R. Sizoo, president of New Brunswick Theological Seminary, topped the "most frequently invited" list, and preachers of national renown—such as John Claypool, Carlyle Marney, and Ralph Sockman—continued to fill Riverside's pulpit. It was only natural that McCracken—who himself had been a theology professor before coming to Riverside—would add to the academic guest list a number of faculty from Union Theological Seminary (including noted preachers Paul Scherer, James Smart, and Edmund Steimle) and professors from other schools in the United States and Britain (such as John Baillie of New College, Edinburgh; Ernest Gordon from Princeton University; and D. Elton Trueblood from Earlham College). McCracken also invited well-known international and ecumenical leaders to fill the pulpit, such as Martin Niemoeller (a leader in the German Confessing Church, who also served as one of the presidents of the World Council of Churches) and D. T. Niles (a noted evangelist and ecumenist from India).

Outstanding African American preachers also mounted the Riverside pulpit with greater frequency during this era, including Benjamin Mays (president of Morehouse College), Howard Thurman (dean of the chapel at Boston University), Gardner Taylor (pastor at Concord Baptist Church of Christ in Brooklyn), and Samuel Proctor (pastor at Abyssinian Baptist Church in Harlem).

Certainly no preacher had a greater impact on changing the course of the nation in the twentieth century than did Dr. Martin Luther King Jr., who preached from the Riverside pulpit six times between August 1961 and

April 1967. King, who had a standing invitation to preach at Riverside during the 1960s, used its pulpit to proclaim his gospel of nonviolent resistance, love of enemies, and racial justice in the years immediately preceding his death.

In a 1962 sermon entitled "The Dimensions of a Complete Life," King
declared his lifelong message:

> God is not interested merely in the freedom of black men and brown men
> and yellow men, but God is interested in the freedom of the whole human
> race and the creation of a society where all men can live together as broth-
> ers and every man will respect the dignity and worthy of human personal-
> ity. This is why I believe so firmly in non-violence. This is why I believe so
> firmly that the ethic of love must stand at the center of any movement
> that is seeking to break loose from some unjust order and move to a just
> order. . . .
>
> And so we have been able to say, in very difficult moments, to our most
> violent opponents, "We will match your capacity to inflict suffering by our
> capacity to endure suffering. We will meet your physical force with soul
> force. Do to us what you will and we will still love you. We cannot in all
> good conscience obey your unjust laws because non-cooperation with evil
> is as much a moral obligation as is cooperation with good.
>
> And so throw us in jail and we will still love you. Bomb our homes and
> threaten our children and we will still love you. Send your propaganda
> agents across the country and make it appear that we are not fit morally,
> culturally or otherwise for integration and we will still love you. Send your
> hooded perpetrators of violence into our communities at the midnight
> hour and drag us out on some wayside road and beat us and leave us half
> dead and, difficult as it is, we will still love you. Be ye assured that we will
> win our freedom. We will not only win freedom for ourselves, but we will so
> appeal to your heart and conscience that we will win you in the process and
> our victory will be a double victory.[119]

In a sermon given at Riverside in 1966, King challenged the church—
"an institution which has often served to crystallize, conserve and even
bless the patterns of majority opinion"—to rise above its own self-interest
and blessing of the status quo, and to dare become "transformed noncon-
formists."[120] And on April 4, 1967, King gave an address from the Riverside
pulpit for a gathering of Clergy and Laity Concerned for Vietnam (a
group formed in 1965 to work within Catholic, Jewish, and Protestant

communities to oppose the Vietnam War), entitled "Beyond Vietnam."[121] In that speech King first publicly expressed his own opposition to the war and linked militarism abroad to human rights at home. It was exactly one year to the day after delivering this address that King's own life was taken by an assassin's bullet.

Phyllis Taylor was the first woman ordained at the Riverside Church (on November 29, 1959), but there is no record that she ever preached during Sunday morning worship in the nave. It was not until May 5, 1968— during the interim period between the ministries of McCracken and Campbell—that Dr. Cynthia Wedel, associate general secretary for Christian Unity of the National Council of Churches, became the first woman to preach from the Riverside pulpit. Her sermon, delivered on the Festival of the Christian Home Sunday and entitled "Love, 1968," encouraged the church to move beyond paternalism in its understanding of love (especially toward youth and the poor) and to recognize that "the task of parents today is to stop feeling guilty about not reproducing earlier patterns of family life, and to look for new ways of building and expressing love within the family."[122]

During the late 1960s and early 1970s, when Ernest Campbell served as Riverside's senior minister, guest preachers and speakers of national renown included Andrew Young (then executive vice-president of the Southern Christian Leadership Conference) and Cesar Chavez (of the United Farm Workers Organizing Committee). Ecumenical leaders Eugene Carson Blake and Philip Potter (each of whom served as general secretary of the World Council of Churches); seminary professors James I. McCord (Princeton Theological Seminary), Letty Russell (Yale Divinity School), Martin Marty (University of Chicago Divinity School and editor of *The Christian Century*), and Phyllis Trible (Union Theological Seminary); and pastors Wyatt Tee Walker (Canaan Baptist Church in New York) and William A. Jones Jr. (Bethany Baptist Church in Brooklyn) were also among the invited guests.

Riverside's ministerial staff members Robert Polk (minister of urban affairs and Riverside's first African American minister) and Eugene Laubach (executive minister) also preached at least once a year during this period. Laubach, who first joined the Riverside staff in 1961 under McCracken, preached around one hundred sermons during his thirty-year tenure at the church.[123] He also helped open the very traditional worship services at Riverside to greater liturgical renewal and innovation during the turbulent 1960s.[124]

In June 1976, just before Campbell's departure, Riverside called Evelyn Newman to be minister of pastoral care and social service. Newman, who served until May 1980, was the first woman on the ministerial staff to regularly share in preaching and worship leadership on Sunday mornings. Riverside also called its first interim senior minister during this period, Jitsuo Morikawa, who regularly preached and led worship at Riverside for one year before Coffin arrived.

When Coffin took over in November 1977, the guest preacher list became much more diverse. First, Coffin invited a far more international group of preachers and activists to the Riverside pulpit than had previously come. Church and human rights leaders from South Africa (Desmond Tutu, Allan Boesak, Beyers Naudé), Latin America (Dom Helder Camara, Orlando Costas), South Korea (Dong Whan Moon), and China (K. H. Ting) joined activists from the United States (Jesse Jackson, Andrew Young, Benjamin Chavis) and western Europe (Sydney Callaghan) in bringing a broader world and its concerns into Sunday morning worship at Riverside.

Second, Coffin expanded the ecumenical makeup of the guest preacher list by adding to it Roman Catholic theologians and church leaders of note (such as Hans Kung, Dom Helder Camara, and Joan Delaplane), as well as by inviting two Jewish rabbis to preach the Sunday morning sermon.

Third, Coffin's list of women invited as guest preachers included white clergy and lay women with feminist concerns (such as Elizabeth Bettenhausen, Isabel Carter Heyward, Phyllis Trible, and Barbara Brown Zikmund), as well as African American clergy women and "womanist" theologians (including Thelma Adair, Katie G. Cannon, Yvonne Delk, and Valerie Russell). Because there already were two women on the ministerial staff who regularly preached and shared in worship leadership during this period (Evelyn Newman and Patricia de Jong), the congregation became far more accustomed to women's leadership in worship.

During the Forbes era (1989–present) many of the trends toward greater diversity in the pulpit that were begun in the Coffin era have continued or have been expanded. Women—including many who served on Forbes's staff (Mariah Britton, Fanny Erickson, Sally Norris, Brenda Stiers)—continued to preach occasionally from the Riverside pulpit. Openly gay men and lesbian women (Mel White, Jane Adams Spahr) also preached at Riverside, especially on Gay Pride Sunday (annually celebrated in June). Local and national politicians, including Bill Bradley (former senator from New Jersey), David Dinkins (former mayor of New York

City), Jesse Jackson (founder and president of the National Rainbow Coalition and U.S. presidential candidate), and Marian Wright Edelman (president of the Children's Defense Fund in Washington, D.C.)—were occasional pulpit guests, as were noted playwrights (Ossie Davis) and authors (Jonathon Kozol, Cornel West).

The multicultural list of guests contained such outstanding preachers and theologians as Joan Brown Campbell, Joan Chittister, James H. Cone, Ada Maria Isasi-Diaz, Peter J. Gomes, Chung Hyun Kung, J. Alfred Smith Sr., Jeremiah Wright, and Prathia Hall Wynn. The list of homileticians expanded (given Forbes's own history as a teacher of preaching) to include scholars like Barbara Lundblad, Cleophus LaRue, Thomas G. Long, Eugene Lowry, Henry Mitchell, and Ella Pearson Mitchell. Riverside also continued expanding its interfaith guest list during the Forbes era. Muslim leaders were invited for the first time to preach on Sunday morning, and Buddhist, Muslim, and Jewish religious leaders joined Forbes in leading the "American in Healing" service after September 11, 2001.

Looking Toward the Future from the Perspective of the Past

The Riverside pulpit has always been a *free* pulpit (highly resistant to any attempts to control or manipulate it), a *liberal* pulpit (in regard to social and political issues), a *relevant* pulpit (consistently bringing the Christian faith into dialogue with personal and societal issues), and an *activist* pulpit (urging its listeners not only to reflect on critical issues but also to promote its liberal ideals). Since its founding, this church, which was built on the preaching reputation of Harry Emerson Fosdick, has placed a high priority on worship and proclamation and has called to its pulpit leaders whose reputations as intelligent, courageous and eloquent spokespersons for the faith have also resulted in their serving as teachers and role models for other ministers in the United States and elsewhere.

Paul H. Sherry, a longtime participant in the life of the Riverside Church and editor of *The Riverside Preachers*, observed that all the Riverside preachers gave their best to the church during their tenure there and that all also "grew with the job."[125] From Fosdick to Forbes, the Riverside preachers not only brought their own distinctive gifts, life experiences, and perspectives to the pulpit; they also grew and expanded those gifts during their Riverside tenure. All have had enormous respect and admiration for their predecessors.

FIGURE 2.7: The resurrection angel. *Used by permission of the Riverside Church Archives.*

Indeed, Sherry suggests that preaching "may be *the* most significant element in shaping the [Riverside] congregation's life and ministry. It has been so powerful, so profound, so innovative and so courageous that it has had a major influence—far more so than in other congregations."[126] Not only has Riverside called serious preachers to its pulpit; Riversiders themselves have also taken preaching with the utmost seriousness, allowing the witness of the pulpit and the weekly experience of worship in the nave to guide their own vision for Christian witness in the larger city, nation, and world. If you want to find the "heartbeat" of the church called Riverside, listen to what goes on in worship on Sunday morning in the nave. It is there that the church finds vision, encouragement, and empowerment for living out more faithfully its corporate and individual call to discipleship in the world.

Perhaps that is why the future of the Riverside pulpit is so important. The decision regarding who will become the sixth Riverside preacher after Forbes retires is not simply a matter of deciding whether or not the church will continue its long trajectory of excellence. Nor is it simply a question of deciding on the racial-ethnic identity or gender of the next preacher.[127] The real question for Riverside in the twenty-first century is who will be the person best equipped to give leadership, vision, encouragement, and guidance from this free, liberal, activist, pulpit?

On the roof of the Riverside Church building is a "resurrection angel" standing guard, blowing a trumpet, and looking out toward the city. In a recent interview, James Forbes spoke of the angel as a herald who "knows what time it is and speaks a word that points the way we should go."[128] Whatever Riverside's future is, many people in the United States and beyond are hoping that this forward-looking church on the hill will continue calling to its pulpit messengers who, like the angel on the roof, "know what time it is" and "speak a word that points the way we should go."

NOTES

1. Robert Moats Miller, *Harry Emerson Fosdick: Preacher, Pastor, Prophet* (New York: Oxford University Press, 1985), 336.

2. Ibid., vii.

3. Harry Emerson Fosdick, *The Living of These Days: The Autobiography of Harry Emerson Fosdick* (New York: Harper & Row, 1956), 33.

4. Fosdick, *The Living of These Days*, 53.
Fosdick particularly credits William Newton Clark, professor at the Theological Seminary at Colgate and author of *An Outline of Christian Theology*, for helping shape his liberal religious thought. See *The Living of These Days*, 55–56, 66–67.

5. Fosdick, *The Living of These Days*, 74–75.

6. Ibid., 94.

7. Ibid., 78.

8. Fosdick's famous quotation in this regard is "Only the preacher proceeds

still upon the idea that folk come to church desperately anxious to discover what happened to the Jebusites." Fosdick, *The Living of These Days*, 92.

9. Fosdick, *The Living of These Days*, 94.

10. For a classic statement of Fosdick's approach to preaching, see "What Is the Matter with Preaching," reprinted from *Harper's Magazine* (July 1928), in *Harry Emerson Fosdick's Art of Preaching: An Anthology*, compiled and edited by Lionel Crocker (Springfield, Ill.: Chas. C. Thomas, 1971), 27–41.

11. Fosdick, *The Living of These Days*, 99 (italics added).

12. Fosdick, *The Living of These Days*, 100.

13. In his autobiography, Fosdick recalls that there were virtually no personal counseling courses offered during his days as a seminary student at Union. He was self-taught in this field, reading the classic works of people like Freud and Jung and texts in psychology and religion such as William James's *The Varieties of Religious Experience*, Starbuck's *Psychology of Religion*, Coe's *Psychology of Religion*, Pratt's *Psychology of Religious Experience*, and Ames's *Psychology of Religious Experience*. See *The Living of These Days*, 214. In the introduction to *On Being a Real Person* (New York: Harper Bros., 1943), Fosdick acknowledges his personal indebtedness to Dr. Thomas W. Salmon, a personal friend and "the leading American pioneer in the field of mental hygiene," with whom he consulted on numerous cases (viii). Anton T. Boisen, the founder of the modern Clinical Pastoral Education movement, had also been one of Fosdick's students at Union, and doubtless Fosdick read much of the emerging literature in the new field of pastoral counseling.

14. Miller, *Harry Emerson Fosdick*, 101.

15. The Park Avenue Baptist Church published a brochure entitled "Dr. Harry Emerson Fosdick's First Sermon as Pastor Elect Park Avenue Baptist Church." This quotation is from p. 1 of that brochure.

16. Fosdick as quoted in Miller, *Harry Emerson Fosdick*, 200–1.

17. The fire, on December 21, 1928, began when a carelessly strung electrical wire set fire to wooden scaffolding in the nave. It significantly set back progress on the church building, delaying the completion of its construction by more than a year.

18. Fosdick, *The Living of These Days*, 191. For a more detailed account of the architecture of the Riverside Church, see chap. 3 of this book.

19. "Visiting Throng Sees Riverside Church Opened: 5000 Turned Away after Standing Room Is Exhausted at Solemn Devotionals. Rockefeller Jr. Is Absent. 4000 of All Faiths Hear Dr. Fosdick on Christianity." *New York Herald Tribune*, October 6, 1930.

20. H. Augustine Smith, ed., *Hymns for the Living Age* (New York: Century Co., 1923).

21. Milligan served as organist, director of music, and conductor at Riverside Church until 1940, when Frederick Kinsley succeeded him. The Riverside building

also had in its tower an excellent carillon, the Laura Spelman Rockefeller Carillon, and Kamiel Lefévere was hired as the carillonneur, a position he held for more than thirty years.

22. "Fosdick Church Dean of Ushers Has Staff of 92," *New York Herald Tribune*, November 28, 1931.

23. These statistics are from "The Record of Marriages at the Riverside Church 1926–1948." In 1943, when the church also served as the Sunday afternoon worship location for the Navy Midshipmen's Training School, as many as twenty weddings took place on the same day and at the same time, with a navy chaplain officiating.

24. See, for example, his sermon, "The High Use of Memory," preached on May 31, 1931, at the Riverside Church. "Sometimes I think the best argument against war is laughter. . . . The adjective which condemns war is 'silly.' It is insanely silly. . . . What did it settle?"

25. See Fosdick, "The Unknown Soldier," in *The Riverside Preachers*, edited by Paul H. Sherry (New York: Pilgrim Press, 1978), 49–58.

26. One person, who was a seminarian at Union Theological Seminary when the attack on Pearl Harbor occurred, remembers Fosdick leading a group of Japanese theological students through an underground tunnel that extended from the seminary to Riverside Church, in order to give them a place of safety in the wake of anti-Japanese sentiment.

27. For example, in 1932 Fosdick began his sermon, "A Religious Faith for a Discouraging Year," with an honest acknowledgment of the economic depression that "overshadows everything." He asserted that the real threat to U.S. national security came not from without but from within, namely, from the nation's own lack of large-scale social and economic planning. Yet in his very next sentence Fosdick hastened to defend the business leaders who were members of his congregation: "I suppose that this challenge to a creative faith comes particularly to you men and women in responsible positions in the business world. The radicals are denouncing you. I think that is nonsense. You are human like all the rest of us, carrying terrific burdens and puzzles, as everybody else is, about the way out, and many of you are doing everything you can think of in this confused situation to make it well for the common man."

28. McCracken was forty-two when he became Riverside's pastor.

29. Fosdick's words as quoted in the *New York Herald Tribune*, May 23, 1946.

30. Fosdick's words spoken during McCracken's installation service on October 2, 1946, were quoted the following day in the *New York Herald Tribune*.

31. Fosdick's words as quoted in the *New York Herald Tribune*, October 3, 1946.

32. Meditation given by Laubach at McCracken's memorial service, March 25, 1973.

33. Robert J. McCracken, *The Making of the Sermon* (New York: Harper Bros., 1956), 62.

34. Ibid.

35. McCracken also published a book of his sermons entitled *Questions People Ask* (New York: Harper Bros., 1951).

36. McCracken, *The Making of the Sermon*, 15.

37. Ibid., 15, 17.

38. Ibid., 24.

39. Despite McCracken's frequent references to the Trinity, the Holy Spirit is largely underdeveloped as a topic in his preaching. I could find only one sermon title that referred to the Holy Spirit ("Belief in the Holy Spirit"), whereas many, many titles refer to God or Christ.

40. Eugene Laubach said of McCracken: "There was an expression around the church which said 'Jim McCracken is at his best on Easter.' And indeed that was so. He was most alive and most vital then because this was the time of year which served best to dramatize all that he most deeply believed. The Easter resurrection experience was the central experience of his life." Meditation given by Rev. Eugene Laubach at McCracken's memorial service, March 25, 1973.

41. Meditation given by Laubach at McCracken's memorial service, March 25, 1973.

42. Ibid.

43. Ibid.

44. Robert J. McCracken, "Discrimination, the Shame of Sunday Morning," a sermon preached at the Riverside Church on February 21, 1954.

45. Ibid.

46. Robert J. McCracken, "The Christian Attitude to Communism," a sermon preached at the Riverside Church on October 10, 1948.

47. Robert J. McCracken, "The War in Vietnam," a sermon preached at the Riverside Church on January 9, 1966.

48. The groundbreaking service for the Interchurch Center took place on October 12, 1958, with President Dwight D. Eisenhower laying the cornerstone. The building was completed and dedicated in 1959.

49. Meditation given by Laubach at McCracken's memorial service, March 25, 1973.

50. McCracken had two reasons for wanting the font: first, so that the service of baptism could move out of the chapel and into the morning worship service in the nave, and second, so that those baptized in the nave would have an option for baptism in a mode other than immersion.

51. Many of these reflections are from an interview with Ernest Campbell by Marianne Rhebergen on January 28, 1999.

52. Interview with Campbell.

53. Interview with Campbell.

54. Ernest T. Campbell, "The Case for Reparations," in *The Riverside Preachers*, 118–31.

55. Ibid., 119. The italics are Campbell's.

56. Ernest T. Campbell, "An Open Letter to Billy Graham," in *The Riverside Preachers*, 127.

57. Paul H. Sherry, editor of *The Riverside Preachers*, added this word as a footnote to Campbell's sermon, p. 131.

58. This sermon was preached at the Riverside Church on May 20, 1973.

59. Ernest T. Campbell, "Overheard in Room 738," in *The Riverside Preachers*, 110–17.

60. Ernest T. Campbell, "Forty Years on the Heights," a sermon preached at the Riverside Church, October 4, 1970.

61. Ernest T. Campbell, *Christian Manifesto* (New York: Harper & Row, 1970), ix (italics in original).

62. Campbell, however, was not a lectionary preacher during his Riverside years and, in fact, opposed lectionary-based preaching on the grounds that (a) the lectionary covers only 65 percent of the Bible, and (b) he believes in a "free" pulpit, that is, one that is not constrained by the lectionary. Interview with Ernest T. Campbell by Leonora Tubbs Tisdale and Marianne Rhebergen, March 19, 2001.

63. Ernest T. Campbell, "The Silence of the New Testament," *Christian Manifesto*, 50–56.

64. Interview with Campbell by Rhebergen.

65. Ernest T. Campbell, "Experience, Expectation, and Surprise," in *The Riverside Preachers*, 104–9.

66. Campbell confirmed that the element of indirection was important to him as a preacher, especially when addressing controversial issues. "If you're looking for results, you don't go hard and alienate people." Interview with Campbell by Tisdale and Rhebergen.

67. Minutes of the Riverside Church Worship Council, February 27, 1969. Historically, children's worship at Riverside had taken place separately as a part of the Christian education program.

68. June 24, 1976, Riverside Church news release. For the first time in its history, the Riverside Church called a senior interim minister after Campbell's departure. Previously, guest preachers and other members of the ministerium took over administrative duties. Dr. Jitsuo Morikawa, a professor at Union Theological Seminary, served in this capacity from November 1, 1976, to October 30, 1977.

69. This is how Coffin himself described their home in his autobiography, *Once to Every Man: A Memoir* (New York: Atheneum, 1977), 3.

70. William Sloane Coffin Jr., "Why I Became a Minister," a sermon preached at the Riverside Church, October 5, 1986.

71. Ibid.

72. Ibid.

73. Coffin, "A World Fit for Children," a sermon preached at the Riverside Church, November 20, 1977.

74. Coffin, "After Rocky's Funeral," a sermon preached at the Riverside Church on February 4, 1979.

75. Coffin, "And Pray for the Iranians, Too," a sermon preached at the Riverside Church, December 23, 1979.

76. Coffin, "Report from Tehran," a sermon preached at the Riverside Church, December 30, 1979.

77. Cora Weiss had previously organized a shipment of ten thousand tons of wheat to go to Vietnam for the Church World Service. Also see chap. 5.

78. Coffin, "Homosexuality," a sermon preached at the Riverside Church, July 12, 1981. For more information on the Channing Phillips sermon and the church's response to the homosexuality issue, see chap. 5.

79. "It has even been said that a woman's right to an abortion is an absolute right. Whether that means a legal or a moral right is not always clear. What is clear is that whether legal or moral an absolute right—one right taken out of the framework of all other rights—is what gets us into trouble." William Sloane Coffin, "Abortion," a sermon preached at the Riverside Church, July 26, 1981.

80. Coffin, "Acting Our Consciences," a sermon preached at the Riverside Church, April 15, 1984.

81. Coffin, "AIDS," a sermon preached at the Riverside Church, January 26, 1986.

82. Coffin, "Alex's Death," a sermon preached at the Riverside Church on January 23, 1983. The sermon has been reprinted in *A Chorus of Witnesses: Model Sermons for Today's Preacher*, edited by Thomas G. Long and Cornelius Plantinga Jr. (Grand Rapids, Mich.: Eerdmans, 1994), 262–66.

83. Ibid.

84. William Sloane Coffin Jr. as quoted in *The Riverside Preachers*, 143.

85. Campbell, however, says that he preached from an outline and then edited the transcribed sermon tape before it was printed. Interview with Campbell by Tisdale and Rhebergen.

86. Interview with William Sloane Coffin Jr. by Marianne Rhebergen, June 18, 1999.

87. Interview with Coffin by Rhebergen, June 18, 1999.

88. "The Spirit of Power and Love," Coffin's inaugural sermon preached at the Riverside Church on November 6, 1977. Coffin pledged to the congregation that he would try to heed this first recommendation during his tenure as their pastor.

89. Coffin, "Born to Set Thy People Free," a sermon preached at the Riverside Church, December 4, 1977.

90. Coffin, "Burn Out," a sermon preached at the Riverside Church, March 8, 1981.

91. Coffin, "Acting Our Consciences," a sermon preached at Riverside Church, April 15, 1984. The sermon urges the church to become involved in the sanctuary movement.

92. Coffin, "Fiftieth Anniversary," a sermon preached on the fiftieth anniversary of the Riverside Church building, October 5, 1980.

93. The divide was made public when one of Coffin's ministerial associates, Dr. Channing Phillips, preached a sermon on May 5, 1985, that placed him in direct opposition to Coffin's own open and affirming stance on the issue. For more on this incident and the church's response, see chap. 1.

94. "Statement of Openness, Inclusion and Affirmation of Gay/Lesbian Persons," voted affirmatively at a meeting of the Religious Society of the Riverside Church on June 2, 1985.

95. The first official policy was adopted by the Worship Council in 1997.

96. Forbes told and reenacted these stories in an interview with me, March 25, 2002.

97. James A. Forbes Jr., *The Holy Spirit and Preaching* (Nashville: Abingdon Press, 1989), 14.

98. Yonat Shimron, "Two Brothers Share Vision," *Raleigh News & Observer*, January 14, 2000.

99. "Matters of the Heart: Reflections from a Preacher and Theologian," *Sojourners*, May 1989.

100. Forbes told the story about his call in one of his early sermons at Riverside Church. He actually sang the melody and beat out the rhythm of the music at the appropriate time in the sermon. See James A. Forbes Jr., "Why I'm a Member of the Church," a sermon preached at the Riverside Church on April 23, 1989.

101. Forbes, "Why I'm a Member of the Church."

102. Forbes, *The Holy Spirit and Preaching*, 14.

103. This is the same phrase Fosdick used to describe himself.

104. James A. Forbes Jr., "Release Your Song," a sermon preached at the Riverside Church on February 5, 1989.

105. Interview with James A. Forbes Jr. by the Riverside Church History Project authors, June 11, 2000.

106. James A. Forbes Jr., "A New Strategy for Peace," a sermon preached at the Riverside Church, June 4, 1989.

107. James A. Forbes Jr., "Affirmative Action for Rich and Poor," a sermon preached at the Riverside Church on July 23, 1995.

108. Ibid.

109. James A. Forbes Jr., "Emancipation from Poverty," a sermon preached at the Riverside Church on January 19, 1997.

110. See James A. Forbes Jr., "Repent, Believe, Receive," a sermon preached at the Riverside Church on December 9, 1990; "Would Your God Want to Be Called 'Mother'?" a sermon preached at the Riverside Church on March 18, 1990; "A Christian Conversation on Sexuality," a sermon preached at the Riverside Church on June 25, 1989, and "More Light from the Spirit on Sexuality," a sermon preached at the Riverside Church on April 20, 1997; "The High Cost of Peace," a

sermon preached at the Riverside Church on May 3, 1992; and "Prophetic Patriotism," a sermon preached at the Riverside Church on July 4, 1989.

111. Forbes believes that preaching is a shared responsibility of the pulpit and the pew. "No more than 50 percent of a sermon rests with the preacher and the preacher's imagination. The other 50 percent is up to the congregation." Consequently, he often seeks to be suggestive and evocative in his preaching (rather than directive), leaving it to the listeners to complete and carry out the implications of the message he initiates. My interview with Forbes.

112. My interview with Forbes.

113. Cleophus J. LaRue, *The Heart of Black Preaching* (Louisville: Westminster John Knox Press, 2000), 6.

114. Only one year into his tenure at Riverside, Forbes preached a sermon defending the use of "Amen" in worship. See "Say a Serious 'Amen,'" February 11, 1990. The sermon not only called for freedom of expression in worship; it also challenged those who voice their "Amens" to follow through with action in the world.

115. Timothy E. Smith, organist and director of music, and Helen Cha-Pyo, conductor and associate director of music, oversee an extensive and diverse musical program at the church. A new hymnal was adopted for use in 1990 as a part of the church's sixtieth anniversary celebration: *Hymns, Psalms and Spiritual Songs* (Louisville: Westminster/John Knox Press, 1990).

116. Specifically, they charged that Forbes's preaching was too focused on matters of personal piety, treated social issues superficially, and lacked the intellectual rigor of his Riverside forebears. They also complained about shifts in the tone and tenor of the worship services, arguing, for example, that "altar calls . . . are from a theological and worship tradition that is quite different from Riverside's" and that "applause is at odds with the dignity and beauty of the nave space." See the second letter addressed to the congregation of the Riverside Church from the "Riversiders for Riverside," October 13, 1992.

117. A long-standing tradition at the Riverside Church is that the preaching year for the senior minister ordinarily runs from mid-September to mid-June, with the minister taking at least two of the summer months away from the pulpit (and often away from the city itself) for rest, renewal, and preparation for the church year ahead.

118. Johnson's sermon was entitled "The Defense of Democracy." Unfortunately there is no written or recorded copy of his sermon in the archives of the Riverside Church. Records indicate that he was probably the first African American to preach in the Riverside nave.

119. Martin Luther King Jr., "The Dimensions of a Complete Life," a sermon preached at the Riverside Church on November 18, 1962, and reprinted on p. 6 of *Sermons at Riverside*, a collection of sermons of the Riverside Church Archives published in 1996 in celebration of the church's sixty-fifth anniversary.

120. Martin Luther King Jr., "Transformed Nonconformist," a sermon preached on January 23, 1966, at the Riverside Church. This sermon also appears in M. L. King Jr., *Strength to Love* (New York: Harper & Row, 1963), 8–15.

121. The speech was reprinted under the title "Beyond Vietnam: Dr. Martin Luther King's Prophesy for the 80's," in celebration and remembrance of King's birthday by the Riverside Church, January 15, 1988.

122. Cynthia Wedel, "Love, 1968," a sermon preached at the Riverside Church on May 5, 1968.

123. Laubach's sermons frequently had creative titles like "Crust into Batter," "An Elephant's Ballet," "Holiness and Hustle," "Seven Cents Worth of Love," and "Riot in the Streets" (Palm Sunday, 1968).

124. In an interview with the authors of this book on June 10, 2000, Laubach stated that during 1965/66, when McCracken was absent from the pulpit for an extended period (due to illness), he and organist Fred Swann introduced a great deal of liturgical innovation, including regular adherence to the church year calendar, the first Tennabrae service, and the first Ash Wednesday and Epiphany services. Laubach estimated that during that time, he preached or spoke more than forty-five times at Riverside. When asked what he considered to be his greatest success during his thirty-year tenure, he replied that it was his influence on the church's worship life.

125. Interview with Paul H. Sherry by the Riverside Church History Project authors, June 10, 2000.

126. Ibid.

127. Certainly, issues of race and gender will be significant in the next round of conversations. Can this congregation—which is now predominantly African American in membership and has grown accustomed to a more Afro-centric preaching and worship style—happily call a senior minister who does not, to some degree at least, continue that tradition? Can this congregation—which has had a number of women associate pastors in recent years but never a woman senior minister—cross that frontier as well?

128. Interview with James A. Forbes Jr. by the Riverside Church History Project authors, June 10, 2000.

3

A Christian Vision of Unity
An Architectural History of the Riverside Church

John Wesley Cook

An Impressive Sanctuary

This church believes in the ministry of beauty, and
makes no apology for building as impressive a sanctuary
as it was able.
    —*The Riverside Church in the City of New York:*
    A Handbook of the Institution and Its Building, 1931

As people rushed toward the new Riverside Church building along Riverside Drive on Sunday morning, October 5, 1930, they saw looming before
them a beautiful and monumental neo-Gothic building, still in the last
stages of construction. The exterior symbolized tradition, stability, ele-
gance, and expense (see figure 3.1).

Upon entering the spacious, vaulted narthex (vestibule) and finding a
seat in the sanctuary, they saw that a twentieth-century version of the
Gothic tradition had inspired the overall spatial concept as well as the
small details. As the worship service began, it became clear that this architecture represented not only a rich and significant past but also, at the
same time, a truly modern living church for the present and for the future
(see figure 3.2).

The Riverside Church building integrates the historic with the modern.
In the construction phase, the decisions that determined the spatial
arrangement for the central worship space reflected theological priorities.
Rather than the three-aisle plan that one would find in the medieval

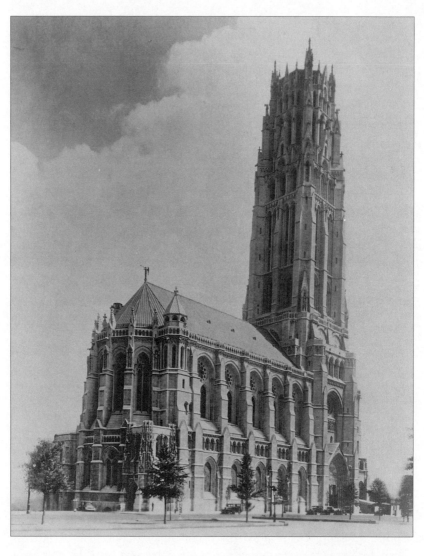

FIGURE 3.1: The Riverside Church in 1930. View of the north end and the west side. *Used by permission of the Riverside Church Archives.*

FIGURE 3.2: The opening service of the Riverside Church, October 5, 1930.
Used by permission of the Riverside Church Archives.

Gothic style, a preaching hall was created. In the medieval Gothic style, the traditional three-aisle basilica is laid out proportionally. That is, the side aisles are usually one-half the width of the nave (center aisle), and the interior walls are usually laid out proportionally, with the height of the columns and the height of the clerestory (the upper window section) being equal. The galleries (the smaller middle part of the wall) are one-third the height of the colonnade and the clerestory.

But the medieval Gothic style served a different kind of sacramental theology than did that of the Riverside Church. The hearing of the Word is central to the concept of Riverside's ministry and therefore central to the architectural planning of the sanctuary space. Preaching is the primary sacrament administered in the Riverside space, that is, the primary mode of encountering God. In traditional Baptist theology the sacraments were redefined as ordinances, and regularly taking bread and wine in the context of worship was a mode of remembering. Preaching at Riverside is a way of knowing God's revelation through the life, death, and resurrection of Jesus Christ.

The Riverside Church was built as a preaching hall in a modified Gothic form that borrowed heavily from the style of the cathedral at Chartres, France. What the architects did with their model makes the Riverside structure unique. The Chartres building is situated on an ancient sacred Druid spring and was built at the end of the twelfth and well into the thirteenth century on the ruins of a burned-out Romanesque church. In the Middle Ages, the site had been an important center of pilgrimage. In contrast, the Riverside Church building was situated on Riverside Drive after a few, less important, buildings had been removed. It was to occupy one of the highest points on Manhattan Island and, as an urban presence, was to relate to a community of important intellectual and religious institutions in the Morningside Heights area of New York City.

The architectural techniques employed at Chartres Cathedral were among the most up-to-date of the late medieval period. Likewise, the construction of Riverside Church used some of the most modern building techniques of the early twentieth century. Because medieval builders believed that certain proportions had spiritual significance, Chartres Cathedral was laid out according to strict mathematical formulations in order to produce ratios of one to two in the nave and one to three in the interior walls. In contrast, Riverside Church's side aisles are reduced to mere passageways in order to make room for the open, central space for proclamation, hearing, and seeing. The medieval vaulting system at Chartres was calculated in order for the stone-on-stone construction to remain stable at greater heights. The Riverside building, however, is a steel-framed structure with Gothic features, and so its vaulting system is decorative rather than structurally essential. The method of construction at Chartres allowed for large windows to provide more light, which passed through painted scenes. In the Middle Ages, people believed that the light of stained-glass windows had sacramental value. But the windows of Riverside Church, though produced at Chartres and copied in large part from the medieval prototypes, are merely decorative. And although they depict religious scenes and religious figures and include non-Christian and modern figures, they have none of the sacramental meanings attached to medieval windows. In other words, the more mystical elements of the Chartres building are reformulated in the Riverside structure. The theological goals achieved in the modern church building are different from those realized in the medieval model. In addition, different theological ends are served in their modern architectural expression.

Besides the variations in Riverside's structure from those of its medieval model, other variations from the so-called neo-Gothic norms of its (Riverside's) own times are apparent as well. The neo-Gothic style was invented in the nineteenth century when churches' building programs renewed their interest in medieval planning and the assertions that the rebuilding of Gothic forms realized a particular religious priority. For instance, in Germany the brothers Boiseree finished building Cologne cathedral in the nineteenth century according to their studies of the original drawings. In England, A. W. N. Pugin published *The True Principles of Pointed or Christian Architecture* in 1841 and *An Apology for the Revival of Christian Architecture in England* in 1843. For Pugin, "Christian architecture" was synonymous with "Gothic architecture."

In the United States, when these forms were used for religious purposes, they were more successful for Roman Catholic worship than for Protestant worship. The greatest difference is in the role of the Eucharist in Roman Catholic worship and the role of the sermon in Protestant worship. Copying medieval models creates problems for modern worship. Sightlines are obscured; seating patterns are less flexible; and acoustical properties are generally muted and less distinct in the high-vaulted stone surfaces of neo-Gothic sanctuaries. Movement to an altar (Roman Catholic) is easier to accommodate than clarity of the spoken word (Protestant) in neo-Gothic architecture.

Riverside was even a variation on the modern Protestant uses of neo-Gothic designs. At Riverside, the sightlines are open; the acoustics are clear for the spoken word and for music; and the auditorium, with its narrower side aisles and two balconies, center the congregation in the space for worship. Because they set out from the beginning to accommodate a preaching ministry, the architects at Riverside avoided many of the problems inherent in Gothic and neo-Gothic designs.

Riverside's Past: An Architecture for Hearing the Word

To understand the historical place of Riverside's ministry on a national and even an international scale, one must understand that from the beginning, its sermonic voice has been its primary mode of communication and impact and that this church's architecture has served that purpose. One of the principal architectural contributions is the way that Riverside presents a very modern religious concept in medieval dress.

As discussed in earlier chapters, the congregation responsible for this new place previously worshiped in the Park Avenue Baptist Church, a neo-Gothic building. The preaching ministry, the educational ministry, and their social concerns led the congregation to invest in architects who could combine their values and interests and bring fresh insights to the new Riverside commission.

The Riverside Church Handbook of 1931 states,

> Nearly one hundred years have passed since a small group of Christian men and women laid the foundations of the institution which was to become long afterward the Riverside Church. The Church traces its history back to 1841 when the life of New York centered in the lower part of Manhattan Island.[1]

The early history of the congregation illuminates the path that led to Riverside's construction.

In the mid-nineteenth century, one of the best-known preachers of New York City was Dr. George Benedict, pastor of the Stanton Street Baptist Church. Under his vigorous ministry the church membership increased beyond the capacity of the Stanton Street building. It became apparent that to accommodate the pastor's following, Dr. Benedict's ministry would need a larger church building, and in 1841, several hundred members of the Stanton Street Church acquired a more commodious building not far away and organized a new church called the Norfolk Street Baptist Church, with Dr. Benedict as pastor.

Another commanding figure in the religious community was Dr. Thomas Armitage of Albany, New York, who succeeded Dr. Benedict in 1848. His appointment marked the beginning of a pastorate that continued for forty years of progressive church development. The church had dedicated a new edifice in downtown New York in 1850, and in those early days the city was undergoing a rapid transformation. Commerce invaded the once quiet streets of the Lower East Side, and the rising tide of population altered the character of old-time neighborhoods.

Before the end of the 1850s the church had begun a journey northward through the city, a journey lasting more than seventy years that took it to Fifth Avenue, to Park Avenue, and, finally in 1930, to Riverside Drive.[2]

The Fifth Avenue Baptist Church, located on the corner of Forty-sixth Street and Fifth Avenue, opened in the spring of 1860. Between that time and 1912, when Dr. Cornelius Woelfkin became the pastor, four pastors led the congregation. By 1917 the church began plans for constructing a new building on Park Avenue and Sixty-fourth Street, to be named the Park Avenue Baptist Church. The architectural style would be neo-Gothic. The first public worship service was held in April 1922. The highly respected Dr. Woelfkin retired in January 1926 and was succeeded by Harry Emerson Fosdick. At this same time, the Park Avenue congregation already was interested in building a new church on a new site.

The Need for a New Church

As discussed earlier, John D. Rockefeller Jr. was instrumental in the creation of the Riverside Church. Architecture was a profession about which he knew a great deal. That is, he knew what he liked, and he supported the incorporation of a Gothic vocabulary of form as he understood it in the early twentieth century. The Rockefeller family, and especially John D. Jr., was involved in the campaign to construct a new building in a unique neo-Gothic style.

Rockefeller had believed for some time that New York City needed "a great Protestant cathedral." He had supported plans for the construction of the Cathedral of St. John the Divine in Morningside Heights. Bishop William T. Manning had emphasized that that cathedral would be "a shrine of prayer and worship for all people" and a "common center for the religious life of our whole city." Rockefeller's generosity was particularly remarkable given the fact that he was not an Episcopalian but a devoted Baptist and a loyal member of the Park Avenue Baptist Church.

By 1925, however, Rockefeller was attracted to a broad, inclusive view of Christianity that was not limited by the doctrines of a particular denomination. As a result, he became closely involved in an ecumenical movement that sought to bring all Christians together in the service of a better and more peaceful world.

But Bishop Manning declared that the time had not yet arrived when members of other denominations could join the board. Although he accepted Rockefeller's gift of $500,000 toward building the Cathedral of St. John the Divine, he refused his application for board membership. Bishop Manning's rejection thus prompted Rockefeller to support the construction on Morningside Heights of what became known as the Riverside Church.[3]

Rockefeller offered Harry Emerson Fosdick the position of pastor of the Park Avenue Baptist Church, and Fosdick accepted on the condition that a church building be erected near Columbia University. He also insisted that the new church be given a name with no specific denominational connotations. "Fosdick desired 'an inclusive church' with an interdenominational congregation open to all Christians. . . . The independent congregational structure of the Baptist Church, with no control from a higher central ecclesiastical authority, permitted the new congregation to embrace Fosdick's vision of an ecumenical church."[4] Rockefeller shared this same vision.

Within a year Rockefeller was negotiating to buy a site for the new building and selecting the architects and an architectural design. In the spring of 1926, he bought a site on the south side of West 122d Street between Riverside Drive and Claremont Avenue, including the entire 200-foot frontage on West 122d Street and 225-foot frontages on Riverside Drive and Claremont Avenue. To make room for the church, three apartment buildings, as well as a mansion and a stable that had been built in 1880, had to be removed.[5]

Originally, Rockefeller hoped that the apartment buildings would generate income for the project. Even some of the early church building plans incorporated the apartment units into the design in the hope that they might generate income. In 1925 the famous architectural firm of McKim,

Mead and White presented an illustration of how a church building and a high-rise apartment building could be integrated (see figure 3.3).

After studying the McKim, Mead and White plan, however, it was clear to all involved that "the church structure was lost in the massive apartment complex." Rockefeller, especially, realized that creating a church of great monumentality in a building that combined the church with an apartment building was impossible. Accordingly, he proposed removing the income-producing element and provided a large donation to cover any additional costs.[6]

Rockefeller donated $8 million toward the purchase of the site on Riverside Drive and the initial design, a considerable sum for any time and especially in 1925. The failure of this first design led Rockefeller to Charles Collens, a partner in the Boston firm of Allen and Collens, and also the New York architect Henry C. Pelton. They were the team that had designed the Park Avenue Baptist Church. Influential in the decision to plan a neo-Gothic church building was the fact that the nearby Union Theological Seminary was in a Gothic style. Rockefeller himself was enamored with the classic French cathedrals, and for a short time Ralph Adams Cram, a famous neo-Gothic architect, was associated with the project. "Sensing Rockefeller's interest, Collens and Pelton decided to avail themselves of an offer made by Rockefeller to fund a trip to France and Spain for the study of Gothic churches."[7]

Building a church in the neo-Gothic style was a great challenge. The architect's mandate was to build a modern church with modern technology that would serve the preaching style of Fosdick and the liberal program of the church. The architecture was to transcend even the conventions of traditional Protestantism.

In the *Church Monthly* of December 1926, architect Charles Collens described the plans then under way:

A simple bold type of Gothic architecture has been used, the inspiration for which has come largely from Chartres Cathedral. This involves the elimination of tracery motifs in the fenestration and throughout the Tower openings, replaced by the engaged collonette and flattened arch, and the use of plate tracery rose windows with great areas of stained glass framed in heavy metal bars and leadings.

The selection of the style was not a matter of chance. At the time when this problem was first suggested to the architects, they decided that the

FIGURE 3.3: An early rendering of a Riverside Church concept by McKim, Mead and White architects. *Courtesy of the Avery Architectural and Fine Arts Library, Columbia University.*

matter was of such magnitude that the only solution lay in a first-hand examination of the cathedrals and church architecture of France and Spain to select those elements best adapted to this particular Church.

Charles Collens is quoted as saying, "He who designs a great church in anything but Gothic has lost a divine spark in the structure itself which only that great art can supply."[8]

These architects regarded the decision to use Chartres as a model for planning as exceptional when compared with the usual uses of Gothic models in neo-Gothic styles. As Collens wrote,

> There were two especial reasons for this selection: First, so much of the modern church design in New York and throughout the country has made use of the traceried types of the later French and English Gothic that it appeared advisable to obtain a certain individuality by employing this noble and imposing type of sturdier design. Secondly, the erection of a great tower in which every floor is used for some practical purpose required a fenestration devoid of tracery, which the superimposed and offset arcades of the older of the two Chartres towers furnishes in an admirable manner.
>
> The Cathedral of Chartres [1194–1260] which many think represents the best phase of church design of a period in the history of architecture notable for its outstanding ecclesiastical structures, was selected therefore as the prototype to be followed in designing the new Riverside Church. The type of construction design on the other hand was to be distinctly modern in every way, that is, the modern steel frame enclosed with masonry. The completed building thus represents the best traditions of religious architecture with the most modern thought in economical and lasting construction.[9]

The architects' early decision to adapt the Gothic model to a Protestant preaching hall is noted in another section of Collens's 1926 commentary:

> Following closely the dimensions of the interior of Albi Cathedral in Southern France, the Church Auditorium has a span of 60 feet and a clear height to the ridge of the vault of 100 feet. This interior is planned with narrow vaulted airless, triforium and clerestory, the northerly end terminating in an apsidal treatment, with Choir and Ambulatory, and the southerly end in a double gallery motif made necessary by the requirements of fitting a seating capacity of 2400 to a restricted New York lot.[10]

FIGURE 3.4: The steel construction of the Riverside Church's nave.
Used by permission of the Riverside Church Archives.

The major part of the stone sculpture program was executed by Piccir-illi Studios, John Donnelly & Co., M. H. Keck, and Charles H. Humphries. Clifford Swan was the consulting engineer in all questions involving acoustics. Meyer, Strong and Jones was the engineering firm for the electrical, ventilating, heating, and elevator installation. The amplifying apparatus was installed by Bludworth and Co., Inc., whose engineers also were advisers on the mechanics of the building's sound amplification and reproduction.

The theological interpretation of the architecture thus was the simultaneous embodiment of two different convictions. First, the Gothic vocabulary that is the building's dominant visual message refers to a tradition well known to the ecclesiastical history of architecture. It evokes a memory of the past that is somewhat familiar to the general public. The style of the building says "church" to even the casual observer, given the limited knowledge of the time as well as the recent memory of the neo-Gothic style, which had become a popular form. Second, the building incorporated the most recent and most modern technology available in order to create a monument held together and held up by steel, concrete, and stone. All that was new in the experience of building skyscrapers in New York City was available to the architects and builders of the Riverside Church, in which the tension of the medieval and the modern is held together in harmony (see figure 3.4). This dynamic mirrors the similar tension between the church's teaching based on ancient scripture and its preaching based on the contemporary human condition. Or put another way, both the historical and the modern are a part of the ministry and the architecture of the Riverside Church.

Another factor that greatly influenced the design of the new church was the need for a tower to house the bells. They were to be dedicated to the memory of Laura Spelman Rockefeller, the mother of John D. Rockefeller Jr. Since 1924 they had been in the tower of the Park Avenue Baptist Church where "the music of the carillon was heard for the first time in New York City."[11]

The Tower

The design of the tower had to resolve two major problems. The tower has twenty-one working floors below the bell chambers, which in themselves account for the equivalent of five additional floors. The tower has four elevators, two of which go to the tenth floor and two to the twentieth floor. One major consideration for the tower's construction was the design for the Laura Spelman Rockefeller Memorial Carillon (the bell collection) (see figure 3.5).

The tower was to be 392 feet high to accommodate the nearly one hundred tons of specially wrought bells. Because of the height, weight, and stress caused by the placement and playing of the bells, the tower contains some of the heaviest steel columns and beams used in the church's entire structure.

The second major problem in the tower's design was the necessity of carrying one edge of it over the back of the nave. The juxtaposition was necessary because the desired seating in the nave needed to accommodate 2,400 people. This meant that the entire north wall of the tower had to be carried on one truss beam resting on upright columns placed on either side of the nave. The cross truss is 68 feet long and weighs 60 tons.

FIGURE 3.5: The Laura Spelman Rockefeller Memorial Tower. *Used by permission of the Riverside Church Archives.*

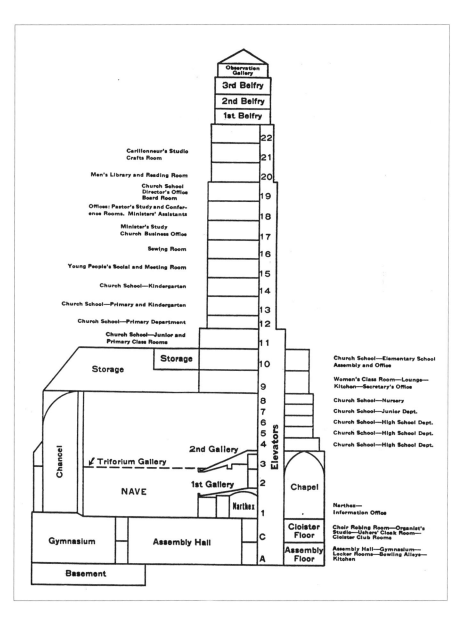

FIGURE 3.6: A cross section, by floors, of the first building campaign. *Used by permission of the Riverside Church Archives.*

The tower has twenty-two floors, most of which are devoted to the specialized uses of the various church groups and to the church offices. In addition, two floors cover the entire area of the building beneath the Riverside level for the common uses of the members and friends of the church (see figure 3.6).

> Ample facilities for every department of the church life will be provided. The tower itself will have about twenty available floors for Church School work, Young People's activities, the varied program of the Women's class, the Women's society, the Church Offices, etc. The Men's Auditorium will be in the same relative position as in the present building. On that level also will be the main recreational features for which provision is being made, including a most ample gymnasium and four bowling alleys.[12]

Within a year, in 1927, construction was begun on the first campaign. Although the exterior, an unapologetic Gothic massing, was described early on as having an entrance on the south side, by the time of the first service in 1930 the decision had been made to put the main entrance on the western side, that is, on the Riverside Drive side, opening to the narthex. The main door therefore is the west portal (see figure 3.7).

> Patterned after the great doors at Chartres, the West Portal contains the figures of forty-two scientists, philosophers, and religious leaders of the ancient and modern world. These figures line the three central arches that begin on a level with the top of the doors and rise to an apex above the figure of Christ. The first and fifth arches contain figures of angels.[13]

In the tympanum (the triangular panel above the door) framed by these arches is a seated figure of Christ. At Christ's right hand are an angel and a lion, symbols of Matthew and Mark; at Christ's left are a bull and an eagle, symbols of Luke and John. At Christ's feet are two bands of sculpted figures in low relief. The upper band presents three scenes depicting Christ's birth, and the lower band shows the twelve apostles flanked by a single figure each on the left and the right.

The statue columns to the left and right of the two central doors are nearly life size. On the left are the prophets Isaiah, Jeremiah, Hosea, Amos, and Micah, and at the right are Saints Simeon, Stephen, Paul, Barnabas, and Timothy. On the trumeau, or central pier between the doors, stands John, the beloved disciple.

FIGURE 3.7: The West Portal of Riverside Church. *Used by permission of the Riverside Church Archives.*

While the format of the sculpture in the west portal was decidedly Gothic, based on the Chartres model, the figures were original to the New York site and included modern figures selected by the iconography committee.

A Modern Figure in the Church's Iconography

According to Dr. Eugene C. Carder, in his unpublished manuscript "The Riverside Church As I Have Known It," "the decision to include Albert Einstein among the fourteen great scientists to appear in the 'Arch of Scientists' at the West Portal occasioned much comment" (see figure 3.8).

Actually, the committee on iconography had not intended to choose a contemporary personality to represent any category, and when they submitted a preliminary list of some twenty scientists to the faculty members of various universities for their recommendation, the name of Albert Einstein was not included. The faculty members, however, pointed out that any list of fourteen great scientists should include the name of Einstein, which persuaded the committee to have him represented in the arch. Einstein himself was a bit surprised to learn that he was to stand at the portal of a Protestant church in New York City.

The day after he reached New York on this first visit, Dr. Einstein appeared at the church and with characteristic modesty and simplicity indicated that he had been led, in part, by curiosity to see himself enshrined in the symbolism of a Christian church. It was the writer's privilege [Dr. Eugene Carder] to join Dr. Fosdick in conducting him through the building. He did not linger long before his own statue but was soon inside where he exhibited a keen and highly appreciative interest in the inclusiveness of the philosophy of the church as exhibited by the persons portrayed in sculptured stone and stained glass. Standing before the Philosopher's Window in the east aisle, his eye was caught by the portraiture there of Emanuel Kant, the great German philosopher, walking in his garden in evident meditation and followed by his servant carrying an umbrella. As he looked at the galaxy of philosophers and realized that, like himself, they did not belong, for the most part, to the same creed as the builders of this church, he said, "This could not happen in Europe. I am afraid it may never happen there." Then he asked, "Am I the only living person in all the symbolism?" On being told that he was, he seemed to

FIGURE 3.8: A detail of the West Portal's sculptural program. *Used by permission of the Riverside Church Archives.*

speak to himself as he said, "I'll have to be very careful as to what I say and what I do for the rest of my life."[14]

The story of the Riverside Church's iconography also is related in Collier and Horowitz's book about the Rockefellers: "To symbolize the inter-denominational spirit and its further reconciliation of religion and science, the tympanum arching the main portal contained the figure of non-Christian religious leaders and outstanding heroes of secular history, Confucius and Moses, Hegel and Dante, Mohammed and the dread Darwin."[15]

The Chapel Door

South of the west portal is the door leading to the Christ Chapel. Today, it is seldom opened. In the tympanum above the doors, a stone carving shows the adoration of the Magi, a scene similar to that of the medieval period in the right portal of the west facade at Chartres cathedral (see figure 3.9). Bordering this scene at Riverside are arches that hold figures representing the twelve months of the year. These and other symbols on the portal emphasize the eternally recurrent nature of life as recorded in history, religion, science, and the arts.[16]

The Narthex

The west portal leads to the narthex. Directly ahead, over the stairwell on the far wall, are four lancet windows of stained glass that depict the story of Christ. These windows are early-sixteenth-century works of art that originally appear to have been created for a cathedral in Bruges. For a while, these windows were the chancel windows of the Park Avenue Baptist Church. They appear to be well preserved and represent a technique that suggests that they were made by the Antwerp School of Glass Painting.[17]

The narthex uses heavy Gothic forms. Springing from the massive stone columns, without a break in the form of the column for a capital, these forms rise in a more organic manner to form low four-partite vaults. Although the details of the narthex seem to be late Gothic in style, its layout seems more Romanesque in its spatial concept. (The Romanesque was a pre-Gothic, medieval style of construction primarily in stone and borrowing heavily from earlier Roman methods.) This mixed design leads one immediately into the nave's soaring vaults while maintaining the explicit Romanesque concepts of the architectural style of Christ Chapel, located to the immediate right of the narthex. That is, the narthex subtly reflects simultaneously the two styles that flank the entrance space to the north and to the south.

Christ Chapel

A passage from the narthex goes to Christ Chapel, located to the right side of the entrance. The architects patterned the chapel after the eleventh-century Romanesque Church of Saint Nazaire in Carcassonne, France. Its walls of warm-color Brier Hill sandstone form a rich setting for the intricately carved reredos (a large screen) behind the altar. The top section of this stone screen is bisected by a cross bearing the inscription: "I am the

FIGURE 3.9: The chapel door and its sculptural program. *Used by permission of the Riverside Church Archives.*

Door; by me if any man enter in, he shall be saved, and shall go in and out, and find pasture." A flock of sheep at the left of the cross is tended by a shepherd in Palestinian garb, and a flock on the right is tended by a pagan boy. They recall: "Other sheep have I that are not of this fold."

A transfigured Christ appears at the center of the composition beneath the cross, with Moses, Elijah, Peter, James, and John beside him. The lower panel of the reredos depicts the Last Supper. On the altar front are carved major scenes from Christ's ministry.

Above the altar is a rose window whose central figure is the Paschal Lamb surrounded by emblems of the Twelve Apostles. The stained-glass windows along the south wall tell the story of the life of Christ, beginning with the Annunciation in the window nearest the altar and concluding with the Resurrection in the rear window.[18]

Although much has been made of the cathedral at Chartres as a model for the design of Riverside, the nave, for example, is in many ways different from that of the cathedral. It is open and broad, housing a preaching space that underplays the role of the sacramental theology prevalent in the medieval model. As mentioned earlier, the act of preaching as an engagement with the Word of God is the primary mode for a relationship with God, and this is expressed in the nave's architecture. The twentieth-century accommodations created by the architects are illustrated in some very practical design decisions. First, the side aisles are small in proportion to the width of the nave, ignoring the role of numerology in medieval planning. Second, the galleries are decorative rather than liturgically functional. Third, the four-partite vaulting over the central space creates a light, lofty, billowing impression but is not a structural, supportive device. Fourth, the back wall of the nave rises to two layers of balconies that are, architecturally, a complete break from the medieval, Gothic aesthetic. Fifth, the visual focus in the room is primarily on the pulpit area and the reading stand rather than on the altar. Finally, the place of the choir is not like a medieval choir loft but is more in keeping with the Protestant tradition (see figures 3.10a and b).

The nave is a remarkable integration of motifs that serve both the symbolic purposes of a neo-Gothic plan and a decidedly Protestant function. The 1931 guidebook to the Riverside Church's architecture claims that it is "a simple and bold design that endows the structure with the profound appeal of mediaeval religious art, without diminishing its utility as a building."[19] The architectural style has not escaped criticism, however. Early on, "the massive Gothic edifice of the Riverside Church, whose effort to bridge the gap between traditional and modern architecture, was derisively styled 'neo-eclectic' by its critics."[20] Wallace A Taylor of the American Institute of Architects, in an article entitled "A Criticism of the Riverside Church, New York" for the June 1931 issue of *Architecture*, asked: "Is America's last word in church architecture to be a violation and betrayal of both Gothic tradition and steel construction?" He then asserted that the building represented "bewildered eclecticism, of cultural servitude to Europe, and a travesty on Thirteenth Century Gothic."[21]

Modification and integration were not among the values that all critics esteemed in the first half of the twentieth century. Even though many neo-Gothic buildings dotted the landscape by the time the Riverside Church was finished, few if any, reached the heights of "harmonic tension" so beautifully created in the first campaign of this building.

The stonework is exemplary for its time. Sheathed in Indiana limestone on the exterior and interior, the detailing is exquisite. Clustered shafts rise from the base of the nave's piers through the gallery zone into the clerestory area to the springing points of the ribs of the wide arches that span the nave. Tracery for the stained glass is reserved for the choir, while the aisle and clerestory windows of the nave's side walls reflect their sources in Chartres cathedral. The double-wall construction exposed in the gallery area extends the support elements in the walls of the massive structural weight above. The blind arcading of the gallery areas on both sides of the nave and throughout the choir reflect Chartres's early Gothic style. Even though the pointed arch motif is maintained throughout the structure, everything is modified to serve the purposes of a twentieth-century preaching hall.

The Pulpit

Within the nave, a few elements are worth noting. First is the pulpit, which was dedicated to the memory of the beloved pastor of the Park Avenue Baptist Church, the Reverend Dr. Cornelius Woelfkin. He did not live to see the completion of the new church.

The symbolism of the pulpit consists of major and minor prophets of the Old Testament who, in this setting, emphasize the prophetic utterance that this pulpit represents. In addition to the slender columns that rise from the floor at the outer edge, the pulpit consists of three parts. The entire work is made of solid limestone, and each of the three blocks weighed

Figure 3.10a: The Riverside Church's nave. *Used by permission of the Riverside Church Archives.*

FIGURE 3.10b: An early architectural concept of the nave.
Used by permission of the Riverside Church Archives.

three tons before it was carved. The theology of the pulpit's iconography emphasizes the prophetic role of preaching. The preaching of the current minister, Dr. James Forbes, is an appropriate fulfillment of this iconographic promise because it exemplifies the kind of preaching that draws much from Scripture and strikes deeply at the values of contemporary society.

The Chancel Rail, the Choir Stalls, and the Labyrinth

Twenty quatrefoil medallions cover the face of the rail that frames the choir. The low-relief carving of the medallions represent the interests, emphases, activities, rites, and ceremonies expressed in the chancel and in the worship and service of the people. Just as the subject of the medallions is appropriate to the chancel area, the carved oak images of the choir stalls are equally appropriate to the place of music in worship. The dominant theme underlying all the carvings is the praise of God. For example, on the ends of the stalls are elements that the psalmist calls for in Psalm 148. The misericordi (wooden carvings in the choir seats) and armrests tell of the majesty and providence of God, referring to Psalms 104.

Between the choir stalls in the center of the chancel, the labyrinth is embedded in the floor in three kinds of marble. Although smaller in scale, it is similar to the one at the back of the nave at Chartres cathedral. The original use of such a pattern in the floor may have been for penitential prayer and may have referred either to the way of Christ on the way to his crucifixion along the Via Dolorosa or to an abstract journey for those who could not go on a crusade. In any case, the medieval labyrinth in the nave floor at Chartres is copied here. Its location here, however, is problematic, and its size raises even more questions about its use, if any, in Protestant worship in the twentieth century. The writings of the early planners of the Riverside Church do not reveal their reasons for this configuration, so it may be best to regard it as decorative. Under the direction of a minister, the labyrinth may have been used for private devotions, but nothing explicit is reported in the sources.

The communion table was carved from a single block of Caen stone. It is centrally located, and behind it is the baptismal pool. Both the table and the pool are screened in such a way that they are not strong public symbols to be read as part of the vast vocabulary of iconographic motifs or liturgical opportunities in the space.

A Design Element Introduced and Then Discarded

In an early description of Riverside Church, Charles Collens wrote: "As a focal point to the whole composition the usual reredos has been replaced by an intricate Gothic canopy or baldacchino covering the Baptistry and communion table at the rear of the Chancel."[22]

The "canopy or baldacchino" seems to have been a medieval feature that appealed to the architects in their travels but, as a design concept, created problems for the ministers. It must have seemed extremely "high church" for a Protestant building. Against this feature Eugene Carder used an argument based on movement and distances:

> The Committee made no objection to the proposed treatment until it began to appear that the very bold and beautiful altar was going to pose a serious problem. For in the conduct of the regular worship services, as well as the service of the Lord's Supper, and the Baptismal Service, there must be some room for free movement from one side of the chancel to the other without necessarily passing in front of the altar and before the view of the congregation.
>
> The architects were understandably reluctant to abandon their original proposal and there developed a long series of discussions about this one feature. For weeks the matter was brought up when the current agenda for that day had been disposed of. Finally, on one well-remembered day, the writer [Dr. Calder] recalls having once more pointed out his objections to the baldacchino, stressing particularly the fact that to cross the chancel from one side to the other without passing in front of the altar or in view of the congregation, one must go down one flight of stairs, walk half a block along a corridor, cross over at the cloister level between the assembly hall and the gymnasium—a distance of about forty feet, proceed north again for half a block, climb a flight of stairs and there find himself on the other wide of the chancel, about thirty feet from his starting point.
>
> So it had been going for weeks, and so far as the writer knew no hint had been dropped by the chairman [John D. Rockefeller Jr.] as to his own thinking. However, on this occasion as the writer left the drawing board where he had demonstrated the traffic problem, Robert Eidlitz, the builder, to who[m] differences between building committees and architects was not a new experience, said quietly, "Don't you say another word."

The architects then took up their rebuttal to the traffic argument, and when they were finished the chairman turned toward the writer and said, "What do you have to say to that?"

"Nothing, Sir," was the response. "After all, the alternative proposal of a chancel screen treatment would cost a great deal more than the baldacchino." It seemed useless to push the matter further.

But the chairman responded, "I thought you might feel that way, nevertheless, we'll have the chancel screen."[23]

The Chancel Screen

The chancel screen is a large and complex wall of iconographic figures that represent the theology at the time of construction and remain a strong statement as a dominant focal point in the worship space. Seven panels of white limestone make up the screen. Its location and scale make it a major feature, and the careful iconographic arrangement offers a visual theology that is central to the church's ministry. To describe it, the original pages that the Reverend Eugene Carder prepared in order to make clear what the chancel screen signifies are reproduced here. The figures represent the seven phases of Christ's ministry, based on the understanding that the figures in some way personified Christ's ministry in their own lives. Although the choice of some of the figures is surprising, the purpose of the collection is to show that Christ's mission and ministry are continued into the present through exemplary examples.

The seven panels are (from left to right): the physicians' panel, the teachers' panel, the prophets' panel, the humanitarians' panel, the missionaries' panel, the reformers' panel, and the lovers-of-beauty panel. Although Carder's listing is fascinating in regard to the selection of figures that, at the time, seemed appropriate, it is the total form that serves worship in a specific way.

The figures face the congregation as a constant reminder of those who have given their lives in service, particularly in the seven panel categories. One of the goals of Riverside's ministry is to call all its members and visitors to a life of service that will create a better world and praise God. Part of the theology of the building's iconography is the visual statement that God works in the productivity and service of the lives of his people. The

FIGURE 3.11: The Riverside Church's chancel screen. *Used by permission of the Riverside Church Archives.*

Reverend Carder's commentary on the chancel screen explains how the iconography relates to the concept of Riverside's ministry.

A delicately carved screen of Caen stone standing in the seven arches of the apse, with the Cross as the focal point, constitutes the central symbolic feature of the Nave of The Riverside Church. Each of the seven panels presents a figure of Christ surrounded in each instance by painstakingly sculptured representations of men and women of the ages who have faithfully followed Christ's pattern in these respective fields—Physicians, Teachers, Prophets, Humanitarians, Missionaries, Reformers, and Lovers of Beauty.

The panel on the extreme left behind the pulpit represents Christ in the character of the Great Physician. Standing with him there in this category are the following:

1. Andreae Vesaıius (1514–1564), founded the science of human anatomy.

2. Sir Joseph Lister (1821–1912), introduced the antiseptic principle into surgery.

3. Robert Koch (1843–1910), discovered the tuberculosis and cholera bacilli.

4. Hippocrates (ca. 460–388 B.C.), the "Father of Medicine."

5. Luke the Beloved Physician.

6. Christ the Healer.

7. Thomas Sydenham (1624–1689), the "English Hippocrates," anticipated modern medical practice.

8. Louis Pasteur (1822–1895), revolutionized medicine by demonstrating the principle of bacterial infection.

In the next panel, the Christ who stands in the center is he whom we think of as the Supreme Teacher. With him in this panel are found six of the greatest teachers of all time.

1. Saint Thomas Aquinas (1225–1274), the Dominican scholar and theologian, founder of medieval scholasticism.

2. Henry Drummond (1786–1860), taught the beauty of love.

3. Thomas Arnold (1795–1842), "in whose nature the moral and spiritual elements were supreme."

4. Socrates (470–399 B.C.), in his questioning search for truth, made an enduring contribution to the development of moral standards.

5. Christ the Teacher.

6. Desiderius Erasmus (1465–1536), worked for the reformation of the Church through the enlightenment of men.

7. Johann Heinrich Pestalozzi (1746–1827), Swiss teacher, reformed the methods of education.

The Prophetic Christ stands in the center of the third panel from the left and with him are ten others whose lives and words have been touched with the prophetic spirit. Savonarola and John Ruskin are found here with a group of the Biblical prophets.

1. Girolamo Savonarola (1452–1498), denounced vice and corruption in the Church and State, saying "Your sins make me a prophet."

2. John Ruskin (1819–1900), apostle of beauty, truth and righteousness, "taught us how to see."

3. Moses, like unto whom there arose not a prophet since in Israel.

4. Christ the Prophet.

5. Isaiah, second only to Moses among the Hebrew prophets.

6. John the Baptist, forerunner of the Messiah.

7. Micah, "prophet of the people."
8. Elijah, the Destroyer.
9. Elisha, the Healer.
10. Amos, the Social Reformer.
11. Hosea, prophet of the divine compassion.

In the center bay, the focal position was given to Christ in his character as a Humanitarian, the Supreme Friend of mankind. Immediately below our Lord, on the same mullion, appears the Good Samaritan. At the top of the extreme left hand mullion of this bay is a figure of Abraham Lincoln standing here for the enduring service he rendered to the Negro race. Corresponding to his position on the other side of the panel is a figure representing the Family Doctor who is given a place not particularly to honor any one individual but rather to recognize the friendly service which every family doctor has rendered.

1. Christ the Humanitarian.
2. Saint Francis of Assisi (1182–1226).
3. Saint Elizabeth of Hungary (1207–1231) devoted to charity her life of self-denial.
4. Valentin Hauy (1745–1822), founded the first school for the blind.
5. Ann Judson (1789–1826), a missionary's wife.
6. Abraham Lincoln (1809–1865).
7. Booker T. Washington (1858–1915), pathfinder of the Negro race.
8. General Samuel Chapman Armstrong (1839–1893), founded Hampton Institute.
9. The Good Samaritan.
10. Earl of Shaftesbury (1801–1885), champion of labor and philanthropist.
11. Florence Nightingale (1820–1910), founder of the first school for nurses.
12. The Family Doctor.
13. Walter Reed (1851–1902), discovered the cause of yellow fever.
14. Edward Jenner (1749–1823), discovered vaccination.
15. John Howard (1726–1790), prison reformer.
16. General William Booth (1829–1912), founded the Salvation Army.
17. Mary the Mother of Jesus.
18. John the Beloved Disciple.

Christ as a Missionary, together with a group of the great missionaries of the church, people the panel immediately to the right of the altar. The two large figures at the base are St. Paul and David Livingstone.

1. Saint Philip the Evangelist, "preached to the hated Samaritan, the swarthy African, the despised Philistine, the men of all nations."
2. Saint Stephen (ca. 977–1038), king of Hungary, spread Christianity through his country.
3. John Eliot (1604–1690), first to preach the Gospel to the American Indian.
4. Christ Missionary.
5. William Carey (1761–1834), "the inspired cobbler," pioneer missionary to British India.
6. Saint Augustine (354–430), "Apostle of the English."
7. Saint Francis Xavier (1506–1552), "Apostle of the Indies."
8. Robert Morrison (1782–1834), the first Protestant missionary to China.
9. Adoniram Judson (1788–1850), one of the first foreign missionaries commissioned from the United States.
10. Saint Paul, "Apostle of the Gentiles."
11. David Livingstone (1813–1873), prototype of the early missionaries to Africa.

To the right of this panel we find Christ in the character of a Reformer with the following standing with him there:

1. George Fox (1624–1691), founded the Society of Friends.
2. John Knox (1505–1572), organized the Presbyterian Church.
3. John Wesley (1703–1791), founded Methodism.
4. John Wycliffe (ca. 1324–1384), the "Morning Star of the Reformation."
5. Christ the Reformer.
6. Martin Luther (1483–1546), the "monk who shook the world."
7. John Calvin (1509–1564), exponent of the right of conscience to rebel against authority."

The extreme right hand panel, just behind the lectern, features Christ who reveals himself as a Lover of Beauty. It is he who loved little children, the flowers of the field, the birds of the air. Here he is surrounded by men who have given themselves primarily to expressing their love for beauty and life in poetry, music, and art.

1. John Greenleaf Whittier (1807–1892), poet of nature.
2. Fra Angelico (1387–1455), whose frescoes breathe still the spirituality and mystical charm of a great religious painter.
3. John Milton (1608–1674), in his blindness saw the "beauty which the eye cannot see."

4. Giovanni Palestrina (ca. 1524–1594), father of modern church music.
5. Leonardo da Vinci (1452–1519), "the most versatile genius of the Renaissance."
6. Christ the Lover of Beauty.
7. Michelangelo (1475–1564), the greatest sculptor of the Renaissance.
8. Johann Sebastian Bach (1685–1750), the greatest composer of organ music.

. . . When the plans for the structure had proceeded to the point where it was apparent that the treatment of the Chancel would call for an ornamental screen of significant proportions and of central importance, Mr. Hoyt [the chief designer] was dispatched to Europe to make a detailed study of the chancel screens of the churches and cathedrals of England, France, Spain, and Italy. When he returned after many months in his research assignment, he brought with him hundreds of sketches of everything that had appealed to him and also an outline of the plan that was evolving in his mind and in his artist's soul. What the observer sees in this Chancel is what came from his drawing board after months of intensive and highly rewarding work with his pencil and fingers. We say "fingers" advisedly, for over and over again, when he could not satisfy himself that a particular motif, as drawn on the flat surface, would be right, he would resort to clay and reproduce the detail before his eye in proper scale, proportions and dimensions. . . .

Another artist who took great personal interest in the Screen and who had immeasurable satisfaction in its development and erection was Mr. Piccirilli, the senior member of the famous family of sculptors in whose studio the screen and its fascinating company of statues and statuettes were sculptured. In modeling and carving the figures representing the characters in the seven panels, Mr. Piccirilli went to all possible limits to make truly life-like characterizations. His questions about the biblical figures were often difficult if not impossible to answer because of the total absence of any full length portraits of Amos and Moses. One instance will reveal the realistic and intelligent nature of his search for information before he would attempt to reproduce in clay and stone a representation of any given personality. A statue of General Armstrong, the founder of Hampton Institute, stands in the Humanitarians' Panel as one of the figures in the trilogy of the friends of the Negro, the other two being Abraham Lincoln and Booker T. Washington. His characteristic question was "What did this man look like—what kind of a man was he?" Well, in this case we could really help. General Armstrong's widow was living at the time in New York and it was easy to arrange to call on her at her Madison Avenue apartment.

The sculptor's eye fell upon a portrait of the general which Mrs. Armstrong assured Mr. Piccirilli was a good likeness. Before the call was over, the son of the general came in and the sculptor's interest and attention shifted at once to a study of the son, his posture, and his proportions. He seemed completely satisfied that the questions his artist's soul was asking were answered sufficiently when the mother said that the son was very like the father. These statues stand here in cold stone, but the artist who produced them was concerned with the spirit that lived in them and was striving to be faithful to it.[24]

The Windows

One of the glories of the Riverside Church is its stained-glass windows (see figure 3.12). There are fifty-one stained glass windows in the first building, not counting various smaller windows with geometric grisaille, or gray-glass, patterns. The nave alone has thirty-four magnificent windows, and all but six depict figures and stories. The nave has three stained-glass programs. The theme of the apse clerestory windows (those highest in the interior wall) is the communion of God with persons of all time through Jesus Christ. In the ambulatory or hallway around the rear of the apse behind the baptismal pool is the "mercy" window, flanked by two windows of grisaille. In an early photograph of the first worship service in October 1930, the view of the choir reveals the arrangement before the chancel screen was in place, so the ambulatory windows can be seen more clearly.

The subjects of the side aisle windows of the nave range from agriculture to material creation and from children to the international character of religion. Outstanding among the windows are those above the triforium gallery, which are reproductions of the windows of Chartres cathedral. For the most part they deal with the lives of saints and, in some instances, recognize the guilds that donated the original glass at Chartres. Various sources in the history of Riverside point out that the color values of the windows influenced their placement. For instance, the richer colors fill the spaces on the left, or light, side of the nave, whereas the lighter colors tend to be concentrated on the right, or shady, side. The high clerestory windows in the choir have the darker colors because they have

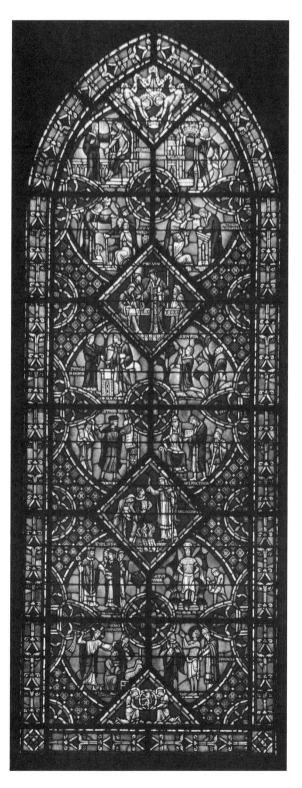

FIGURE 3.12:
A stained-glass
window in the
Riverside
Church's nave.
*Used by permission of
the Riverside Church
Archives.*

more exposure to the light. The intricate symbolism of the entire window program is included in figure 3.13, a chart from *The Visitors' Guide to Riverside Church*.

As James Hudnut-Beumler observed in *The Riverside Church in the City of New York*,

> Riverside was on its way to becoming, at least in the hearts and minds of ordinary people throughout the United States, the national cathedral of mainline Protestantism. . . . Not ten days after its opening, it was hailed as the most important attempt to bring the Christian Gospel to modern urban America.
>
> The entire building was filled from end to end and from top to bottom. That included the great tower. It has been pointed out that no tower in medieval architecture ever served the many functions that one finds at the Riverside Church. At the same time that a full ministry and a full program filled the new church building, it led to an almost immediate need to expand the size of the building.[25]

The Second Campaign

Although the early drawings from the 1920s showed an extension of the building from the west facade to the edge of 122d Street, more than twenty years passed before the building as originally conceived was completed (see figure 3.14).

The pastor at the time, the Reverend Robert J. McCracken, explained, "Construction of the parish house is designed to serve the needs of the church for the next twenty-five years, by the architects who have served the church from the beginning." The Reverend Harry E. Fosdick noted, "The original plans for the church building embodied a southern wing which architecturally would have balanced the nave to the north and the Gothic tower, but its construction then seemed unjustified. Now it is a real necessity."[26] (The new addition was originally referred to as the South Wing.) Francis S. Harmon also referred to "the ever increasing growth of the Riverside outreach, especially in such fields as foreign students, youth work, religious education and community projects."[27]

In 1955, plans to add a parish house were seriously considered. The new building was to provide space for expanding and new programs. John D.

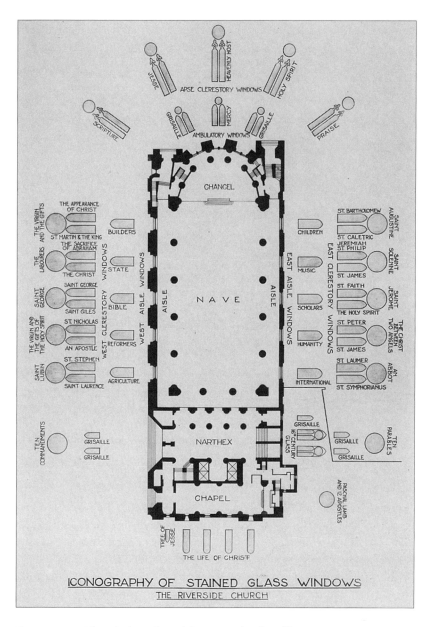

FIGURE 3.13: The window plan of the Riverside Church's nave. *Used by permission of the Riverside Church Archives.*

FIGURE 3.14: An early drawing of the Riverside Church's exterior west elevation. *Used by permission of the Riverside Church Archives.*

Rockefeller Jr. offered to build, furnish, and fully equip the parish house as a gift to celebrate the twenty-fifth anniversary of Riverside's dedication. The design was a simplified version of Allen and Collens's earlier scheme, creating what was seen as a modern Gothic design. The firm of Collens, Willis and Beckonert, the "modern" successor to Allen and Collens, designed the addition, with Harold Willis as the principal architect. The builder was Vermilya-Brown. Completed in 1959, the seven-story parish house, called the "South Wing," contained classrooms, an assembly hall, a radio station, recreation rooms for use by the increasingly large Spanish-speaking community on Morningside Heights, and a two-story underground parking garage. The building was entirely underwritten by John D.

Rockefeller Jr. and was dedicated on Sunday, December 6, 1959. Then on January 12, 1985, the congregation voted to rename the South Wing the Martin Luther King Jr. Memorial Wing (see figure 3.15).

The 1997 Master Plan

Riverside Church continues to view its architecture as both an opportunity and a challenge. "The Riverside Church Master Plan," submitted in October 1997 by Body Lawson, Ben Paul Associated Architects and Planners lists the church's basic architectural principles: "(a) creating a welcoming and inviting atmosphere in the Church; (b) opening the Church to the Community; (c) upgrading the Church for the new information age; (d) being aesthetically appropriate, and (e) being sustainable and

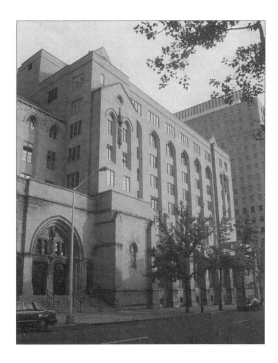

FIGURE 3.15: The Riverside Church's Martin Luther King Jr. Memorial Wing. *Used by permission of the Riverside Church Archives.*

efficient."[28] The master plan retains those principles that were dear to the founders but is sensitive to the needs to modernize, to technology, and to environmental issues.

Approximately thirty years elapsed from the opening of the first construction campaign for the Riverside Church in 1930 to the dedication of the second campaign in 1959, and approximately forty years have passed since then to the present. In these seventy-plus years, the innovations in the twentieth-century neo-Gothic style of the Riverside Church have served the shifts in its ministry's leadership, mood, and emphasis in such a manner as to be a remarkably compatible and stabilizing entity in which beauty, symbol, space, and liturgy have consistently pointed to both the need to serve the human condition and the reality and presence of God.

NOTES

1. *The Riverside Church in the City of New York: A Handbook of the Institution and Its Building* (New York, 1931), 23.

2. Ibid.

3. Andrew S. Dolkart, *Morningside Heights: A History of Its Architecture and Development* (New York: Columbia University Press, 1998), 71.

4. Ibid., 73.

5. Ibid., 74.

6. Ibid., 75.

7. Ibid., 75.

8. Charles Collens, "The Riverside Building," *Church Monthly*, December 1930, 5.

9. Ibid., 11.

10. Ibid., 4.

11. Eugene C. Carder, "The Chancel Screen: Seven Aspects of the Life of Christ," unpublished manuscript, 94.

12. Charles Collens, "The New Riverside Building," *Church Monthly*, November 1926, 32.

13. *The Riverside Church*, 26.

14. Carder, "The Chancel Screen," 94.

15. Peter Collier and David Horowitz, *The Rockefellers, an American Dynasty* (New York: Macmillan, 1976), 154.

16. *The Riverside Church in the City of New York.*

17. *The Flemish Windows of the Park Avenue Baptist Church*, author and date unknown.

18. *A Visitor's Guide to the Riverside Church.*

19. Ibid., 25.

20. Collier and Horowitz, *The Rockefellers*, 154.

21. Wallace Taylor, "A Criticism of the Riverside Church," *Architecture*, June 1931, 14.

22. Charles Collens, *Church Monthly*, December 1926, 11.

23. Carder, "The Chancel Screen," 39.

24. Carder, "The Chancel Screen," 39–42.

25. James Hudnut-Beumler, "The Riverside Church: A Brief History of Its Founding, Leadership and Finances" (New York: Riverside Church, 1990), 8.

26. Robert J. McCracken and Harry E. Fosdick as quoted in "Riverside Plans a Parish House," *New York Times*, April 25, 1955.

27. Francis S. Harmon as quoted in "Riverside Votes for a Parish House," *New York Times*, May 6, 1955.

28. Body Lawson and Ben Paul Associated Architects and Planners, "The Riverside Church Master Plan," October 1997, 4.

4

Universal in Spirit, Local in Character
The Riverside Church and New York City

Judith Weisenfeld

> History may run to universals but it is essentially local in
> character. The local church is equipped through its ties
> with a particular community to relate the gospel of Jesus
> Christ to history in a way that matters. All churches have
> the same mission. Every church has its own mission.
>
> —"Report of the Program Staff to the
> Board of Deacons," June 1972

In the fall of 1951, Robert J. McCracken, then pastor of the Riverside
Church, met with a representative of *The Christian Century* as the magazine was preparing a portrait of the church for its "gallery of great
churches." At one point McCracken led the reporter to a window in a
room in the church's distinctive tower, and the two looked southward, taking in a view of New Jersey across the Hudson River and the expanse of
Manhattan down to the Empire State Building.

> The visitor looked at the spectacle beyond the window and then at the silent
> man beside him. "How," he finally ventured to ask, "can a man preach to
> *that*?" The answer came instantly, yet in a voice so low one scarcely heard it.
> "What right has any man to preach to *that*?"[1]

The reporter concluded that McCracken might indeed be up to the task
precisely because he dared to ask this question and attempted to measure
his own suitability to preach and minister to "this city where the power of
a continent comes to focus."[2] In many ways, the men's exchange encapsu-
lates the long history of challenges and expectations inherent in the life of

this prominent and privileged congregation. For the *Christian Century* reporter, the task of preaching from Riverside to New York City perhaps would be a burden, and so his question focuses on how. How could anyone manage a job of this magnitude? Surely this city, rendered so often, as Robert A. Orsi noted, "as the site of moral depravity, lascivious allure, and the terrain of necessary Christian intervention," presents an impossible task for a Christian minister.[3] McCracken's interrogative response dramatically shifts the perspective on the relationship of the church, its minister, and the city. The challenge for Riverside's ministry, McCracken insisted, is not merely approaching the city as a problem but also understanding the power and promise of the urban context to the church. What individual merits the position that Riverside offers for tapping into the city's possibilities, McCracken asked, turning us away from envisioning the city as a site of unrelenting peril.

Riverside has always been a church that turned its gaze, ear, and prophetic voice toward the nation and the world. In some ways, it appears to be *in* but not *of* New York City, and one wonders whether its significance should be marked only in these sweeping terms. As the *Christian Century* reporter noted in 1951, "Everybody knows Riverside. That is to say, everybody who knows anything about American churches knows the cathedral-like fane [sanctuary] with its soaring massive tower that crowns New York's Manhattan island." The reporter continued, "Just as the commanding physical location makes it one of the sights of New York, so the fame of its pulpit and the projection of its ministries make it a beacon in American Protestantism."[4] William Sloane Coffin, Riverside's fourth senior minister, remarked that from the minister's perspective, there were two great kinds of churches, the small-town church, where the minister can know and call on everyone, and the very large church with a national profile, "where you can get anyone you want."[5] Figures of national and international significance come to Riverside, Coffin implied, because throughout its history Christians and non-Christians alike have listened to the words preached from the church's pulpit and watched the actions its congregation has taken in its campaigns for social justice grounded in Christian principle.

This chapter focuses on the Riverside Church as a local religious institution, charting major themes in the interactions between the congregation and the unique urban environment of New York City. As we shall see, the Riverside Church is unquestionably both in and of the city of New York, and its urban sensibility suffuses the life of the congregation in ways that contribute to its distinctiveness. The importance of the city to the church's identity is underscored in the recounting of the church's history to new members. "The history of this congregation goes far back into the history of New York itself," members are told,[6] and the church's official name—The Riverside Church in the City of New York—makes it impossible to forget its urban connection. Issues and concerns peculiar to urban contexts and to New York City in particular have shaped the experiences of congregants in important ways, and New York's racial, ethnic, religious, class, and sexual diversity has challenged Riverside's understanding of itself as a Christian community.

At the same time that its development as an urban congregation has shaped Riverside, the church and its members have often found the pressing national and international issues more compelling and perhaps less difficult to engage than local ones. William Sloane Coffin asserted that during the 1980s, for example, it was much easier to find members willing to be arrested outside the South African embassy in a protest against apartheid than to organize congregants to lobby and protest in Albany or Washington, D.C. on behalf of the homeless in New York City.[7] Riversiders have often exhibited extraordinary courage in speaking about their ethical and theological commitments on issues like peace, nuclear disarmament, U.S. involvement in Central America in the 1980s, and apartheid in South Africa. Yet Riverside's status as a church of prosperous and financially secure residents of the New York metropolitan area has sometimes meant that engaging the nearby realities of economic and racial discrimination has proved threatening and too challenging for some, whereas taking up broader and more distant political issues was less so. I focus here on broad trends, using a number of case studies to illuminate them. Of course, the fact that Riverside is such a large church and that this chapter deals with the entire span of the church's history means that not every member's experience conforms to the community's general trajectory. In the broadest sense, however, the picture that emerges is of a congregation shaped in profound ways by its urban location, whose members have deeply rooted and strongly held commitments to urban life and whose lives as Christians have been lived through New York City's lenses.

In Riverside's earliest years the church was concerned largely with its status as a good institutional neighbor with a sense of responsibility to care *for* others. Engagement with the city entailed identifying needs and providing services through volunteer work and benevolent giving, approaches that were often paternalistic and tended to keep the congregation safely insulated from difficult issues like urban poverty and racism. From the late 1950s through the 1970s, Riverside became more deeply involved in the crises facing American cities and sought to care *with* those in need in ways that required a great deal of research and study of urban issues and a concerted attempt to allow urban residents to articulate their needs and help determine the shape of Riverside's activism. Throughout the 1980s, concern with the local was balanced by, and sometimes became overshadowed by, the demands of broader, international issues like disarmament and the United States' involvement in Central America. William Sloane Coffin observed about his years at Riverside that his goal was to show "that traditional Christian faith and progressive thought and action are linked and that faith undergirds the action."[8] Coffin felt that he could take for granted the spiritual grounding of Riverside's members and therefore focused on finding ways to impel these people of faith into activism. At the century's end and into the twenty-first century, the congregation is maintaining its engagement with urban issues but is much more concerned with the spiritual development of individuals and the church as a community as the starting point for whatever activism—local, national, international—may follow. Rev. James A. Forbes Jr. was attracted to Riverside in part because he felt that "he could strengthen the faith commitment that undergirded Riverside's tradition of activism."[9] Rather than taking for granted that spiritual commitment preceded activism at Riverside, as Coffin had, Forbes assumed that activism was an integral part of Riverside's identity and that the spiritual grounding for that activism needed to be deepened.

A Neighborhood Parish

The story of Riverside's special position in the city and its power to function as a beacon of liberal American Protestantism must be told in relation to the Morningside Heights neighborhood of Manhattan in which the church is located. Morningside Heights covers the area between 110th and 125th Streets on the west side of Manhattan from Morningside Drive on the east to Riverside Drive on the west. As Andrew Dolkart notes in his architectural history of the Heights, the eastern and western boundaries of the neighborhood are determined by the area's topography—Morningside Cliffs and Morningside Park on one side and the Hudson River and Riverside Park on the other—with its location on a plateau creating a "topo-graphic isolation" that caused the neighborhood's development to take place at a different pace from that of the rest of the island. The neighbor-hood came to be characterized by a set of institutions, whose presence (in conjunction with the accessibility of the subway under Broadway after 1904) motivated residential development in the early twentieth century, "resulting in Morningside Heights becoming the city's first middle-class apartment-house neighborhood."[10]

A religious institution—the Episcopal Cathedral of St. John the Di-vine—began the institutional development that marks Morningside Heights to this day. Bishop Henry Cadman Potter began gathering sup-port for the project in 1887, and the cornerstone was laid (on property at 110th to 113th Streets and Amsterdam Avenue) in 1892.[11] Over the next thirty years, St. John the Divine was joined on Morningside Heights by a variety of relocated or newly formed religious, educational, and cultural institutions.[12]

It made sense, then, that when the time came to select a location for the community that would gather at the Riverside Church, Morningside Heights would prove especially attractive. Reflecting on the search for a lo-cation for the new congregation he had agreed to lead, Harry Emerson Fosdick wrote, "It was clearly going to be one of the foremost cultural cen-ters in the nation, and no adequate Protestant parish church was there to minister to the countless thousands who were being drawn to the neigh-borhood by its unique opportunities."[13] Not only would Riverside be able to involve newcomers to the neighborhood, but it also would be able to connect even more directly with the members of the Park Avenue Baptist Church—its constituent congregation—the majority of whom at that time lived in Morningside Heights.[14] Moreover, according to Fosdick, the Morningside Heights location also suited other members because it was situated "almost exactly in the geographical center of the widespread dwelling places of [the church's] members." While Fosdick did acknowl-edge that Riverside would not be the first Protestant church in Morning-side Heights, in his estimation Riverside would quickly become the neigh-borhood's Protestant parish, even though St. John the Divine had pre-ceded it.[15] There is no question that Fosdick and others involved in the founding of Riverside would consider broad theological, national, and in-ternational social questions in pursuing the church's mission. Its founding pastor also, however, understood Riverside's charge as one of ministering to the residents of Morningside Heights, as would any other local church. In the church's 1956 self-study, prompted by Dr. McCracken's sermon "A Design for Living," members insisted that

> the Riverside Church was not built on Morningside Heights to provide a spiritual haven for its members. The move from Park Avenue twenty-five years ago was a bold, deliberate decision to establish a liberal, dynamic Christian enterprise where the preaching ministry and the progressive program of the Church could influence the faculties, students, and residential neighbors of a group of important institutions.[16]

Although "there is no evidence of a deliberate, coordinated effort among the leaders of these various organizations to create a unified institutional center," a strong sense of mission developed among the institutions to establish an environment in which they would minister to mind, body, and spirit. With the construction of the cathedral, a variety of observers began to refer to the neighborhood as "the Acropolis," an image that was enhanced over time by the large gathering of institutions.[17] Riverside made a point of locating itself ritually in this constellation of institutions shortly after the congregation occupied the building. In February 1931 Riverside's services focused on dedicating the new church and did so in relation to a variety of constituencies, including children and youth and the community. Henry Sloane Coffin, then president of Union Theological Seminary, preached the sermon at the February 8, 1931, afternoon community service which representatives from neighborhood organizations and institutions attended.

While the optimism of the "Acropolis's" institutions led them to see the urban environment as salvageable and, indeed, the appropriate location for their work, others reflecting on Riverside's urban identity saw the city as irredeemable and detracting from the church's ability to meet its goals. One week after the first service was held at Riverside in October 1930, the *Christian Century* assessed the church's consequence in terms clearly connected to the perceived problems of its urban environment. The article's perspective emphasized an understanding of the city as a secularizing, and therefore debilitating, element in the lives of Americans.

> This project is one of the most fateful, and it is one of the most daring, ever undertaken by a Protestant congregation. It is an attempt to bring the gospel in an impressive and convincing way to those who have dismissed it

as of no importance. That multiplied thousands of city dwellers have so dismissed it is depressingly clear.

The article's author also saw the secular intellectual environment of Morningside Heights as an obstacle to the work of the church: "Paul faced no more skeptical, no more aloof audience on Mars Hill than Dr. Fosdick faces on the heights of the American metropolis."[18]

Education on Morningside Heights

This "aloof audience" challenged the church over the years. When Riverside arrived on Morningside Heights, it joined a number of institutions with which it had a great deal in common—elite institutions that valued learning—as well as distinct differences in their missions. Even though Harry Emerson Fosdick had studied philosophy with Nicholas Murray Butler, who was president of Columbia University from 1902 until 1945, relations between Riverside and the university were strained during Butler's tenure. Riverside's relationship with Columbia was not unique to the relations between Protestant institutions and institutions of higher education in the early twentieth century.[19] Dorothy C. Bass argued that "colleges tied to the leading Protestant denominations not only showed quantitative losses in the earlier twentieth century, they also lost the authority to define the character of higher education, even for themselves."[20] Columbia's Anglican connections had long since faded, and Butler had little interest in shaping the university's image in relation to Riverside. But by the time the *Christian Century* produced its profile of Riverside in 1951, Robert Mc-Cracken "was in high spirits at the changed attitude toward religion which . . . marked the passing of the [Butler] regime at the university."[21] He noted the increasing numbers of Columbia professors, especially from Teachers College, who were members of Riverside and was pleased that a Riverside minister had been included among the university's religious counselors.

In May 1951 Riverside appointed Rev. J. Gordon Chamberlin, a 1938 graduate of Union Theological Seminary, to work on the Columbia campus with the university chaplain's office. Chamberlin joined a staff of eight other counselors responsible for students' religious activities.[22] Chamberlin also organized the Student Forum, held at 9:30 on Sunday mornings and attended by students from various schools and colleges in the city. In

1952 Riverside established its Campus Relations Committee, chaired by Professor Harry Jones, in order to carry out "a more specific ministry" toward the university. In articulating its goals to the Riverside community, the committee stated that it hoped to provide a flexible, engaging environment for students to approach religious questions. The committee further emphasized that it was "*not for students only*. Christianity's primary concern in higher education always . . . centers on the religious dimensions of the academic pursuit and areas of knowledge."[23]

While the relationship between Riverside and Columbia University over time was a local question about how neighboring institutions would share the space of Morningside Heights and exercise authority in the neighborhood, the significance and place of the church in a secular educational environment had farther-reaching implications. Fosdick reflected on the broad questions that secular education raised, noting that he had

> lived into a generation where not science alone but education too "has created a world in which Christianity is an imperative." Facts without values, fragmentary specialties with no integrating philosophy of life as a whole, data with no ethical standards for their use, techniques either with no convictions about life's ultimate meaning or with corrupting convictions— here, too, a panacea has turned out to be a problem. What quality of faith and character is going to use our educated minds?[24]

In its role as a neighborhood parish, Riverside Church has remained engaged with the intellectual community of the Heights, influencing it in ways consistent with its understanding of liberal Protestantism.

A number of historians whose work focuses on the relationships between higher education and American religious institutions have observed that the development of campus ministries to serve Christian students was one way in which Protestant denominations tried to reorient their influence in American higher education in light of the severed ties between universities and denominations. In addition to concentrating on university pastorates, denominations contributed to the support of student Christian associations, campus Young Men's Christian Associations and Young Women's Christian Associations.[25] The Riverside Church participated in this trend through its financial support from the 1930s through the 1960s of the Student Christian Associations of City College and Columbia University and of the Intercollegiate Branch of the YMCA.[26]

FIGURE 4.1: Participants in Riverside's ministry to Columbia University on the steps of Low Library, n.d. *Used by permission of the Riverside Church Archives.*

The request from the Christian Association at City College for financial support generated a great deal of debate among the members of Riverside's Benevolence Committee, the group responsible for dispersing the church's charitable funds, about the relationship of Riverside to its immediate environs and its attendant obligations to assist neighbor groups over those in other areas of the city. The church decided not to contribute to New York University's Christian Association in 1948 despite the finding of a survey that more Riverside members lived in the vicinity of the two NYU campuses than lived in the City College area.[27] Nevertheless, the Benevolence Committee and the church's ministers felt that it was more important to maintain and build the connection with City College because it was geographically closer to Riverside. Similarly, in 1951 the committee refused a request from the 135st Street African American Harlem Branch of the YMCA (at Lenox Avenue) on the grounds that it already supported the 104th Street Uptown Branch (near Columbus Avenue), which was closer to the church.[28] Thus in a number of instances, Riverside's members defined the church's identity in relation to the neighborhood and expressed a strong commitment to the residents of the area over a broader connection to the city at large. The members of Riverside's Benevolence Committee saw the church's engagement with and commitment to the local environment as an important part of its function as a "neighborhood parish."

Community Connections and Urban Service

In addition to fashioning a working relationship with the university, the church tried to shape the life of the Morningside Heights community in other ways. The question of how best to serve the neighborhood public schools to make them attractive and acceptable to Riversiders motivated the members of the church community to become involved in a number of ventures over the years, including Morningside Heights, Inc., a nonprofit consortium founded in 1947 to provide a range of services for the neighborhood. Its Committee on Schools focused on supplementing the resources available at Public School 125, the local elementary school on 123d Street between Amsterdam and Morningside Avenues. The committee outlined its purposes as follows: "The interest of Morningside Heights, Inc. in enriching P.S. 125 is two-fold: firstly, it is concerned with any social program looking toward the improvement of the whole community; secondly it is concerned with developing a public school to which institutional personnel will feel happy to send their children."[29] Funding for the program initially came from equal contributions from six neighborhood institutions, with others consulting at first and later making financial contributions.

The group's approach to improving the local elementary school began with the first grade and, with an initial budget in 1947 of $3,000, provided a salary for a part-time educational consultant, supplementary materials for the first-grade classes, and support for a parent's group for the grade.[30] The following year the organization increased the budget to $4,500 in order to add a similar program for the third grade, as well as seminars through Teachers College for the first-grade teachers and, later, all the school's teachers. In subsequent years the group turned its attention to another nearby elementary school and considered additional programs in junior-high and high schools because P.S. 125 served only those children living above 116th Street and only up to the seventh grade.[31] Morningside Heights, Inc., also sponsored the Play Schools Association, an after-school and vacation program based at P.S. 125, to which Riverside contributed financially throughout the 1950s and 1960s.[32]

Riverside's involvement with Morningside Heights, Inc., and its schools committee grew in part from its desire to engage the neighborhood and its residents in a constructive manner and to provide material and human resources. Then as now, the difficulties facing urban public school systems were much on the minds of concerned parents and urban residents, and the work of Riversiders in this regard sits in a long tradition of activism to improve New York City's public schools. But a strong element of fear and dissatisfaction with the changing demographics of the local public schools and with the church's proximity to Harlem was present as well. Could the church find a way to persuade its staff members and church members to remain in the neighborhood and help them feel comfortable educating their children in the public schools? Morningside Heights, Inc., is a good example of cooperation between Riverside and other institutions on "the Acropolis" because it demonstrates the church's strong commitment to participate fully in the life of the community—as communicated through a desire to send the children from these institutions to the local public schools—and, at the same time, gives evidence of these elite institutions' paternalistic control of the neighborhood. Although the principal and teachers of P.S. 125 expressed their appreciation for the work and financial support of Morningside Heights, Inc., in many ways, the school never seemed to be able to do enough to satisfy the organization's institutional members. By the late 1950s, Riversiders saw "adequate public school facilities" as "the greatest single unmet need on Morningside Heights" but placed that concern in the context of the postwar "flight to the suburbs" by white Riversiders and not in relation to the needs of the less wealthy residents of color.[33] Indeed, Morningside Heights, Inc., had already decided to investigate the possibility of "institutional interest in a private school located within Morningside Heights."[34]

Eventually, Morningside Heights, Inc., turned to issues other than education and increasingly concentrated on programs for young people in the neighborhood, administration of the Stone Gymnasium (which occupies a space adjacent to the church), and housing activism, particularly the construction of low-income public and middle-income cooperative housing in the area.[35] This development reflects a concession by the organization to the area's changed demographics and represents a shift from trying to stem the tide of white flight to offering services to the black and Latino newcomers. Learning how to live as neighbors in an environment undergoing a transformation in its racial and class structure proved to be one of the most pressing challenges to the Riverside community and its mission as a witness to the progressive possibilities of Christian faith.

Beyond the immediate environs of Morningside Heights, the Riverside Church has become important to shaping the development and direction of social service work in New York City. Throughout the 1930s and 1940s, Riverside and its members participated in an extraordinary range of social service organizations in the city, primarily through benevolent giving, although as we shall see, this involvement was in no way limited to financial contributions. Riverside's members also maintained strong connections with these organizations through both volunteer and paid service, demonstrating their commitment to practicing their Christian beliefs to improve social conditions. Like that of the Park Avenue Baptist Church, Riverside's program of benevolent giving materialized at first as a large, undifferentiated donation to the Northern Baptist Convention and a number of other Baptist groups. Then in 1935 Riverside stopped giving to the convention and began to choose projects on its own, administered through the Benevolence Committee.[36]

With this turn away from allowing the denomination to determine how to use the church's benevolence funds and toward a financial commitment to religious and social service organizations that grew organically out of the interests and concerns of Riverside's members, the benevolence program began to assume greater importance. A report by the Benevolence Committee in 1937 made explicit its understanding of the theological importance of benevolence and its connection to Riverside's broader goals for its members.

> The benevolence program of the Riverside Church is but one of the many activities which make up the total program of the Church. Easily the benevolences are viewed too narrowly as constituting a list of agencies—a service outside the church through gifts of money by members to deserving enterprises. But a satisfactory and effective program of benevolence involves much more than that; it involves education and interpretation within the church—to the end that the spirit of benevolence among members may be encouraged, that opportunities for expressing the spirit of unselfishness and Christian stewardship may be effectively presented, and that a greater degree of voluntary cooperation and giving by members may be secured.[37]

FIGURE 4.2: Poster from the 1936 budget exhibit showing Riverside's support of the Henry Street visiting nurses and calling for donations to the Benevolence program. *Used by permission of the Riverside Church Archives.*

In the early years the church's giving program concentrated on particular kinds of projects, such as work with the elderly, children, or students. Increasingly, however, those people determining Riverside's benevolences began to think of the work according to a geographic division, with the majority of the money and resources going to local community service projects and the rest to national and foreign services.[38] At various points over the years, the dominance of community services in the overall benevolence budget caused concern for members of the committee, and they tried to maintain the proportion of local giving at 50 percent in order to increase the amount for foreign missions.[39] Nevertheless, from Riverside's early years until the present, giving to community service organizations across the city has occupied a large portion of the attention of members of the Benevolence Committee.

Channeling financial contributions through the Benevolence Committee was not the only way in which Riversiders exercised their philosophy of urban service. From the beginning, volunteer work has been a part of the church's life, with members working on such projects as the Every Member Canvass, which brought in the funds disbursed by the Benevolence Committee, and in many organizations outside the church. In the early years, two of the church's women's groups—the Women's Society and the Business and Professional Women's Club ("the B & P's")—provided volunteers for such activities as serving coffee and sandwiches to service men during World War II, "sewing and knitting for community service groups and homes, doing White Cross work assigned by the mission boards, [and] making surgical dressing for the Visiting Nurses."[40]

In 1956 the B & P's, which had mainly organized social activities, provided support and a sense of belonging for working women in the congre-

FIGURE 4.3: Members of the Riverside Auxiliary rolling bandages, n.d. Photograph by Lilo Kaskell Photo. *Used by permission of the Riverside Church Archives and Lilo Kaskell Photo.*

FIGURE 4.4: Dr. Fosdick with children at the
Manhattanville Neighborhood Center, n.d. Pho-
tograph by Warman. *Used by permission of the
Riverside Church Archives.*

gation, and established the Community Service Group as a conduit for
regular volunteer service in local institutions. Members worked at St.
Luke's Hospital, Manhattanville Community Center, Columbia-Presbyter-
ian Medical Center, the Baptist Home for the Aged, and the Grant Houses;
visited the Women's House of Detention; and joined both the Friendly
Visitors' Program in the prison and groups involved in prison reform
more broadly. Indeed, community service through volunteer work had become such an important part of the B & P's identity that by the early 1970s
the group's statement of purpose was amended to include functioning as
"a channel of service to the Riverside Church *and the Community*" in addition to creating fellowship and offering cultural and social activities.[41]

In 1951 Riverside formed the Social Service Guild to "provide avenues of
expression for our concern for our neighbors . . . our concern for people

who need our help. Its objective is to implement the Guild purpose 'to use avenues of practical service to express the spirit of Christ.'" The guild assigned interested members to volunteer work at St. Luke's and Bellevue Hospitals; to teach English at the Mariners' Temple downtown; and to work in day care at the Manhattanville Neighborhood Center, in the church's tutoring program for public school children, and in the Toy Workshop, in which members made and repaired toys for children who participated in the activities of the Manhattanville Neighborhood Center.[42]

The church's earliest years were thus characterized by a range of engagements with the neighborhood: attempting to shape local institutions for the benefit of Riversiders, extending the church's influence through benevolent giving, and expressing the spirit of a neighborhood parish through volunteer work.[43]

Institutional Influence and Control

The Riverside Church's engagement with various social service organizations in New York represented both a financial and a personal commitment through a donation of time and other personal resources. In addition to supporting programs of already well-established organizations, the church also sometimes attempted to shape the course of these organizations and occasionally tried to reform their practices by imposing standards of professionalization. It is certainly understandable that Riverside's Benevolence Committee would want assurance that the money that members donated to support social service work would be used efficiently and productively. But this sometimes made it difficult for financially strapped organizations that did not have the resources for professionally trained staff to meet the church's standards. In other cases, the church used its influence to try to persuade organizations to make their practices more socially just.

In one case in which Riverside intervened in the work of a social service organization, the church began by supporting the work of the Union Neighborhood Center located at 123d Street and Broadway and founded in 1931 by students at Union Theological Seminary.[44] In 1935, for example, the Women's Bible Class donated money to help send thirteen African American boys from the neighborhood to the New York Urban League's summer camp. The Benevolence Committee continued to make donations over the next ten years to support programs that included sending neighborhood children to summer camp, operating a local summer play school, as well as various events for families in the summer.[45] Despite Riverside's commitment to the center, members of the Benevolence Committee expressed concern about the impermanent and unprofessional nature of the neighborhood center's programs. Mrs. John A. Fitch, a committee member, visited the center in 1936 and was impressed with the work that it did with local boys and girls but recommended that the Benevolence Committee "express its interest in the objectives of the organization and its desire to help when the Center has set up an organization somewhat permanent in nature and can show plans which will stand examination by professional social service workers."[46] The Benevolence Committee's report on the center also indicated concern about the large number of programs to which the small organization had committed itself, as well as its poor record keeping. The staff at the Union Neighborhood Center made several changes in response to Riverside's report, such as reducing the number of programs—following an evaluation of what the center could best handle—and reorganizing its records. Accordingly, Riverside and other local institutions renewed their commitments to the center. Union Theological Seminary "placed a number of scholarship men at the Center to help carry on the work," and more than fifteen Barnard College students volunteered. Union, Barnard, and various women's groups at Riverside pledged funding, and Mrs. John D. Rockefeller Jr. and Harry Emerson Fosdick made personal contributions.[47] In this case, Riverside's insistence that a local organization meet the highest professional standards resulted in considerable benefit for the Union Neighborhood Center.

While exchange and interaction with local social service organizations were important ways in which the church has served the community, the Benevolence Committee has generally refused to contribute to local churches to help them develop programs or defray their operating expenses. The church's files are full of refused requests, many from African American and Latino churches, for help rebuilding after a fire; for general assistance for work in Harlem, the Bronx, and Queens; and with Spanish-speaking Protestants.[48] In 1941 Rev. Egbert Ethelred Brown, pastor of the Harlem Unitarian Church, wrote to Riverside to request assistance, describing his church as "in every sense a missionary church trying in measure to do for our race what you are splendidly doing for yours." He continued, "We are working especially among the so-called radicals and are succeeding fairly well in recommending religion to our group." The

Benevolence Committee did not contribute, and the report to the committee by the associate minister, Eugene Carder, outlines what seems to have become the church's general approach to such requests.

> I cannot imagine that the philosophy of the Benevolence Committee leaves an opening for such an appeal as this and am assuming that it will get no financial response. This is a *local* church—probably no better and possibly much worse than any one of the scores of local congregations in Harlem. My own opinion is that response in money to any local congregation to pay expenses is outside our perview [*sic*].[49]

The Benevolence Committee did fund programs sponsored by a number of local churches, but these tended to be explicitly interdenominational or nondenominational churches in the city or programs housed in one of the larger established churches of the Upper West Side. For example, Riverside contributed to a summer program for the elderly that the Cathedral of St. John the Divine organized in the 1970s.[50] The Church of the Open Door—which was founded in Brooklyn in 1953 and sponsored by the NYC Mission Society, the Protestant Council (Brooklyn Division); Baptist Church, Congregational Christian Church, Methodist Church, Presbyterian Church, and the Reformed Church in America—was among the interdenominational religious projects that Riverside funded.[51] Although its interracial membership was a noteworthy aspect of the Church of the Open Door, Riverside seemed to be especially interested in the fact that Rev. William Sterling Cary, the church's pastor, intended to downplay "the interracial slant" and emphasize "what can be accomplished when the Protestants unite."[52]

While it seems clear that at various points of deciding to which institutions to make donations, Riverside shied away from associating itself with some black and Hispanic churches. In some instances, Riverside's benevolence program reached out beyond its large, established Upper West Side neighbors, whose congregations were principally white, to support churches that served poor, multiracial neighborhoods. Riverside contributed to the Neighborhood House at First Street and Second Avenue on the Lower East Side of Manhattan, for example, run by the Church of All Nations. The Neighborhood House's program helped residents who were "predominantly Italian, Puerto Rican, Slavic, and southern Negro in background." A large portion of the Neighborhood House's work was with young gang members.[53] The United West Side Parish, an interdenominational project that covered the neighborhood between Forty-eighth and Sixtieth Streets from Broadway to the Hudson, provided a similar connection for Riverside in the late 1950s and early 1960s. It outlined its goals as including presenting "an ecumenical witness to the community," helping young people and their families, uniting "all people regardless of race or ethnic background in the Christian fellowship," and "lead[ing] people from the isolation of the block to the communion of the Church, there to be transformed by the Grace of God so that they may act as agents in this area."[54] The combination of an interdenominational enterprise and one assisting a multiracial neighborhood made the United West Side Parish compelling for members of Riverside's Benevolence Committee.

Urban Ministry

Although from the start Dr. Fosdick and other members of the church staff and community recognized that Riverside would function as a "neighborhood parish" and should develop some sense of what it meant to be a good neighbor, the church began to develop a much broader sense of urban ministry in the late 1940s and early 1950s. In Fosdick's summary statement about the church's mission, written upon his retirement in 1947, he emphasized that the church should be concerned with "trying to meet the needs of the neighborhood which cannot be met within the church's walls."[55] Robert McCracken, Fosdick's successor, certainly set the tone for such engagement with his insistent preaching on the sin of racism and on the need to go beyond a concern about racial justice and the elimination of racially biased thinking to a deeper level of engagement between white and black Americans.[56] Riverside's pursuit of an urban ministry in the 1950s and 1960s also was influenced by the fact that Ernest T. Campbell, who served as senior minister after McCracken, was a native New Yorker who had grown up in Morningside Heights, went to school at P.S. 125, and attended the nearby Broadway Presbyterian Church. Campbell presided over particularly turbulent years for the nation, the city, and the congregation, during which urban issues proved especially challenging. Riverside's approach to urban ministry in this period, with all its successes and failures, was characterized by an attempt to do ministry *with* the diverse populations of the city rather than ministry *to* or *for* them.

While developing its own sense of what it meant to be an urban congregation, Riverside participated in the emerging field of the study and training of an urban ministry. Although Riverside's approach was unique, given its location in Morningside Heights and the particular history of the congregation, many other religious institutions were facing similar issues in the later 1950s and early 1960s. The urgency of doing ministry in the urban environment in a new way—that is, adding to and moving beyond the kind of control evinced in the Morningside Heights's initiative in the public school and in forging connections through financial giving—became apparent when Riverside conducted a self-study that resulted in the 1956 "Riverside Church Survey Report." Riverside's responsibility to the neighborhood was a clear concern to many. In outlining the church's special mission and attempting to forecast what would be required to continue to live up to it in the future, the committee noted the sometimes negative consequences of a vibrant congregational life for the church's connection to the city. "There is a real and besetting danger," the report observed,

> that Riverside, demanding of time, energy, loyalty in its own right, may become ingrown and self-centered. Stress on service to the local parish should not be at the expense of its metropolitan functions. The ministers of the Church, and members with influence and gifts of leadership, ought increasingly to be active in the affairs and concerns of the City. In this respect we must keep on extending our borders and widening our horizons.[57]

Demographic changes in Morningside Heights and general issues of urban poverty emerged as a central concern in the survey report.

> The declining character of portions of the neighborhood imposes on the Church the duty of taking a position of affirmative leadership in ascertaining the causes of the decline and in seeking to eliminate them. This involves cooperative efforts directed toward the improvement of housing, schooling, security, and social conditions. The heterogeneous character of the neighborhood imposes the duty of Christian social action to serve the needs of the less fortunate and peoples of all nationalities and races.[58]

In addition to noting that it was critical to take account of the more gradual racial and economic demographic changes in Morningside Heights, the report also considered future changes in light of the imminent construction of middle- and low-income housing in the neighborhood. In 1952 the New York City Planning Commission approved the construction of Morningside Gardens, a complex of six cooperative apartment buildings for almost 3,500 middle-income residents, and of the General Grant Houses, a federal low-income housing project for more than 8,000 residents.[59] Riverside and other local institutions that were members of Morningside Heights, Inc., expressed their support for the addition of housing stock for the neighborhood and expressly for the racial and economic diversity that the new residents would bring. In a press conference in December 1952, Dr. Fosdick spoke on behalf of the neighborhood's major religious and educational institutions:

> "We represent over forty different nationalities," Dr. Fosdick said. "The whole community is interracial; all the institutions are interracial; and the result is that we can have there in unique fashion non-segregated interracial housing. . . . I am convinced," said Dr. Fosdick, "that what you are considering today is not just the fate of one housing project but the possible future of one of the City's most important neighborhoods. . . . It is a pioneer neighborhood where the American city confronts some of its most characteristic problems and where, if we solve them at all well, the whole world will know it."[60]

Members of the Riverside Church had a history of interest in and activism on behalf of better housing in the city, dating back to the congregation's early years in Morningside Heights. When the Grant Houses opened in the summer of 1956, Riversiders joined others in Morningside Heights, Inc., to welcome their new neighbors. The summer newsletter reported:

> Riverside is actively sharing in a special Committee for the Community which will provide a genuine welcome to our new neighbors. . . . The Committee for the Community will be represented on moving day with hostesses to help the newcomers and to give needed assistance. . . . In addition, there will be a lounge [at the houses] open every day, a friendly place for newcomers to get acquainted. A directory of the community will be given to each family.[61]

Despite the anxiety of many longtime Morningside residents and members of Riverside, the church based its response to the opening of the Grant Houses on its ongoing commitment to function as a good neighbor and to envision itself as an interracial congregation.

The church identified the new residents of the middle- and low-income housing complexes as constituting a mission field, recommending that Riverside prepare to "capitalize the opportunity so near at hand."[62] But to the church's credit, it did not interpret the demographic changes solely in terms of the possibility of evangelistic work. Eugene Laubach, for example, insisted that "when the neighborhood changed the church either had to change or become obsolete. It had to follow the neighborhood or become like the 'avenue churches' where people only come for services."[63] To that end, the expansion of the church's facilities and the ministerial staff, the development of a Hispanic-American ministry, and the opening of the Sunday school to neighborhood children proved centrally important to Riverside's approach to an urban ministry that fully engaged the city, rather than as a mission field or from the potentially paternalistic perspective of stewardship.

From its inception, Riversiders understood the plan to expand its physical plant—which resulted in the construction of the South Wing, renamed the Martin Luther King Jr. Wing, in 1986—as necessitating a new relationship with the surrounding community. In the 1956 "Riverside Church Survey Report" the committee noted: "As to the new South Wing, majority opinion indicates that it should *not* be regarded as a settlement house. Social activities will undoubtedly be a feature of its use but they should be clearly church-centered. The distinction must carefully be drawn between a social agency and a church program."[64] Here we see the anxiety generated by both the demographic changes in the neighborhood and the potential of the South Wing to bring in a broader range of people to the church. Clearly, many Riversiders wanted to engage the neighborhood and its new residents, but only on Riverside's terms and in ways that would keep the life of the church at the center.

Among the most significant developments enabled by the new South Wing was the expansion of the Sunday school. Eugene Laubach recalled that this transition came with a great deal of difficulty, beginning with the fact that "many of the rooms [in the South Wing] were poorly set up for educational purposes" and that the opening of the Sunday School to children from the Grant Houses in 1961, increased attendance from 231 to 1200. Laubach concluded that although the church had long been committed to diversity and had been successful in some small measure in this regard, "Riverside integrated itself [racially] when the kids came and their parents followed them."[65] In a powerful sermon, "Holiness and Hustle," Laubach asked the congregation:

What is it worth for us to have a church program that is open to all who come? It is not an educational, but a total church question. . . . Three out of five of the children who come are not from families who are members of the church. Many of them come from homes where there is no support at all of their even coming to church. What is it worth to undergird a child who gets himself up and dressed and gets his own breakfast and gets to church school on time every Sunday morning? How's *that* for holiness and hustle?[66]

Laubach continued to argue that this case and those of other church programs pushed the congregation to a critical moment of decision about "whether we will sit down on the side of holiness, whether we will choose hustle, or what it will mean for us to live up to combining the two." And in a consistent and fundamental way, the newly constructed South Wing kept these issues active and challenging to Riversiders.

Hispanic Ministries

Riverside's Hispano-American ministry, which was in existence from 1959 until 1971, was an unsuccessful attempt to meet part of the challenge of the new urban diversity by bringing Protestant members of New York City's largely Puerto Rican, Spanish-speaking population into the life of the church. The development of this ministry took place in light of the demographic changes in the Morningside Heights neighborhood and in East Harlem, which saw the number of Puerto Rican residents grow dramatically. The church took its first steps to make contact with these new residents in April 1959 when, in conjunction with the Church of the Good Neighbor, it appointed Luis A. Flores, a former member and deacon of the Baptist Church in Caguas, Puerto Rico, and a Korean War veteran, as a lay visitor. Flores, who had been conducting missionary work in the Bronx and in Stamford, Connecticut, was charged with "attracting a core of interested men and women who would become the nucleus of a Spanish-language group within Riverside when the church is ready to call a full-time Spanish minister." Flores set part of the pattern for the activities of the Hispano-American ministry by starting a Sunday school class and a worship service, the first of which took place in May 1959 with Rev. Rafael Cotto, a local minister and native of Puerto Rico, presiding.[67] Bible study and a prayer group later also became staples of the ministry's activities. Throughout the summer and early fall, this small group met and worshiped together as Flores began to build a small constituency.

In November 1959 Riverside formalized its commitment to developing a ministry among Spanish-speaking New Yorkers when it called Rev. Pablo Cotto, the brother of Rev. Rafael Cotto, to take charge of the Hispano-American ministry beginning in February 1960. The ministry's new pastor, who came to Riverside from a pastorate in Brownsville, Texas, was educated at Eastern Baptist Theological Seminary and the Biblical Seminary in New York City. Pablo Cotto had considerable experience at building new congregations, having done so in New York City and in Brownsville. Luis Flores continued in his work as lay visitor.[68]

With Cotto's arrival, the Spanish-language group began to hold Sunday morning worship in the Christ Chapel, at the same time that the English-language service took place in the nave. In developing this ministry, the church's aim was to bring Spanish-speaking worshipers into the main congregation; they never envisioned the project's becoming a separate congregation. From the outset, however, the relationship of this group to the larger Riverside congregation was uncertain, as Spanish-speaking participants tried to exercise agency in determining their place and role at Riverside. Only a few months after Cotto's arrival, Riversiders read a report in the *Carillon* about the growth of the ministry and learned that some fifty people attended the Spanish-language Sunday service and that twenty Spanish-speaking people had become full members of Riverside.[69] At the same time, it had become clear that commitments to both anguage and culture made participants in the ministry anxious to keep their identity separate from that of the primary congregation. The difficult task of balancing independence and integration was part of Cotto's work. On the first anniversary of the ministry, for example, the *Carillon* marked the event with a report, in Spanish, that declared,

> In breaking the ice of separation, many Spanish-speaking people have found a true place of worship at Riverside. They have become affiliated with the congregation and so have come to constitute an integral part of its program. . . . Gradually, they have come to form a part of the body of ushers, of committees and of different organizations in the church. Everyone has taken an active part in their regular contribution to sustain the total program of the church.[70]

Because the article was published in Spanish, it seems more an attempt to convince participants in the Hispanic American ministry that they were and should want to be an integrated part of the Riverside congregation than as a report to the congregation at large about the ministry's activities. One of the ways in which the members of the Hispanic American ministry tried to strike this balance and assert themselves as congregants rather than a mission field was to provide a number of services to the English-speaking members. The ministry offered regular Spanish-language instruction, hosted a range of events for the congregation during the Christmas season, and later offered a flamenco dance class.

The issue of funding caused a significant conflict between the trustees and participants in the ministry. Cotto's and a secretary's salaries, as well as other general expenses, initially came from "an oversubscription" of the 1957 Every Member Canvass (EMC) goal, but by 1960, these funds had been exhausted. From 1961, the Hispanic American ministry's financial needs, as determined by the board of trustees, became a regular part of the EMC. From the perspective of the congregation's Spanish-speaking members, the allotment was never sufficient, and with a large budget cut in 1969, Cotto and those he served became increasingly dissatisfied with the arrangement, despite the insistence by C. Harvey Williamson, chairman of the board of deacons, that the church remained committed to the ministry.[71]

In October 1970, in the midst of Riverside's attempt to deal with the developments in the aftermath of James Forman's presentation of the Black Manifesto to the congregation,[72] Rev. Pablo Cotto resigned his position on the Riverside staff. Participants in the ministry immediately lodged a complaint with the broader congregation in which they expressed support for Cotto's decision, given the insufficient support provided them in a congregation in which "other programs get all the support and all the supplies they want," and pressed for a real commitment from Riverside to a Hispanic ministry. The group demanded almost $35,000 in annual support for a full-time minister, a bilingual secretary and social worker, the assignment of a seminary student to the group part time, an organist and choir director, money for preaching for five Sundays and money for fellowship, cultural affairs, and evangelism.[73] In its public disclosure of Cotto's resignation and the future of the Hispanic American ministry, Riverside's leaders did not acknowledge the disaffection of its Spanish-speaking members and, in the issue of the *Carillon* to which the printed protest was attached, simply reported Cotto's resignation without reference to the members of the ministry or their apparent desire to develop more along the lines of a congregation within the larger body of Riverside than to continue functioning as a ministry from Riverside to Spanish-speaking New Yorkers. When Riverside's ministers and lay leadership attempted to honor Rev. Cotto at the annual meeting in December, as it generally did for departing staff members, Cotto declined to attend, indicating in writing that he felt that it would not be in the best interests of the church or the members of the Hispanic congregation for him to be present. Hispanic congregants read Cotto's letter at the meeting and walked out en masse for a period of time to protest Riverside's treatment of their minister.[74]

The next year, the board of deacons appointed a task force to make recommendations about the Hispanic ministry and hired Rev. Fernando Garcia Castano of the Spanish Evangelical Church (Presbyterian) and a graduate of Union Theological Seminary as interim minister for the group. Finally, in December 1971, with the task force recommending that the Hispanic ministry be discontinued, the board decided that the focus of "any new program . . . be related to, not separate from, the church's Urban ministry." The task force also recommended that the church appoint an associate in urban ministry who had a Hispanic background.[75] This turn meant that Riverside's engagement with Spanish-speaking Protestants in New York would take place "largely outside the walls of the church,"[76] an approach that necessarily made it difficult to envision the congregation as ever including Hispanic Protestants. Since the dismantling of the ministry that Cotto had built to serve Hispanic New Yorkers, Riverside has not focused on issues of diversity other than the concerns of its African American members. In 1984 a group called Latinos at Riverside, coordinated by Carmen Alicia Nebot, was formed to educate Riversiders about Latin American and Latino issues, as well as to provide support for Latino members of the congregation who continued to feel marginalized within their church community. This was a lay initiative and never received the kind of support from the institution that the Hispanic ministry had and so remained small and informal.[77]

Urban Affairs Ministries

In considering the meaning of its location in New York, Riverside added another minister to focus specifically on urban questions. Robert L. Polk, the first African American minister on Riverside's staff, began his tenure in 1960 as the minister to youth, a position he held until 1966. A native of Chicago, Polk had pastored a congregation in North Dakota and worked as director of youth services at a North Dakota YMCA before moving to Riverside.[78] In 1966 Polk left Riverside to serve as dean of the chapel at Dillard University and then returned in 1968 as minister of urban affairs, a position that he characterized as an undefined "one-man operation." Polk understood his task as balancing issues of particular concern to Riverside with his own deep commitment to urban communities, a commitment that was sometimes at odds with Riversiders' concerns. Reflecting on his first few years as the urban affairs minister, Polk felt that he was at a disadvantage from the start because he became associated with a number of new groups within the congregation that had begun to assert themselves against the comfortable old guard, especially the Black Christian Caucus, which was founded in 1969, the New Priorities Movement, and with Group Interested in Power Sharing (GRIPS), a group aimed at young families and interested in "intrachurch communication" and a more open decision-making process.[79] Polk wrote a few years later that "now, in retrospect, this can all be seen as a part of the emerging fear of ethnic and cultural change which always accompanies churches and communities in transition."[80] In addition to the hostility he felt from the outset, Polk asserted that the church's commitment to the issues that had led to his hiring seemed to wane considerably once he began the job, with the congregation seeing him as taking care of urban issues and problems and, therefore, absolving them of any action on their part. He also noted that some members saw his job as his becoming involved on behalf of the church in the urban environment and in urban issues and causes but not dealing with such problems within the Riverside community.

Upon taking the job of minister of urban affairs, Polk identified the critical needs of urban communities, with special attention to housing, health and welfare, education, and revenue sharing. In 1972, when Polk felt that the congregation's interest in urban issues had waned, he convened a "think tank on urban ministry," bringing together Riverside staff and members with expertise or involvement in urban affairs, as well as some specialists in Christian social services. The participants expressed concern that in Riverside's structure at the time, the urban ministry was positioned as a marginal, adjunct endeavor rather than as a central part of the congregation's life and mission. They proposed to the board of trustees that Riverside might consider urban ministry as in truth the heart of its total ministry—the ministry out of which all ministries evolve. In other words, Riverside is a church in the midst of urban life. It ministers to urban people. Whatever its relation to the world, it is through the life of an urban congregation. The question of urban ministry is the question of the church's role in the life of urban people.[81]

The think tank motivated Riverside to undertake a large-scale "metropolitan mission study" in 1972, which resulted in 1974 in a report of a well-researched survey of conditions faced by urban dwellers nationwide and urban congregations generally in an attempt to identify "emerging models for mission." In evaluating conditions and making recommendations, it is clear that the members of the committee and the authors of the report tried to affirm Riverside's historic strengths, take stock of its weaknesses, and chart new directions that could use Riverside's traditions and leave behind outdated attitudes and practices.

Several noteworthy themes and concerns emerged. First, the ongoing issue of the neighborhood's changing demographics and its impact on the congregation loomed large, and the fear of white members becoming the minority at Riverside was palpable. The report expresses this concern as an interest in maintaining "a pluralistic congregation," something its writers felt would not be the case if Riverside became a predominantly black congregation. Nevertheless, the question of how to deal with the racism deeply embedded in the institution and in some of its members was a pressing concern. Second, the report considered the problems of dealing with the "myth of Riverside Church as a self-supporting institution" and finding new ways of thinking about stewardship ("of time, talent, space and money"). The members of the committee wanted to impress on the church's members the centrality of service and stewardship to Riverside's mission and theology and to elevate it in order to promote cutting-edge ministries. The third major theme was determining the direction of these new ministries in ways that would take advantage of Riverside's resources and apply them to the pressing needs of urban residents.

The Urban Affairs Committee (URBAFAC), founded in 1974 under the auspices of Robert Polk's office, was the institutional entity that emerged from the study. Its program encompassed "the organization of volunteer services, an in-church seven-week series to enhance the urban awareness of Riverside members, and a series of field trips within the city to further the educational process."[82] URBAFAC coordinated volunteer opportunities for Riversiders in hospitals, in tutoring programs, visiting the elderly, mentoring young people, in thrift shops, and in youth programs. Its educational programs took up such issues as housing, welfare, and food advocacy.

The focus on a metropolitan mission also resulted in a renewed commitment to a number of other Riverside endeavors. The Council on Christian Social Relations expressed particular interest in prison reform in New York City and elsewhere and formed a task force on prison reform and rehabilitation. In the fall of 1971 the council began educating Riversiders about the conditions in local prisons, by conducting field trips to the Tombs city jail in Manhattan; Riker's Island; Greenhaven Correctional Facility in Stormville, New York; and the adolescent facility on Riker's Island. The task force also established a relationship with the South Forty Corporation, a social service organization that works with ex-offenders, to form the Post–Prison Adjustment Committee to solicit members of Riverside to give jobs to former inmates.[83] In 1974 the prison task force embarked on a remarkable cooperative enterprise with the newly formed Performing Cooperative of the Theatre of Riverside (for a more thorough discussion of theater and dance arts at Riverside, see chap. 6). The theater established as its resident company The Family, a troupe of former inmates who brought with them a production of Miguel Piñero's *Short Eyes: The Killing of a Sex Offender by the Inmates of the House of Detention Awaiting Trial*. Piñero had been an inmate at the Ossining Correctional Facility when he wrote the play, and he took the prison slang term for a child molester as his title. The production at Riverside received extremely favorable notices from critics Mel Gussow and Clive Barnes in the *New York Times*, and it eventually moved, with the original cast of former inmates, to the Joseph Papp Theater and then to the Vivian Beaumont Theater at Lincoln Center, winning many prestigious theater awards and nominations for others.[84] In addition to this unusual focus on life in prison, Riverside continued a prison ministry throughout the last years of the twentieth century and does so still, with an emphasis on helping prisoners return to life in the community and on improving conditions in prison.

In this period of intense focus on urban issues in the late 1960s and early 1970s, Riverside developed or took advantage of new funds to help the congregation make a greater impact on urban social service organizations. The Weeks Fund, the result of a bequest from George K. Weeks to the church, had been available to Riverside's Benevolence Committee for some years and, according to his wishes, had been used "to enlarge the contribution by the Church to benevolences in the City of New York, thus broadening the influence of the church in the civic and religious life of the community outside its own constituency."[85] In contrast to the regular benevolence program in which Riverside established ongoing relationships with organizations, gifts from the Weeks estate provided "seed money rather than recurring items, and for items which would not usually fit into traditional institutional patterns."[86] Moreover, the majority of Weeks's gifts were to secular organizations that dealt with such issues as drug addiction, urban education, and helping local girls to qualify for admission to elite colleges. Other grants from the Weeks Fund went to Native American, Latino, African, African American, and Asian groups in the city.[87] The Weeks Fund provided flexibility with regard to funding and permitted the congregation to "respond to the cries of justice, empowerment, liberation, and self-determination . . . and to enable people to turn to this Christian fellowship with hope that they might not have in turning elsewhere."[88]

The Riverside Fund for Social Justice, which developed as part of Riverside's response to James Forman's Black Manifesto, was another important avenue in the 1970s for distributing funds to community organizations. The goal was to raise $450,000 in three years. Although the goal was to raise most of the funds from within the church, a secondary aim was to encourage other churches to take similar actions, by seeking the participation of individuals and groups outside Riverside. Some Riversiders did not think that the church and its members should be held responsible for the American system of racism or the economic exploitation of African Americans, as the Black Manifesto charged. As one member of the Benevolence Committee wrote: "I have asked myself, to what extent does the characterization of the church in this report apply to the majority of the members of Riverside? Involvement in a system I can understand, but I do not think that Riverside can be called a 'racist' church."[89] Despite the concerns or objections of some members, the congregation approved the Riverside Fund for Social Justice, and within the first two years of its existence, the committee was able to offer grants to organizations that dealt with housing and urban renewal, the mentally retarded, entrepreneurship in black communities, recently released prisoners, and New York City's Latino population.[90]

Riverside's Radio Ministry

In a number of important cases, Riverside pursued its mission in ways that were not explicitly religious but involved a broader attempt to inculcate in New York City's public life the principles that animate the congregation. Riverside's foray into broadcasting from its own radio station, from 1961 through 1976, represents an important—if sometimes controversial within the congregation—instance of the church's commitment to an innovative urban ministry. In response to the conclusion that the church was insufficiently engaged with the media, particularly television and radio, and after a long period of research in which Riverside submitted an application to the FCC for the last unassigned FM frequency in the New York metropolitan area, the church was awarded a license for a noncommercial radio station to be broadcast at 106.7 FM. It hired John D. "Jack" Summerfield, who had ten years of experience as station manager of Boston Public Radio's WGBH, and a staff of twelve.[91]

The major obstacle to getting the station up and running was not establishing a program schedule but the tremendous controversy over whether the station's antenna would mar the aesthetics of Riverside's tower, which housed the Laura Spelman Rockefeller Memorial Carillon. John D. Rockefeller Jr. again offered to provide the financial resources to ensure the tower's architectural integrity. After considerable effort and expense, the church purchased a specially designed antenna that would be hidden inside the tower and chose the station's call letters—WRVR—in accordance with the antenna's model designation.[92] In 1971 the station switched its broadcast antenna to the Empire State Building to increase its signal's range.[93] Another impediment to WRVR's early success was the fact that FM radio was still quite new at that time and its future was still unclear. Jack Summerfield was optimistic, however, reporting during the station's first years that of the eleven million residents of the New York metropolitan area, more than two and a half million homes had one or more radios that could receive an FM signal, a higher percentage than in any other part of the country.[94]

WRVR began broadcasting in January 1961 and presented New Yorkers with a lineup of shows that included public affairs programming, broadcasts of classical music and jazz, discussions of fine arts, cultural programs, and a small number of Spanish-language programs.[95] In establishing a schedule of programs, the church obtained commitments from neighboring institutions, including Union Theological Seminary, Barnard College, Juilliard School of Music, Jewish Theological Seminary, and International House, to produce shows for the stations or to participate in programs. Among the regular, locally produced, programs on WRVR were *Just Jazz with Ed Beach; Gordon Gilkey Views the News*, a fifteen-minute current events show; and *Voices of UNESCO*, broadcast in both Spanish and English and hosted by Sally G. Swing, the United Nations Educational Scientific and Cultural Organization's information officer, and Asdrubal Salsamendi, chief of the New York City office of UNESCO's Mass Communications Unit. Union Theological Seminary offered *People or Puppets*, during which guests discussed "values and concepts fostered by modern mass media as compared with values and concepts rooted in our moral-religious traditions," and Barnard College presented the Danforth Lectures, a series of talks "on the religious heritage of the Jewish, Roman Catholic, and Protestant faiths." Later the Juilliard School of Music, New York University, Cooper Union Forum, and other New York City cultural and educational institutions helped produce programs for the station.[96] WRVR broadcast in Spanish on Tuesday evenings and presented other programs on Hispanic history and cultures. These included programs like *New York: Hispanic City, Radioteatros, Redecubriendo America (Rediscovering America)*, and *El Servicio de Adoration*, a broadcast of the previous Sunday's Spanish-language service.[97] The station also relied on programming from WGBH-FM, Boston Public Radio, and Puerto Rico's Department of Education, among other sources. Most popular among the shows from outside sources was *Father O'Connor's Jazz*, a WGBH program.[98] In addition to reaching an audience in the New York metropolitan area, WRVR programs also were broadcast on the Voice of America, Radio Sweden, Radio Free Europe, Radio Nederland, and BBC; in New Zealand, France, Japan, and Canada; and syndicated on a wide range of U.S. stations.[99]

While the station's programming was varied and discussed religious, political, social, and cultural issues, it did not fail to represent its connection to the Riverside Church. For example, WRVR broadcast the Sunday service of worship, the station's second most popular program according to a 1969 audience survey.[100] In reflecting on the importance of the station for Riversiders, Fosdick wrote,

> From the beginning I was enthusiastic about the possibilities of Riverside Radio WRVR. Now, however, with old age seriously limiting our activities,

WRVR has become to Mrs. Fosdick and myself not simply valuable but downright indispensable. All week long the galaxy of institutions on Morningside Heights makes possible an enriching series of programs. But to us Sunday is the climax when, unable to attend Riverside Church in person, we can join in the worship and listen to the magnificent preaching here at home.[101]

In addition to the broadcast of the service, Riverside's ministers were represented regularly on the air with spots like *Fosdick at Five* and *McCracken at Midnight*, in which the station aired recordings of prayers by the two clergymen. In April 1961, Dr. McCracken began a daily reading of the newly published New English Bible, which was aired Monday through Friday at 9:45 P.M. and rebroadcast at midnight.[102] At various times WRVR aired lectures and sermons by McCracken and Fosdick, and in 1969, Eugene Laubach hosted a series of shows on New York City's theater.[103] Beginning in 1970, WRVR featured Laubach's fifteen-minute Sunday evening *Riverside Report*.[104] In 1972 Paul Sherry, a member of the board of deacons for many years and chair of the church's radio committee, hosted *Always on Sundays*, an hour-long live call-in show focusing on religion and "current social concerns" and during which Sherry interviewed a guest about a particular issue. His guests included Margaret Mead, Arthur Schlesinger, Rollo May, R. Buckminster Fuller, Harvey Cox, Pete Seeger, Cesar Chavez, Ralph Abernathy, and Alan Paton. Sherry recalled, "I saw the program as part of the church's social ministry. . . . Through the program we hoped to inform persons about issues addressed by our guests and perhaps get them involved."[105]

In establishing a public, noncommercial radio station, Riverside was using mass media to engage the residents of the New York City metropolitan area with programs that "reflect the basic philosophy and objectives of the Church: liberal and dynamic in its approach to religion; inter-racial in its fellowship; international in its outlook; inter-denominational in its inclusive fellowship; and intercultural in its concern."[106] Those involved made it clear from the start that the station would not function as a means of recruiting members to the church or even of making converts to Christianity. As Robert McCracken told the congregation,

Our venture into broadcasting is not simply an attempt to create a favorable impression of the Riverside Church, nor, primarily, to recruit members for the church; it is rather an attempt to relate the sacred to the secular, to have the sacred permeate the secular, to bring the insights of Christianity to bear on every province of society. It is an attempt rooted in the conviction that a sound personal life and a sound national life are impossible without the habitual vision of greatness.[107]

In addition to affirming a commitment to an interdenominational approach to Christianity in the station's broadcasts, WRVR's leadership insisted that its broader approach to religion be grounded in esteem for other religions. In promotional material for the station, Jack Summerfield wrote,

> In a real sense, WRVR is *your* station, whether you belong to Riverside or not. As a station licensed to serve the public interest WRVR is *your* station whether you are Protestant or not. In our stewardship of WRVR we wish to demonstrate both the deeply held Christian commitment of the Church and the respect which the Church feels for religious convictions other than its own. In a real sense, WRVR is an inter-faith station.[108]

In later years, WRVR aired series like the 1966 broadcasts on Jewish holidays and ways of life, produced in cooperation with the Jewish Theological Seminary. The *Carillon* provided a strongly worded rationale for the station's interest in religions other than Christianity: "Living with our neighbors involves not only tolerance, but understanding. Recognizing that knowledge is the only basis for true understanding, WRVR has undertaken a series of programs to present authentic information about one group of our neighbors, the Jews."[109] Listeners from a variety of backgrounds responded to this interfaith approach to religion. One listener wrote in to inquire about a piece of classical music played on a WRVR show but soon turned to other issues.

> I ought to bring in religion here, too. Since your headquarters are in the Riverside Church, it is natural for you to program "Christian" programs. But, let me commend you for your "Portion of the week" at midnight, and other programs for other faiths. I am Jewish, but if being situated in a church does this good, all F.M. stations should have their headquarters in a Church.[110]

One of the most significant elements of WRVR's impact on the life of New York City was its role as an important interpreter of the civil rights movement for members of the Riverside community and city residents at large. Taking an activist stance, a press release for one of the station's multipart programs on the civil rights movement asserted that "as the radio station of the Riverside Church in the City of New York, WRVR felt the need not only to acquaint its listeners with this spirit [of the civil rights movement], but also to suggest the basic Christian ethics that are the backbone of the civil rights effort."[111] Perhaps the most widely acclaimed and distributed show ever produced by WRVR was the six-hour documentary *Birmingham: A Testament of Non-Violence,* first broadcast in the summer of 1963. Jack Summerfield, the station's director; Walter E. Nixon, WRVR's news and public affairs director; and Rev. Robert L. Polk, Riverside's youth minister, produced the documentary that took listeners first inside St. John's Church on May 10, 1963, to hear Martin Luther King Jr., Ralph Abernathy, and others at a celebration of an agreement to integrate the buses and then to a Ku Klux Klan meeting the next day. The WRVR team then covered the aftermath of the bombing of the Gaston Motel and the home of King's brother, Rev. A. D. W. King, later that night.[112] Many reviews evaluated the series as representing a milestone in radio journalism, imagining that in an age in which television images of the civil rights movement had captured the American imagination, radio might still have the capacity to challenge the newer medium.[113] This series brought a great deal of attention to Riverside, and the station was overwhelmed by requests for information on the radio programs and for additional coverage of the civil rights movement more generally. WRVR continued its coverage of civil rights issues and, on the day of Dr. Martin Luther King Jr.'s funeral, broadcast live from Atlanta and New York with "Dial-in for Non-Violence," which brought together "experts in the non-violence movement and listeners at home" to talk about the movement's future. WRVR's historic programming on this occasion was carried by thirty-six stations and earned it an Armstrong Certificate of Merit for Community Service in 1969.[114]

Similarly, the station aired a number of impressive series over the years on other important and sometimes controversial topics. On Mondays and Thursday evenings in the fall of 1965, for example, WRVR broadcast a series of programs, *The Homosexual: A New Minority?* which included interviews with gay men and lesbians, a discussion by Dr. Albert Ellis on "the causes of homosexuality," and coverage of the legal, civil, religious, and theological issues facing gay men and lesbians.[115] In the summer of 1970 Studs Terkel's regular show on WRVR focused on women's liberation and featured interviews with members and leaders of the National Organization for Women. The station also aired a number of programs on Vietnam.[116] At various points in its history, WRVR paid special attention to the needs of urban youth with series like *Pass the Youth*, which, in the summer of 1970, presented a five-part program on the problems of urban youth and included segments on the Stone Gym, Harlem youth, black students, and youth culture more generally.[117] In the winter of 1970 the station broadcast *Attitude*, a five-part series on African American culture developed by Ron Johnson, a graduate of Dillard University and an intern at WRVR, who came with some experience in radio.[118]

WRVR also served as a conduit for informing Riverside members about developments regarding particularly difficult in-house issues. In the aftermath of James Forman's presentation of the Black Manifesto, various members of the church and representatives of community agencies spoke about their reactions to Forman's demands, and WRVR taped and broadcast the event the following Tuesday evening.[119] And later in 1969 when the "new priorities movement," which arose "as part of a grass-roots effort to give greater importance in federal government spending programs to the current economic and social inequities," held a conference on the military-industrial complex, WRVR taped and later aired the proceedings.[120] Thus, while the radio station's major contribution was providing a forum for Riversiders and other New Yorkers to discuss and learn about broad social issues from a multidenominational and ecumenical religious perspective, it also helped shape developments of particular interest to church members.

In 1971 Riverside transformed WRVR from a noncommercial station to "a limited commercial operation which preserve[d] time for broadcasting church services and other church programs of major importance." The church had been losing money from the start.[121] For many, the drain on church resources during a period of general financial crisis was difficult to justify, even though WRVR had accomplished a great deal with its small budget. With the change to a limited commercial station, WRVR also changed its format to emphasize public affairs programming and news interpretation but retained its broadcasts of the service, the services of music, and Ed Beach's *Just Jazz*, consistently the station's most popular program.[122] By 1974, with WRVR $1.8 million in the red, the station's management decided to discontinue the public affairs format and instead focus on jazz, especially the new fusion jazz. The station's board also fired a number of on-air talent, and other hosts quit, leading Helen Kruger of the *Village Voice*, one of the city's progressive weeklies, to comment: "Now they've gone, and with them a dream of an alternative radio station devoted in significant part to news and public affairs."[123]

Riverside's contribution to broadcasting in New York City ended when the church sold the station in November 1976, as church staff and members began to feel that the station increasingly had little to do with the life of the church. By this time it had also become embroiled in a controversy over management's treatment of its black and Hispanic radio hosts. In the early 1970s, WRVR received letters from listeners complimenting the station on the diversity of its programming and personnel. One listener wrote to commend the station for airing Felipe Luciano's show:

> Your radio is responding to a need among Puerto Ricans for radio programs that deal with them as people in an intelligent manner. The other radio stations deal with Puerto Ricans as a market. . . . Your radio station has just touched the tip of this unquenchable need among Puerto Ricans for self expression. It has the right format, that of engaging your audience in dialogue. I would like to see more Puerto Ricans broadcasting on your station. There is an audience waiting for them.[124]

Rob Crocker, a jazz DJ with a background hosting shows for Radio Free America and the Pacifica Network, also was the subject of many positive letters from listeners. By 1974, however, the station had fired Luciano and Crocker, as well as Tony Batten, the station's music director, a black news anchor, and Adam Clayton Powell III, who had been the assistant news director in 1971/72.[125] Crocker had reportedly been fired after posting a list of staff salaries on an office bulletin board to highlight inequalities in pay.[126] The press coverage following these firings was not positive, and the station received many letters of protest from listeners who saw the dismissals as part of a pattern of exploiting black music and failing to include people of color in the station's administration.

The 1976 decision to sell the station's license came amidst this tension among the staff, the inability to find a format that could overcome operating losses, and Riversiders' growing sense that the station was not truly connected to the church. Although Riverside was proud of WRVR's accomplishments in its years of operation, and many members and New Yorkers listened to the music, news, and cultural programming, the question of whether they should continue to make a major financial investment in WRVR prompted a reexamination.[127] The board of trustees decided to sell the broadcast license for $2.3 million in an attempt to recoup some of the losses that had come from advances made to the station from the building endowment fund. Sonderling Broadcasting Corporation, the new owner of the license, changed the station's format to country and western music but agreed to continue the live broadcast of the service.[128] But this arrangement remained in place for only a few months until the new station began to broadcast the service on tape on Sunday evenings.[129] As of 2002, Riverside's Sunday service is broadcast from 5:00 to 6:00 A.M. on WLTW, the station that now owns the license to 106.7 FM. Despite WRVR's relatively short lived history, it had a lasting impact on discussions of public affairs in New York City in its time, on many listeners over the years, and on the future of noncommercial radio in the United States. Many New Yorkers still recall WRVR's forthright and probing shows on social and political issues and its insistent support of jazz and fusion as important art forms. Some of its staff have gone on to have productive careers in media and continue to influence the shape of radio broadcasting in America.[130]

The Urban Church in an International Era

During William Sloane Coffin's tenure as senior minister from 1977 to 1987, the congregation's interest turned, in large measure, to a number of compelling national and international issues. In addition to addressing international peace issues through disarmament convocations, demonstrations, lobbying, and petition writing, during these years Riversiders focused on the situation of Haitian refugees, on apartheid in South Africa, and on the United States' involvement in Central and South America, especially through their participation in the sanctuary movement, providing protection to a Guatemalan family. Riverside's commitments to urban questions and other issues continued through these years, but with the inauguration of the disarmament campaign, its attention turned to international peace and the church's self-representation through the *Carillon* emphasized national and international over local issues. At various times, Riverside worked to bring the disarmament issue to the local level, as in a 1984 series of discussions on the connections between the United States' large and growing military budget and urban poverty. In addition, the church became a vocal opponent of Columbia University's plan to activate its TRIGA-Mark II nuclear reactor, located in the School of Engineering on 120th Street between Broadway and Amsterdam Avenue. One week before the accident at the Three Mile Island nuclear plant, Riverside's Religious Society voted to oppose Columbia's operation of the reactor "as being too great a risk to a densely populated area, with the possibility of unforeseen accidents because of trainee or other human error or malfunction of the facility." In response to the widespread opposition, Columbia's President William J. McGill and the engineering faculty agreed not to activate the reactor.[131]

Coffin himself was always concerned about the city's problems, having spent his earliest years there. Years after he left Riverside, when asked what surprised him most when he returned to New York to become the church's senior minister, Coffin replied that the misery was more pervasive and profound than he expected. He saw the failure, on both his part and that of the congregation, to do more about the problems of New York City as the main disappointment of his tenure as senior minister and what he would change if he could serve again. What they were able to do was good, he concluded, "but so inadequate."[132] Despite the focus on disarmament and other issues of global militarism, Riverside's commitment to the problems and promises of urban ministry remained strong throughout this period and moved in important new directions, spurred by the alarming rise in homelessness and poverty in New York City—results of the economic policies of the Reagan administration—the emergence of the AIDS crisis, and the growing importance of the city's gay rights movement.

The Clothing Room and Food Pantry services, which had long been staples of the work of Riverside's Social Services Department and originating in a sewing project of the Women's Society, became overwhelmed in the 1980s as they tried to meet the emergency needs of New Yorkers.[133] By 1983, a group of Riversiders had organized a food and justice task force and had begun working with the church's Food Pantry to explore other options to meet the food needs of the city's poor. That year the *Carillon* reported that almost one hundred people a day were coming for emergency food relief, a quadrupling of the demand.[134] The church cosponsored Food for Survival, Inc., which was "designed to serve all of New York City by providing surplus food to food pantries, soup kitchens, day care, senior centers and city shelters at a cost far below what these services are now paying."[135]

In addition to encountering the pressing needs of the working poor with regard to finding food and clothing, Riversiders and other New Yorkers also saw the problem of homelessness become, in Coffin's words, "unbelievable" during these years.[136] In the winter of 1984, Riverside joined fifty other New York City metropolitan area churches that had opened small shelters for homeless men, with Riverside accommodating up to ten men each night, joined by two volunteers from the congregation. Originally intended to last only through the winter, by the early spring of 1984 the church had decided to continue the shelter program through June. The Riverside shelter remained open for ten years, closing finally because of the declining need and the increasing difficulty of finding Riverside volunteers to staff the program year-round.[137] Although Coffin supported the Food Pantry and homeless shelter work, he did so reluctantly, as he felt that it was an easy solution permitting the congregation to take its customary route of "[allowing] charity to take the place of justice."[138] Despite the congregation's ambivalent relationship to the project of sheltering homeless men, the shelter represented an important way in which Riverside kept the local issues of poverty and homelessness in sight during this period of significant attention to international issues.

In an attempt to move beyond charity and toward justice in developing a thorough and thoughtful urban ministry, in 1979 and 1980 Riverside organized a series of forums on the city's problems, which were intended to bring in specialists familiar with issues such as housing, education, prisons, hunger, mental illness, drugs, the elderly, and federal money for New York City to educate members and suggest strategies and solutions. These were followed by a number of "study-action" courses for the congregation: "Riverside Past and Future: Re-envisioning the City" and "The City and Its People."[139] Out of these sessions emerged a plan for a conference in March 1981, "The Church and the City: Signs of Despair, Signs of Hope," which coincided with the church's fiftieth anniversary celebration. Among the participants were Harvey Cox of Harvard Divinity School, Letty Russell of Yale Divinity School, and James A. Forbes Jr., then of Union Theological Seminary, speaking on the theme of "Liberation Theology for Urban People." The conference also featured presentations by the prominent socialist activist Michael Harrington on "What Ever Happened to the Other America?" and Shirley Chisholm, Democratic member of the House of Representatives from Brooklyn, on "Urban Prospects for the Future." Additional participants included Rev. Gardner Taylor, H. Carl McCall, Studs Terkel, Herman Badillo, and William Sloane Coffin, and resource persons from a range of city organizations and political offices were available for consultations with those in attendance.[140]

FIGURE 4.5: Riversiders collect food for the Food Pantry, n.d. *Used by permission of the Riverside Church Archives.*

In general, the conference was a success, with more than one thousand people attending, and it achieved its goal of educating members and encouraging them to become involved in urban issues. Despite the successes, however, the issue of the place of Riverside's Hispanic members in the congregation's consciousness once again became a major issue. A group of disaffected Latino members of the congregation interrupted the conference's Friday morning session to read a statement of protest that in some ways echoed the Black Manifesto that James Forman presented in 1969. It read, in part,

> The American religious establishment must assume its share of responsibility for the decay of urban areas and the deplorable conditions under which Hispanic must live. The church's policy . . . has been to neglect, desert or undermine the resources of the Hispanic people. The only churches that have remained to service the spiritual needs of Hispanic people in the inner cities are the indigenous, independent Hispanic churches.

The protesters further charged that Hispanics had been inadequately represented in both the planning of the conference and the list of speakers. The *Carillon* reported, "In response the delegates passed a resolution acknowledging neglect on the part of major denominations and promising encouragement and efforts to correct the situation. The proceeds from the Friday evening service of worship were allocated to Hispanic church efforts."[141] The irony of the Riversiders' attention to political issues in Central and Latin America in this period, as well as the church's participation in the sanctuary movement in light of its long history of conflict with or neglect of Hispanic members, was not lost on the protesters. In the end, the response to the requests of Latino congregants remained superficial, and the sources of their complaints persisted.

An initiative by Riverside in 1982 to combat racism in the congregation, the community, and the nation did lead to some additional attention for Latino congregants. Seeking to make the elimination of racism as central a priority for Riverside as disarmament had been under Coffin's direction, the congregation explored the possibility of an affirmative action policy among the church staff, of new ways to interact with the city's black churches, and of "ways by which Riverside can become more relevant to the Hispanic community."[142] This brief attention to the particular needs and desires of the congregation's Latino members was followed by the formation in 1984 of a group called Latinos at Riverside.[143] Nevertheless, finding ways of creating a feeling of belonging in an interracial congregation that constructs its identity along the racial axis of black and white remains a problem.[144] In 2001 Riverside's social justice ministry included a Latino/a ministry that "brings political, cultural and spiritual issues of . . . Latino/a members and neighbors before [the] Riverside congregation," an indication that despite the difficult experiences of Latino Riversiders, the church community is still looking for ways to address these issues.[145] It seems, however, that the church has not been entirely successful in moving beyond imagining Riverside as an interracial community to being a multiracial one.

Gay and lesbian members of Riverside constituted another constituency that began to assert itself within the congregation in the late 1970s and early 1980s. Although WRVR had demonstrated courage and foresight in producing a series on homosexuality and religion in 1965, and Eugene Laubach and others had participated in a series of courses on religion and sexuality in 1973 at which the issue was raised of finding ways to support and affirm gay and lesbian members,[146] no formal mechanisms to recognize gay and lesbian Riversiders took shape until 1978. The first tentative moves came with a forum sponsored by the Adult Ministries Committee, which invited members to explore "the relevance of the gay rights movement to the church's ministry and congregational life as well as to the larger society and the Gospel imperative for social justice."[147] Shortly after the Adult Ministries' forum, the *Carillon* announced to the congregation the formation of Maranatha, a group with a range of goals combining politics, education, and spiritual development. At the outset, its members set out three goals:

> (1) to combat, through the example of Christian living and education, the distrust, cynicism, fear, violence, and hatred directed toward gay men and women; (2) to provide gay men and women, who may feel somewhat alienated from the Riverside community, an opportunity for acceptance and encouragement in Christian living; and (3) to provide gay men and women who may be confused and/or suffering an opportunity to find solace, understanding, and help within a framework of Christian friendship.[148]

With the formation of Maranatha, its members arranged a variety of activities for gay and lesbian members and for the education of the broader congregation, from interreligious worship services and participation in New York City's annual June Gay Pride march to special events at Riverside's Fosdick Preaching Convocation to provide resources for clergy wishing to minister to gay and lesbian Christians.[149]

The most difficult and controversial events related to the emergence of gay and lesbian members of Riverside as a visible constituency resulted from the church's 1984 educational theme of "Church in the City." This exploration of urban church issues took much the same form as had past initiatives at Riverside, beginning with a period of education and moving into one of practical planning. The recommendations for the future included a request for the Adult Education Committee to begin working with Maranatha, "to develop a statement affirming rights of gay and lesbian persons" to be presented to the board of deacons and then the congregation at large in the spring of 1985.[150] We should note that the Riverside members and clergy who drew up the statement of affirmation of gay and lesbian congregants explicitly connected the broad issues of religion and sexuality and the challenges and promises of urban ministry. Once the Adult Education Committee began writing the statement, it also provided a number of educational sessions to help Riversiders decide how they would vote when the statement was put before the congregation. These sessions focused mainly on the daily realities of life in New York for gay men and lesbians, with particular attention to housing and job discrimination, antigay violence, and the unwillingness of the New York City Police Department to include antigay violence in the category of bias crimes. While the Adult Education Committee was offering a range of information for Riversiders to make a decision on their own, the committee made clear its belief that adopting the affirmation statement would be the right thing for Riverside to do as a New York City institution.[151]

The Religious Society of the Riverside Church ultimately did vote to accept the "Statement of Openness, Inclusion and Affirmation of Gay/Lesbian Persons," on June 2, 1985. The process of adopting the statement of openness and the tensions that arose as Riversiders considered the social and theological implications of the path on which the church was embarking reveal a great deal about the limits of liberal theology and the willingness of some members to move beyond them. As has been the case with so many conflicts at Riverside, for better or worse, the resolution sometimes serves to mask the ongoing underlying disagreements. Thus, although the issue of taking an official stance of inclusiveness has been resolved, the congregation has not necessarily reached consensus on the religious meaning of its members' various approaches to human sexuality. Senior Minister James Forbes has spoken out against homophobia in the black church and among Christians more broadly, trying to keep the congregation thinking about these questions, asking whether it is "appropriate for any congregation to celebrate at God's table if all God's children—gay, lesbian, bisexual included—are not at the table?"[152]

By the mid-1980s, as the incidence of AIDS infection had reached crisis proportions in New York City, Riversiders began to look for ways to minister to people with this disease, especially following a special service that took place in January 1986 in which a member of the congregation gave testimony about living with AIDS. In addition to focusing on gay men with AIDS, one of the most visible and activist AIDS constituencies, Coffin made sure that the congregation also considered the impact of AIDS on drug users. Coffin recalled that a chorus from Reality House, a drug rehabilitation program in Harlem, opened the special service by singing "Go Down, Moses." "You could just see Pharaoh as that fucking needle," Coffin said, remembering this as the most moving service in his time as Riverside's senior minister.[153] Many Riversiders took up the cause of ministering to people with AIDS by visiting patients, taking care of people dying of the disease, counseling drug addicts, visiting AIDS babies in New York City hospitals, and, through the Gay Men's Health Crisis, working as "buddies" to people with AIDS.[154]

Thus, despite Riverside's intense focus during Coffin's tenure on national and international issues, many members of the congregation continued to work hard to carry their faith commitments into the life of the city in what they understood to be uniquely Christian ways. Although outsiders no doubt remember Riverside in these years as a disarmament and a sanctuary church, it is clear that it was also a church that tried to deal with issues ranging from race and racism, housing, urban poverty, sexuality, and AIDS on a scale beyond what it had in the past.

Spiritual Development and Urban Disciples

With Rev. James A. Forbes's acceptance in 1989 of the call to become Riverside's senior minister, the church's focus began to shift gradually from the national and international activism that Coffin had promoted to individual and communal spirituality. Just as Coffin had announced his major disarmament initiative early in his tenure, so Forbes called Riversiders to make spiritual development the center of the community's life. Forbes insists that coming from an evangelical and Pentecostal background, the message he wants to give to the liberal Protestant tradition is "a bridging message" to enable this venerable activist congregation to undergird its political commitments with a strong spiritual base. Forbes hopes to see a spiritual revival in America that will lead to social transformation and believes that Riverside can be at its forefront.[155]

In many ways, Forbes's early years at Riverside were marked by tensions within the congregation over his shift in emphasis. Some members felt that his preaching was too biblical and that his focus on spirituality would distract from the activist work in which the church had long been engaged. Members of the Social Justice Commission were particularly concerned about this possibility and called a number of meetings asking Forbes to justify his understanding of the relationship between spirituality and activism.[156] Although a more inward-looking approach to spirituality has characterized James A. Forbes's tenure as Riverside's senior minister, the tradition of urban activism that had become so much a part of Riverside's life has continued, encouraged by both Forbes and lay members of the congregation.

To provide a more concrete structure for Riverside's urban activism in conjunction with the congregation's focus on spirituality, Forbes established a number of new "action initiatives" in February 1992. He told the congregation that the existing work continued to be important but that new approaches also were necessary.

> We affirm, are most grateful for and need to continue current mission initiatives—food pantry, clothing services, PS 165, Harlem Valley Churches, etc.,—and then we need to act on additional initiatives to help solve some of the deep-seated crises impacting urban life in New York. A myriad of issues surround us—housing issues, our "lost generation" of youth, unemployment amid recession, social bias, health care are a few.

Selecting the Sunday before Martin Luther King Day, he announced to the congregation plans for four new groups to organize the work of Riversiders, focusing on youth crisis, unemployment, health care, and racial justice. Some 275 people expressed interest in becoming involved in these projects, with most interested in working with young people.[157]

Addressing the needs of New York City's poor has been a major focus for Riverside during Forbes's tenure, building on a history of service and ministry. The Emancipation from Poverty initiative, begun in 1998 and responding directly to Martin Luther King Jr.'s call to address poverty, seeks to understand "the spiritual, economic, social, and cultural needs of all groups" and to help Riversiders take "effective action that will lead to a healthy and caring society, free of all the oppression of poverty in its various forms."[158]

As of 2002, the only program operating under the auspices of the Emancipation from Poverty initiative was an eight-week barber-training course. The social services ministry runs a number of programs to aid impoverished New Yorkers, including the Job Center (which provides listings and referrals), Direct Aid, Food Pantry, and Clothing Distribution services, all long-standing Riverside endeavors. Through the Direct Aid program, Riverside distributes federal funds and private donations totaling approximately $20,000 a year to assist people with such problems as paying their rent.[159] In May 2000, in conjunction with other institutional members of the Upper West Side Colloquium Against Poverty, the ministry also founded the Shower Project. This program provides access to a hot shower and clean clothing for anyone in need of them, and the social services ministry also provides referrals for employment, medical needs, shelters, and soup kitchens.[160] The church's Thrift Shop has attracted many volunteers from the congregation and offers a selection of clothing and shoes ranging in price from five dollars for children's sneakers to fifty dollars for a tuxedo.[161]

By investing considerable money and volunteer resources, Riverside has been able to continue to provide limited services to New York City's homeless men and women as well as the working poor throughout the 1990s and into the twenty-first century. Despite Forbes's emphasis on setting out in new directions with the "action initiatives" announced in 1992, the general shape of this urban service has been very much in keeping with Riverside's traditions of engagement and shares their benefits and limitations. Forbes's emphasis on building a spiritual base for activism seems to have heightened the congregation's spiritual dimensions. Throughout most of the 1990s, its impact on reshaping and reinvigorating activism has been less clear, but the congregation began investigating innovative forms of spiritually grounded activism at the end of the century in ways that continue today.

Beginning in 1999 Riverside's Church Council and Commissions began formulating a plan that could combine the best of Riverside's history of urban ministry and chart new directions that will have a positive impact on the life of the city. As part of the Five-Year-Plan for the New Millennium, a $10 million Jubilee Fund was created with the goal of making "tangible the Gospel of Jesus as outlined in Luke 4:16–21, to help make substantial changes in the quality of life of those living in the Greater Harlem community."[162] The work of the Jubilee Fund is organized around Community Development, Public Education, Health, and Youth Outreach, and the money will go to create and support programs outside Riverside. The first phase of the project was researching these areas of concern and building alliances with existing organizations and institutions in the Greater Harlem area. In setting goals for the new millennium and developing the plan for the Jubilee Fund, the Riverside community is trying to find a way to place "the well being of the local community at the center of [the church's] mission" and to do so in ways that remain grounded in a process of spiritual development.[163] This program thus combines Rev. Forbes's emphasis on the process of spiritual maturation with Riverside's evolving sense of urban mission in new ways and also seeks to engage the needs of the neighborhood and the city in ways that derive less from what Riversiders decide should be done than from what residents want to be done.

Just like other active engaged citizens, Riverside's clergy and congregants have been involved in electoral politics in New York City. From Fosdick's endorsement of Socialist Norman Thomas's campaign for mayor (over Republican Fiorello H. LaGuardia) to McCracken's call for Protestants to run for office, Riversiders have always been concerned with finding ways for the church to influence the city's political order.[164] The church entered into a new relationship with the city's elected officials during the administration of David Dinkins, when James Forbes formed a close relationship with the mayor during his four-year tenure, meeting with him shortly after his election in 1989 and consulting with him periodically thereafter. Along with other clergy in the city, Forbes participated in a campaign to ease racial tensions in the city and was one of the prominent figures in the January 1990 "Good Neighbor Week," which began with an interfaith prayer service at Riverside, coinciding with the observances of Martin Luther King Jr.'s birthday. Mayor David Dinkins read a proclamation before those gathered for the service, which was greeted with great enthusiasm. The goal of the campaign was to share meals across racial and religious boundaries and to facilitate discussions among participants about the racial tension in their neighborhoods.[165]

By the end of Dinkins's term in office, however, the city had experienced serious racial divisions over such events as the 1991 death of seven-year-old Guyanese American Gavin Cato (after having been hit by a car driven by a Hasidic driver), the murder of visiting Australian scholar Yankel Rosenbaum by a group of black men, and the subsequent unrest among blacks in Crown Heights, Brooklyn. According to Sheryl McCarthy, a reporter for the *New York Times*, following Dinkins's failed bid for re-election and his loss to Rudolph Guiliani in 1993, Forbes told the congregation that he considered the results a "moral defeat for the people of New York City and a victory of the forces of racism and elitism over more high-minded values for the city."[166] McCarthy responded to Forbes's religious analysis of Dinkins's defeat and his assessment of the loss as entirely the result of racism, by looking at the degree to which she saw "personal disappointment take a sharp departure from reality." McCarthy's concern centered on the potential of Forbes's engagement with the racial politics of New York City's electoral politics to divide the Riverside community. As she noted, "If [Riverside's] racially mixed congregation voted anything like the rest of the city, then half of them may have voted for Guiliani." Providing a public forum for politicians to speak with black congregants—most frequently politicians affiliated with the Democratic Party—is traditional among black ministers, and Forbes's interest in and support of New York City's first African American mayor is fully in keeping with this tradition. McCarthy raised the question of how such a tradition will function in a congregation as diverse as Riverside, an issue that the church will certainly face for many years.

Even though the senior minister's involvement in partisan politics might cause some members to feel disaffected, Forbes has continued to be active and to support candidates and elected officials whom he feels advocate racial healing and racial justice, the economic empowerment of the poor, and a range of other issues. He has opened Riverside to Senate candidate Hillary Rodham Clinton and to Fernando Ferrar, whose candidacy for the Democratic nomination in the 2001 mayor's race he eventually endorsed, and has visited Al Sharpton's National Action Network in Harlem, often a controversial move for any public figure in New York City.[167] In 1996, Riverside held a special Sunday service celebrating "the sacredness of black men," during which the congregation honored Bronx district attorney Robert T. Johnson, who had refused to seek the death penalty—which had recently been reinstated in New York State—in a case involving the death of a police officer, resisting pressure from the mayor and governor to do so.[168] In addition to participating in partisan and electoral politics, James Forbes and Riverside have continued to address broader political issues in New York City and beyond. Welfare reform, drug policies, and AIDS have been of particular concern to the congregation during Forbes's tenure, and Riverside also participated in an interfaith project to encourage New Yorkers to vote, with Forbes insisting that the act of voting be understood as a "moral responsibility."[169] Despite its decidedly liberal and activist stance on so many social and political issues, Riverside's involvement with electoral politics has not always reflected a clear or easy consensus on how to translate its liberal theology into political choices.

September 11, 2001

With the destruction of thousands of lives in the horrific attacks on the World Trade Center and the Pentagon on September 11, 2001, many New Yorkers, along with other Americans, turned to one another for comfort and often did so in religious contexts. In the first few days after the attack, much of New Yorkers' grieving took place in public spaces as residents gathered in parks and squares and streets to affirm the importance of human contact, to reclaim the city, and to create informal, spontaneous memorial sites. Communities organized candlelight vigils to offer support to one another and to the colleagues and families of those who died in the attacks. New York's religious institutions responded to the city's needs by opening their doors for individuals to seek solace and counsel and by organizing formal worship and memorial services. Riverside's response to New York's need in the wake of the terrorist attack reveals a great deal about the church's vision of religion for the city and about many New Yorkers' image and expectations of Riverside. It was fitting that Riverside be a major institutional venue in which city residents from a range of religious backgrounds tried to begin to make sense of the attacks and to prepare themselves spiritually for whatever future would emerge from the events.

On Sunday, September 16, New Yorkers gathered at Riverside Church for a service of healing that included both religious leaders and artists and asked all participants to do more than simply acknowledge the religious diversity of the city and the nation but to experience that diversity in genuine ways.[170] In addition to a brief sermon by Rev. James Forbes, the service featured prayers and words of comfort and guidance from two Muslim leaders, a Reconstructionist rabbi, and a minister from the New York Buddhist Church. Riverside's service of healing was attentive to religious specificity, as those gathered heard prayers from a variety of traditions recited in Arabic, Hebrew, English, and Japanese, and many there seemed to engage all the prayers as equally meaningful and spiritually productive. Indeed, the participants did not simply sit and listen respectfully to prayers from traditions other than their own but prayed comfortably in whatever mode was made available to them throughout the service. This kind of involvement in interfaith worship, rather than a simple inclusion of representatives of different traditions, differentiated Riverside's service from most of the others that took place in the weeks following the attack, and this perspective seems to derive naturally from the church's open sensibility. Even though interdenominational has a technical meaning in the Riverside context—denoting its affiliation with two Protestant denominational structures—in practice, the interdenominational part of the congregation's identity has cultivated a commitment to religious openness, engagement, and exchange that was clearly in evidence at the September 16 service of healing as participants celebrated New Yorkers' various religious traditions.

While the service was attentive to religious specificity, it also pointed to broader religious issues in an effort to highlight what binds us together as human beings. In his brief sermon, Forbes spoke of the body's ability to help us deal with grief and counseled listeners to be active in their grief when necessary but also to take the time to be quiet, to listen to the wisdom of their bodies, and to follow the directions that this wisdom offers. In perhaps the most emotional moment of the service, singer and actress Lillias White performed Duke Ellington's "Come Sunday" (1943), beseeching through each repetition of the refrain, "Lord, dear Lord above, God almighty, God of love, Please look down and see my people through," and declaring with extraordinary power and conviction, "I believe God is now, was then and always will be. With God's blessing we can make it through eternity." Many who were present expressed their grief and hope through tears during White's performance, and Ellington's lyrics seemed to affect listeners of all backgrounds that morning.

Since the service of healing, Riverside has begun a formal program to offer support to the community, providing counseling and other services to survivors of the World Trade Center, bereavement counseling, ecumenical meditation, Christian healing prayer, and adult education classes on Islam. Reconstructionist Rabbi Lester Bronstein's remarks at the September 16 service exemplify the attempt of those who participated in the service that day and of Riverside as a congregation to make sense of the events and to find ways of connecting through religious means when he insisted, drawing on a metaphor from the teachings of Rebbe Nachman,

> God cannot have sent us this terror. But we can see that God has given us a world that is a very narrow, precarious bridge—so narrow, so precarious, that one would logically . . . fear falling into the abyss and simply choose not to cross the bridge. But we must not fear to cross. We must believe that this bridge of life becomes ever wider and safer when thousands of us gather, across all the lines and definitions that divide us, to become the agents of God's goodness.[171]

The events of September 11, 2001, and the various ways in which New Yorkers expressed their grief revealed some of important issues that Riverside will face in the twenty-first century. The church's work will take place in a city of extraordinary religious diversity and a high level of religious commitment, despite the stereotype of urban environments as secularizing. Immigrants to the United States who arrived after national quotas were eliminated in 1965 brought an array of religions that fall outside the bounds of the older traditional definitions of American religion and also contribute to the ethnic and theological diversity within New York's communities of Protestants, Catholics, and Jews. The sensitivity of Riverside's members to religious diversity in their reaching out to New York in the aftermath of the terrorist attack on the city derives from the congregation's long-established commitments to liberal Christianity, interreligious dialogue, and ethnic diversity. These deeply held values place the church in a strong position to continue its work in the city's complicated religious terrain. Even as the Riverside Church has changed its leadership, governance structures, and emphases in ministry, the congregation has always maintained an engaged urban ministry as a central part of its mission, and its location in New York City will continue to be an important element of the congregation's identity.

NOTES

1. "New York's Riverside: What Is Happening Today in This Mighty Church in a Great City?" *Christian Century*, November 28, 1951, 1372. McCracken served as senior minister from 1946 to 1957.

2. "New York's Riverside," 1372.

3. Robert A. Orsi, ed., *Gods of the City: Religion and the American Urban Landscape* (Bloomington: Indiana University Press, 1999), 6.

4. "New York's Riverside," 1369.

5. Interview with William Sloane Coffin by the Riverside Church History Project authors, June 8, 2000. Coffin's tenure as senior minister ran from 1977 to 1987.

6. Eugene Laubach, "Church History Tape for Membership Classes," 1990, RCA. Other internal histories of the church emphasize its roots in colonial New York. See, for example, Mina Pendo, "A Brief History of the Riverside Church" (New York: Riverside Church, 1957).

7. Interview with Coffin. Randall Robinson and TransAfrica, the organization he founded to help shape U.S. policy in Africa and the Caribbean, organized more than a year of daily protests outside the South African embassy in which some five thousand people (many celebrities and political figures) were arrested. See Randall Robinson, *Defending the Spirit: A Black Life in America* (New York: Dutton, 1998).

8. Interview with Coffin.

9. Interview with James A. Forbes Jr. by the Riverside Church History Project authors, June 8, 2000. Forbes accepted the call to be senior minister at Riverside in 1989.

10. Andrew S. Dolkart, *Morningside Heights: A History of Its Architecture and*

Development (New York: Columbia University Press, 1998), 2–3. Dolkart points to the additional factors of lack of public transportation and the presence of the Bloomingdale Insane Asylum on the land now occupied by Columbia University as major deterrents to residential development in the nineteenth century.

11. Dolkart, *Morningside Heights*, 37–40.

12. These institutions included Teachers College (1894), St. Luke's Hospital (1896), Columbia University (1897), Barnard College (1897), Jewish Theological Seminary of America (1903), Woman's Hospital (1906), Union Theological Seminary (1910), Institute of Musical Art (which later merged with the Juilliard School of Music) (1910), and International House (1924). See Dolkart, *Morningside Heights*, 4–5.

13. Harry Emerson Fosdick, *The Living of These Days: An Autobiography* (New York: Harper Bros., 1956), 188.

14. Pendo, "A Brief History of the Riverside Church," 44.

15. Fosdick, *The Living of These Days*, 188.

16. "Riverside Church Survey Report" (New York: Riverside Church, 1956), 45.

17. Dolkart, *Morningside Heights*, 1.

18. Quoted in James Hudnut-Beumler, "The Riverside Church: A Brief History of Its Founding, Leadership and Finances" (New York: Riverside Church, 1990), 8.

19. On Fosdick's course work at Columbia, see Fosdick, *The Living of These Days*, 70. On Protestant churches and higher education, see Dorothy C. Bass, "Ministry on the Margin: Protestants and Education," in *Between the Times: The Travail of the Protestant Establishment in America, 1900–1960*, edited by William R. Hutchison (Cambridge: Cambridge University Press, 1989); George Marsden, and Bradley Longfield, eds., *The Secularization of the Academy* (New York: Oxford University Press, 1992); James Tunstead Burtchaell, *The Dying of the Light: The Disengagement of Colleges and Universities from Their Christian Churches* (Grand Rapids, Mich.: Eerdmans, 1998); D. G. Hart, *The University Gets Religion: Religious Studies in American Higher Education* (Baltimore: Johns Hopkins University Press, 1999).

20. Bass, "Ministry on the Margin," 50.

21. "New York's Riverside," 1371.

22. *Riverside Church News Letter*, May 16, 1951; *Church Monthly*, September and November 1951.

23. *Church Monthly*, September 1953.

24. Fosdick, *The Living of These Days*, 271. Fosdick quotes Nobel Prize–winning physicist Arthur H. Compton, who asserted that "science has created a world in which Christianity is an imperative."

25. Bass, "Ministry on the Margin," 57–58.

26. Benevolence Committee Reports, May 1, 1936–April 30, 1937, RG 9.21; B. Carroll to Dr. King, Interoffice memo, August 5, 1948; B. Carroll to Dr. Tibbetts, Interoffice memo, August 15, 1948; B. Carroll to Mrs. Bailey, Interoffice memo,

October 19, 1948, Benevolence Committee records, RG 9.21, box 244, 1935–1972 A-
C, RCA.

27. At this time, New York University's main campus was uptown at 181st
Street and University Avenue, and it had a satellite campus downtown in Green-
wich Village, which has since become its sole site. City College, now part of the
City University of New York, is located at 138th Street and Convent Avenue.

28. C. D. King to Riverside Church, May 1951; Interoffice memo, May 3, 1951.
Declinations file, Benevolence Committee records, RG 9.21, box 238, RCA.

29. Morningside Heights, Inc., "Meeting of the Committee on Schools, Men's
Faculty Club," April 19, 1951, "Supplementary Program and Budget for PS 125 for
1951–1952." Benevolence Committee records, RG 9.21, box 239, RCA.

30. Morningside Heights, Inc., "Meeting of the Committee on Schools."

31. Morningside Heights, Inc., Minutes, Deanery, Barnard College, April 23,
1952. Benevolence Committee records, RG 9.21, box 239, RCA.

32. Play Schools Association, P.S. 125. Benevolence Committee records, RG 9.21,
box 239, RCA.

33. "Riverside Church Survey Report," 1956, 46–47.

34. Morningside Heights, Inc., "Meeting of the Committee on Schools."

35. Mrs. Margaret Shipherd, associate director, Morningside Heights, Inc., to
Carroll B. Fitch, October 30, 1959; Mrs. Theodore Dilday to Mr. Edward C.
Solomon, executive director, Morningside Heights, Inc., December 7, 1965; John V.
Butler to Mrs. Theodore Dilday, February 1, 1966; Morningside Heights, Inc., Press
release, December 12, 1952. Benevolence Committee records, RG 9.21, box 239,
RCA.

36. George J. Heidt to John D. Rockefeller Jr., May 12, 1938. Benevolence Committee records, Minutes and Budgets, Binder 1936–1974, RCA.

37. Report on the Riverside Church Benevolences, May 21, 1937. Benevolence
Committee records, Minutes and Budgets, Binder 1936–1974, RCA.

38. Benevolence Committee Reports, May 1, 1935–April 30, 1936; May 1,
1936–April 30, 1937; May 1, 1937–April 30, 1938. RG 9.21, RCA.

39. See Arthur W. Packard, "Benevolence Report," October 1935; and Benevolence Committee Reports, May 1, 1937–April 30, 1938, RG 9.21, RCA. The Packard
Report was commissioned to investigate ways of funding foreign missions in particular.

40. "Riverside Church Survey Report," 1956, 34.

41. Riverside Business and Professional Women's Club Historical Committee,
"In Celebration of Our Sixtieth Year, 1990," suppl., RCA; *Carillon*, February 19,
1959.

42. *Church Monthly*, March 1951.

43. Dr. Paul H. Sherry emphasized this aspect of Riverside's benevolence work
throughout his years of involvement with the church, arguing that the Benevolence Committee tended to support social service rather than social activist

groups. Interview with Paul H. Sherry by the Riverside Church History Project authors, June 8, 2000.

44. *Church Monthly*, March 1935.

45. Rex Pierce Butler to Katherine Miller Eddy, August 19, 1935; Hayden S. Sears to Ivar Hellstrom, May 6, 1936. Union Neighborhood Center file, Benevolence Committee records, RG 9.21, box 238, RCA.

46. Mrs. John A. Fitch, May 5, 1936. Union Neighborhood Center file, Benevolence Committee records, RG 9.21, box 238, RCA.

47. Hayden Swift Sears to Benevolence Committee, November 20, 1936. Union Neighborhood Center file, Benevolence Committee records, RG 9.21, box 238, RCA.

48. See Declinations file, Benevolence Committee records, RG 9.21, box 238, RCA.

49. Egbert Ethelred Brown to Riverside Church, November 25, 1941; Eugene Carder to Dr. Atwater, December 11, 1941. Declinations file, Benevolence Committee records, RG 9.21, box 238, RCA. On Brown and the Harlem Unitarian Church, see Juan Floyd-Thomas, "Creating a Temple and a Forum: Religion, Culture, and Politics in the Harlem Unitarian Church, 1920–1956" (Ph.D. diss., University of Pennsylvania, 2000).

50. Cathedral of St. John the Divine Senior Citizen Summer Program file, Benevolence Committee records, RG 9.21, box 251, RCA.

51. Church of the Open Door file, Benevolence Committee records, RG 9.21, box 244, RCA.

52. Notes on the Open Door," n.d., Church of the Open Door file, Benevolence Committee records, RG 9.21, box 244, RCA.

53. Florence Burnett to Robert W. Hudgens, February 17, 1958. Church of All Nations Neighborhood House file, Benevolence Committee records, RG 9.21, box 244, RCA.

54. "United West Side Parish" pamphlet, n.d., United West Side Parish file, Benevolence Committee records, RG 9.21, box 238, RCA.

55. Quoted in Dr. Eugene Laubach, "Historical Statement," June 1972, 2. Metropolitan Mission Study, RG 9.1, RCA.

56. For an extended discussion of McCracken's preaching on racial issues, see, for example, Robert J. McCracken, "Discrimination, the Shame of Sunday Morning," a sermon preached at Riverside Church on February 21, 1954; and chap. 2 of this book.

57. "Riverside Church Survey Report," 1956, 12–13.

58. Ibid., 12.

59. "Riverside Church Survey Report," 1956, 49; Morningside Heights, Inc., Press release, December 12, 1952. Benevolence Committee records, RG 9.21, box 239, RCA. The Morningside Gardens complex is located from 123d and 124th Streets between Broadway and Amsterdam Avenue. The Grant Houses border

125th Street from Broadway to Morningside Drive, with one section meeting Morningside Gardens at 124th Street and the other bordering Morningside Park at 123d Street.

60. Morningside Heights, Inc., Press release, December 12, 1952. Morningside Heights, Inc., file, Benevolence Committee records, RG 9.21, box 239, RCA.

61. *Riverside Church Summer Newsletter*, July 1956.

62. "Riverside Church Survey Report," 1956, 49.

63. Interview with Eugene Laubach by the Riverside Church History Project authors, June 8, 2000.

64. "Riverside Church Survey Report," 1956, 12.

65. Interview with Laubach.

66. Eugene E. Laubach, "Holiness and Hustle," sermon delivered at Riverside Church, November 1, 1964.

67. *Carillon*, April 2, 1959.

68. *Carillon*, November 19, 1959.

69. *Carillon*, August 18, 1960.

70. *Carillon*, March 16, 1961. The translation is my own.

71. See *Carillon*, May 21, 1969.

72. For a more detailed discussion of Forman, the Black Manifesto, and Riverside's response to it, see chap. 5. See also Robert S. Lecky and H. Elliott Wright, eds., *Black Manifesto: Religion, Racism, and Reparations* (New York, Sheed & Ward, 1969).

73. *Carillon*, October 24, 1970, and attached memorandum.

74. *Carillon*, December 19, 1970.

75. *Carillon*, June 5, July 10, and December 4, 1971.

76. *New York Times*, January 2, 1972.

77. *Carillon*, March 2, 1984.

78. *News-Times* (Danbury, Conn.), May 18, 1998.

79. See *Carillon*, June 6 and July 18, 1969, and March 6, 1970. For more on the Black Christian Caucus, New Priorities, and GRIPS, see chap. 5.

80. Robert L. Polk, Paper for Metropolitan Mission Study, n.d., Metropolitan Mission Study, RG 9.1, RCA.

81. "Report on the Think Tank on Urban Ministry," Meeting at "Grey Dunes," Long Island, Friday, March 18, to Sunday, March 20, 1972. Metropolitan Mission Study, RG 9.1, RCA.

82. *Carillon*, March 28 and April 20, 1974.

83. *Carillon*, February 5, 1972, and June 9, 1973.

84. *Carillon*, January 31 and May 18, 1974.

85. Charles G. Peterson to Mr. Francis Fisher, January 27, 1977. Benevolence Form Letters file, Benevolence Committee records, RG 9.21, box 251, RCA.

86. Benevolence Committee, Minutes file, March 26, 1971; Benevolence Committee records, RG 9.21, box 249, RCA.

87. Benevolence Committee Minutes file, May 25 and June 7, 1971. Benevolence Committee records, RG 9.21, box 249; Memorandum from Benevolence Committee to Board of Trustees, October 2, 1972; Benevolence Committee–Steering Committee file, Benevolence Committee records, RG 9.21; Mrs. Elinor Kajiwara to Mrs. Mifaunwy Shunatona Hines, June 24, 1974; Densford Fund, Riverside Church, September 1977; American Indian Community House file, Benevolence Committee records, RG 9.21, box 251; "Benevolence Committee Appropriations in 1976," Benevolence Form Letters file, Benevolence Committee records, RG 9.21, box 251, RCA.

88. "Guidelines and Factors to Be Reviewed in Evaluating Requests for Funds" (draft, for discussion only), February 28, 1972. Benevolence Committee–Steering Committee file, Benevolence Committee records, RG 9.21, box 259, RCA.

89. Tabia Korjus to Rev. Robert L. Polk, February 9, 1970. Riverside Fund for Social Justice Task Force Report file, Benevolence Committee records, RG 9.21, box 239, RCA.

90. *Carillon*, March 6, 1970; Riverside Fund for Social Justice, "A Report to the Members of the Riverside Church," February 6, 1970; Riverside Fund for Social Justice Task Force Report file, Benevolence Committee records, RG 9.21, box 239, RCA; *Carillon*, May 1, 1970; March 4 and 25, 1972; and July 10, 1973; *New York Times*, April 9, 1972.

91. "Riverside Church Survey Report," 1956, 53, 74; *New York Herald Tribune*, July 23, 1960; see interview with John D. Summerfield by Burt Harrison, July 27, 1978; National Public Broadcasting Archives, Special Collections Department, University of Maryland Libraries.

92. *New York Times*, August 24, 1960; "Facts about Riverside Radio WRVR," *Christian Broadcaster*, January–April 1961.

93. *Carillon*, July 6, 1971.

94. Jack D. Summerfield, "Riverside Radio WRVR: Purpose and Direction," n.d., History and Miscellaneous file, WRVR records, RG 6.5, box 109, RCA.

95. *Broadcasting*, January 23, 1961; *Carillon*, December 8, 1960.

96. See interview with Summerfield.

97. "WRVR Audience Survey," 104; "La Voz Hispana de Riverside," n.d., History and Miscellaneous file, WRVR records, RG 6.5, box 109, RCA.

98. See "1969 Audience Survey," 104. History and Miscellaneous file, WRVR records, RG 6.5, box 109, RCA.

99. See interview with Summerfield.

100. See "1969 Audience Survey," 104. History and Miscellaneous file, WRVR records, RG 6.5, box 109, RCA.

101. Harry Emerson Fosdick, n.d., History and Miscellaneous file, WRVR records, RG 6.5, box 109, RCA.

102. *WRVR Fine Arts Guide*, January and April 1961.

103. *Carillon*, July 30, 1963, March 26, 1965, and February 7, 1969.

104. *Carillon*, January 30, 1970.

105. Paul H. Sherry, personal correspondence with me, March 15, 2001. *Carillon*, November 11, 1972.

106. "A Statement of Policy for the FM-Radio Station, with Special Comments concerning Programming," January 1960, History and Miscellaneous file, WRVR records, RG 6.5, box 109, RCA.

107. "On Giving the Public What It Wants (Suggested by the F.C.C. Television Hearings)," sermon by Rev. Robert J. McCracken, minister of Riverside Church, February 11, 1962. History and Miscellaneous file, WRVR records, RG 6.5, box 109, RCA.

108. Jack D. Summerfield, "Riverside Radio WRVR: Purpose and Direction," n.d., History and Miscellaneous file, WRVR records, RG 6.5, box 109, RCA.

109. *Carillon*, February 5, 1966.

110. Charles Blum to WRVR, August 16, 1962. The "Portion of the Week" presentation on WRVR included the Torah reading, as in synagogue, along with rabbinic commentary by "spiritual leaders in the Metropolitan NY Area." The commentaries were provided by rabbis from Orthodox and Conservative congregations in New York and New Jersey. Press release, n.d., History and Miscellaneous file, WRVR records, RG 6.5, box 109, RCA.

111. Press release for broadcast of "We Shall Overcome: An Affirmation of Freedom," n.d., History and Miscellaneous file, WRVR records, RG 6.5, box 109, RCA.

112. For a detailed description of the series, see David Cort, "The Voices of Birmingham," *The Nation*, July 27, 1963.

113. *New York Herald Tribune*, June 16, 1963. See also *Saturday Review*, June 20, 1963; *Variety*, June 12, 1963.

114. *Carillon*, May 9, 1969.

115. See the listings of WRVR programs in the *Carillon* throughout the fall of 1965.

116. *Carillon*, July 24, 1970.

117. *Carillon*, May 15, 1970.

118. *Carillon*, March 27, 1970; Ronald E. Johnson, "Report on WRVR Communications Trainee Program for 1969–1960," n.d., History and Miscellaneous file, WRVR records, RG 6.5, box 109, RCA.

119. "Special Communication to the Congregation," *Carillon*, May 16, 1969; "Riverside's Recent Strawberry Festival Airs Congregation's Feelings," *Carillon*, May 30, 1969.

120. *Carillon*, October 17 and November 14, 1969.

121. "WRVR Background," Metropolitan Mission Study, RG 9.1, RCA; *Carillon*, November 21, 1969, and February 21, 1971.

122. *Carillon*, July 19, 1968, and July 6, 1971.

123. *Village Voice*, March 7, 1974.

124. Efrain Aviles to John Wicklein, August 14, 1972. WRVR records, RG 6.5 box 285, RSC.

125. On Powell, see *New York Times*, August 13, 1972.

126. Helen Kruger, *Village Voice*, March 7, 1974.

127. Paul Sherry felt strongly that the station's mission never diverged from that of the church but that Riverside's more theologically conservative members did not understand this approach to outreach. Eugene Laubach, however, agreed with those who thought that the radio station's management no longer sought to fulfill the church's mission. Looking back on the period that preceded the sale of the license, station personnel Walter P. Sheppard and Martha Sheppard were rather scornful of Riverside and its members, viewing the congregation as more interested in turning a profit than in sponsoring a progressive radio station. Interview with Paul H. Sherry with the Riverside Church History Project authors, June 8, 2000. Dr. Eugene Laubach, "Historical Statement," June 1972; interview with Walter P. and Martha Sheppard by Burt Harrison, October 13, 1978, National Public Broadcasting Archives, Special Collections Department, University of Maryland Libraries.

128. Years later, guitarist Al DiMeola reflected on the demise of WRVR: "I was driving down the Palisades Parkway one day . . . turned on the jazz station WRVR and Dolly Parton was on. I started switching the dial, thinking I wasn't tuned in right. The DJ came on and said with enthusiasm 'That was Dolly Parton and next we're gonna have Tex Ritter!' I pulled over and called the station. They put me through to the booth and my friend there said 'Al, I can't talk now. I'll call you in a couple of hours.' Everybody was calling the house; it was like Black Sunday. He called that night. 'It was awful: A semi trailer truck pulled up at 10 in the morning and they told us that we're changing to country music. Whoever stays will get a raise. A couple of us left, but some of us had nowhere to go.' I said, 'At least tell the people who've been listening all these years that you've made a change. You're freaking people out.' 'We're not allowed to mention anything about it.' That was the beginning of the end here in New York, the death of the progressive period and transformation of jazz to an easy-listening format; what followed were many years without a progressive jazz station." See *Musician*, July 1992.

129. *Carillon*, September 6, 1975, November 12, 1976, and January 28, 1977.

130. Rob Crocker, the station's popular jazz DJ, continued to work as a DJ in New York City after his dismissal from WRVR and moved to Tokyo in the 1990s to continue his work as a jazz DJ. Robert Siegel, who has been a major figure in the development of National Public Radio (NPR), was a reporter, host, and director of news and public affairs at WRVR from 1971 until 1976. His career at NPR has included working as senior editor in its London bureau and as general public affairs editor, serving as director of the News and Information Department and hosting its *Weekend Edition* news program. Walter Sheppard went on to become manager

and later vice-president of programming for WITF-FM and TV in Hershey, Pennsylvania.

131. *Carillon*, April 27, 1979.

132. Interview with Coffin by Riverside Church History Project authors.

133. See, for example, *Carillon*, January 28, 1980.

134. *Carillon*, November 4, 1983.

135. *Carillon*, June 30, 1983. Interview with Emmett Montalvo, Riverside Food Pantry Coordinator by me and Lawrence Mamiya, June 27, 2000.

136. Interview with Coffin.

137. *Carillon*, January 13 and April 6, 1984, and February 1995. Interview with Norma Rolon, assistant director of social services, Riverside Church, by me and Lawrence Mamiya, June 30, 2000.

138. Interview with Coffin.

139. See *Carillon*, February 15, 1979, June 11, 1980, and September 29, 1980.

140. *Carillon*, November 29, 1980, and February 27, 1981.

141. *Carillon*, September 29, 1981.

142. *Carillon*, March 30, 1982.

143. *Carillon*, March 2, 1984.

144. Answering a question about his goals for diversity at Riverside in the twenty-first century—particularly with regard to Hispanic and Asian New Yorkers—James Forbes argued that relations between black and white Riversiders must take precedence and that until these issues are resolved, the congregation cannot move on to think about diversity in broader ways with any productive results. "Getting to the second semester of Calculus is hard if calculus is about to kick your butt," he said, using the comparison to indicate the work he felt was still ahead with regard to African Americans and whites at Riverside. Interview with Forbes by Riverside Church History Project authors.

145. http://www.theriversidechurchny.org, September 6, 2001.

146. *Carillon*, April 16, 1985.

147. *Carillon*, April 10, 1978.

148. *Carillon*, September 2, 1978.

149. *Carillon*, September 1, 1979, October 15, 1981, and December 9, 1982.

150. *Carillon*, January 11, 1985.

151. *Carillon*, March 11, 1985.

152. *Denver Post*, July 20, 1996. Forbes also appeared in *All God's Children* (1996), a documentary exploring the often difficult relationships between lesbian and gay African Americans and their churches.

153. *Carillon*, February 1986; Interview with Forbes.

154. See, for example, *Carillon*, October 1987.

155. Interview with Forbes; *Carillon*, October 1991.

156. Interview with Forbes.

157. *Carillon*, January 1992.

158. http://www.theriversidechurchny.org, July 16, 2001. See also, for example, *Carillon*, January/February 2001.

159. Interview with Rolon.

160. http://www.theriversidechurchny.org, July 16, 2001; interview with Rolon. See also, for example, *Carillon*, January/February 2001.

161. The Riverside Church Thrift Shop, "Pricing List," n.d.

162. http://www.theriversidechurchny.org, July 16, 2001.

163. See Riverside Church Budget and Planning Committee, "Jubilee Five-Year Plan for the New Millennium," draft 4, April 16, 2000.

164. *New York Times*, October 18, 1929; *New York Times*, February 26, 1962.

165. Interview with Forbes; *New York Times*, January 14, 1990.

166. Sheryl McCarthy, *New York Times*, November 8, 1993.

167. *New York Times*, March 6, 2000, and *New York Times*, August 20, 2001; *Amsterdam News*, January 14, 1999.

168. *New York Newsday*, August 29, 1996.

169. *New York Newsday*, November 1, 1998.

170. The service was broadcast live on PBS stations and rebroadcast many times in subsequent weeks.

171. On Rebbe Nachman, see, for example, Chaim Kramer, *Crossing the Narrow Bridge: A Practical Guide to Rebbe Nachman's Teachings* (Jerusalem: Breslov Research Institute, 1989).

5

The Public Witness of the Riverside Church

An Ethical Assessment

Peter J. Paris

It is very easy for liberal-minded Christians to fall in love with the Riverside Church because few churches in the world offer such a dynamic combination of architectural splendor, diverse membership, prophetic preaching, meaningful programs, ecumenical spirit, aesthetic creativity, and courageous action as does this twentieth-century phenomenon in the heart of New York City. From the beginning, this church has viewed its life and mission as a public enterprise.[1] In contrast to the parochial aims of most congregations, Riverside's mission has always been to reach beyond its own walls to serve the needs of a broader humanity. Its early motto of being interdenominational, interracial, and international rapidly distinguished it from all other congregations in the city. Its liberal theology, progressive teaching, and courageous activities combined to make it a public church that took pride in being free from every heteronomy, whether religious or otherwise.

Such a public enterprise implied no radical separation between the church's internal life and its external witness. Hence, it was hoped that its members' spirituality would be manifested in the daily activities of their various workplaces and the many and varied social services of the church itself. In short, Riverside has consistently been outward in its orientation and has always measured its spiritual life by its public mission. Thus, it has tended to view all its activities as contributing directly or indirectly to its public mission of making the world a better place.

First and foremost, Riverside's motto has always functioned as a beacon welcoming the creation of enduring spaces for the exercise of freedom and tolerance. Over the past decades it has developed and nurtured an environment that has been increasingly interethnic, interclass, gender inclusive, and intercultural. Those combined qualities were rare elements in American Protestantism during the first half of the twentieth century. It would remain to be seen how such a church, sheltered and distinguished by its symbols of wealth and influence, would be able to express all aspects of its motto in its congregational life. Gradually and, at times painfully, the diversity of its membership presented many challenges. By recognizing itself as a microcosm of the larger public arena, the church resolved from time to time in the midst of considerable conflict to make appropriate modifications in its lifestyle so as to create the necessary conditions for doing justice and expressing love and goodwill toward all its peoples.

Since its beginning Riverside has been in the vanguard in creating public spaces for the spiritual development, educational enlightenment, and moral formation of children, youth, men, women, seniors, gays, and lesbians. In addition, it has encouraged the development of programs in the arts, athletics, social services, neighborhood relations, and coalitions for various forms of social justice advocacy. In each of these programs, participants have had to discern and accept their responsibility for a broader humanity.

Riverside also has created public spaces for the study and discussion of various social issues through the sponsorship of conferences, consultations, rallies, lectures, and plays. Similarly, the church has created public spaces by allowing its facilities to be used by community groups, institutions, and many others promoting causes commensurate with its public mission. In close alliance with these ventures, the church also has created public spaces to celebrate the numerous moral and political struggles that it embraces and blesses as well as public spaces for its own worship life, including many ecumenical and interreligious celebrations.[2] It also continues to provide space for the nurture and development of several diverse worshiping communities.

Origins

Undoubtedly, Riverside's mission was determined in large part by its founders, Harry Emerson Fosdick and John D. Rockefeller Jr. United by their common spiritual vision, both believed that the church's teaching and mission could and should be harmonized with contemporary thought

FIGURE 5.1:   The Riverside Church supports gay and lesbian rights. *Photograph by John Frederick Herrold © 1998. Used by permission of the Riverside Church Archives and the photographer.*

in general and especially with modern science. In fact, both believed that scientific methods should be applied to all dimensions of the Christian faith, including the Bible itself. Most important, they both embraced the cardinal moral principles of liberalism: the inviolability of the individual person; freedom of thought; personal liberty; toleration of religious differences; benevolence toward the poor; and moral and social progress through education, international peace, and improved race relations.

Even a casual observer quickly discerns that the Riverside Church has not departed very far from the vision of its founders, who hoped that it would be cathedral-like in its life and mission, unique in its architecture, aesthetic in its liturgy, glorious in its music, persuasive in its preaching, faithful in its benevolence, and pace setting in its ministry. Each new generation of leaders has reconfirmed that hope. Consequently, as must have become clear by now to the readers of this book, the Riverside Church continues to be a strong prophetic presence in the city of New York and beyond.

Conceived in the optimism of the mid-1920s, the Riverside Church was destined to spend its first decade in the gloom of the Depression, the greatest economic crisis that the nation had ever experienced. Ironically, this amazing architectural symbol of wealth and beauty was dedicated to the glory of God on a cold, windy day in February 1931. Reports state that more than six thousand people gathered to celebrate this spectacular achievement and to pray for God's blessing on a sacred mission undertaken by a transplanted congregation bent on rooting itself firmly in the environs of Manhattan's upper west side. Even so, Harry Emerson Fosdick is remembered as having said while it was being built that whether or not the church would be wonderful was not yet settled. "It depends on what we do with it."

Although little thought seems to have been given at the time to the generation of new ideas concerning the church's program in its new location, none doubted that preaching and worship would remain central to the congregation's life. While it was assumed that many of the programs of the Park Avenue Baptist Church would be continued in the new location, it was obvious that the size of the new building demanded a major recruitment endeavor whose success would inevitably lead to a corresponding development of new programs designed to meet the needs of the newly enlarged congregation.

As indicated earlier, this congregation had been nurtured for more than a generation in an ethos that discerned no radical opposition between Christianity and modern culture. Contrary to the sensitivities and beliefs of the earlier Protestant orthodoxy, this liberal viewpoint implied a synthetic relationship between religion and culture. The new theology being institutionalized in the Riverside Church, however, was revealed in the following concrete ways: (1) a sculptured iconography in the chancel comprising ancient and modern Jewish, Christian, and humanist figures; (2) twenty-two floors of office and meeting rooms in the Tower and two underground floors equipped with a gymnasium, bowling alleys, a theater, and an auditorium; and (3) multiple ministries organized in accordance with the church's functional principles. Riverside organized its ministries similarly to those of the nineteenth- and early-twentieth-century so-called institutional churches. Programs were sponsored seven days a week in the mornings, afternoons, and evenings to serve the needs of the neighborhood and the larger city.[3]

Even though most of its former Park Avenue Baptist members lived in the Morningside Heights area, the Riverside Church was a newcomer to the neighborhood in 1930. Like all new arrivals, its first action was to plant roots in the community and to make a home for itself in the renowned academic, religious, and social institutions that were its immediate neighbors. Those neighbors included Columbia University, Barnard College, Jewish Theological Seminary, Teachers College, Union Theological Seminary, International House, St. Luke's Hospital, the Cathedral of St. John the Divine, and Riverside quickly welcomed their participation in its worship services and other programs.

As has been previously discussed, Riverside has always been troubled by the social and economic distance between its own membership and the impoverished poor at its southern and northern borders. That concern was heightened after the Depression and even more after the World War II when the area's changing residential patterns resulted in the migration of many poor and working-class families into the Morningside Heights area.

Having moved far uptown in advance of the rapidly expanding commercial and industrial interests of midtown at Fifth Avenue to the solidly middle- and upper-income environment of Morningside Heights, the church thought that it had found at last a permanent location in a stable environment. As predicted, its membership grew rapidly, with large numbers of professionals, teachers, students, and many connected with the arts joining the church.

Interestingly, however, the Riverside Church failed to attract either the very wealthy or manual workers. It is possible that the very wealthy sought other alternatives in churches that were not as progressive as the Riverside Church on social issues. For example, Fosdick was an outspoken pacifist, a position that many could not embrace, especially following the Japanese attack on Pearl Harbor. Whereas working-class people in Roman Catholic churches are not intimidated by cathedral-like edifices, the Protestant pattern of residential churches ensures racial and class homogeneity, both of which discourage working-class people from attending churches outside their residential neighborhoods.

Responding to Human Needs

From the beginning, the Riverside Church has searched for adequate expressions of its faith in its programs. Its readiness to respond to human needs has always been a primary concern. During the Depression it started a cooperative program with the state's employment service to help meet the needs of the unemployed. Through women's volunteer services, hundreds of people were interviewed and channeled into jobs provided by the church membership. The newly formed Charity Organization Society located the jobs and matched them with the applicants. Similarly, a sewing workshop was started which paid women three dollars a day and prepared them for work outside the church. The church also organized an arts and crafts program to help people learn skills that would help them find jobs. Similarly, it organized a symphony orchestra to provide an income for unemployed artists. These activities marked the beginning of the church's Social Service Committee.

The demographic features of the Morningside-Manhattanville community began changing rather abruptly in the early 1940s owing to the exodus of middle-class and professional families who had been associated with the community's various institutions. Many of the former homes of these suburban-bound residents were divided into multiple single and family units that were rented mainly to low-income African Americans and Puerto Ricans. Thus, the number of racial and ethnic minorities in the area increased between 1940 and 1950 at a much higher rate than did that of either Manhattan or the city as a whole. With incredible speed, unscrupulous landlords hastened the transformation of a middle-class community into a densely populated slum.

After World War II, Riverside participated in the rehabilitation effort in Europe through its Fund for World Service. More than anything else, its involvement in the overseas program inspired some of its members to begin looking at the needs of the poor closer to home. In fact, the immense impoverishment evident in all parts of Harlem implied the need for a major domestic rehabilitation program, which led, as we have seen, to Riverside's involvement with Morningside Heights, Inc., for the purpose of "developing a balanced community."

The following year, 1948, the church joined its neighbor institutions in organizing the Manhattanville Neighborhood Center. These nascent organizations gave the church some limited access to the world of the urban poor. In 1946, the year of his retirement, Dr. Fosdick founded and served as president of the interracial board of the Manhattanville Neighborhood Center. Its effectiveness eventually led to its becoming the Manhattanville Community Centers, Inc.

Clearly, the Riverside Church welcomed the opportunity to address the needs of the poor in its community. But the only way it knew how to render that service was to join others of like mind in what is viewed as "char-

itable paternalism." In what the church unwittingly labeled as benevolence, charity, social service, and community development, the poor themselves were conspicuously absent from all the decision-making processes
affecting their life and destiny. From the church's perspective, however,
this type of "charitable paternalism" encouraged its members to demonstrate their discipleship by becoming personally involved in a variety of
voluntary services to the community.

The Riverside Church's Committee on Christian Service was organized
in 1956. Volunteers were recruited, trained for specific functions, and sent
to their respective areas of service in the community at large. Liaisons
were organized between the church and the outside agencies requesting
assistance, and periodically follow-up work was performed. In its recruitment, the committee sent information to new staff members of Columbia
University, Barnard College, and City College as well as the General Grant
Homes inviting them to affiliate with the church.

The committee also worked closely with various existing organizations
in the church whose primary functions were the provision of certain community services, like the Business and Professional Women's Club,
Women's Society, Guild, Men's Class, and Parents Fellowship, as well as
with groups organized for specific services such as the choir, Christian education, Zone Organization, Every Member Canvass, and the ushers. Each
of these groups and organizations provided opportunities for individuals
to offer Christian service in both the church and the community, such as
the Morningside Community Center, General Grant Houses, Baptist
Home for the Aged, and the new Garment Guild. For reasons that are not
completely clear, the Christian Service Committee changed its name on
November 14, 1960, to the Volunteer Service Committee.

Riverside's community service programs were enhanced by the opportunities offered by the nascent Interchurch Center, whose dedication
Riverside hosted on May 29, 1960. Many of the clergy and laity on the staff
of the Interchurch Center soon became members of the Riverside Church,
and in time, several were elected to its official boards.

In 1968 the chair of the church's Long-Range Planning Committee reit-
erated the church's social mission as a lay-training program to help people
express their faith in their daily living. In his report he wrote:

> It is my conviction that the purpose of the church is to be a center of re-
> source and of enabling experience for lay people in terms of their lives in
> the world. This is based, of course, in the conviction that the lay people are

the church, and that their ministry is in the world rather than in the church as an institution. The church is seen as the matrix for training persons, enabling and equipping them for their living. In this respect, Riverside offers a magnificent opportunity for such help. There is a richness in the cultural "mix" which replicates the world more nearly than most churches. There is a breadth of program which enables a person to find many avenues of approach.[4]

The report acknowledged the dependence of the church's social mission on two interpretative images of the Riverside Church, of "cathedral" and "parish." The report contended that the Riverside Church functioned like a cathedral for those who, though widely dispersed round the city and beyond, were attracted by specific purposes and programs. Yet, it also functioned like a parish for many others who lived nearby and had needs that the church could satisfy.[5] Further and most important, the report concluded that Riverside should synthesize both the cathedral and parish images and not sacrifice either for the other. In fact, the report claimed that the church's cathedral function was a necessary condition for the parish functions because it provided basic leadership and material resources. Thus, the report viewed both functions as necessary. That conclusion led the report to claim a need for balancing the church's membership between those who could serve and those who needed the services. Such a perspective symbolized the desire for a membership that would comprise some mixture of the city's social and economic classes. The paternalism implied in that understanding, which soon sparked various degrees of internal conflict within the church itself, was apparently not yet recognized.

The Decision-Making Process at Riverside

For all controversial issues at Riverside, the church long used the method that Dr. Fosdick had proposed many decades earlier. In 1946 Fosdick proposed in a lecture the following strategy for what Riverside should do when it could not agree on a subject: "Have lots of sermons on it, lots of discussions and church group statements; then together work out a congregational statement on it."[6] The church used this method effectively on several occasions, including the conflict over issues pertaining to the Black Manifesto, sexual orientation, and disarmament.

Whether or not he was oblivious to Fosdick's teaching on resolving conflicts, the Reverend Dwight C. Smith, chair of the Morningside Renewal Council and a member of the Riverside Church, wrote an open letter in March 1968 to the members of the church entitled "A Request to the Trustees and Deacons of the Riverside Church." In the letter he chided the church for not having a formal process by which the church could address social issues. He reminded the church of the embarrassment of many of its members because it had no mechanism by which it could express its public endorsement of the 1964 Civil Rights Act.

> The logical inference of our enforced silence as a church was that while we would allow our Minister to speak with eloquence and passion about this issue so closely related to human dignity we must abstain as a church from expressing any support for this specific application of the Christian gospel to an immediate issue.
>
> . . . Before extending a call to any man we owe it to him as well as to ourselves to make certain that we can give enthusiastic and public expression of approval as he points ways in which our Christian convictions may be declared in current and urgent issues. Otherwise, we shall, in effect, say to the man we call, "Brother, we want you to preach with prophetic power, while we promise that we will never as a church, utter one word of support for the things you advocate." I submit that to be thus gagged as a church is both unthinkable and intolerable. The situation cries out for a rational and urgent solution.[7]

Smith's letter reminded the church of its responsibility to its neighborhood when residents were being steadily evicted from their homes in order to give Columbia University space for its own institutional expansion. He asked, "Who determines whether, and how the church's right hand shall know what its left hand is doing, and whether the church's influence among those who live in its close vicinity is to be that of a good neighbor or a bad neighbor?"[8]

As implied earlier, it is ironic that the church should discover a dilemma regarding its two principal concerns: its responsibility for the African Americans, Puerto Ricans, and Asians who were gradually replacing the former middle-class white residents in the neighborhood;[9] and its complicity with Columbia University's policies, which was based on its interest in maintaining a close relationship with the university. That dilemma became clear at midcentury when the university's plans for expansion led to the eviction of many poor people in the area because of the continuous razing of tenement buildings. Although the Morningside Tenants Committee joined other community organizations to try to force the university to be more respectful of the poor and to devise more creative policies that would meet its needs while preserving and improving the neighborhood, the Riverside Church played only a small role in the conflict. By doing so, it demonstrated that it felt a greater kinship with the university and its educational interests than it did with the housing needs of the poor ethnic and racial minorities who were being forced to leave the community. Clearly, both the church and the university cherished their reciprocal relationship, one that was highly praised as early as 1951 by the vice-provost in his address that year at the "church family dinner." Rather than risk embarrassing the university by taking a public stand on the conflict, the church seemed to take refuge in its mission of helping prepare men and women to apply their individual faith to their responsibilities as citizens.

The church's lack of deliberate engagement in such a major transformation of Morningside Heights greatly reduced the depth of its identification with the neighborhood despite the various social services it continued to provide. The many changes in the area during the first twenty-five years of the church's presence there increased at an exponential rate during the 1940s and 1950s.[10]

Reportedly, many people viewed the basic problem underlying the conflict as one of class prejudice rather than racial prejudice. Although it is difficult to separate the two completely, many of the opponents to the university's policies felt that the majority of whites at the university were not opposed to living in a racially integrated area. Rather, they objected to living in close proximity to the poor, regardless of their race or ethnicity.

No observer could fail to notice the great cultural divide between the members of the Riverside Church and the poor residents of Morningside Heights. Despite the church's rhetorical commitment to welcome all people regardless of their economic, denominational, racial, or national status, the class difference was obvious to all visitors at the Sunday worship services, as evidenced in the ushers greeting them in formal morning dress. In fact, concerning the ushers' dress, the church's self-study of January 20, 1968, stated the following:

The Board is weighted in favor of retaining cutaway coats and have resisted many attempts to change. But many new men on the Board do not own these and cannot serve on the main floor. A decision about this has been long overdue; and depending on its direction the composition of the Board might be expected to shift.[11]

Both Fosdick and McCracken approved of the formal dress code because they saw it as adding dignity to the worship service. Ironically, the debate over the ushers' attire occurred nearly a decade after the formation of the Committee on Social Service, whose aim was to persuade all its neighbors to consider affiliating with the church. In order to provide a more welcoming atmosphere, the Committee on Hospitality to Visitors made plans to greet a large number of summer visitors to the church. In order to make the so-called colored people feel welcome, the committee considered having a "Negro" placed in the narthex to help with that part of the program. From the vantage point of hindsight, we can now see the obvious conflicts between the church's internal cultural life and its outreach to the poor.

Although the Riverside Church played only a small role in the Morningside Heights urban renewal conflict, it did express itself rather clearly on a number of other social issues. For example, in 1965 the board of deacons requested the Council on Christian Social Relations to study the issue of capital punishment in the state of New York and to make recommendations to the board and the members of the church. Accordingly, the *Carillon* carried the following report:

> After consideration the council passed a resolution, to be sent to the state officials, urging the abolition of capital punishment in New York state. The council also expressed its concern that members and friends of the Riverside Church write now to their elected officials, expressing their personal convictions on the matter.[12]

The church's response to this and many other issues clearly indicated both then and now its greater openness to collective protest action on issues that were somewhat removed from its own neighborhood. In addition to the various institutions, programs, and ministries that the church has supported consistently through its annual benevolences, it also has sponsored numerous educational programs on a broad range of moral issues. In fact, the annual calendar of church events is overwhelming in its multiplicity of activities.

As described elsewhere, Riverside's acknowledgment of being a part of the progressive liberal Christian tradition has been expressed clearly over the years in its benevolence program. In 1947 the church joined other churches across the country in an effort to relieve suffering and restore conditions for a Christian mission worldwide. The Riverside Fund for World Service was established for that purpose, and annual allocations were made to assist various kinds of Christian service throughout the world. In 1950 its name was changed to the Riverside Fund to Help Build a Christian World, thus signaling its embrace of the central aim of the Social Gospel movement in America, namely, of helping build a Christian world. From the earliest days until the present, the Benevolence Committee has undertaken financial drives to raise money for widespread distribution in support of causes in the city, nation, and the world at large.

Although the church did not have a congregational mechanism for taking controversial stands on public issues, certain parts of the church did express themselves from time to time on a number of public issues. Foremost among these was the powerful Men's Class, which issued several political resolutions either supporting or opposing specific social policies. These were made without consulting the board of deacons and were sent directly to mayors, U.S. representatives, senators, and the like on behalf of the Men's Class on such issues as supporting an emergency increase in immigration (1947 and 1952), supporting the Marshall Plan (1948), supporting the World Health Organization (1949), supporting aid to migrant workers (1959), supporting legislation to reduce narcotics availability and addiction (1960), opposing aid to parochial or church-related schools (1960), supporting the expansion of foreign aid (1960, 1961), supporting the removal of all racial restrictions from immigration and nationality laws, supporting compensation for losses sustained by Japanese Americans during their forced evacuation from the West Coast, and supporting Federal Support of the Arts (1963). Even though the Men's Class did not formally speak for the church as a whole, its members represented some of the city's most socially distinguished and politically influential persons. An analysis of the Men's Class's resolutions, however, reveals positions commensurate with the consensus of most liberal-minded citizens on the issues addressed.

It was not until the mid-1970s that the church found a way for significant numbers of its members to make public statements short of official

FIGURE 5.2: March against police brutality on
the Brooklyn Bridge. *Used by permission of the
Riverside Church Archives.*

acts of the church per se. In fact, its model was what had been used in the
past by various groups in the church. From time to time, those groups, like
the Men's Class, had issued statements expressing their particular view-
points on certain issues. But the act of getting ad hoc groups of members
and friends to do so was new.

Following the Palm Sunday service in May 1977, a letter was signed by
three hundred members and friends of the church and sent to President
Jimmy Carter praising him for his stand on human rights and urging him
to press for their protection wherever they were violated.

We, the undersigned, members and friends of the Riverside church, New York city, want you to know that as Christians we applaud and intend to support in anyway we can the strong stand you have taken on human rights.

We believe that in emphasizing this issue in relation to other political negotiations you are assuring us and the total global community that the original principles upon which our nation was founded are still the basic principles determining your leadership and the actions of your administration. For this we are profoundly grateful.[13]

The Riverside Church and Racial Justice

As just discussed, the combination of powerful social, economic, and political forces significantly changed the basic composition of the Morningside Heights neighborhood. The policies of expansion by the various existing institutions (including the Riverside Church), coupled with their tacit approval of the plan to concentrate racial and ethnic minorities in low-income public-housing units, gradually attracted more professional people to the area. Riverside's mission of offering an array of religious and social services for the whole neighborhood enabled many of its members to interact with racial and ethnic minorities for the first time in their lives. Riverside soon became adept at providing the necessary training and organization for such a ministry. Thus the church soon found itself offering one sort of ministry to the academic communities in its midst and another type to the many newcomers to the neighborhood occupying the General Grant Houses, Morningside Gardens, and Manhattanville Houses and working in the various institutions. In fact, the newly constructed housing units soon became the locus for a major concentration of social services provided by the various institutions in the area and especially by the Riverside Church. As has been mentioned, the addition of Robert Polk and Pablo Cotto in 1960 as senior pastors signaled Riverside's commitment to a ministry offering social services to the African American and Puerto Rican communities in its midst.

Polk and Cotto represented the church's administrative and pastoral vanguards in race relations. Their social ministries did more than anything else to educate the church about the problems and concerns of the African American and Puerto Rican communities in New York. Distinguished African American preachers began appearing with greater frequency as guests in Riverside's summer preaching series, including Gardner Taylor, senior minister of the Concord Baptist Church of Christ in Brooklyn and president of the Protestant Council of the City of New York; Martin Luther King Jr.; and James H. Robinson, minister of Morningside Heights Presbyterian Church and founder of the Operation Crossroads Program. Further, Ossie Davis's play *Purlie Victorious* premiered in 1961 in the theater at Riverside, and in 1966 Thurgood Marshall received the distinguished Charles Evans Hughes Award at the Men's Class's sixty-ninth annual dinner. Undoubtedly, these events legitimized the African American leadership in the Riverside Church.

On April 29, 1962, the renovated Stone Gymnasium was dedicated to the service of the community's youth. As time went on, it became clear that a high percentage of those who attended Sunday school, the weekday nursery and kindergarten programs, and the athletics program were from nonmember families living in the neighborhood. Clearly, Polk's work as youth director was enormously important in promoting the church's expanded ministry to African Americans. He himself started the renowned athletic program and inspired Ernest Lorch to become its esteemed athletic director.[14] Through its sports program and other community services, the church soon demonstrated a spirit of friendliness toward the racial and ethnic minorities in its midst.

In concert with the spirit of his predecessors, the senior minister, Ernest Campbell, led his congregation to take a stand in the nation's struggle for racial justice. He quickly translated his preaching and teaching into commensurate practices of societal reform both inside and outside the church. By doing so Campbell declared that for the first time Riverside was taking history seriously, and it became evident in his ministry.

In the spring of 1970 Campbell initiated a series of Lenten programs in the form of five open conversations with experts in a variety of fields on subjects relevant to the church's ministry. His conversational partners included the following prophetic figures: Dr. Otis Maxwell, director of training for the American Foundation of Religion and Psychiatry, who focused on the needs of the total person; Dr. Milton A. Galamison, former vice-president of the New York City Board of Education, on the current state of public education; Dr. Gayraud Wilmore Jr., chair of the Division of Church and Race of the United Presbyterian Church USA, on race relations; Edward J. Logue, president of the New York State Urban Development Corporation, on housing problems and their solutions; and Dr.

Richard R. Gilbert, executive director of the Division of Mass Media of the Board of National Missions, United Presbyterian Church, U.S.A., on mass media opportunities for the church. Each of those conversations was open to the public and also aired on WRVR. In short, they demonstrated Campbell's commitment to relating the church to the racial struggles of the day.

The Black Christian Caucus

In response to the impact of the black power movement on African Americans in predominantly white institutions, the organization of a black caucus at Riverside began in February 1969. Nearly sixty African American members seized the initiative to define and celebrate the meaning of their heritage for the Riverside Church. They decided to stop being mere spectators in a predominantly white church and resolved to claim that the church belonged also to them and not to whites alone. Above all, that decision implied the creation of a space for the African American religious experience in the Riverside Church. Even though African Americans had been minimally represented on the church councils, committees, boards of deacons and trustees, and as Christian education teachers, they rightly felt that they had had little impact on the life of the church as a whole. Accordingly, they officially announced the formation of the Black Christian Caucus in June 1969 as their immediate response to that watershed event in race relations at Riverside commonly referred to as James Forman's Black Manifesto.[15] The caucus was "composed of black members and friends of the Riverside Church organized for the purpose of fellowship, identification and understanding [and] hopes to make a unique and significant contribution to the life and ministry of this church and the community."[16] Most important, the caucus declared its readiness to guide the church in the critical decisions it would need to make in response to this troublesome event.

> As a group of individuals from the black membership of the Riverside Church, we feel that we should prepare ourselves to play an active role in the choices which this church will make in the matter of the Manifesto. We are a part of the situation out of which the Manifesto emerges; therefore, we would like to be recognized as a liaison capable of feeding into the dialogues of this church the intelligent identifications which are imperative in arriving at wise decisions. To this end we have formed our caucus.[17]

FIGURE 5.3: The Black Christian Caucus. *Front row*: Mary Lake, Bernice Scott, Sadie Wilson, Alice F. Jones, Hylda Clarke, Elyse White, Shartan Harper, Ruth B. A. Britton. *Back row*: Rafael Delgardo, Howard Irvin, Calvin Bass, Fannie P. Finch, Romell Finch, David Connell. *Used by permission of the Riverside Church Archives.*

Thereafter, the Black Christian Caucus sponsored a variety of programs for the spiritual and cultural enrichment of the whole church. These included events like a black arts festival, Odetta in Concert, the "Evolution of Black Music in America," an annual Martin Luther King Jr. memorial service, special worship services, two festivals of music by black composers, a series of forums on South Africa, discussions of health care in the black community, a festival of gospel music, a scholarship program, a humanitarian award, and many other events.

The caucus also sponsored workshops for the church's self-examination aimed at developing strategies to rid itself of its racism. The workshops were led by people like Myles Horton, founder of the Highlander Center in Tennessee; Anna Arnold Hedgeman, national and international human rights worker; Maya Angelou, renowned writer and poet; Will Campbell, writer, theologian, and civil rights advocate; and Philip Potter, general secretary of the World Council of Churches. The caucus also assumed responsibility for identifying African American members for positions in the church's decision-making processes. Whether or not it was the first to do so, the caucus was in the vanguard of those who began raising questions about what was being pejoratively called an *elite* form of governance[18] at the Riverside Church.

James Forman's Black Manifesto certainly shifted the focus of Riverside's approach to race relations. Before that, with respect to the issue of racism, the church had focused on sponsoring programs to sensitize the congregation to issues pertaining to race relations, coupled with the provision of social services to African Americans, Puerto Ricans, and other minority groups. The Black Manifesto and related events forced the church to consider, for the first time, its complicity with racism and the many and various issues associated with the empowerment of African Americans both inside and outside the church. While its earlier activities in race relations had prepared the church somewhat, the summer of 1970 marked a radical turning point in its life and mission. Among other things, the African American membership in the church came of age.

In the early 1960s Riverside fully embraced the civil rights movement. Martin Luther King Jr. had preached several times in the nave during and following that period, and as discussed in a previous chapter, WRVR broadcast its series *Birmingham: A Testament of Non-Violence*. In fact, the National Council of Christians and Jews named Riverside's WRVR-FM one of the 1964 winners of its National Media Brotherhood Award for the documentary. The church also hosted five hundred volunteers from the city and various parts of New Jersey in "Operation Sack Lunch," when the group made eighty thousand sandwiches that were sacked with an apple and a piece of cake and taken to the March on Washington, August 28, 1963.[19] In 1964 the church nominated its first black, Dr. Benjamin F. Payton, the director of the Commission on Race at the National Council of Churches, for election to the board of deacons. It was not until 1967, however, that the church succeeded in electing its first black, Rev. Carl Flemister, to its board of deacons, and in that same year it appointed Rev. Robert Polk as its minister of urban affairs. All these events, along with its excellent educational programs sponsored by the Task Force on National Issues under the Council on Christian Social Relations, helped prepare the church for its role in meeting the moral demands implied by Forman's Black Manifesto.[20]

But despite the best efforts of the Black Christian Caucus, many members at Riverside believed that the caucus had no right to exist in the church. Others had mixed feelings about it, and still others supported it in principle but criticized its function in the church. To clarify its rationale, the board of deacons asked the Reverend Robert Polk, whom they trusted, to comment on its background and philosophy. His comments were published in the *Carillon* on July 18, 1969. In his address he took care to explain why the caucus would be Christian, political, and black. His was one of the best rationales for the presence of a black caucus in a predominantly white denomination.

The caucus was interested in identifying the needs and problems of the urban community, especially as it related to the black people, for the life and ministry of this church and in interpreting the concerns of this church to the black community.

Mr. Polk commented that between 1965 and late 1968, the number of black members in the church had fallen, and the caucus was interested in bringing these people back into the church.[21]

The church's archives contain an undated statement in which the Black Christian Caucus specified its support of the basic premise of the Black Manifesto, namely, that the church had failed to fulfill its responsibility as a moral leader in the nation's struggle against racism. The purpose of the statement was to report the consensus of the Black Christian Caucus and to indicate the approach that the church should take. The statement reads as follows:

> Though there is no one position that is unanimously endorsed by all the members of the Riverside Black Christian Caucus group, in essence, we agree that: (1) the basic premise of the Manifesto is valid and just—that incalculable damage has been done to this country's Black citizens and other minority groups and (2) the Church has failed to fulfilling its responsibilities as moral leader of the country and by this failure has contributed directly and indirectly to the injustices and sufferings inflicted upon minority groups. We feel that just as Alaska is now paying millions of dollars to the Eskimo citizens, reparation is indeed due to the Blacks. There should be no talk of moderation or alternatives since we, in this country, are over 100 years late in starting.
>
> We feel the spirit of reparation has been born out of a deep source of discontent which we, in this group, not only understand but share. It makes a poignant plea for justice which must not, indeed CANNOT, be ignored or overlooked. It is the message of this confrontation, not the messenger, which must be examined and acted upon. It is the message that requires attention. We must overlook the spokesman and the blackness of its supporters and the vehicle which bears the message. We must look instead within ourselves as Christians for self-examination and action.

We as Christians cannot stand on the quick sand of self-righteousness, holding on to what good we have done. We must look creatively and imaginatively at the great possibilities of good yet to be done and use ourselves and our resources to bridge these gaps. We strongly urge the Church to recognize IFCO[22] as a responsible body founded in justice, love and integrity. In addition, we also feel that the Church's meaningful support of more community based organizations in the Harlem or local community is an essential beginning.   —Members of the Black Christian Caucus

The impact of the Black Manifesto on the Riverside Church has been felt up to the present day. It is interesting to note in this context that Dr. Campbell's first book was published in 1970 under the title *Christian Manifesto*. Both the timing and title of the book reveal the source of their influence. Apparently too, the senior minister and many others wanted to help the church assume a more prophetic role with respect to the struggle against not only racism but also the war in Vietnam. One year after the Black Manifesto, those two problems were discussed together in "A Declaration of Christian Conscience," prepared for congregational discussion by a group of students and faculty at Union Theological Seminary and endorsed by Dr. Campbell in the *Carillon*. The declaration stirred enormous controversy, in large part because many people thought that Dr. Campbell's endorsement of it meant that he was its author. Rather, the declaration was intended merely as a basis for congregational discussion about the church's role in the nation and the world.

Awakened by recent events to the inhumanity of our nation's policies, we as American Christians make this declaration. Our call to life in Christ places us under obedience to Him who bears the life of God among men and is Lord of conscience and of nation. This call to life brings to light our religious idolatry, for we have substituted the rightness of our nation for the righteousness of God.

In the name of legitimate authority our nation misuses its power. Its continuing racism oppresses blacks and other minorities at home. It scorns dissent. Agencies of government threaten, persecute, even kill those who protest injustice. The judicial process is subverted for purposes of political repression. Pride in country prevents us from admitting our failure in Southeast Asia. Our aggression against nations of the world community violates international and national norms of conduct. Hiding behind the language of peace, justice and freedom, our nation inflicts war, injustice and enslavement.

The church too often has tolerated and even supported immoral actions of our government. Most Christians have presumed the will of this nation to be the will of the righteous God of all history. Our American way of life, our political power have become false gods. In our worship we have used high-sounding moral phrases to rationalize political repression and social injustice. We have sanctified wealth but not human life. We have exalted individual piety but not communal justice. We have sought institutional self-perpetuation but not the liberation of the oppressed. We have proclaimed our faith but have not lived it. . . .

"Therefore I will judge you, O house of Israel, everyone according to his ways, says the Lord God. Repent and turn from all your transgressions, lest iniquity be your ruin. Cast away from you all the transgressions which you have committed against me, and get yourselves a new heart and a new spirit! Why will you die, O house of Israel? For I have no pleasure in the death of anyone, says the Lord God; so turn and live" [Ezekiel 18:30–32]. We in the church stand under and draw our hope from these words. We believe that God in his grace is now judging the church and nation. We stand under God's judgment for acquiescing in the wholesale slaughter of Vietnamese men, women and children, the defoliation of their land and the destruction of their homes. We stand under God's judgment for the invasion of Cambodia, without its prior consent and in violation of its neutrality. We stand under God's judgment for our silence at the erosion of justice in the persecution of the Black Panther Party. We stand under God's judgment for the lives of our precious youth, both overseas and at home.

That the church may turn and live, that the nation may be called to righteousness and justice under God, we call on other Christians to join us in repentance and action in the belief that God will bring healing to the church and to the nation. We who affirm this declaration of conscience commit ourselves to actions now to reverse our nation's inhuman policies at home and abroad.[23]

War and Poverty

In his sermon on the church's fiftieth anniversary, the senior minister, William Sloane Coffin, emphasized two things that the church must always keep high on its agenda: its concern for the poor and its work to abolish war.

This church is rooted in the city and its decency is at stake. I said I loved this building and I do. But a rich, proud building that is also a church cannot decently exist unless its preachers and members become humble before the poor, and bold on their behalf. . . . Dearly beloved parishioners, we have no choice, we must work for the redistribution of wealth We must abridge our luxuries for the sake of others' necessities. . . .

Secondly, on this World Wide communion Sunday, let us pledge to continue to work for the abolition of war. Fosdick himself was a pacifist. Most of us are not, if by pacifist you mean one who believes that all war is always morally wrong, and always has been wrong. Nevertheless, I think most of us see war as an avoidable tragedy, and believe that the problem of solving international conflict without massive violence has become the number one problem of our time.[24]

Long identified with its liberal pacifist founder, Harry Emerson Fosdick, the Riverside Church had been well nurtured in the tradition of Christian pacifism. Throughout World War II, Fosdick had taken the unpopular stand of advocating pacifism and speaking out against the war. He also encouraged the church to think about the principles and art of just peacemaking. His 1943 sermon "Toward a Just and Durable Peace" grew out of the forum section of the Men's Class, which met once a week for five months with men of national and international reputation to discuss the conditions needed for a lasting peace with justice. The result was a set of resolutions adopted by the 117 men in the class and sent to the nation's leaders. "Replies were received from eight departments of the Government, from fourteen senators, and from twenty-four representatives and from the Governor of New York."[25] The Men's Class both endorsed the six pillars of peace that had been adopted by the Federal Council of Churches of Christ in America and went beyond them in setting forth additional conditions for the total abolition of war.

On April 4, 1967, exactly one year before his assassination, Martin Luther King Jr. delivered his historic address at the Riverside Church to a meeting of Clergy and Laity Concerned. In his address, entitled "A Time to Break Silence," he linked the Vietnam War to the struggle for civil rights in this country. Clearly, the Riverside Church was viewed by all concerned as a friendly place in which to issue such a protest.

In 1969 at the height of the anti–Vietnam War demonstrations, Dr. Mc-Cracken preached a sermon in which he supported the call by the church's

Council on Christian Social Relations for a moratorium on the bombing in Vietnam. He did make it clear, however, that he was not speaking for the church, which was as divided over the issue as the nation was. Nonetheless, Riverside's participation in the moratorium was greatly influenced by his sermon, together with the recommendation of the Council on Christian Social Relations. On October 15, the day of the moratorium, the carillon bells were rung several times during the day, and two services were held for the congregation.

On the one-hundredth anniversary of Fosdick's birthday, the deacons endorsed Coffin's initiative to establish a national disarmament program at the church. At a church meeting on May 16, 1982, a large majority of the members approved a resolution for a mutual nuclear weapons freeze. Coffin's reputation as a national and international leader in the nuclear disarmament movement had been confirmed a month earlier when *The Christian Century* named him one of the five most influential persons in the field of religion in our day.[26]

On June 12, 1982, the United Nations held its second special session on disarmament, and the Riverside Church helped organize the massive march. Four hundred people marched under the Riverside banner. Coffin was one of the principal speakers and, along with Cora Weiss, served on the Central Planning Committee. Avery Post, the president of the United Church of Christ and a member of Riverside Church, prayed. In his sermon at Riverside two weeks earlier, Coffin stated:

> We will march because the nuclear arms race is madness. We will march because people beg and starve, which they shouldn't have to do, and because in no country should a person's hardest job be to find one. We will march as victims of the forces of history and the forces of destiny, compelled by indignities of days gone by and by aspirations of generations yet unborn. . . . We will march because we want to heed the injunction and know the promise of Scripture, "Cast away from you all the transgressions which you have committed against me, and get yourselves a new heart and a new spirit. Why will you die, O house of Israel? For I have no pleasure in the death of anyone, says the Lord god, so turn and live."[27]

Despite the rhetoric, the Riverside Church has placed much greater emphasis on the issue of war than that of poverty. As discussed elsewhere, Forbes's ministry has tried to change that imbalance.

Gender Inclusion

Both European American women and African American women played important roles in helping raise the church's consciousness about gender issues. In May 1968, Cynthia Wedel became the first woman to preach in the nave at Riverside Church.[28] This marked the beginning of a series of events that eventually culminated in a conference, "Emerging Womankind," which was held at the church in April 1973 with more than one hundred women from all ages in attendance. An internal survey had revealed that the most salient women's issues centered on lifestyles, jobs, legal rights, parenthood, sexuality, and loneliness. Norma Barsness, director of children's work at Riverside, became the first coordinator of "Emerging Womankind." The programs resulting from the nascent Women's Center included summer rap sessions dealing with the role of women at Riverside and in the United States at large; a series of workshops on women and jobs; a series of films and discussions on birth, aging, and death; publicity for the Memorial Society's program on widows; the library's book discussion of women's books; the formation of a single parents' group that met on Sundays following the worship service; and the church's support in sending representatives to women's conferences on women counseling women and on black feminism.

Reformation Sunday, October 27, 1974, was a momentous occasion at the Riverside Church. The Reverend Carol Anderson preached at a special service celebrating women in the ministry, along with three Episcopal women priests who had been ordained in an irregular ordination service in Philadelphia that previous July, Anderson officiated at the Eucharist. More than two thousand people attended the service that united feminist theological consciousness with ecumenical celebration.

On March 15, 1975, a minority women's conference was held in cooperation with the U.S. Labor Department Women's Bureau, the Opportunities Industrialization Corporation, and the Ministerial Interfaith Association of Harlem. The keynote speaker was Eleanor Holmes Norton, New York City's commissioner for human rights. The theme was "Celebrating the Role of Black Women in the Struggle for Peace and Justice." That year, 1975, was the Women's International Year. Judith Jamison danced "Cry," which was choreographed by Alvin Ailey and dedicated by him to all black women. In that year also, the Reverend Evelyn Newman was appointed the first female member of the ministerial collegium at the Riverside Church.

She succeeded the Reverend Jesse Lyons who had retired after nineteen years of service to the congregation.

Riverside's Refugee Program

Undoubtedly, Riverside's Disarmament Program had an immense impact on the church, not least of which was the provision of protection for refugees. On May 30, 1978, fifteen Chileans living in New York City began a hunger strike in sympathy with several hundred strikers in Chile protesting the government's withholding information about the whereabouts of political prisoners. Riverside Church gave them a place to stay. On Sunday, June 11, Dr. Robert MaAfee Brown, professor of ethics and world Christianity at Union Theological Seminary, delivered a powerful sermon based on Luke 24:13–35 in support of the Chilean hunger strikers and argued that the United States was responsible for the present situation in Chile because the CIA, the federal government, and corporations like ITT helped financed the coup against the Allende government.[29]

In 1980 the Christian Social Action Commission and Council IV established Riverside's Refugee Resettlement Task Force with the aim of sponsoring at least one refugee family. The church sponsored Mr. Liem and his three nephews and assumed responsibility for every detail of their relocation. The congregation also sponsored two Haitian refugees. The same task force organized a major conference on South Africa in 1981 and was instrumental in persuading the church's board of trustees to withdraw its operating account of approximately $6 million from Citibank[30] as part of its support of sanctions against South Africa. The church's withdrawal was the first such action by a major local congregation in New York City. In its announcement the senior minister, William Sloan Coffin, stated:

> Citibank is America's most important financial lifeline to apartheid South Africa. Citibank's funds support the white supremacist policies of the South African government. Riverside's trustees decided in good conscience that this church cannot continue its long-standing business relationship with Citibank while the bank continues an open-door policy of loans to South Africa. . . .
>
> Riverside church will continue to hold Citicorp stock in its portfolio so that, through participation in shareholder resolutions and proxy votes, the

church can continue to register opposition to the bank's financial support of the Republic of South Africa.[31]

The Disarmament Program was also instrumental in persuading the church to house a sanctuary group. After three months of careful discussion, many hearings, study, and deliberation, the church voted on June 10, 1984, to become a sanctuary church for Salvadoran and Guatemalan refugees who were being denied refugee status by the U.S. Immigration and Naturalization Service. In doing so, the Riverside Church became part of a national sanctuary movement against the U.S. government's policy of deporting such persons because the church believed that they were seeking refuge from terror and possible death in their home countries. Soon thereafter a Guatemalan family—Federico, Ana, and baby Carlos[32]—arrived at the church and was welcomed. The family would live at the church until they became self-sufficient enough to live in this country. A very colorful worship service[33] was held in the sanctuary on October 1, 1984, to welcome them officially.

Another impact of the Disarmament Program was the national observance of the Peace Sabbath that was cosponsored with the Clergy and Laity Concerned, the Religious Task Force of Mobilization for Survival, and the Fellowship for Reconciliation. As time went on, the sponsors were joined by Sojourners, and Pax Christi, a Roman Catholic peace group. In its first year, 1979, more than a thousand churches and synagogues joined in the observance, and that number rose to many thousands in the ensuing years. By 1984, twenty thousand congregations were participating, with the program handing out to congregations packets with sermons, worship aids, posters, and action suggestions.

The Relation of War and Racism

Although many people feared that during Coffin's tenure, the church's focus on nuclear disarmament might reduce its commitment to the fight against racism, there is little evidence to support that fear. Coffin's own sensitivity to the issue, coupled with the vigilance of the Black Christian Caucus, prevented any diminution. Moreover, Coffin never lost sight of the relationship of war, poverty, and racism in America, South Africa, and elsewhere.

In the fall of 1981 the church's emphasis was on racism. In keeping with that commitment, twenty-one deacons, eight trustees, and two collegium members met at Stony Point, New York, for a weekend to devise a plan to help the church overcome racism within its own institution and in the city. Elinor Galusha, chairperson of the board of deacons, reported:

> Our process at Stony Point was amazingly open and honest, our sharing deep, and at times truly moving. A commitment growing out of the weekend was to make the elimination of racism a visible priority in the entire life and work of Riverside . . . even as the church already commits this to its other priority, peace and justice through the "Reverse the Arms Race Program."[34]

Among the highlights of the retreat, Galusha listed the following: (1) to name a committee to write a staffing proposal to make Riverside better equipped to deal with racism in its church and society; (2) to develop an affirmative action policy and program for all salaried and volunteer positions, with an effort to make all the church's committees and programs as inclusive as possible; (3) to orient all new members to the reality of racism and to Riverside's commitment to its elimination; (4) to engage deacons and trustees annually in a program to examine and assess Riverside's progress in eliminating racism; (5) to study ways by which Riverside can become more relevant to the Hispanic community; (6) to expand areas of cooperation by Riverside with other churches in New York City, especially black churches, so as to increase its ecumenical effectiveness in working against racism at Riverside and in the city; and (7) to take some specific steps in particular program areas in order to make the entire program more relevant to the concerns of a racially and culturally diverse congregation. Other areas of concern were taking steps to overcome the compartmentalization that exacerbates, and is exacerbated by, racism and naming a small committee of deacons, trustees, collegia, and building staff to monitor the process and report regularly to both boards.

The president of the board of trustees, Ernest Lorch, added the following goals: (1) to consider the use and allocation of some of the new and projected endowment funds for business ventures intended to create or increase minority employment opportunities, business ownership, and other broad-based community involvement; (2) to explore the possibility of establishing the funding of or participation in a financial enterprise such as a small business investment company or a church credit union; and (3) to remain sensitive to and aware of the problems and pervasiveness of racism and its effects on Riverside's decision-making process.

The congregation was also advised to read the booklet "The Broken Body" prepared by the Adult Education Program for the church's educational focus on racism. In January 1982 two buses went to Washington, D.C., from Riverside to protest South Africa's apartheid policies. Senior minister Coffin and Channing Phillips accompanied the ninety-eight persons who participated. Seventy Riversiders, including Coffin and Phillips, were arrested[35] for protesting within fifty feet of the (South African) embassy.

Clearly, the church tried to remain faithful to its commitment to eradicate racism from the church's internal life and throughout the society at large.

The Church's 1980 Mission Statement

In 1980 the Riverside Church began giving a rational account of itself through a mission statement that integrated the church's own understanding of its past and its hopes for the future. The statement was called "Agenda for the 80's: The Riverside Church." After long and careful study the two governing boards approved the statement, which was later read by the congregation as a litany following Dr. Laubach's sermon of the same title.

> It is the mission of the Riverside Church to proclaim the good news of God's redeeming, liberating and transforming presence as we experience it in Jesus Christ and to help persons respond in faith and love.
>
> To become a loving, caring community in which persons may experience the liberating fullness of the gospel.
>
> To nurture persons in the meaning of the Christian faith to the end that they commit themselves to Jesus Christ and his mission in our world.
>
> To strive for justice and reconciliation at every level.
>
> We believe God calls us. . . .
>
> To be a liberal, Protestant voice in the city and nation to the end that the gospel and its relevance for life may be proclaimed.
>
> To achieve more effective church growth in order that more persons may participate in the community and ministry of this church.

To provide a program of effective pastoral nurture for members and constituents of the church so that they may become a living, caring community.

To provide nurture for all ages leading to growth in Christian faith so that persons may understand the meaning of their faith and make it relevant in their lives.

To become a truly intercultural/interracial community of faith to the end that our programs will be inclusive of all social/economic levels in the congregation.

To formulate some new visions for the city to the end that the church may become an instrument in creating a more human city in which to live.

To help formulate some new visions of the role of the Christian as an international citizen in order that persons may express that ideal in their daily lives.

To establish a firm financial base for the church and its programs.[36]

These statements comprised the church's agenda for the 1980s. The congregation discussed how it should implement the eight goals, proceed with the fiftieth-anniversary celebration, determine priorities, and identify those areas needing further study and expansion. As always, the church strove to be as expansive and progressive as possible in education, pastoral care, volunteer social services, and social justice advocacy. In each area, the church's public witness sought manifestation in its internal life as well as in the neighborhood, city, nation, and world. In other words, the Riverside Church never acknowledged a divide between the goals of its internal life and those of its external life. Rather, it has consistently taught its members that the quality of the Christian's spiritual life should be revealed in his or her daily life. Furthermore, the church has always taught that its proclamation of the gospel implies both pastoral and prophetic functions in the church, city, nation, and world. As a sign of respect for that tradition, the church has always given the senior minister maximum freedom and never tried to muzzle his voice.

Church, Community, and Conscience

At a farewell gathering for Bill Coffin in December 1987, the Reverend Dr. Donald Shriver, president of Union Theological Seminary and a member of the church, asked some questions about the community that makes up

Riverside Church. They were poignant, mirroring the same questions that Riversiders constantly ask themselves. The spirit of Shriver's questions was expressed in an article in *Carillon* in 1988: "Riverside: Church, Community, Conscience."

Who is the community that really makes up Riverside Church? Is it ourselves, the congregation, Dr. Shriver asked, or a wider group of leaders and people served by our message and programs and commitments? If it is a wider group, "is it the community of educational institutions on Morningside Heights" for whom, in part, the church was founded? "Is it the seminary across the street? The religious and civic leaders of Harlem, who look to Riverside for leadership on issues of racial diversity? The homeless persons on every other block on Broadway who, if they know anything at all about Manhattan churches, know that in the pulpit and the congregation of this church they have a friend, an advocate, a burning, conscientious witness against the scandal of homelessness. The people of Nicaragua? Refugees from war and persecution in Central America who have found sanctuary here? The people of South Africa? Or given the debt that every human being on this planet owes to everyone who makes possible a step away from the arms of Armageddon, is it too much to think that the whole human world is part of the Riverside Church community?[37]

The report then discusses others' views on the subject:

Balfour Brickner, senior rabbi of the Stephen Wise Free Synagogue, whose friendship with Riverside is of twenty years duration, puts his feelings about our influence this way: "Through all the period that I've known Riverside, it has always stood for moral presence in the larger community, in a practical way. . . .

When Stephen Wise was first looking into providing sanctuary for Central American refugees, the people we counseled with were people from Riverside, whose sanctuary program was a model for the nation. When we were interested in pioneering a citywide Jewish conference on peace and disarmament, the first group I consulted was Riverside's peace and disarmament program. When we wanted to get into serious issues of housing and race, we looked to you as an anchor in the community. In other words, there is not a social action in which Riverside does not set the example for the rest of us in the religious community."

Without platforms such as Riverside Church the great moral thinkers of America would not have a place from which to be heard in a respected and respectful locus. That's what Riverside has always been.

The report then quoted another observer, Joe Sullivan, auxiliary bishop of Brooklyn:

> To me, Riverside Church represents living incarnational theology—the belief that Christ became a human person, to be enmeshed in the reality of the world and to fashion and reshape the world. It's what the Vatican Council said was the mission of the church in the modern world: faith expressed through charity and social justice. Especially under Bill's leadership, Riverside became the vital center of a truly relevant Christianity—in which witness carried on outside the church brings credibility to worship within.

The same article also quoted Darlene Cuccinello, a Maryknoll sister on the Central American Affairs staff of the Intercommunity Center for Justice and Peace: "Our daily commitment to the community at large—through Riverside's current programs of disarmament, sanctuary, the men's shelter, English conversation, the Food Pantry, and many others—makes us a 'prophetic witness.' The whole city looks to Riverside Church."

Finally, the author returned to Don Shriver's questions and gave his answer in the form of a quotation from Bill Coffin: "Riverside's members are known far and wide for the way they hold the dying in their living flesh, for the way they set a feast for the poor, dance with the lame, put their arms around the assaulted, and continue to preach peace to the nation and the world."[38]

Although the tone of this quotation may seem either hyperbolic or unabashedly romantic, the reader would have no difficulty in finding many members of the church, at any time including right now, expressing similar views of the Riverside Church and its mission. Many people who have been members of the church for several decades almost become euphoric when they contemplate the wide divide between the ethos of the church before the 1960s and that of today. Few in the earlier period could have imagined a time when the Riverside Church would call an African American Pentecostal minister with a passion for social justice to be its senior minister.

On March 17, 1991, the senior minister, Dr. James Forbes, did an extraordinary thing in the midst of the morning worship service. Standing in the center of the chancel, he said:

> With us today is a person who will be significantly featured when the history of Riverside Church is written, a person who, back in 1969, came and

FIGURE 5.4: Interreligious "Americans in Healing" service, September 16, 2002. *Used by permission of the Riverside Church Archives.*

stood right here and let loose a shot heard around the world . . . the day James Forman delivered the Black Manifesto [a declaration that demanded reparations from institutions controlled by whites to the black community for its unacknowledged contributions to this country for over 300 years].

. . . Riverside has never been the same since, nor has our nation. When you stood here those years ago we were not able to receive you with such great joy but history has a funny way of vindicating the truth of justice. You have been used as an instrument and its is not hard at all to rejoice on the gift you brought us. May we carry on in the days ahead the kind of legacy that you have called us to.[39]

Clearly, the increasing centrality of racial concerns in all spheres of the church's ministry has been and continues to be one of the most visible symbolic effects of Forbes's ministry at Riverside Church. This part of the church's social ministry was greatly encouraged by many of Forbes's actions but especially by joining a grassroots organization (Harlem Initiatives Together) in its protest aimed at improving public facilities at the 125th Street subway station, upgrading conditions in Morningside Park,

FIGURE 5.5:
Nelson Mandela behind
Dr. Forbes. *Used by
permission of the
Riverside Church Archives.*

FIGURE 5.6: Martin Luther King Jr. at the nave pulpit. *Used by permission of the
Riverside Church Archives.*

FIGURE 5.7: Rev. Martin Luther King Jr. on WRVR, delivering
his anti–Vietnam War speech, April 4, 1967. *Photograph by
John Goodwin. Used by permission of the Riverside Church
Archives.*

and bringing pressure to bear on area supermarkets to clean up unsafe
and unhealthy conditions. In addition, Forbes's hosting such prominent
racial justice leaders as Jesse Jackson, Mayor David Dinkins, Wyatt Tee
Walker, Calvin Butts, Peter Gomes, Thabo Mbeki, Nelson Mandela,
Coretta Scott King, and many others has enhanced the church's favorable
image on all matters pertaining to racial justice.

Riverside's concern for racial matters has steadily grown from the time
of the Black Manifesto until the present. Forbes's call to become Riverside's fifth senior minister concluded a process that was set in motion
three decades ago to rid the church of every vestige of racism. But Forbes
insists that the primacy afforded the struggle against racism and poverty
under his leadership does not imply any intentional neglect of other social
justice issues. Rather, the church's public witness continues a commitment
to all the various cries for justice, including all who are oppressed by the

terrors of racism, sexism, homophobism, war, poverty, imprisonment, domestic violence, child abuse, and many more.

Riverside's heightened sensitivity to all forms of social injustice has made it a safe haven and a strong advocate for countless numbers of people and their just causes. As the church's many and varied programs readily reveal and as this book has disclosed, Riverside's public witness has been both prophetic and pastoral. The church's activities of worship, study, celebration, protest, counseling, advocacy, and deliberation are united by love and respect for all of God's people. The leadership of its clergy and the ministry of its members unite in affirming the dignity of all of God's creation and the common resolve to do everything possible to enable all of God's people to flourish. The church's future is inextricably tied to that mission.

While Riverside has taken a progressive stance on many social justice issues, it has not as yet spoken prophetically on the economic inequalities that are presently ravaging the so-called Third World and are threatening the security of this nation. How this church will address the structural dimensions of this major global challenge remains to be seen.

NOTES

1. Since I use the term *public* a great deal in this chapter, I should tell the reader its meaning in this context. I am heavily indebted to the thought of both Aristotle and Hanna Arendt for a full understanding of the term. It refers to the common life that human beings construct in their freedom and try to preserve and enhance. The term derives from the Greek *polis*, in which all participants are free citizens and the rightful purposes are the preservation and enhancement of their shared public life. Similarly, the term *public space* refers to those areas in which our common world is the subject matter of all speech, deliberations, and actions. Thus, the church's *public witness* pertains to all those activities of thought and practice aimed at enhancing the quality of our common life, and *public religion* refers to spirituality that drives all such concerns and engagements. See Hannah Arendt, *The Human Condition* (Chicago: University of Chicago Press, 1958), chap. 11; and Aristotle's Nicomacheon *Ethics* and *Politics*.

2. Certainly the most memorable interreligious event was held on September 16, 2002, following the September 11 attack on the World Trade Center and the Pentagon.

3. In a memorial service for Dr. Fosdick on October 12, 1969, Dr. McCracken's superbly crafted meditation spoke about Fosdick's being in the forefront of the

ecumenical movement and the movement for racial integration and his concep-
tion of the church as an institutional church "repeatedly emphasizing the need for
personal and social religion, never concentrating on one and neglecting the other."
Carillon, October 17, 1969, 2.

4. See Report to the Long-Term Planning Committee, March 17, 1968, 1, in
Metro Mission Council, first folder 1, stack F, RG 9.

5. Ibid., 4.

6. *Carillon,* May 1991, 2–3.

7. Dwight C. Smith, "A Request to the Trustees and Deacons of the Riverside
Church," March 25, 1968, 1, in Council IV Metro Mission (unprocessed), stack F,
RG 9.

8. Ibid.

9. For an analysis of the problem from the perspective of an activity faculty
group concerned about the expansion of the university and the preservation of
the community, see "The Community and the Expansion of Columbia University:
A Report of the Faculty Civil Rights Group at Columbia University, December
1967," in Council IV Metro Mission, stack F, no. 1, RG 9.

10. For a detailed analysis of the migration changes in the community, see
Clyde Murray's "Statement on the Morningside-Manhattanville Community," pre-
pared for the Survey Committee of Riverside Church, June 7, 1955. See also its ap-
pendix entitled, "Excerpts from Address Given by Lawrence M. Orton at a Dinner
Meeting of the League of West Side Organizations on January 17, 1955 (FR-907.1,
June 15, 1955).

11. Self-Study Report, January 20, 1968, in Council IV Metro Mission (unprocessed) stack F, no. 1, RG 9.

12. *Carillon,* April 27, 1965, 2.

13. *Carillon,* September 9, 1977, 1.

14. See the article in the *Carillon,* June 30, 1983, on the Riverside Hawks,
Ravens, and Warriors, which Lorch coached for many years. At least two basketball
players from the Riverside team became NBA stars—Albert King and George
Johnson—and Johnson joined the Harlem Globetrotters. Over the years the
Hawks won trophies locally and internationally in Yugoslavia, England, Spain,
France, Russia, and Italy. The many trophies fill display cases in the assembly hall.

15. This document was presented to the National Black Economic Develop-
ment Conference in Detroit, Michigan, and adopted on April 26, 1969. See
Gayraud S. Wilmore and James H. Cone, eds., *Black Theology: A Documentary
History, 1969–1979* (Maryknoll, N.Y.: Orbis Books, 1979), 80 ff.

16. From the program in Commemoration of the Tenth Anniversary of the
Black Christian Caucus of the Riverside Church, "The Evolution of Black Music,"
Saturday, November 17, 1979.

17. *Carillon,* June 13, 1969, 1–2.

18. For a description of this form of governance, see the article by Eugene Laubach entitled "From the Ministers," *Carillon*, March 6, 1970, 3–4.

19. See *Carillon*, October 18, 1963, 2.

20. As the months passed, Forman's message of reparations was embraced by the National Conference of Black Churchmen, Inc., which, on behalf of all black Americans, issued the Black Declaration of Independence on July 4, 1970, which similarly attacked European American Christianity for its racist apostasy. In the midst of these events, James H. Cone's first book, *Black Theology and Black Power*, was published and had a significant impact on theological education in America. In fact, it can be argued that the Black Manifesto event at the Riverside Church led to the initial convergence of the black theology and black power movements, each of which sent shock waves through European American Christianity.

21. See *Carillon*, July 18, 1969, 2.

22. The acronym IFCO stands for the Interreligious Foundation for Community Organization, Inc., of which Rev. Lucius Walker Jr. was the executive director. As a coalition of community organizations, IFCO included the Detroit Conference on Black Economic Development, where Forman first delivered his manifesto.

23. *Carillon*, May 22, 1970, 1–2.

24. *Carillon*, November 29, 1980, 5.

25. See "Toward a Just and Durable Peace," signed by 117 members of the Forum of the Men's Class of the Riverside Church, New York City, October, 1943, 1.

26. *Carillon*, April 3, 1982, 3.

27. *Carillon*, August, 1982, 6.

28. See the report in *Carillon*, May 10, 1968.

29. See excerpts from that sermon in *Carillon*, September 2, 1978, 2.

30. See *Carillon*, May 31, 1981, 1.

31. See *Riverside News*, May 31, 1981, 2–3.

32. See *Carillon*, October 5, 1984, 1, for a picture and description of the family and the sanctuary program at the church.

33. See *Carillon*, November 9, 1984, 1, for a photo story concerning the service.

34. *Carillon*, March 30, 1982, 3–4.

35. See story of the arrest in *Carillon*, March 11, 1985, 3.

36. See "Riversiders Move toward New Goals for the Eighties," *Carillon*, June 11, 1980, 1.

37. See "Riverside: Church, Community, Conscience," *Carillon*, May 1988, 1.

38. Ibid.

39. *Carillon*, April 1991, 3–4.

6

Congregations within a Congregation

Contemporary Spirituality and Change at the Riverside Church

Lawrence H. Mamiya

Paul Tillich, the famous German theologian who taught at the Union Theological Seminary across the street and was an occasional visitor and lecturer at the Riverside Church, was once shown a copy of *Time* magazine. He looked at the table of contents, including its various categories of Arts, Entertainment, Politics, Economics, Sports, and Religion, and scoffed, "They're all religious." Tillich meant that each area of life can express a person's "ultimate concern," or what elicited that person's devotion, loyalty, and respect.[1] He recognized that the "secular" areas of life, such as the stock market, politics, science, sports, music, and the arts, can have their own religious dimension as an expression of a person's ultimate concern.

Tillich's broad view of religion and contemporary spirituality is relevant to the variety of people who come to the Riverside Church as members or as visitors. For example, Betty Davis said that she was attracted to Riverside's arts and crafts program and participated in it for more than ten years without attending a worship service or joining the church. Then, under Dr. James Forbes's pastorate, she eventually joined, became active in church committees, and eventually was elected as the chair of the Church Council and a member of the History Project Committee.[2] Davis's story has been repeated many times in the lives of members or visitors who come to Riverside for its famous preachers, worship service, music concerts, theater events, social justice concerns, majestic architecture, or even its sports teams.

Contemporary spirituality at the Riverside Church of New York City is diverse, pluralistic, and complex. It reflects the current trends of religion in America, which is composed of multiple centers and expressions of faith and spirituality. The main argument of this chapter is that there are multiple congregations at the Riverside Church or "congregations within a congregation," of which the main Sunday morning congregation at the 10:45 A.M. worship service in the nave is but one example. The term *congregation* refers to a group of people gathered around a particular faith concern. Accordingly, *to congregate* means "to gather." The simplest definition of a church congregation is found in the New Testament: "Where two or three are gathered in my name, there I am in the midst of them" (Matthew 18:20). Many New Yorkers who would never cross the threshold of a church, synagogue, or mosque try to meet their need for transcendent spiritual experiences by going to a concert at Lincoln Center, visiting the Metropolitan Museum of Art, seeing a play or a movie, or vicariously participating in a sports event with the Knicks, Yankees, Mets, or Jets. In events with large numbers of people, whether in a sports stadium or a large hall, the collective enthusiasm of the crowd, or what the sociologist Emile Durkheim called "collective effervescence," can create an uplifting experience that is similar to a religious experience.[3] From a Christian perspective, Tillich would ask whether these concerns and experiences are really ultimate.

Riverside can be classified as a "megachurch," a very large church with a membership of two thousand or more with multiple ministries.[4] As we have seen, Riverside is a "megachurch" with a liberal theological heritage, whose ministerial and lay leaders have often blurred the distinctions between the religious and the secular by creating programs to meet secular needs within the confines of the church building. The goal has been to create a holistic ministry covering all facets of human life. Over the years, each of these program areas has developed its own following. Thus, there are the theater, drama, and dance congregation, the arts and crafts congregation, and the congregation drawn by Riverside's musical events and concerts. There also are congregations for employees and staff, senior citizens and the elderly, the Black Caucus, Maranatha for gays and lesbians, the social justice and prison ministry, and the Riverside Hawks basketball team. Congregations can overlap but they also can stand alone. Membership in one of these congregations does not necessarily include church membership, although it can sometimes lead to it.

This idea of not requiring church membership in order to participate in the church's programs reflects Riverside's liberal heritage. For example, the poor people who come to the church's Food Pantry program for baskets of food or clothes from the clothing bank are not forced to sit through a religious service or a homily as they are with the Salvation Army or the more conservative fundamentalist churches who expect participants to "catch the Gospel on the fly." Instead, the tolerance and openness of Riverside's liberal heritage allow the city's "secular" people to participate in its programs without having "religion" forced on them. Often the only religious identification is that the programs usually take place in the church building. Because of its large size and multiple meeting rooms and chapels, Riverside follows the "parish model" found in the Catholic tradition, in which the central cathedral draws people to the building.

This view of the Riverside Church as composed of "multiple congregations" is not new but was suggested in the "Report on the Think Tank on Urban Ministry" meeting at Grey Dunes, Long Island, in March 1972. Commenting on the Riverside Church's need for a "new identity," the report concluded: "This will require that Riverside consider itself not as a single homogeneous congregation but a *collection of congregations*, each cultivated and respected for its importance to the whole. There would be periodic gatherings at which the whole body would be gathered together in a kind of cathedral function."[5]

The idea of "congregations within a congregation" has implications for the future of the professional ministry and lay leadership at the Riverside Church during a new century when the population projections forecast a much more diverse American society, both racially and culturally. At the beginning of the new millennium, the population of California—a bellwether state—is already more than 50 percent minority, with the minority populations (African American, Asian American, and Hispanic/Latino American) growing and the European American population declining. This chapter examines some of the similar demographic changes in Riverside's neighborhood and church membership and gives some examples of the multiple congregations in the life of the church. It also looks at some of the conflicts and controversies of the 1990s and the dynamics of change at the Riverside Church, a subject to which we now turn.

From the "Negro in the Narthex" to the Black Preacher in the Pulpit

In the mid-1950s, Riverside considered stationing a Negro usher, dressed in a morning suit and white gloves, in the narthex of the church to greet the growing numbers of Negro worshipers and visitors.[6] The social and psychological distance was great between the largely elite white congregation on Morningside Heights in its towering cathedral structure and the Negro masses in the Harlem Valley below it.[7] The ensuing decades saw considerable turmoil and conflict in American society and at the Riverside Church with the emergence of broad movements for social change and empowerment: civil rights, antiwar, feminist, black power, gay and lesbian, the disabled, the elderly. In 1989 the board of trustees ratified the Search Committee's choice of Rev. James Forbes as the senior minister and pastor of Riverside, the first black preacher to formally occupy its pulpit.

The selection of Jim Forbes to lead America's Protestant cathedral was historically significant and set into motion a series of events and controversies. As Forbes himself observed, "Every day I get up and walk through the front of this church, with my black self, with my Afro-American being, with the uniqueness of my culture, is a major political statement about God's call to a community that transcends the limitations of race and class."[8] Whether the Riverside Church could transcend the limitations of race and class in America was a hopeful and optimistic assessment of the controversies that followed.

The Search Committee and the Formation of a New Church Council

When Rev. William Sloane Coffin resigned as the senior minister of the Riverside Church on December 31, 1987, a search committee of twenty members, chaired by Richard Butler, was formed. The extensive search process for a new minister lasted for thirteen months, and five thousand letters were sent out to clergy and churches in the United States and abroad. During this time, Rev. George Hill served as the interim senior minister.

The committee created listening groups to determine the mood of the main congregation. According to Butler, the job description is always aimed at the last person to occupy the office, and Bill Coffin was a great preacher who did not like church administration.[9] So the plan was to hire a preaching minister as the senior minister and an executive minister to deal with the administration. This same division of labor was used in the 1960s when Rev. Ernest Campbell was the preaching senior minister and Rev. Eugene Laubach was the executive minister.

The pool of hundreds of applicants was reduced to twelve candidates, and each one was visited at his church on a weekend by three members of the Steering Committee. Four finalists were chosen. Each was invited to the Riverside Church and extensively interviewed by staff clergy, the Search Committee, and other constituencies in the church over two evening sessions.[10]

The consensus of all the meetings was to invite Rev. James Forbes Jr., who had been the Joe R. Engle Professor of Preaching at the Union Theological Seminary for thirteen years, to become Riverside's fifth senior minister. The boards of trustees and deacons and the congregation also ratified the Search Committee's choice. According to Butler, the central question regarding Forbes was "whether the congregation was ready for this." Forbes would be the first African American, the first southerner, and the first with a Pentecostal background. The change of senior ministers at Riverside was always a major event, accompanied by changes in the main congregation. Since Harry Emerson Fosdick, each senior minister has been a famous preacher, drawing his own constituencies, and every time the preacher changed, the makeup of the congregation in regard to race, geography, and the like changed as well. Each senior minister also is confronted with problems, turmoil, and change.[11]

Besides changing senior ministers, the Riverside congregation also faced significant changes in its internal governance. According to Dr. Katherine Wilcox, from 1989 until early 1990 the church shifted from a bicameral to a unicameral system of governance. Since its establishment, the Riverside Church always had a board of deacons, which was responsible for the church's programs, and a board of trustees, which controlled the church's finances and property. By controlling the purse strings, the board of trustees always had the ultimate power.[12] In the past, there was considerable conflict between the two boards. The trustees, who tended to be both fiscal and social conservatives, often undercut the more liberal, social activist programs proposed by the deacons. Fearing that these conflicts could inflict "lasting damage to the church" and that confrontation could result in "litigation between the boards," a study commission headed by

Timothy M. Taylor recommended the formation of a "unicameral" board as early as October 28, 1970.[13] However, for a variety of reasons—such as the history of the governance of American Baptist churches which included both deacons and trustees, the opposition of Riverside's trustees to any "drastic changes" in their fiscal authority, and the uncertainty of New York state laws about the legality of a single board—Taylor's recommendation for unicameralism was shelved.[14]

Riverside's fiscal problems in the late 1980s and Coffin's resignation created a crisis at the church. There were tensions between the congregational lay leaders and the clergy staff and also tensions on the fifth floor, the church's administrative offices. According to Butler, each clergy person has a "separate congregation." For example, the ministers of social justice and parish life have their own constituencies.[15] This also was a time when deep budget cuts had to be made and the "friction between the two boards increased." The crisis atmosphere led to a push for the creation of a unicameral board, the Church Council. In October 1989 at a corporate membership meeting, the congregation approved the change in the unicameral board with new elections to the twenty-six-member council taking place on January 21, 1990.[16] Nine of the Church Council's members were trustees; another nine were elected by the congregation; and eight represented the four program commissions.[17] These various tensions also affected Jim Forbes's ministry during the first five years. Jeffrey Slade, a longtime member and theologically trained lawyer, became the first chair of the newly formed Church Council. One of his pressing concerns was the creation of new bylaws for the Riverside Church, which were completed in 1995.[18]

The Controversies of the Early 1990s

On June 1, 1989, Rev. James Forbes was installed as the fifth senior minister of the Riverside Church. According to Forbes, it was a "symbolic moment, a Gospel vignette."[19] The installation service was attended by more than five hundred preachers, many of whom were regarded as the leading preachers in the United States. It was this collection of great preachers that gave Forbes the idea of establishing an annual preaching workshop at Riverside.[20] The inaugural period was also a brief honeymoon, devoid of the conflicts and tensions that later became all-consuming. One of the "most glorious and memorable moments" of Forbes's pastorate was the visit by Nelson Mandela in June 1990, five months after Mandela had been freed from twenty-seven years of incarceration by the South African government.

After nearly a decade of Coffin's emphasis on social activism, during which Riverside had become a national center for peace activities and nuclear disarmament, members of the Search Committee wanted to turn to a deeper spirituality in the church's ministry, to seek a balance between the claims of spirituality and social justice.[21] The common adage across the street at the Union Theological Seminary was to "hold the Bible in one hand and the *New York Times* in the other," paraphrasing the Swiss theologian Karl Barth. Just as Union's students and faculty had difficulty finding the correct balance between the Bible and the *New York Times*, so did many congregants at Riverside. Some Riversiders preferred that their preacher begin sermons with the headlines from the *New York Times* than with Bible stories or scriptural passages for exegesis.

For members of the Search Committee, the deep spirituality of Forbes's Pentecostal background was an attractive feature, but for some members of Riverside's Social Justice Commission, Pentecostalism was a signal that the church's traditional commitment to issues of social justice would disappear. Unfortunately, stereotypes of Pentecostalists as "pie-in-the-sky," otherworldly salvation seekers were prevalent. The first signs of discontent with the choice of Forbes as senior minister came from the Social Justice Commission. Called to two Sunday meetings of the commission in 1990, Forbes was seated in the middle of the room while members vented their criticisms and anger. Some complained that his sermons did not include commentary on the latest current events as depicted in the headlines of the *New York Times*. Others questioned his commitment to social justice. In his own defense, Forbes tried to explain that his goal was to find a balance between social activism and social justice and biblical faith. Activism for the sake of activism often led to burned-out lives, a common phenomenon in the social movements of the 1960s. His goal was a faith-based activism at Riverside, one that could endure the peaks and valleys of social activism and movement politics. After his explanation, a woman member in the audience sent a check for $50,000 to support the church's ministry. Looking back, however, Forbes also felt that this was a time of mourning, especially by members of the Social Justice Commission, for Coffin's sudden departure.[22]

The period from 1991 to 1995 was one of the most tension filled and controversial in the history of the Riverside Church. The controversies involved the resignation of Rev. David Dyson as the executive minister and the formation of a group called "Riversiders for Riverside."

In August 1990 Jim Forbes selected Rev. David Dyson to be Riverside's executive minister. Dyson, a Presbyterian minister, came with strong credentials as a community and labor organizer with Caesar Chavez's United Farm Workers Union and an executive with the Amalgamated Clothing and Textile Workers Union. He also had pastored two congregations. He appeared to have all the skills and qualities needed to fulfill the job description for executive minister: to be the chief operating officer of the church and to assist the senior minister in fulfilling his responsibilities to the Church Council and the Religious Society, among other requirements. Dyson's combination of urban social activism and administrative experience were appealing to Forbes.

In less than fourteen months, however, the working relationship between Forbes and Dyson had deteriorated. When Forbes continued to reduce the scope of Dyson's responsibilities as executive minister, both men agreed on December 10, 1991, that the relationship was not working. In January 1992 Forbes tried to have Dyson dismissed as the executive minister, a request that the Church Council's Executive Committee turned down. Instead, the Executive Committee recommended a course of reconciliation and mediation between the two embattled leaders.[23]

The clash between the two strong personalities, the internal tensions from creating a unicameral Church Council, the repercussions of the financial crisis of the late 1980s which resulted in Dr. Coffin's sudden resignation, and the mobilization of groups either supporting or attacking Forbes eventually led to a conflict that spread throughout the congregation and became the focus of media stories in the New York Times, New York Post, and The Westsider.[24] On the Church Council's recommendation, both Forbes and Dyson signed an agreement on March 2, 1992, to try mediation and reconciliation by an outside mediator.[25] Dr. Douglas Lind, president of the TriSource Group and an ordained Presbyterian minister, therapist, and organizational consultant, was the first choice of both parties for the mediation sessions.[26] The men met in five sessions from March 13 to April 24, 1992, but the mediation attempts ended in failure with no resolution reached.[27] In a letter dated May 26, 1992, addressed to the Members of the Riverside Church Council and Dr. James A. Forbes Jr., senior minister, Rev. David Dyson wrote the following:

At the same time it is painfully apparent to me that a crisis of personal confidence exists between Dr. Forbes and myself which we may not be able to bridge, and which Dr. Forbes may—for reasons good or bad—be unwilling to bridge. As you know, since this turmoil arose there have been two long sets of mediation which, by all accounts, have failed completely to achieve any reconciliation. . . . If we cannot successfully resolve this problem in the next few weeks, then I believe we must turn to the task which Dr. Forbes requested me to address in January—the terms on which I would be prepared to withdraw from my position as executive minister of the Riverside Church.[28]

With a generous severance package, Rev. Dyson resigned from the Riverside Church and left in August 1992. He became the pastor of the Lafayette Avenue Presbyterian Church in Brooklyn.

In the first months of 1992 as the conflict was being played out, a small but vocal group called the "Riversiders for Riverside" began organizing and circulating to members of the Riverside Church congregation newsletters that made clear they were strong supporters of David Dyson and highly critical of Jim Forbes. The Riversiders were quite effective in mobilizing discontent in a sector of the main congregation, church staff, and members of the choir. Their criticisms included Forbes's preaching and its content (a "Southern Baptist" style, too biblically based and not intellectual enough); the length of the sermon (going beyond noon); "ad hoc interjections" of Amen! during the worship service; changing the choir's and service's music program by adding gospel music and performances; a dictatorial and authoritarian style of leadership; declining membership and church contributions; resignations of key staff members such as John Walker, the director of music; and poor morale throughout the congregation and church staff. Some members of the choir sent a letter of complaint, as did some members of the church staff.[29]

Some discontented Riversiders were not satisfied with writing letters and began to picket and hand out leaflets at the worship services. During a service, one member threw leaflets from an upper balcony onto the main floor of the nave. These organized protests also contributed to a temporary decline in membership and finances during this period. In January 1993, the Riversiders for Riverside issued a call for Forbes's resignation.[30] They also began to hold their own worship services in Christ Chapel at

9:30 A.M. on Sundays so they would not have to hear Forbes preach. Dissenting members of the church staff led the services.

Forbes was, however, supported by most members of the congregation—which by then had become 50 percent African American—and the main body of the Church Council, as well as groups like the Black Caucus. Some members of the church staff also signed a letter supporting Forbes, openly criticizing the anonymous letter sent by their colleagues who opposed him.[31] Professor James M. Washington of Union Theological Seminary was a strong supporter and close adviser to Forbes during this tumultuous period. Washington and other key leaders—such as Geoffrey Martin, Jeffrey Slade, Dr. Katherine Wilcox, and Betty Davis, all of whom became chairs of the Church Council—helped devise a plan to keep Forbes in office.

In retrospect, Jeffrey Slade, chair of the Church Council during part of this period, noted that every senior minister at Riverside had had difficulties during his term at the church, for example, the James Foreman reparations protest during Rev. Ernest Campbell's term or the controversy about homosexuality during Rev. William Sloane Coffin's pastorate. But it was important to remember that "no other senior pastor had to endure the severity of protests and criticisms that Jim Forbes did." Although a few black members were critical of Forbes's leadership, Slade asserted that there was an "underlying racial tone" to many of the criticisms, such as the style and content of sermons, ad hoc interjections, the length of the service, the addition of gospel music to the service, altar calls, and authoritarian leadership style.[32] According to Rev. Brenda Stiers, executive minister at Riverside from 1994 to 2000, the few blacks who opposed Forbes were largely from the Caribbean. Most of them came from a high church Anglican tradition and preferred the Western canon of music. They thus were "supercritical" of attempts to introduce African American gospel music into the worship service.[33] The controversial events at Riverside underscore the difficulty of changing a church's worship culture. Indeed, studies of American congregations indicate that the greatest conflicts are over attempts to introduce change into a church's worship patterns.[34]

The years from 1995 to 2000 represented a complete reversal of fortune for both Forbes and Riverside. By 1998 the congregation's membership began growing again, adding new members each week. The spectacular bull market through the second half of the decade and careful investing by Riverside's financial advisers more than doubled the church's endowment, from $67 million in 1988 to more than $150 million in 2001. Annual contributions also rose, exceeding target goals each year. The racial composition of Riverside's membership also changed. Under Coffin, African Americans made up 38 percent of the congregation.[35] During Forbes's early years it rose to 50 percent and is currently between 60 to 70 percent.[36]

The transition from the "Negro in the narthex" to the "black preacher in the pulpit" has been long and arduous, full of controversies, problems, and difficulties. It is reflected in the composition of the congregation, the church staff, and the shifting power relations among lay members in the Church Council and other church commissions and committees. The presence of African Americans is stronger and is apparent throughout the church, especially in the worship culture. The 1990s was crucial to the emergence of a new and different Riverside. African Americans have achieved a level of empowerment unprecedented in the church's history.

Riverside's Formal Congregations

The Riverside Church's "formal" congregations are anchored by worship and ritual practices and activities like preaching or communion services, which usually are defined as part of a church congregation. In contrast, the church's "informal" congregations are groups coalescing around a special interest or particular faith concern, such as dance, drama, music, sports, the Black Caucus, gay and lesbian issues, and social justice concerns. They may also include age-graded cohorts such as teenagers or older adults. The informal congregations usually do not have worship at their center, although they may perform ritual practices such as prayer or meditation. While some informal congregations have stable memberships like the older adults, others have much more fluid, changing constituencies, like the audiences for music concerts or theater events. At Riverside, many of these informal congregations are called *ministries*, for example, the music ministry, the youth ministry, the older adults ministry, and the prison ministry.

The formal congregations encompass the Sunday morning nave worship service, which is usually identified as the "main" congregation; the Wednesday evening "Space for Grace" congregation; the congregation at the early Sunday morning "meditation" service in Christ Chapel; and the youth congregation that meets on its own on Sunday. Other formal congregations also use the church building for meeting space but are not a part of the main congregation. These include the Chinese Christian

Fellowship, which meets on Sunday afternoons, and the Ethiopian Orthodox Tewahedo Church of Our Savior, which has its worship service from 9 to 11:00 A.M. on Sunday mornings. Both congregations meet in the Martin Luther King Jr. Wing of the church building.

The Demographic Characteristics of Riverside Church Members

At its first public worship service on October 5, 1930, about six thousand people attended to hear Dr. Fosdick preach.[37] This first service was a major public relations event that attracted many curious New Yorkers and visitors who wanted to be at the opening of the new Gothic building and see the results of the restoration, after a fire in the scaffolding in December 1928 had destroyed the entire interior of the nave and damaged the tower structure. The rebuilding had taken more than one year, and during that time the congregation met at Temple Beth-El on Fifth Avenue.[38] The six thousand attendees were the largest number to attend a morning service at the Riverside Church during its seventy-two-year history at the Riverside Drive location. It also was reported that 846 members transferred their membership from the Park Avenue Baptist Church.[39] After that glorious opening celebration, Riverside's church attendance for morning worship services has generally averaged between twelve hundred and two thousand. Attendance has been affected by factors such as the weather (lower during bad winter weather), transportation difficulties, illness, the school year (higher in the fall), ritual holidays (highest during Christmas and Easter), and sometimes the reputation of the Sunday morning preacher as an orator (higher for better-known speakers).

Church attendance is the number of people who attend a morning worship service, and *church membership* refers to those people who have joined the church as members, pledging by faith to support it financially and be active in its programs. From its first service in 1930 to the present, the regular core of ushers, who are present at the morning worship service and do a head count, have provided a fairly accurate count of church attendees. However, the definition of who is a member of Riverside has shifted over the years and has sometimes included categories like "associate members" or "affiliate members" who have moved away from the city and no longer attend services or are active in programs. Sometimes during political conflicts in the church, attempts have been made to mobilize the associate members in order to express the "general will of the member-ship." Moreover, depending on who is in charge of the Office of Church Membership, the efforts to prune and keep accurate church membership records have not been consistent over the years. Political influence also can affect the reported church membership. Thus, at Riverside, church atten-dance figures have generally been more accurate than church membership reports.

Riverside's international reputation as a leader of American Protes-tantism has also affected its church attendance. It is estimated that visitors continue to make up between 40 to 50 percent of the attendees on a Sun-day morning. For example in 1956, it was reported that "almost half of those at Sunday morning services are nonmembers, many attending for the first time."[40] Between 1938 and 1954, the average annual church atten-dance for morning worship services was about 2,000.[41] At its twenty-fifth anniversary in 1955, the reported total membership for the quarter century (1930–1955) was just over 7,000 members. In 1955 there were 3,621 regular members and 252 affiliate members.[42] A comparative view of the church surveys of 1955/56 and 1999/2000 helps show who made up the main con-gregation of the morning worship service in the nave and the differences and changes over time. All the data and comparisons should be accepted with qualifications, however, since the surveys were only partially filled out by members and attendees, different questions were asked, and the methodology of collecting the data was not always the same. The later sur-vey in 1999/2000 asked more questions and had a more refined analysis of the results.

The Riverside Church Surveys of 1955/56 and 1999/2000

One of the problems of using church survey data from the 1950s is that it was the decade of the most explosive growth of church membership and building of new churches in the United States in the twentieth century as religion became a major way of joining the American mainstream.[43] Peo-ple attended church or synagogue not only for religious reasons but also for social status, "to see and be seen." The 1950s also was an optimistic time for the country, with the victory in World War II in the background and a vigorous economy emerging from the Great Depression. The char-acteristics of this period were described by the authors of the 1956 River-side church survey:

Finally, it is obvious that we are in a period marked by an awakened religious interest throughout the country. This is not the place to diagnose the reasons for the phenomenon. It can be said that behind it is the craving for personal and national security and the growing realization that the future well-being of mankind does not rest wholly with science, social science, political strategy, or scientific research. Already apparent is the fact that religious interest can be abused and exploited. Religion can be offered as a means of achieving purely self-regarding ends. With the mental climate what it is, Riverside's task is to seek to present the Christian Gospel in its full dimensions as relevant to human need, and credible as well as relevant. In particular it must be shown that Christianity not only provides spiritual sustenance but makes a moral demand. Its Gospel is at one and the same time social and personal and brings assurance of the regeneration of both the individual and society.[44]

After this peak period of "awakened religious interest" which resulted in church growth, the turmoil over racial issues and the Vietnam War in the 1960s and 1970s led to major declines in the membership of mainline Protestant denominations and churches, some of which lost more than 40 to 50 percent of their membership.[45] In the 1980s and 1990s, this loss of membership and the ensuing financial losses contributed to some of the major denominations, such as the United Methodists, members of the United Church of Christ, and the Presbyterians, to move their headquarters from the Interchurch Center on Riverside Drive to other parts of the country. This move of denominational headquarters also affected the Riverside congregation, since many denominational church officials and staff members had joined the church.

The reported membership in 1955/56 was about 3,600 regular members plus 252 affiliate members. In 2000, the membership was estimated at 2,500, with no breakdown between regular and affiliate members. However, church attendance during both periods continued in the range of 1,200 to 2,000 persons at the Sunday morning worship service.

The most apparent difference between the periods is the racial composition of the congregation. In 1956 the Riverside Church was more than 90 percent white with a scattering of African American and Asian members. But in 2001 the church membership was between 60 to 70 percent African American. The contrast between the periods is seen clearly in the photographs of the usher boards (see figures 6.1a and b). In 1956 the usher board is composed entirely of white males in formal dress, whereas in 2001 the board contains both males and females and African Americans make up nearly half the ushers. The first black ushers were Theodore R. Britton Jr. in 1960 and Bernard Freeman in 1965.[46] The informality of the ushers' dress in 2001 also reflects differences in class and social status. The inclusion of women as ushers at Riverside, which began in 1973 with T. Floyd Lenart, was one of the more visible changes regarding the role of women.[47] Riverside's main congregation today is more racially diverse than it has ever been, thus fulfilling its goal of becoming an "interracial" congregation.

The feminist movement of the late 1960s and early 1970s provided the leverage for a breakthrough for women in all aspects of leadership roles at the church, including the ministerial staff.[48] In the 1950s all the chairs of the boards of trustees and deacons were white men, but in 2001 the chair of the unicameral board, the Church Council, was a black woman.

The ratio of male and female members of the congregation in both periods is similar, with men making up one-third of congregational members and women, two-thirds.[49] For example, in 1956 it was reported that "approximately 70 per cent of those attending are women." The average age of worshipers in 1956 was forty-five, "somewhat older for women than men."[50] The question about the worshipers' age was not asked in the 2000 survey, so no comparable age figure can be given.

The 1950s was also a time for the growth of suburbs. The GI bill, which provided both educational opportunities and low-cost home loans for veterans, helped accelerate the move out of the city to newly built, mass-produced suburban housing such as Levittown on Long Island. The U.S. Congress also provided massive funding for constructing highways that bypassed cities and led to the explosive growth of the suburbs. This suburbanization affected the Riverside congregation as well. In 1955, it was reported that "more than 600 of our membership [out of an estimated 3,600] live in suburban areas, and, driving to church on Sundays, have found it almost impossible to find a parking place. When the new South Wing is completed, with parking facilities for 300 cars, the number of suburban families may be greatly increased."[51] The 16.5 percent of the congregation that lived in suburbs in 1955 had expanded to 41.1 percent of Riverside members in the 2000 survey who said that they needed a car to get to church. The growth of the black middle class to one-third of the total U.S. black population means that suburbanization also includes African Americans. According to the 2000 survey, almost a quarter of the members were able to walk to church; slightly more than one-quarter

FIGURE 6.1a: The Riverside Church's board of ushers, 1958. *Photo by Empire Photographers, New York City.*

FIGURE 6.1b: The Riverside Church's board of ushers, 1997. *Photograph: Steve Friedman © 1997.*

came by bus and one-fifth used the train; and about 12 percent traveled by taxi or limo.

Church-Growing Views by Gender and Sexual Orientation

In 2000 the main congregation at Riverside was more diverse both racially and in terms of sexual orientation. The church endured extensive debates and struggles during the early 1980s over the acceptance of homosexuals and lesbians. Even now, Riverside's position is far more liberal than that of most major black and white denominations that are still struggling with the acceptance of gay and lesbian members in their congregations and ministries. The gay and lesbian movement has had a profound impact on American society and the Riverside Church. Although there were gays and lesbians in Riverside's congregation in the 1950s, they remained closeted. In contrast, the 2000 survey recognized the diversity in sexual orientation in some of the questions it asked.[52] Table 6.1 shows the growth of Riverside's membership by both gender and sexual orientation. Most of the respondents (heterosexual, gay, lesbian, bisexual, and transgender), between 70 to 80 percent, felt that Riverside's total membership was growing. This perception of church growth is important because one of the complaints in the 1990s was that the church's membership was declining.

Religious Background of Church Members

The results of the 2000 survey demonstrate that the main congregation has continued to uphold Riverside's tradition of being an "interdenominational" church. Riverside is an official member of two denominations, the American Baptists and the United Church of Christ. Table 6.2 shows the diverse religious background of the 815 persons who responded to the survey. Methodists (16.5%), American Baptists (14.4%), and Presbyterians (13.3%) led the way, for a combined total of 44 percent of the congregational members. The United Church of Christ was the previous denominational background for 7.5 percent of the members, and Pentecostals were 2.2 percent. Members with a Jewish or Buddhist background made up less than 1 percent.

Church Growing Views by Gender and Sexual Orientation

Do you believe the numerical Membership of Riverside Church is:

Male
Total = 154 Responses

	Heterosexual	Gay	Bi-Sexual
Growing	75	28	4
Staying	22	4	1
Declining	11	3	6

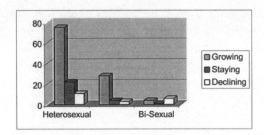

Female
Total = 321 Responses

	Heterosexual	Lesbian	Bi-Sexual	Transgender
Growing	208	16	5	1
Staying	55	6	0	0
Declining	29	1	0	0

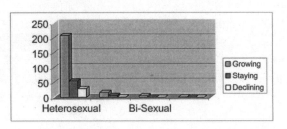

TABLE 6.1.

Religious background of church

Total = 815 Responses

Prior Religion	Number	Percentage
Methodist	125	16.50%
Amer. Baptist	109	14.40%
Presbyterian	101	13.30%
Episcopalian	79	10.40%
No Prior Religion	77	10.10%
Other Baptist	70	9.20%
Roman Catholic	69	9.10%
U C C	57	7.50%
Lutheran	35	4.60%
Unitarian	21	2.80%
Other	19	2.50%
Pentecostal	17	2.20%
Protestant	15	2%
Disciples of Christ	10	1.30%
Jewish	6	0.80%
Buddhist	5	0.66%

*Please note members may have chosen more than one answer.

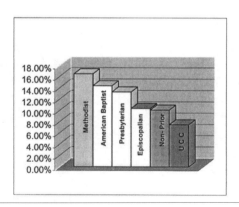

TABLE 6.2.

Comparison between Income and Education

Table 6.3 compares the education and income of 664 respondents. In 2000, Riverside's members were largely middle and upper-middle class in education and income. The median education for Riverside respondents was at the master's degree level, or the completion of one to three years of graduate work. The high number of respondents with doctorates (21.1%) reflects the milieu of higher educational institutions on Morningside Heights. The median income level was between $50,000 and $75,000. The data indicate that only seventy-four (11.14%) of the respondents fell into the "under $20,000" category, which is an indicator of poverty. So even though the Riverside congregation has become a bit more diverse in terms of class, the overwhelming majority are middle or upper middle class. There were no comparable data on education and income from the 1950s, although the presumption is that the congregation then was also well educated and comfortably middle and upper middle class. There were probably a few more patrons of wealth during this early period, such as John D. Rockefeller Jr., who was still an active member in the 1950s, than there are now.

Church Attendance

Table 6.4 shows the answers of 759 respondents in regard to church attendance. About one-third replied that they attended church "more than once a week." In the parlance of the sociology of religion, these attendees would be labeled *superchurched*; that is, they are much more active in their church and participate in other programs each week besides attending worship service on Sunday. Riverside's programs and ministries seem to be highly dependent on the "superchurched" for volunteer help and lay leadership. Another third claimed that they attended church "more than once per month" or at least twice during the month. A little over one-quarter said they attended church "a few times per year." About 5 percent were "no responses." Again, comparable data on church attendance in the 1950s are not available. The surveys of 1955/56 mainly counted the number of people attending the morning worship service and did not ask them about their frequency of church attendance and participation.

Comparison of income to education

Total = 664 Responses

	8th	%	H.S.	%	2 yrs	%	4 yrs	%	MA/	%	DR. or	%
under $20.000	1	1.20%	11	13.40%	12	13.90%	18	20.90%	27	31.40%	5	5.80%
$20.000-30.000	0	0%	6	7.90%	14	18.40%	27	35.50%	23	30.20%	1	1.30%
$30.000-40.000	0	0%	6	5.50%	22	20%	29	26.40%	34	30.90%	10	9.10%
$40.000-50.000	0	0%	4	4.70%	9	10.50%	23	26.70%	37	43%	11	12.80%
$50.000-75.000	0	0%	4	2.60%	9	5.80%	23	14.90%	74	48.10%	43	27.90%
$75.000-100.000	0	0%	1	1%	5	5.20%	15	15.60%	49	51%	22	22.90%
$100.000-150.000	0	0%	0	0%	0	0%	10	18.50%	15	27.80%	25	46.30%
$150.000+	0	0%	0	0%	1	2.30%	5	11.60%	10	23.30%	23	53.50%

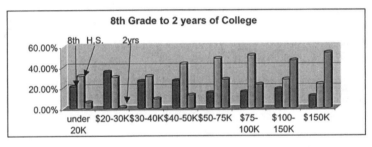

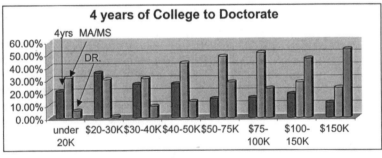

TABLE 6.3.

What Brought Members to Riverside?

Table 6.5 asked, "What brought you to Riverside?" Out of the 1,050 respondents, more than 60 percent replied that they were attracted by worship. Indeed, the Sunday morning worship service has remained the most important reason for persons coming to the Riverside Church throughout its history, from Fosdick to Forbes. Slightly less than one-quarter felt that the church's reputation was important to drawing them. Shopping for churches was the main motivation for almost 10 percent of the respondents. About 7 percent were attracted to non-church-related activities like political events and speeches, while another 7 percent went to Sunday school. Six percent cited the building, and 5 percent came because of the weekly music concerts on Sunday afternoons. Theater events drew about 2 percent, and the older adult programs also attracted 2 percent. About 1 percent came to Sunday morning Bible study classes. One percent came because of the Food Pantry, and the Wellness Center attracted another one

Church Attendance

Total = 759 Responses

Attendance	Number of people	Percentage
More than once per month	259	34.10%
More than once per week	258	34%
A few times per year	205	27%
No answer	37	4.90%

Church Attendance

TABLE 6.4.

What brought Members to Riverside?

Total = 1050 Responses

Brought to Riverside	Number of people	Percentage
Worship	468	62%
Church's Reputation	166	22%
Shopping for church's	70	9%
Non Church related activities	55	7%
Sunday School	50	7%
The Building	45	6%
the Concert	37	5%
Volunteer Opportunity	23	3%
Week day School	17	2%
Baptism	14	2%
Theater Event	14	2%
Older adult Programs	12	2%
Arts and Crafts	11	2%
Bible Study	9	1%
Food Pantry	7	1%
Wellness Center	5	1%
Counseling center	2	0.10%
Job Center	0	0%

*Please note that there are more than one answer to this question.

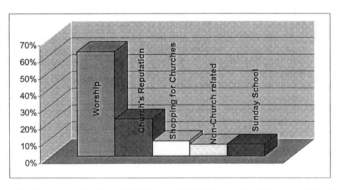

TABLE 6.5.

percent. We should point out that the survey was filled out largely by church members and not the visitors to or attendees of musical concerts or theater events. The results thus reflect the diverse interests of Riverside members. Again, no comparable data from the 1950s are available.

Conclusions from the Demographic Overview

This demographic overview thus shows some of the similarities and differences in the congregational surveys of 1955/56 and 1999/2000. In both periods, the attendance during Sunday morning worship ranged between 1,200 to 2,000. The ratio of one-third males and two-thirds females has not changed. The social class of the majority of congregation members (middle and upper middle class) is similar. Therefore the main differences between both congregational periods are race (now 60 to 70% African American membership), more leadership roles for women, and a greater diversity of sexual orientation, with more gays and lesbians in all phases of congregational life.

Adult Bible study classes are now held before the Sunday morning worship service in the nave. The group has taken the name "Kerygma," and in the winter/spring of 2000/01, fifteen-week class sessions were held on "Discovering the Bible," "The Bible and Theology," "The Book of Revelation: Visions for the Church in Crisis," and "Amazing Grace: A Vocabulary of Faith." On Tuesday evenings another session of "Discovering the Bible" was held. The adult classes supplement the biblical and theological substance of the main worship service.

As mentioned earlier, the main congregation on Sunday morning in the nave is not the only formal congregation at Riverside.

Creating a Space for Grace Congregation

In many American churches, Wednesday evening has usually been reserved for Bible study and prayer meetings. However, at Riverside the Wednesday evening lectures were held in order to attract the university community on Morningside Heights. Dr. Fosdick began the tradition by lecturing on themes of Christian dialogue with the emerging popular fields of psychology and psychotherapy. His successor, Rev. Robert James McCracken, who was not quite as adept at talking about psychology, began bringing in other speakers. Topics of intellectual interest or current events attracted a following of twenty-five to fifty persons, and a well-known lecturer or controversial topic might even bring an audience of one hundred. During his tenure as senior pastor, however, Dr. Campbell eventually did away with the lectures, and Wednesday evenings were sporadically used for special services or Lenten events. In September 1998, an experimental worship service called "Creating a Space for Grace" began to be held regularly on Wednesday evenings in the lower Assembly Hall. A communal meal of soup and bread is served first, with the worship service afterward.

The Space for Grace service is much more informal in both its ritual practices and its style of dress than the main service on Sunday morning. Its cultural style is more in the African American worship mode, which reflects the heritage of about 85 percent of the participants and leaders. The service consists of gospel songs and spirituals, prayer, Scripture reading, and personal testimony, and at the beginning, special prayer requests are made. The atmosphere is enthusiastic, with some shouts of "Amen," handclapping, and the lifting of hands in praise. Occasionally, modern dance pieces are choreographed as part of the service. The senior pastor's wife, Bettye Franks Forbes, leads the Amazing Grace choir, and several of Riverside's associate ministers participate in the service and sometimes preach. The main preacher for the Space for Grace congregation has been Rev. James Forbes, the senior minister who also gives the Sunday sermon. This successful service attracts between one hundred and two hundred participants, including many non-Riversiders and students from Union Theological Seminary. As Rev. Kanyere Eaton, the associate minister in charge of the Food Pantry and Thrift Store, pointed out, the Space for Grace services have also attracted some poor people, who like its informality and "less daunting style." The elderly, needy people, and those recently released from prison come as well. "It's quite attractive to people who don't have a church or don't usually go to one."[53]

At one of the services, the congregants warmly applauded an Asian American youngster who belted out gospel choruses while his mother smiled approvingly. The Riverside handbell choir and the youth choir also sometimes perform. The service usually ends with an invitation to those who need spiritual healing or counseling, with clergy available to meet those requests.

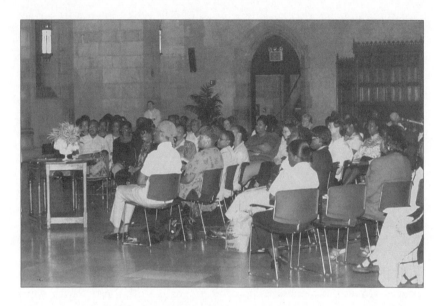

FIGURE 6.2a. Space for Grace congregants.

FIGURE 6.2b: Rev. Bernard Wilson at Space for Grace. *Used by permission of the Riverside Church Archives.*

The Morning Light Meditation Congregation

The Morning Light Meditation service, led by Rev. Fanny Erickson, meets early on Sunday mornings in Christ Chapel during the year and in the Wellness Center in the summer. Beginning with a period of silent meditation and prayer, the service has a full complement of Christian rituals, including Communion (breaking bread and sharing the cup), responsive readings, Scripture, and a homily. There is also a brief healing ritual in which the person needing healing kneels on a cushion and all those in the room are invited to lay their hands on him or her and pray. Although the Meditation congregation is small, attracting only about a dozen persons, mainly women, it meets the needs of those who want to meditate and reflect quietly in a small-group setting. Its emphasis on the healing ritual is also attractive to those who are suffering and beset by personal problems. Weekly prayer and meditation services are also held on Monday and Thursday evenings.

The Meditation congregation and the Wellness Center are the Riverside Church's main points of contact with the Eastern religions and New Age religiosity. Meditation techniques come from both the Christian tradition and Zen Buddhism's sitting and breathing exercises. The Wellness Center, on the nineteenth floor of the Tower, has sponsored such programs as "Mindfulness Meditation," "Community of Mindfulness Weekly Sitting," "Sound Healing," reiki and touch therapy, massage therapy, and classes on tai chi and bodily movement.

Although they are not formally connected, I have included here the Riverside group that walks the labyrinth on Tuesday evenings because of its emphasis on meditation. Created in 1220 at the French cathedral at Chartres, Riverside's architectural forebear, the labyrinth was originally cut into the cathedral's floor and walked as a substitute for the pilgrimage to Rome or Jerusalem. A smaller labyrinth can be found in the chancel area of the nave at Riverside, although it has not been used. Instead, a cutout of the labyrinth is laid on the floor in one of the rooms at Riverside to guide the participants on their spiritual pilgrimage. The hour-long walk, leading to the center and back, is a meditative and spiritual Christian experience.

Although most Christian churches would be reluctant to include non-Christian meditative techniques and spirituality, Riverside's tradition of liberal Christianity has led it to embrace the universal qualities of the world's religions through its emphasis on "internationalism." The architectural figures in the chancel area of the nave, which include those of Moses, Muhammad, Buddha, and Albert Einstein in the West Portal, lend legitimacy to the quest for a universal spirituality.

The Chinese Christian Fellowship

Formed in March 1950 as the only Mandarin-speaking congregation in New York City among the numerous churches where the southern Chinese dialect of Cantonese predominated, the Chinese Christian Fellowship celebrated its fiftieth anniversary in November 2000. The CCF, as it is called, began its relationship with the Riverside Church during the Christmas season in 1951, using the chapel on the third floor of the South Wing for its late afternoon services. On its thirtieth anniversary in 1980, Rev. Eugene Laubach wrote the following:

> One of the pleasures of having been at Riverside for a long time is that of having known Dr. Harry Emerson Fosdick. It was his dream that came to pass in creating this church building and providing a place where persons of great diversity could come together, recognizing that we serve the same Lord. He was fond of reminding people that this church was to be a place where people should not be asked to deny their religious traditions, but to share them for the enrichment of all. . . . This is the spirit that, in my judgment, has guided the relationship of the Chinese Christian Fellowship and Riverside Church.[54]

According to its founder, Mr. Heyward Wong, a retired engineer, the primary reason for the fellowship was to serve Chinese students from mainland China who spoke Mandarin, because all the other Christian services in Chinatown were conducted in Cantonese. Beginning with a small core of thirty to forty members, its membership has grown to more than one hundred. But the CCF has remained a fellowship rather than becoming a formal church. It has no pastor and is staffed by unpaid volunteers. Most of its members retain their membership in other churches, with only about one-quarter of the fellowship having joined the Riverside Church. Its services are scheduled in the late afternoon so that the CCF will not compete with other church services.

The CCF's services follow a traditional Christian worship format with hymns, prayers, Scripture reading, performance by a choir, and a talk by a guest speaker, usually from another church. A Chinese dinner is served after the service. Besides its Mandarin service, the congregation has acted as an intermediary between churches and other groups in the United States and China. It also emphasizes Christian evangelism among non-Christian Chinese and trains young people for missionary work. One of its members translated the New Testament into modern Chinese. The fellowship has a Bible study every Friday evening and sponsors a Sunday school, a choir, and young adults' and older adults' groups. In addition, it holds spring and fall retreats, a summer conference, and occasional outings. The CCF has helped people get jobs and has assisted newcomers with immigration problems. It has also established a scholarship fund for students going into the ministry.[55]

The Hispanic Ministry and Congregation (1960–1970)

Although it no longer exists, Riverside's Hispanic ministry was one of its many formal congregations. Originally called the Hispanic American ministry, this congregation began meeting in February 1960 after a Hispanic minister, Rev. Pablo Cotto, was hired.

The Hispanic American ministry was one of the plans of Riverside's urban ministry task force. in the 2000 survey. The Hispanic congregation held a separate service in Spanish in Christ Chapel and joined the main congregation in the nave on Communion Sundays. Cotto organized various classes taught in Spanish and other programs for Spanish-speaking members. An adult Bible study class was held on Sunday mornings, and worship services took place in the afternoon. Spanish classes and a class to learn English were held during the week, and in 1968 the congregation started a flamenco dance class. Despite these attempts at outreach to the Hispanic neighborhoods in New York City, the congregation remained fairly small and did not grow much during the decade.

In 1968, the Riverside Church had a major financial crisis. In his remarks to the Hispanic American Committee meeting on September 22, 1968, Mr. C. Harvey Williamson, chair of the board of deacons, said that for fiscal year 1969,

There is very little left to cut in this fashion and the prospective deficit is so large that the deacons' Budget Committee has found itself obliged to select a number of program areas for major cost reductions. These reductions will require either the curtailment of these programs or a shift from full-time paid staffing to part-time and volunteer staffing.

The deacons recommended that the full-time bilingual secretary work only part time and Cotto's budget be cut. Notwithstanding the numerous letters of protest and Cotto's meetings with members of the congregation, the budget reductions stood.

In November 1970, Rev. Cotto resigned from Riverside. The worship services continued with guest ministers until December 1971, when the Hispanic congregation decided to move to another location. In an angry letter, dated October 25, 1971, to the church's board of deacons, several members of the Hispanic American task force stated the case for severance from Riverside: "The little flock has thus realized that in the prevailing conditions we cannot grow numerically or spiritually. Therefore, we have reached the conclusion that [it] is more honorable to start our exodus towards an unknown land, than to tighten our chains to this bankrupt institution."[56] There is no record of whether the congregation continued elsewhere or dissolved. Riverside's financial crisis and the Hispanic congregation's lack of growth over a decade were the principal reasons for ending the Hispanic ministry.

After the debacle of the Hispanic American ministry, Riverside's board of deacons decided in November 1971 to create a broader-based program for the Hispanic community, which would be tied to the church's urban ministry program.[57] The vaguely proposed, broader-based program never materialized, however. Riverside Church's current lack of a Hispanic/Latino ministry still remains a large gap at a time when that ethnic population has become the largest minority group in both New York City and the nation.

The Ethiopian Orthodox Tewahedo Church of Our Savior Congregation

Fosdick's vision of Riverside as a place where different people and religious traditions could be celebrated is most applicable to the Ethiopian Orthodox Tewahedo Church of Our Savior. The Ethiopian congregation was organized at Riverside in 1984, first meeting in Christ Chapel and then moving to the fourth floor of the Martin Luther King Jr. Wing. These Ethiopian Christians trace their heritage to the founding of the Ethiopian Orthodox Church in 325 C.E., one of the earliest Christian churches established. The Tewahedo Church of Our Savior rents space from Riverside for its services.

At the 9 A.M. Sunday worship service, which typically lasts for two or more hours, men and women are seated on separate sides of the main aisle. The purpose of gender segregation is to help believers focus on the worship of God. Part of the worship custom is to remove one's shoes upon entering the sanctuary, which is observed by most of the women, some of the men, and all of the five religious leaders in the front chancel area. The theological reason for removing one's shoes is taken from the Old Testament story of Moses and the Burning Bush, in which God commands Moses to remove his shoes and acknowledge that he is on sacred ground. The physical act also symbolizes that one is approaching God with a clean heart. In addition, following St. Paul's injunction in Romans, women members are required to cover their heads with a shawl that also spreads over their shoulders.

At a service that I attended on July 9, 2000, all the worship leaders were men, with three assistants dressed in colorful orange and gold robes. The visiting preacher wore blue and gold robes, and the resident minister had on purple and gold. The founding minister of the congregation, Rev. Tsehai Bernahu, held the incense holder, and incense permeated the room. Most of the service consisted of chanting by the religious leaders and unison recitation by the congregation. The language used was Amharic, the common language of most Ethiopians. Almost all of the three-hour service was conducted with the worshipers standing. Latecomers to the service usually stopped in the middle aisle and bowed toward the front, with some women prostrating themselves on their hands and knees before going to their seats. During the service, congregants moved freely, leaving and returning. While the service seems long according to American standards, it is fairly short and "modern" to the Ethiopians. In their home country, worship services start at 9 P.M. on Saturday night and continue through most of Sunday.

An a cappella singing group, consisting of six men and three women, performed at this fall service, accompanied by a woman who played a large flat drum. At the front chancel area, several icons of paintings of Jesus were hung on the curtains, with one large icon painting of Mother

and Child, who seemed to be Ethiopian because of their darker skin. During one part of the service, the assistants brought out a large red and gold
umbrella under which the preacher stood. According to Rev. Bernahu
Wedneh, the umbrella symbolizes the descent of the Holy Spirit.[58] At the
end of the service, a communion drink and wafers were given to some of
women and children, washed down with a cup of water.

More than one hundred persons attended this fall service, including a
large number of children. About 60 percent of the attendants were women
and 40 percent were men. A brunch for socializing and fellowship is usually held after the service. According to Rev. Wedneh, most of the members represent a variety of middle-class occupations, such as insurance
agents, restaurant owners and workers, doctors, lawyers, and engineers.
Many are intellectuals who fled the communist takeover of the Ethiopian
government in the early 1980s and formed the congregation in 1984 at
Riverside.[59] Patriarch Paulus, who is now the leading archbishop of the
Ethiopian Orthodox Church, helped establish the congregation when he
was studying at Princeton Theological Seminary in the early 1980s.

The Ethiopian Orthodox Tewahedo Church of Our Savior represents
the mixture of religion, culture, language, and family concerns that is
often found among immigrants to the United States. The Ethiopians have
followed the general pattern of coalescing around their religious institutions. As strangers in a strange land, even those who were not particularly
religious in the old country tend to find comfort and security among fellow migrants, especially in singing familiar songs or recitations in their
own language.

The Youth Ministry Congregation and the Riverside Hawks

Under the leadership of Rev. Mariah Britton, the minister for young people, and her staff, the Riverside Church has developed an extensive array of
creative programs for the youth and young adult ministry. On Sunday
morning from 9:30 to 10:30 A.M. the youth group focuses on Christian education and Bible study. The second hour is spent dealing with Christian
identity issues, such as being a teenager and a Christian. The youth group
(grades 7 to 12), which numbers about fifty participants throughout the
year, also conducts its own youth worship services in a contemporary
style, since many of them find the main nave worship service "a bit bor-
ing." Sometimes they visit other churches. The second-hour group also

plans youth fellowship activities for neighborhood kids, like parties or fund-raising events. The youth choir meets after the main nave service and occasionally sings there. A tutoring program is held on Tuesday and Thursday from 4 to 8 P.M. to provide help with homework and for academic enrichment. Volunteer tutors are recruited from the main congregation. The program serves about twenty-five young people from all over the city, not just those at Riverside.[60]

Friday evenings are the most active time for the church's youth programs. The Friday Night Fellowship is the first program for young people in the church's immediate neighborhood. Recreational activities include basketball, Ping-Pong, movies, board games. and fun olympics. Occasionally, rap groups are brought in to sing about what it means to be a Christian. There is little overlap between the Friday and Sunday groups. During the 1960s, the first youth minister, Rev. Robert Polk, used to require those young people who came to the Friday night activities also to come on Sunday morning. But Rev. Britton has found that that strategy no longer works with the more diverse youth population. Sometimes she conducts group discussions on ethical issues, the Ten Commandments, and the life of Jesus. About 150 youth are registered for the Friday Night Fellowship.

The second Friday night program is a girls' group, which was started in 1997. More boys than girls had been attracted to Riverside, largely because of the national reputation of the Riverside Hawks, its basketball team. The girls' group focuses on their own advocacy, support issues, and resources at the church and in the city. Church members are the volunteer female mentors. Meeting from November to May, the girls' activities include three or four overnight retreats, a college trip, and meetings dealing with health and employment issues as well as domestic violence and drug abuse. The girls learn how to write about their experiences in journals, and they meet women from various professions who act as role models for them. Discussions are also held on how the Christian faith can fit into their contemporary lifestyle and the process of becoming a woman. A Friday night boys' group also was formed, with a similar program.

The third Friday night program includes a highly popular four-week Rap Writers Workshop, which attracts between eighty and ninety young people from different ethnic backgrounds. The average weekly attendance is twenty persons. The workshop was founded in 1992 and is taught by Heru Shango (James D. Moody) of Eyecue Consultants and Pee Wee Dance, one of the original "B-boys" from the 1970s.[61] The major goal of Heru and Pee Wee was recovering the original foundation of hip-hop culture as a "positive societal element."[62] The focus was on issues concerning the use of language and responsibility and the craft of rap music, its message and intentionality.

The workshop covers a brief history of rap and invites well-known performers like D. J. Kool Herc, the father of hip-hop, to share their knowledge. Members are invited to make presentations and give performances, with the group offering constructive criticism. Sessions are held on the music industry and opportunities on and off stage, including information about contract negotiations and lawyers. While hip-hop culture, with its own language and style, may seem strange to outsiders (especially to most adults), it is one of the most powerful cultural influences among young people. In applying Paul Tillich's theology of culture to Riverside's ministry with teenagers, hip-hop culture grapples with life and death issues and the realities of the ghetto. The positive call of hip-hop culture is for authenticity and creativity. As Pee Wee Dance said,

> If you are down for the cause then be real with your moves. . . . Most people who are down just because, lack creativity. Rather than exercising their own creativity, they prefer to borrow someone else's. They are biters. Think for yourself and how you want others to view you. We were all born originals. Let's not all die copies. Remember, He who prescribes the diameter of your information, controls the circumference of your activity. Until next time, DANCE TO THE DRUMMERS BEAT![63]

The Rites of Passage program is held on Saturday, covering grades 10 to 12. The program helps young people make the transition from the teen years to become young adults. In the process of leaving high school, they need to develop social skills and independent living skills. Most important, they need to deal with their "inner vision": what they value, how they move, and what their beliefs, values, and actions are. The program extends from November to May and focuses on the internal growth needed to become a man or a woman. Members of the Rites of Passage program also attend overnight retreats and participate in community service activities. When they are ready, they write an essay about themselves, a kind of statement of intent. If they successfully complete the program, they can return as peer leaders. As one parent commented, the Rites of Passage program helped his teenage son navigate through the identity confusion of the teen years. "He was lost and confused but the program helped him find himself."

FIGURE 6.3: Rites of passage: SOS girls' group and Pathfinderz boys' group trip to Princeton University, April 2002. *Used by permission of the Riverside Church Archives.*

One annual event of the youth ministry program is Career Day, held on a Saturday in February for teens from all over the city. The purpose is to encourage young people to explore career opportunities through panels, workshops, and speakers. About three hundred young people attended Career Day on February 10, 2001. The majority of the youngsters were African American and Latino, and they could choose among seventeen career panels, ranging from architecture and aviation to computers, entertainment, law and order, social and human services. Cosponsored by the youth ministry and the Professional and Business Women's Club, Career Day is staffed by sixty to eighty volunteers, mostly from the church. In the panel on law and order, for instance, volunteer lawyers talked about their profession and led the participants in a mock trial. The young people in the panel on entertainment and the music industry learned about some of the harsh business realities of becoming a recording artist. During lunch, well-known media or entertainment personalities performed as special guests. The emphasis throughout Career Day is on providing positive role models of adults who have had successful careers.

The youth ministry's Scholarship Committee offers one-time scholarships for young people who participate in Riverside Church's programs.

The scholarships can be for college or vocational education, with the only requirements being high school graduation and active participation in the church.

Rev. Mariah Britton's philosophy is to reach young people where they are, using a multidimensional strategy and recognizing that fun is an important part of their development. In the beginning, there is not a heavy emphasis on Christian evangelism. "It is important to provide learning experiences for young people," she said, "and show your commitment to them, then work on the Christianity."[64] Future plans include an experimental worship experience in the main sanctuary of the church on Friday nights, called "Spirit Move." It will be a "high-energy" experience with the participation of people from the entertainment industry, liturgical dance, drama, and motivational speakers. Attendance is expected to range from 150 to 1,500 teenagers. Programs on the development of community leadership and the economic empowerment of young people also are on the drawing board.

The Riverside Hawks Congregation

Sports have often been compared to religion in the fervor, passion, commitment, and "collective effervescence" that they elicit from fans, players, and coaches. As Grace Lichenstein wrote in the *New York Times*, "In 1951 when I was a 10-year-old in Brooklyn, baseball was my family's religion; the Dodgers were our denomination, Ebbets Field was the church."[65] Similar comments have been made about "football as the religion of the South." At Riverside, however, basketball is the religion, and the players, families, fans, and coaches form the congregation of the Riverside Hawks.

The Riverside Hawks basketball team is the best known of the informal congregations of the youth ministry's programs. The team's founder, head coach, guru, and lay minister was Ernie Lorch, a corporate lawyer and loyal church member since 1961 when he both joined the church and formed the team. Rev. Robert Polk, who had served a church congregation in North Dakota composed of African Americans and Native Americans, was hired as the youth minister in 1960 and was the first African American clergy on Riverside's ministerial staff. Polk began the effort to attract young people in the church's surrounding neighborhood, especially those in the Grant Houses and in Manhattanville, by forming athletic teams in football, basketball, and softball. At that time, with its upper-middle-class and predominantly white congregation, Riverside was viewed as "the rich white church on the hill." In 1960 the youth program was 95 percent white and Asian, mainly the children of professors at Columbia, Barnard, Union Theological Seminary, and Juilliard. The program was not at all attractive to the children and teens in the neighborhood. Through his friendship with a Congregational minister, Polk recruited Ernie Lorch, a graduate of Middlebury College who had had some interest in the professional ministry before settling on law as a career. Lorch coached the basketball team and also taught Sunday school. In the early years, if a young person played basketball, he or she also had to attend Sunday school, a requirement that was eventually dropped because it did not work very well. As it has developed, Lorch's program is not a proselytizing one, but it "places the church in the community."[66] But in the mid to late 1970s, the football program was eliminated because insurance and uniforms became too expensive and the church decided to concentrate on basketball, which was more popular with the neighborhood's African American and Latino youth.

Lorch's basketball program focuses on good grades, good citizenship, and the development of teamwork via athletics. Over the forty years, more than eight thousand young people have played for Riverside's basketball teams. Each season, three hundred youngsters, boys and girls in different age groups for the seventeen teams, are selected from the thousands who try out. All the coaches are volunteers, and resources come from the church's budget, Nike, and Lorch's fund-raising from corporate colleagues, the Dyson Family Foundation, and his own pocket.[67]

Across the playgrounds and schoolyards of New York's five boroughs, the word is out about "the Church team." "Do you play for the Church team?" is a frequently asked question among youth who claim that they "got game." According to Lorch, all the kids demanded that the name "The Riverside Church" be placed on their Hawks uniforms. "The kids are not embarrassed by the association," he said.[68] The teams practice in the church's gym behind the Assembly Hall. Following the example of some of the New York Knicks, who gather in group prayer on the court after the game, the teams also pray together, especially when they are on road trips around the city to play other teams.

Among the seventeen teams there is one elite traveling team, nationally known as the Riverside Church Hawks, made up of high-school varsity players who play in a summer league. Their first trip was to Phoenix in 1972. Now the team travels to Europe every year and to Canada for a winter tournament, as well as to other contests in the United States. More than sixty professional players for the National Basketball Association have come from the team. For example, Elton Brand of Peekskill, who played for the Hawks in his sophomore year in high school, was the number one pick in 1999 NBA draft by the Chicago Bulls. Mark Jackson, point guard of the Knicks and the Pacers, also was part of the team. The Riverside Hawks have had a phenomenal success rate, with 95 to 98 percent of the players receiving scholarships to go to college. Eighty percent of its players graduate from college. Twenty-nine Division 1 college coaches were members of the Hawks, and hundreds more coached in community colleges, high schools, and other levels. For example, Matt Doherty, who played for the University of Notre Dame and became the head coach for the University of North Carolina, was an alumnus of the team. The Riverside program is one of the country's most prestigious nationally known youth basketball programs.

In March 2000 the NCAA began investigating the role of the Riverside Church's basketball program in helping Erick Barkley, a Riverside alumnus and St. John's point guard, pay tuition at a prep school in Maine. An article in the New York Times, "Looking inside the Church for Answers," by William C. Rhoden, indicated that the NCAA had been looking into the relationship of the church's basketball program, Lorch, and schools like St. John's that have been the beneficiaries of Lorch's largess.[69] The NCAA has been suspicious of any financial support, including plane tickets or the use of cars, given to star players. Lorch claimed that everything was above board and that the $2,000 scholarship was given to Barkley on the basis of financial need, the same reason as other Hawks players have received Riverside scholarships in the past.[70] As Rev. Forbes noted in the New York Times article, these scholarships are not only for athletes but also for other Riverside youth to enhance their educational opportunities, such as the teenage girls participating in the Sister to Sister program. Nevertheless, the publicity and NCAA probe have caused Rev. Forbes and other church leaders to try to bridge the perceived gap between "heaven" in the nave and "earth" in the basement gym.[71]

The Congregation of Older Adults

According to Rev. Sally E. Norris, the former staff minister in charge of the older adults, they form a special congregation of their own. About one-third of Riverside's members are over the age of sixty-five. Although some of them have moved into retirement homes, they still retain their church membership. The majority have been members for a long time, between thirty to sixty years. They also are a very diverse group, racially, ethnically, and economically. Since most of them have retired, the older adults prefer to meet at Riverside during the daylight hours, feeling safer at that time in the big city.[72]

On Wednesdays during 2001/02, two programs were typically held: a French conversation group led by Betty Jones and an Art of Movement class by Eileen Jones. The Tower League, a program designed for seniors, has several meetings on Thursdays: a men's group at 9 A.M., a beginners' group at 10 and 11 A.M., and an advanced group at 10 A.M. After the Tower League meetings, there is a Bible study for older adults at 12:30 P.M. Since most of the Tower League members are women, knitting circles are occasionally formed to knit clothes, which are donated to Harlem Hospital. The Thursday programs also have had sessions on nutrition and health, speakers from the New York City Health Department, museum slide programs, and the Million Man March Singers. The Tower League tried to develop intergenerational programs, such as "Generations against Violence" and "Police Brutality," but they were hard to maintain, since the younger people did not attend regularly. A grandparenting program, with older adults serving as mentors in Riverside's weekday school, worked for a while, but then the participants lost interest.

Older adults at Riverside Church form the bulk of weekday volunteers. During the week, they volunteer in the Food Pantry, the Thrift Store, and the library. On Fridays, they collate the Sunday bulletin for the main nave worship, and they plan and coordinate the annual church Thanksgiving dinner. The Thanksgiving dinner used to be for older adults, but with welfare reform and cutbacks in the social safety net, younger families have become the norm. The older adults also take cultural trips, both in and out of the city, to museums, operas, symphony concerts, and sight-seeing trips to the country.

Rev. Norris explained that the older adults "function like a church," with their own focus on missions, issues of justice, Bible study, and, occasionally, their own worship services. They visit one another, send cards on birthdays and other occasions, and constantly keep in contact by phone. At a vulnerable time in their lives, they have formed a caring community.

Many of the older Riversiders are retired church professionals, some who never married and others who worked as missionaries abroad. There are also lots of retired nurses. Most of them have a "*real* old value of *church,*" which means that they want not only to receive but, above all, to make a contribution. Most grew up in the Depression, so their concept of money is different from that of younger people. They are a very thrifty group, constantly looking for sales. They also take their activities in the church very seriously. Most of them are not rich, but they give generously of their time and talent. They also are very reliable; if they made a commitment, they follow through. Indeed, regardless of their racial background, the work ethic of the older adults is different.[73]

Rev. Norris has worked with the older adults ministry since 1983, and a mutual trust and respect has developed over the years. She regards them as a delight to work with, since there are few power struggles or ego trips. Most have been through so much in their lives that they do not get worked up over insignificant things. For the future, there are plans to get older adults "computer literate," since that is a revolution that has largely passed them by. But many of the elderly are visually impaired, lack mobility, and cannot afford computers.

There also are plans for more arts classes and particularly more advocacy work in the area of health care and benefits. A "drop-in center" for older adults is a significant need for the future, as the number of those over sixty-five will rise quickly with the retirement of the baby boom generation.

The Music Congregation

Music has the ability to transport its audience to another realm, away from the reality of everyday life.[74] Its power can generate ecstasy or quiet, reflective meditation and worship. Throughout its history, the Riverside Church has always had excellent musical programs, with choirs, organ, and instrumental music undergirding the church's worship life. All of Riverside's senior ministers from Fosdick to Forbes have recognized and appreciated what music can add to worship. As Dr. Robert James McCracken observed, "Music has a marvelous power of reaching the soul. It confirms faith, quickens zeal, inspires praise and thanksgiving."[75] The music congregation(s) at Riverside include the performers and the audiences in the main worship services and the numerous concerts held on Sunday afternoons and on other days, especially during holiday periods.

Before the church building on Riverside Drive was completed, the congregation under the influence of Dr. Harry Emerson Fosdick already had an active music ministry at the Park Avenue Baptist Church. In 1924 John D. Rockefeller Jr. gave the fifty-three-bell carillon to the church, which he dedicated to the memory of his beloved mother, Laura Spelman Rockefeller, during the following year. In 1927 classes were held at the Park Avenue church on "The World's Only Carillon School," "The Art of Selecting Church Music," "The Ministry of Music," "A Renaissance of the Hymn," and "Early American Church Music." With the completion of the Gothic cathedral on Riverside Drive in 1930, the interest in the Laura Spelman Rockefeller Carillon was renewed with weekly concerts. The carillon also was expanded from fifty-three to seventy-two bells. The first public recital by Kamiel Lefevere on the carillon was on December 24, 1931. It was said that its music could be heard "far across the river in New Jersey,"[76] and the National Broadcasting Company aired that carillon concert on the radio. In the 1930s other music sessions included "Anthems We Have Used," "The Organ's Place in Worship," "Mendelssohn's 'Elijah,'" "Pioneers in American Music," and "What Does the Carillon Play." In January 1934, the Riverside Symphony Orchestra was formed by Professor Norval L. Church of Teachers College. Its first rehearsal was held in February, and the symphony orchestra's first concert was in April 1934. About fifty members joined for weekly rehearsals, good music, and fellowship. Two concerts were given every year in January and April.[77] During the 1940s, the contributions of the music ministry came to the forefront, including such classes as "Music As a Healing Art," "Our Own Orchestra Carries On," " Music Is Our Worship," "Friends of Music," and "The New Organ Console."

The architecture of Riverside's Gothic cathedral included music in its building plans, with space for a world-class organ in the nave and the Laura Spelman Rockefeller Memorial Carillon and booth for the carillonneur in the Tower. The Hook and Hastings Company of Boston built a 112-stop organ for Riverside in 1929/30. Although Hook and Hastings had a venerable reputation in the nineteenth century for building America's most important organs, it had not kept up with technological innovations. Immediately after the installation of the organ and its pipes, the criticisms started. "As organs went in those 1930s," wrote T. Scott Buhrman, editor of *The American Organist*, "this instrument was not really bad; it just wasn't good." However, it was not until 1948 that the first organ was gradually replaced. After assuming the position of Riverside organist in 1946, Virgil Fox's top priority was a new organ, which was built under his direction by Boston's Aeolian-Skinner Organ Company. The console arrived in 1948, and the installation of the organ began in 1953 and was completed in 1955.

The organ was dedicated with great fanfare, including a concert by the New York Philharmonic conducted by Dimitri Mitropoulos.[78]

Virgil Fox became the best-known and most famous of Riverside's organists. In 1952 he was voted as America's "most popular organist" by the American Guild of Organists. Known as Virgil to his numerous fans, he

> combined talent and flair with equal parts drama and melodrama. Matched to an electrifying technique and a diligent practice regime, Fox handily commanded five decades of capacity audiences all over the world. the Riverside Church was a prestigious pedestal from which to launch a concert career, and the Fox-Riverside marriage seemed an ideal one.[79]

At Riverside, Fox teamed with his friend W. Richard Weagly, the choir director, to produce an ambitious program of musical events. Fox brought the music of Bach to young people in an innovative and exciting way: in 1970, in his most daring concert, Fox gave an all-Bach program combined with a light show at New York's of rock music, the Fillmore East. In 1965 Fox left Riverside to begin a full-time concert career. He died on October 25, 1980, with funeral services held in Palm Beach, Florida, and at the Crystal Cathedral in Garden Grove, California. A memorial service was also held at Riverside. Virgil Fox's reputation as an organist and his impact on the music life at the Riverside Church was so great that a Virgil Fox memorial concert was held on October 8, 2000.[80]

On March 13, 1955, a committee of the music ministry conducted the only known survey of the attendees of a Sunday afternoon concert at Riverside. A member of the committee wrote: "Riverside already performs many special ministries in which people can participate who are not a part of the church's total life. This would include the ministry of music." His insight was confirmed by the survey, since the majority of attendees at the Sunday afternoon concert were visitors. Of the 223 persons who filled out the survey cards (from a total of 347 in attendance), about 83 percent were visitors, and nearly 17 percent were church members. For nearly one-third of the visitors, this was their first visit, and almost half attended "occasionally." About half the visitors indicated that they attended college or university in New York City and lived in the neighborhood.[81] In other words, about half the audience in 1955 were either students or professors from the academic institutions of Morningside Heights. It has always been one of the church's goals to minister to the intellectual community, and the music ministry has been an important way of attracting this group.

FIGURE 6.4: Virgil Fox at the organ. Photograph by Lilo Kaskell. *Used by permission of the Riverside Church Archives and Lilo Kaskell Photo.*

Riverside's music program also took advantage of the musical talent at the nearby Juilliard School of Music and the School of Sacred Music at Union Theological Seminary from the 1930s until the early 1970s, when both schools relocated. The Manhattan School of Music has replaced Juilliard, and sacred music concerts have also been held in cooperation with the music program at St. Paul's Chapel at Columbia University.

Because of his great love of music, Dr. Robert James McCracken's family and the church's Music Committee dedicated a magnificent Steinway concert grand piano to his memory. To be used exclusively in the nave, the Robert James McCracken Memorial Piano was dedicated at a Sunday afternoon inaugural recital by virtuoso pianist Agustin Anievas in 1974.

In the early 1990s, attempts to introduce diversity into the music of the main worship service encountered resistance in some quarters of the congregation. Before his untimely death, Professor James M. Washington spoke about the difficulties of introducing gospel music into the main

Sunday morning service. Although the church's Inspirational Choir sang only one song a month, there were many complaints about missing the standard European classical music.[82] Dr. John Walker resigned in May 1992 as the director of music and organist of the Riverside Church as a result of the controversy over the worship and music programming. Walker was a staunch defender of traditional classical music in worship. But under the growing pressure of the greater African American presence in the congregation, the worship music has gradually changed to include more diversity. In June 1992 Dr. Timothy Smith was hired as Walker's replacement, with a mandate to broaden the church's music program.

According to Dr. Smith, at a lay-staff retreat in 1992 "there was a cry for more diversity." Smith's strategy for change was to maintain a core of Western European music but to introduce other forms of music to match the diversity of the congregation: "There was a desire to keep the international and interracial groups of people in the church." The push for diversity in music has achieved some success. There are many different styles of music now, and it has become "very international." In Smith's view, there are no conflicts now, but "if one style of music dominates then the conflicts would come back."[83]

During the past decade, Dr. Smith estimates that the Sunday afternoon nave concerts have drawn between two hundred and six hundred persons. Christ Chapel, which seats 175 persons, has also been used for chamber groups and smaller events. The excellent historical reputation of the Riverside Church's music programs has made it easier to find musicians to perform there. Smith has found that the most successful musical events in terms of numbers draw on the church members' familiarity with the musicians, with complete outsiders attracting only fifty to seventy persons.[84]

From 1999 to 2002, the music ministry staged programs such as the Riverside Children's Concert Series, the Riverside Choir and Festival Orchestra, the Riverside Inspirational Choir, the Orpheus Chamber Orchestra, the Martin Luther King Jr. Celebration Concert, an opera on Nelson Mandela's life, and "Voices from the East: Music of Asian Women Composers." In 1984 the Friends of Music group was established to raise funds to support the continuation of distinguished musical presentations at Riverside. Paula Larke, a story-teller-gatherer and musician who has been described as "a cross between Nina Simone and James Brown," was chosen as Riverside's "artist in residence" for 2001/02, a position made possible by the Friends of Music.

For the future of Riverside's music program, Dr. Smith sees the need to maintain the diversity, stretching the boundaries, and to strengthen the quality of the programs: "One can always work to improve the quality of the music being offered."[85] He also plans to collaborate more with the other institutions on Morningside Heights, such as the Miller Theater at Columbia, the Manhattan School of Music, and Columbia's St. Paul's Chapel.

While the focus of Riverside's music ministry has always been on the Sunday morning worship service in the nave, the Sunday afternoon music concerts, and special musical performances, other forms of music have been represented in a wide variety of programs. For example, the youth ministry has rap and hip-hop sessions to bring in young people. During its operation, Riverside's FM radio station WRVR was regarded as one of New York City's premier jazz stations. The bells of the Laura Spelman Rockefeller Carillon also provide musical programs by famous carillonneurs. A handbell group known as the Riverside Ringers was formed. The choirs at the Riverside Church include the main Riverside choir led by the associate director of music and choir director, Helen Cha-Pyo; the Riverside Inspirational Choir directed by Nedra Neal; the Ebony Ecumenical Ensemble led by Bettye Franks Forbes; the Riverside Singers under Mark Miller's direction; and the Riverside Children's Choir under Denise Weber's leadership.

The Theater Arts Congregation

When designing the South Wing (later renamed the Martin Luther King Jr. Wing) of the church in 1959, the architects—at the urging of the members of Riverside's Drama Guild—added space for an intimate professional theater and stage with excellent acoustics, lighting facilities, and seating for two hundred. Originally called the Cloister Theater, it became known more widely as the Riverside Theater.[86] Over the years, it has given birth to many fledgling artistic groups in modern dance and ballet, opera, and musical and drama performances. The people who have coalesced around the Riverside Theater have formed an informal congregation made up of those whose primary interests center on the theater. Some are members of the church, but many others are not. This dynamic congregation has been an important part of Riverside's ministry.

A young adult organization, the Riverside Guild was led by Gertrude Fagan of the Riverside staff, who helped develop a very active drama workshop during the 1930s and 1940s. Plays were given during the church's Sunday evening worship services. Drama also was used extensively in the church school and other church organizations, especially the Business and Professional Women's Club. In the 1950s and early 1960s the Committee on Religious Drama struggled to define the boundaries of "religious drama" without being too restrictive (limiting plays to the Christmas or Easter pageants) or overly broad (including everything that passes for drama). One of the guiding ideas was that the plays should emphasize "what is unique and different from Broadway." In 1959, the committee issued its "Report and Recommendations of the Committee on Religious Drama," which recommended the following for a program of "high-caliber" religious drama at the church:

- Presenting celebrational, festival, liturgical or chancel drama as a part of the life of the church and related to the church year.
- Using drama as a means of helping people to think about the relevance of the Christian faith to personal and social problems.
- Using this program as a means of developing fellowship and of enriching the lives of all persons who participate directly or indirectly.[87]

In 1961 Professors Mary Tully and Tom Driver of Union Theological Seminary further reflected on the parameters of religious drama. According to Tully, religious drama can explore the polarities in life (good and evil, life and death), portray the content of tradition and faith, and reveal the dynamics of interpersonal relationships. Driver proposed two types of drama as being religious: "dramas of celebration" relating to rites, events, and stories in the Old and New Testaments and the traditions of the church; and "dramas of exploration" relating to a problem that Christians should think about, an idea or an "area of experience outside our own which would help us to understand how other people feel."[88] Expanding on Tillich's theology of culture, Joseph Duffey wrote, "A book [or a play] is religious if it moves us, shocks us, stirs us to deeper and more serious concern with the fundamental questions of our life's meaning, its hope and despair."[89]

The Riverside Guild was active for two decades before it finally collapsed and went out of existence in 1959, one year before the Cloister Theater was constructed. "Fewer young people were interested in activities within the church," wrote church member Constance Ball.

> Many old Guilders left the city or became older adults. . . . Had the Theater been available a few years earlier, a large and enthusiastic group of young adults who had profited by Miss Fagan's training and direction would have formed the nucleus from which productions in the new program might have been cast.[90]

(Gertrude Fagan served as the director of the program of religious drama from 1936 until her retirement in September 1963.)

During the early 1960s, the newly reconstituted Committee on Religious Drama, led by Constance Ball, presented such productions as *The Prodigal Son*, *King Lear*, *John Brown's Body*, and *Three by Tennessee Williams*. The Tennessee Williams production drew the largest audience, more than one thousand over four performances.

From the late 1960s to early 1970s the dramatic productions became bolder and more experimental. A group called La Famiglia (The Family), which started from Riverside's Prison Ministry Committee's work with inmates, produced the play *Short Eyes*, about the murder of a sex offender at the New York House of Detention. This powerful drama was written by an ex-offender, Miguel Piñero, directed by Marvin Felix Camillo, and featuring The Family, Riverside's company of ex-offenders, in the cast. Scheduled for a three-week run at the Riverside Theater in January 1974, *Short Eyes* won critical acclaim for its dramatic realism. The play moved to Joseph Papp's New York Shakespeare Festival, and after five months it opened to rave reviews on Broadway on May 23, 1974. During a Communion service on June 2 at the Riverside Church, a special salute to The Family was presented by the preacher, Dr. Robert L. Polk, the church's minister of urban affairs, and Colleen Dewhurst, the actress who played a lead role in *Moon for the Misbegotten* on Broadway.[91] Dewhurst had taken a special interest in La Famiglia and helped in the group's climb to success.[92]

Riverside's Dance Festival was most famous during the 1970s and 1980s. The Riverside Church began experimenting with the use of modern dance in worship on December 30, 1934, when the "mother of modern dance," Ruth St. Denis, and her rhythmic choir performed the *Masque of Mary* at an evening service sponsored by the Riverside Guild in the nave.[93] "Little did she know at that time," wrote David K. Manion, director of the Dance

Festival, "that Riverside would become home to so many choreographers and dance companies."[94] Gradually a regular program of dance performances evolved and began to supplant the drama productions, which ended in the mid-1970s owing to fiscal difficulties. In 1968 the Dance Theater Workshop began the formal production of modern dance performances. In the early 1970s among the groups and artists who presented their dance performances were George Faison, Annabella Gamson, Deborah Jowitt, Larry Richardson, the Don Redlich Dance Company, and the Mary Anthony Dance Theater. Sophie Maslow, Phyllis Lamhut, and Joyce Trisler staged their company productions at the church in the mid-1970s.[95] George Faison, who had his first performance at Riverside on April 4, 1974, plans to return in 2004 to celebrate his thirty years in modern dance.[96]

Under the headline "Theater of the Riverside Church Makes Major Commitment to Dance" in the *New York Dance Bulletin* (September 10, 1975), the Riverside Dance Festival was officially formed, with its first performance by the Hava Kohav Dance Theater in November 1975. The Dance Festival typically offered thirty-four weeks of dance, with more than sixty companies appearing during its season. The festival also brought together many young artists in special programs entitled "Choreographer's Night" in order to encourage the development of their talent.[97]

Some of the dance companies that performed at Riverside between 1982 and 1984 were the Mari Kajiwara and Ohad Naharin Company; the Alvin Ailey Repertory Ensemble; the Ballet Hispanico of New York; Dinizulu and His African Dancers, Drummers, and Singers; the Asian American Dance Theater; and the Historic Dances of Ruth St. Denis.[98]

The stock market crash of 1987and the resulting recession and fiscal effects on the church eventually forced the closing of the Riverside Dance Festival after more than a decade of remarkable performances. The church's endowment did not recover until the mid-1990s. Except for occasional productions, the Riverside Theater remained largely inactive until Jewel Miguel was hired as its artistic director in 1997. She began by reviving the dramatic and dance performances. Two of her innovations are the Forum Theater Workshops and the Family Arts Festival. The Forum Theater Workshops sponsor the "Theater of the Oppressed," interactive productions that explore the external and internal conflicts of issues like "emancipation from poverty." Audience participation is encouraged, and participants get up on stage to express their feelings about how things could change. Maranatha, Riverside's gay and lesbian organization, conducted a workshop on gay and lesbian issues, and the Social Justice Commission explored domestic violence and police brutality.

Beginning in 1999, the Riverside Theater has helped cosponsor the New York Family Arts Festival, a month-long summer program from the first week of July to the first week of August, which makes use of different racial and ethnic cultural heritages. Funded by the Chase Manhattan Bank, the festival uses both the theater and an outdoor stage with bleacher seats erected on Claremont Avenue, blocked off from traffic. Events of the festival have included African *griots*, or storytellers; Korean drum and dance; "Kettle Drum Rhythms"; the Wellspring Project, a dance history demonstration workshop; and a special production from Canada on Inuit culture, *Aah-Potee! That's Snow.*[99]

According to Miguel, there is a theater arts congregation, composed of not only regular attendees but also scores of volunteers. Some of the volunteers are from the church and others are from outside, providing a widespread and useful support network for theater productions. Some serve as ushers or help with staging, lighting, and scenery, and others are artists themselves who bring new ideas and requests for space. The theater arts program is beginning to tap into the main Riverside congregation, coming up with ideas of how to support the work of the church through the arts. Miguel has begun to work closely with the youth ministry and the music, arts, and education programs. The Business and Professional Women's Club has requested help from the theater arts program to aid them in reaching young women, and the Social Justice Commission is planning to use the theater to focus on global antiracism. According to Jewell Miguel, she wants to use the creative, artistic avenue to attract more people to the church and connect with them on a different level. "Many of these people may not come to hear Rev. Forbes preach, but they are present at Riverside [in the theater arts program]."[100]

In 2000 there were 175 performances in the Riverside Theater by seventy-five different arts organizations. "All of this occurred without a word of advertising anywhere," said Miguel. "Artists are looking for performance space and many outside groups have had a wonderful time at Riverside so they keep coming back and tell others. There isn't theater of this caliber in the neighborhood and very few venues in the whole upper West Side, including Harlem."[101]

Future plans include the development of a Riverside Youth Jazz scholarship program. The program will be intergenerational, bringing together professional jazz musicians, budding musicians, and youth. It will cover the history and playing of jazz. The jazz program idea was inspired by a nine-year-old Riversider named Macano Dano who attended the Wednesday evening Space for Grace services with his mother, an Asian immigrant. Dano, a musical prodigy who occasionally played the piano for the Wednesday services, won a jazz scholarship to the Manhattan School of Music.

The Congregation of the Poor

Riverside's congregation of the poor is an informal one, consisting mostly of poor people who use the church's social service programs such as the Food Pantry or the Thrift Store. Most of them come during the weekdays to wait on a line of chairs to be ushered into the Food Pantry so they can select a bag full of groceries to take home. They also buy clothes at the Thrift Store at bargain prices. The Food Pantry opened in 1983. Martha Rolon, the associate director of social services, came to work at Riverside first as a student intern in 1986 and joined the staff the following year. Many of her clients expect to be helped "because it is a church," she noted.[102] Rolon and her staff screen the clients by having them fill out a social services evaluation form. The Pantry helps about two hundred people each week, for an average each month of eight hundred. Whereas once they were predominantly African American, the number of Latinos has increased as much as 50 percent. More drug addicts, especially poor men, and more undocumented aliens began coming in the 1980s and 1990s. Even some members of the Riverside Church, especially the elderly, use the Food Pantry during financially difficult times.

The principal concern for many of the poor is surviving from day to day. Food, shelter, and clothing are the basic material requirements for their survival. Although Riverside may be only one stop in a chain of social service agencies they visit, it is an important place because they are treated with dignity by the staff members and volunteers. Poor people who have found their way to the church form an informal congregation, similar to that of the nonchurch members who attend Riverside's music concerts or theater performances. In fact, some of the poor become acquainted with one another as they sit and wait for their turn to be served. They also may come to the church building more often than do concert or theater goers. Nonetheless, the poor at Riverside still remain a largely unorganized group, with no attempts to formally organize them.

Besides food and clothing, Riverside's social services help the working poor with rent payments. Out of an average of twenty requests a week, only five can be helped with the church's limited funds. The rent arrears budget is made up of federal funds and private donations, totaling $20,000 per year. Other programs for the poor are a listing of jobs at the Job Center, help with utilities, and referrals to other social service centers. The only job training Riverside offers is a weekly barbershop class. From 1984 to 1994, the church also provided a homeless shelter for ten men each night. A shower project, in which the homeless can use some of the shower stalls at the church each week, was instituted in the summer of 2000. Most of the programs have been staffed by church volunteers, mainly the elderly and retired.

According to Rolon, the clients of the social services programs always are invited to attend the worship services at the church. Informal conversations with some of them indicate that many of them do not worship at Riverside. Rev. Kanyere Eaton, the former director of the Food Pantry and Thrift Shop, noted that a few clients attend the Wednesday night Space for Grace service because they feel more comfortable there than at the Sunday morning nave service. She also said that a church volunteer started a Bible study session on Sunday mornings, at which poor people can have breakfast and study the Bible. One of the greatest needs for Riverside's social services programs is for more volunteers, especially for the food and clothing drives. During recent food drives, when volunteers sit outside grocery stores and supermarkets to collect food donations, they have discovered that people are less willing to donate food to black than to white male volunteers, so fewer men of color are now volunteering.[103]

The class issue, especially with regard to persuading more poor people to participate in church programs or worship services, has been one of the most difficult problems for the Riverside Church to resolve. While the church has been successful in providing social services for an informal congregation of the poor, it has not yet developed a more formal one. Educational levels, styles of dress, and aspects of culture such as worship style prevent the church from transcending the class issue. As Betty Davis pointed out in her interview, when she grew up in a poor-working class family in central Harlem, her own family did not attend church each week, even though they lived across the street from one, because they could not afford the "Sunday clothes" that were expected at most black churches. However, her mother did allow her to buy a new dress for Easter, which is when she attended church.[104] At Riverside, the wealth of the church and the education and the income of its members have heightened the class barriers which often scare off poor people from actively participating in worship.

The Congregation of Staff and Workers

Most congregational studies tend to ignore the hired help of megachurches like Riverside and instead focus on the main congregation or ministries.[105] Nonetheless, the workers or staff employees at the Riverside Church constitute an informal congregation, numbering about 147, including security guards; building and grounds maintenance workers; cafeteria workers; secretaries and clerical staff; mailroom staff, middle management directors of programs and offices like communications, finance, worship, music, theater arts; and teachers at the Day Care Center. With activities and events scheduled every day and night throughout the week, Riverside could not function without these workers. They also have their own network of relationships, from more formal ones with their "bosses" to informal circles of friendships with fellow workers, eating lunch together and sharing their personal lives and concerns.

All employees at Riverside are now called "staff," and the "All Staff Committee," which includes clergy, meets once a month. The meetings usually do not begin with prayer but include it when appropriate. The committee helps plan events and the annual church retreat. Before 1996 only the clergy and some directors, such as of music and worship, attended the monthly meetings and retreat. But the many programs, events, and uses of the building by outside rentals required that everyone participate. During the past two years, according to Corinne Nelson, chair of the All Staff Committee, the process has become "more inclusive."[106] Before this, many of the staff did not feel connected to the events.

The Riverside staff's major concerns are job stability, fair wage increases and advancement, benefits, working conditions, and relationships with supervisory personnel. Job stability and security are greater concerns now because during the fiscal crisis of 1988 at the church, about one-third of the staff employees were let go. The drastic downsizing made Riverside look more like a secular corporation than a church that cared about people. Fair wages also remain another point of contention because the Hay

Study of Compensation and Benefits at the Riverside Church during 1999/2000 showed that compared with other nonprofit institutions in the city, Riverside's wages were 20 to 22 percent below the average for clerical positions and blue-collar workers. There also were wage inequities in some positions, particularly with blue-collar maintenance workers making more than those in clerical jobs. However, Riverside's benefits ranked in the top 75 to 90 percent compared with those of other institutions. The HayGroup recommended a gradual equalization in wages.[107]

Many of the support staff, according to Nelson, take their jobs more seriously than do their counterparts at other institutions, "because it is a church." They also respect the stature and prestige of the church in New York City and American society. Out of the 147 staff workers, eighteen have joined Riverside as members, although most have decided not to mix their place of employment with their religious life, preferring to worship elsewhere. Besides the ambiguous tension between work and religion, there is tension between the lay members of the church and the professional staff and middle management directors. As a member of both the American Baptist and United Church of Christ denominations, Riverside adheres to a congregational polity, which means that the lay members of the congregation make the major decisions and the staff are expected to carry them out. Often, however, lay persons are not the most knowledgeable about the job or task, even though they have more decision-making power than the professionals on the staff. Such tensions are common in large churches like Riverside with enormous resources. Moreover, according to Nelson, some of the middle management staff feel the tension between being "administrators" and being "pastoral."[108] At one level, they are administrators in a bureaucratic structure that tends to be impersonal, but at another level, they are working in an institution with beliefs and values that support caring about people.

Obviously, workers have their own religious and spiritual needs and daily concerns. But at Riverside, as at other institutions, they tend to be "invisible people" laboring in the background. Nevertheless, they do constitute an informal congregation with its own group life. As the sociologist Emile Durkheim pointed out, groups of people eventually develop their own religious dimension, or the daily symbols, rituals, and values that contribute to their own social cohesion.[109]

The Relationships among Congregations

Throughout this chapter we have seen that a megachurch like Riverside is composed of many different congregations, some formal ones like the main nave congregation, the Wednesday evening Creating a Space for Grace congregation, the Ethiopian Tewahedo Church of Our Savior, and the Chinese Christian Fellowship, as well as many informal ones like the youth ministry, the Riverside Hawks, the older adults ministry, poor people, and the music and theater arts ministries. Many of the "ministries" and smaller groups at Riverside really are informal congregations with a group life and dynamic of their own. The informal congregations are related to the larger church and main congregation in that each of them have a clergy person, staff member, or lay leader either in charge or directly relating to that group. Some church members also are members of the informal congregations and participate in their activities. These informal congregations are an important part of the church's outreach to the secular city, attracting visitors and nonchurch members to its programs. However, at present, there is no organized way in which the members of the formal and informal congregations can meet together.

As we have seen, Riverside's composition of multiple congregations is rooted in its history. In 1972 the church's urban ministry think tank recognized that Riverside was not "one homogeneous congregation" but "a collection of congregations." Furthermore, the task force predicted that "there would be periodic gatherings at which the whole body would be gathered together in a kind of cathedral function."[110] Currently at the Riverside Church there are no periodic gatherings at which the whole body is brought together.

One suggestion is for some kind of "Riverside festival days," during which all the formal and informal congregations are invited to come together, have a meal, and discuss who they are and what they are doing. Since no place at Riverside could accommodate such a large assemblage, tents could be erected on Claremont Avenue on a Saturday or Sunday afternoon. Once a year, all the congregations would be invited to join the main congregation for a morning worship service in the nave.

Other ways of joining the main congregation and the ancillary congregations are through the public announcements during the worship services and in the church bulletin and the newsletter the *Carillon*. Most Riverside members are unaware of these formal and informal congregations. Another way is to have each of these groups sponsor and plan a Sunday worship service and participate in it. The service would highlight some of the group's activities and introduce the main congregation to them. It also would allow nonchurch members and visitors of each group to become acquainted with Riverside as a worshiping community.

Issues for Riverside in the New Millennium

Throughout its history, the Riverside Church has been viewed not only as the "Protestant cathedral," a place to address national concerns, but also as a role model for other churches, particularly those with large memberships and endowments. What Riverside does in the new millennium will therefore influence many congregations across the country.

While it is difficult to forecast what Riverside's future issues will be, a few important ones need to be considered in any kind of long-term planning: The Master Plan, the Jubilee Fund, a Riverside Church community development corporation, fiscal crises, and demographic trends.

The Master Plan

In 1995 the Senior Management and Council commissioned the firm of Body Lawson, Ben Paul Associated Architects and Planners to draw up plans for building renovations at Riverside. In September 1996 the Church Council presented the two-volume Riverside Church Master Plan to the congregation. The plan described the proposed renovations of the church building, which included tearing down a wall to create a new entrance on Claremont Avenue and constructing an eight-story addition to the Martin Luther King Jr. Wing (previously called the South Wing). Part of the construction would include the Cloister Garden. The eight-story addition would replace the Stone Gymnasium, which is deteriorating. The major rationale for the changes is that the Claremont Avenue entrance to the church is used more often than the entrance on Riverside Drive, which is usually closed for security reasons. The plan would upgrade the Claremont entrance significantly, since it symbolically faces and welcomes the city.

Then a controversy over the master plan erupted.[111] A group called "Friends and Members of Riverside Church" mobilized efforts to stop the changes envisioned in the plan. One of its strategies was to have the church building receive a historic landmark designation from the New York State and National Trust for Historic Preservation. In 1997 the group filed an application with the Landmark Preservation Commission for Riverside to be designated a landmark.[112] The ensuing controversy has slowed the planned changes. The senior management and Church Council eventually agreed to have the 1930 Gothic cathedral building designated a landmark but not the South Wing building, which was completed in 1959. This action will allow the proposed renovations of the master plan to be completed sometime in the future.

The Jubilee Five-Year Plan for the Millennium and Jubilee Fund

In October 1999 at a lay/staff retreat, the groundwork was laid for Riverside's celebration of the new millennium and the symbolic idea of jubilee. The idea of jubilee is rooted in the Hebraic tradition that celebrated emancipation and freedom by freeing prisoners and forgiving debts every fifty years. In cooperation with the church groups working on the Jubilee plan, in October 2000 the leadership of the Riverside Church allocated $10 million to the fund to strengthen its outreach capacities and to build stronger internal organizations in the church, undergirded by spirituality and faith. The Jubilee Five-Year Plan for the Millennium decided on twelve goals: mission, pastoral care, worship, significant relational groups, strong leadership resources, solid participatory decision making, competent educational program and activities, accessibility and hospitality, high-visibility programs, use of space and facilities, solid financial resources, and intentional membership development.[113]

The Jubilee Fund will invest $10 million in four core areas of need in the greater Harlem community: community development, health care, public education, and youth outreach. "Riverside is ready to be a catalyst for change," said Dr. Forbes. "We are looking forward to creating partnerships and investing funds that will lead to the fulfillment of big dreams in Harlem." The Jubilee Fund will focus Riverside's efforts at social change and social justice in the local community. According to Rev. Bernard R. Wilson, executive minister, "A lot of what Riverside has done has focused on national or international issues such as the war in Vietnam, the death penalty, apartheid, and poverty. The Jubilee Fund represents a significant commitment to our community and neighbors." The Jubilee Fund Committee, headed by Rev. James Stallings, along with four subcommittees, has been formed to oversee the distribution of funds and the development of innovative ideas and programs.[114]

The Riverside Church Community Development Corporation

For a number of years, the Riverside congregation has adopted "Emancipation from Poverty" as an expression of both its faith and its commitment to social justice. An office also is dedicated to achieving such emancipation in practical terms. But in evaluating the church's programs dealing with the poor, only one really relates to the emancipatory theme, training poor people to become barbers. Although this is an important program, much more can be done to help poor people escape from poverty.

Other churches in the New York City area have developed "community development corporations," which use church funds combined with grants from the city, state, and federal governments to build housing and to establish small businesses. For example, under the leadership of Rev. Floyd Flake, the Allen African Methodist Episcopal Church in St. Albans, Queens, has produced mixed-income housing, small businesses, its own school from kindergarten to grade 12, and various other community projects. Through the Allen Community Development Corporation, millions of dollars in city, state, and federal funds have been used to help lift the area of Jamaica, Queens, out of poverty. The Abyssinian Baptist Church in Harlem, led by Rev. Calvin Butts, has also built housing through the Abyssinian Community Development Corporation. Similar housing and small business projects have been sponsored by the Canaan Baptist Church and the Malcolm Shabazz Masjid in Harlem. The emphasis has been on providing "mixed-income housing" for the poor, working class, and middle class. This type of housing is directed at breaking up the "social isolation of the poor," who often are concentrated in large housing projects like the Grant Houses. Mixed-income housing also ensures that role models of working adults will be available to poor children and teenagers. The founding of small businesses also provides work and career opportunities for the poor as well as training in job skills and attitudes.

The establishment of the Riverside Church Community Development Corporation (CDC) is a vehicle for bringing reform and change to poor neighborhoods. The CDC will be a separate, nonprofit institution that can receive government grants so as to avoid the issue of separation of church and state.

Fiscal Crises at the Riverside Church

A review of fiscal crises at the Riverside Church indicates the need for a more careful and judicious approach to cost cutting and budgetary matters. In the past, the trustees have seemed more interested in protecting the church's large endowment by cutting programs, staff, and constituencies, which has left the church's outreach and ministries with significant gaps. For example, when the Hispanic ministry's budget was severely reduced in 1969/70, the departure of that congregation left Riverside with no significant outreach to this neighborhood constituency for the next thirty-two years. Similarly, by eliminating the FM radio station, WRVR, the church has lost its radio and television constituency, whereas many successful megachurches have profited from their use of the media. The severe downsizing of staff, the elimination of the highly successful Riverside Dance Festival, and the reduction of Riverside's theater performances in 1988 only necessitated their rebuilding later from scratch. Rather than protecting its key programs and outreach ministries during stock market declines, the financial overseers at Riverside have chosen to allow the bottom line to dictate their actions, sometimes acting more like a secular corporation than a church. The leadership at Riverside needs to clarify its values and priorities and act accordingly.

Demographic Trends

For its ministry in the future, the leadership of the church will need to consider two demographic trends: the rapid growth of the Hispanic and the elderly populations. The 2000 census confirmed that the Hispanic population has become the largest minority in the country and in New York City. The Riverside Church needs to consider how it can reach out to Hispanics, particularly the Dominicans who populate the church's immediate neighborhood. The elderly population will more than double in size with the retirement of the baby boom generation and will need the church's ministry and social services. The new building in the master plan may provide space to meet the needs of this growing population, such as a senior drop-in center.

Conclusion

As we have seen, contemporary spirituality at the Riverside Church is diverse and complex. Riverside is not one congregation but many congregations or, as the title of this chapter puts it, "congregations within a congregation," in which different formal and informal congregations attempt to satisfy the spiritual quests of their participants. While the Sunday morning worship service continues to remain a central focus, attracting many adherents, other New Yorkers and visitors find their spiritual fulfillment by attending musical concerts, theater arts events, or visiting prisoners. The Riverside Church has attempted to remain a holistic institution, meeting as many needs as its resources permit.

Riverside's future looks bright because it is continuing to grow and bring in new members. At the present time, it is financially healthy, its endowment having almost tripled in the past decade. But its real strength lies with its talented, dedicated, and hardworking lay leaders, clergy, and staff members. Riverside has continued to provide national and international leadership as America's "Protestant cathedral." It is a much more diverse church than it has ever been in terms of race, gender, and sexual orientation. It has continued to combine both depth in spirituality and commitment to social justice. Despite its own internal controversies, the Riverside Church has remained a solid rock of faith that can provide an example of a congregation meeting the challenges of the new millennium.

NOTES

1. Paul Tillich, *Systematic Theology* (Chicago: University of Chicago Press, 1952), vol. 1, 12–14. Also see James Luther Adams, *Paul Tillich's Philosophy of Culture, Science, and Religion* (New York: Harper & Row, 1965).

2. Interview with Betty Davis, an information technology architect with IBM and chair of the Church Council, July 9, 2000.

3. W. S. F. Pickering, *The Elementary Forms of Religious Life*, in *Durkheim on Religion*, edited by W. S. F. Pickering (Atlanta: American Academy of Religion, 1994), 135–37.

4. Sociologists use the term *megachurch* to describe congregations with two thousand or more members. Megachurches also have other characteristics such as multiple ministries and a large staff. Throughout most of its history Riverside has

had a membership ranging from 2,000 to 3,500. Because most of the megachurches in the United States are conservative evangelical or Pentecostal in theological orientation, the Riverside Church is unusual in having a liberal theological heritage.

5. "Report on the Think Tank on Urban Ministry," 4, meeting at Grey Dunes, Long Island, on Friday, March 18, to Sunday, March 20, 1972. RC Archives, Metropolitan Mission Study, 1972, GG 2, RG 4, box 395. Italics added.

6. Dr. Reginal Atwater, chair of the Hospitality to Visitors Committee, stated that his committee was "formulating plans to greet the large number of summer visitors to the church, especially the colored people, and that a Negro will be in the Narthex to help with this phase of the project." Meeting of the Executive Council on Christian Services, Outreach and Public Information, March 4, 1956, box 141, stack E, RG 9, file 5.

7. For a description of the changing demography of Harlem and Morningside Heights in the late 1930s, see Felix Riesenberg and Alexander Alland, *Portrait of New York* (New York: Macmillan, 1939). Also see John G. Van Dusen, "Morningside Heights, Inc." (B.A. senior thesis, Princeton University, 1954), 27.

8. Rev. James Forbes, quoted in *Ten Great Preachers*, edited by Bill Turpie (Grand Rapids, Mich.: Baker Books, 2000), 56.

9. Interview with Mr. Richard Butler, chair of the Search Committee, February 4, 2001.

10. Ibid.

11. Ibid.

12. Interview with Dr. Katherine Wilcox, chair of the board of deacons and later chair of the Church Council, February 4, 2001.

13. Report by Timothy M. Taylor to "The Riverside Church Study Commission on the Advantages of a Unicameral Board," October 28, 1970, 2.

14. According to the minutes of the Study Commission of the Unicameral Board, January 6, 1971, "legal consultation indicates that a special enactment by the New York State Legislature would be required in order for the church to adopt a unicameral board."

15. Interview with Butler.

16. "Unicameral board" (also known as the Riverside Organization Committee), RG 3.7, p. 1.

17. Riverside Organization Committee, "Proposal Review Package," p. 3.

18. Interview with Jeffrey Slade, February 13, 2001.

19. Interview with Rev. James Forbes, June 9, 2000.

20. Similar preaching workshops had previously been held, during the pastorates of Drs. Fosdick and Coffin.

21. Interview with Butler.

22. Interview with Rev. James Forbes, July 20, 2000.

23. Chronology provided by the "Riversiders for Riverside" letter, November 19, 1992, 2–3.

24. Rocco Parascandola, "'Holy War' of Pastors Rocks Riverside's Congregation," *New York Post*, April 20, 1992; Ari L. Goldman, "Riverside's Pastor at Center of Turmoil," *New York Times*, May 18, 1992; Al Amateau, "Riverside: No to Its Budget; Rift Remains," *The Westsider*, May 21–27, 1992.

25. "A Request to the Church Council of the Riverside Church from the Senior Minister and the Executive Minister," signed by Forbes and Dyson, March 2, 1992.

26. Memo from Will Kennedy to members of the Church Council of the Riverside Church, March 8, 1992.

27. "Riversiders for Riverside" letter, November 19, 1992.

28. Letter from Rev. David W. Dyson, executive minister, to the Members of the Riverside Church Council and Dr. James A. Forbes Jr., senior minister, May 26, 1992.

29. See the collection of letters, "Riversiders for Riverside," which also includes letters from individual members.

30. Newsletter from "Riversiders for Riverside," January 18, 1992.

31. See the letter to the Church Council, "Our Current Leadership Crisis," sent unsigned by some members of the church staff, February 17, 1992. Also see the signed letter supporting Forbes, February 20, 1992.

32. Interview with Slade.

33. Interview with Rev. Brenda Stiers, executive minister, July 8, 2000.

34. See the study by Carl S. Dudley and David A. Roozen, "Faith Communities Today: A Report on Religion in the United States Today" (Hartford: Hartford Institute for Religion Research of the Hartford Seminary, March 2001), 34–38. According to the study, changes in worship patterns and financial crises are at the root of most conflicts in American congregations.

35. According to Rev. Keith Boyer, who was in charge of the Membership Office at Riverside in 2000.

36. Different church staff members have given different figures for the percentage of the African Americans at Riverside. Rev. Keith Boyer, the former minister in charge of the Membership Office, gave an estimate of 70 percent African American members. Rev. Sally E. Norris, the minister in charge of the Membership Office in 2001, estimated a 60 percent African American congregational membership. She said that the total membership includes members who live at a distance from New York City and are predominantly white. The active membership is 70 percent African American.

37. "Riverside Church Survey Report," 1956, 20.

38. (No author listed), *The Riverside Church: One Hundred Years of Historical Background, 1841–1941*, a one-hundredth anniversary edition commemorating the founding of the church, February 1941, 14. Also see James Hudnut-Beumler, *The*

Riverside Church: A Brief History of Its Founding, Leadership and Finances (New York: Riverside Church, 1990), 6.

39. Hudnut-Beumler, *The Riverside Church*, 46.

40. "Riverside Church Survey Report," 1956, 21.

41. D. J. Livermore, "Supplementary Report on Attendance at the Riverside Church," September 22, 1955, 2. Her reported figures on church attendance were totaled and divided by seventeen years for the annual average during this period.

42. "Riverside Church Survey Report," 1956, 46.

43. Will Herberg, *Protestant, Catholic, Jew: An Essay in American Religious Sociology* (Garden City, N.Y.: Anchor Books, 1960).

44. "Riverside Church Survey Report," 1956, 14.

45. David Roozen and Dean Hoge, *Understanding Church Growth and Decline* (Cleveland: Pilgrim Press, 1979).

46. Ushers Directory, 1968, lists the ushers and the date that each was elected; box 263, shelf 25, cage 2.

47. According to Elsa Sharpe, a Riverside Church member since 1952, T. Floyd Lenart became the first woman usher in 1973. The efforts to have women ushers was led by Josephine Bock Jones. Interview with Elsa Sharpe, March 14, 2002.

48. *Carillon*, summer 2001, 3.

49. See Livermore, "Supplementary Report," 3; and "The Riverside Church Membership Census Report," August 2000.

50. "Riverside Church Survey Report," 1956, 21.

51. Livermore, "Supplementary Report," 3.

52. All the tables in this chapter are from "The Riverside Church Membership Census Report, 2000," with artwork by Joel Dautruche and Latisha Dautruche. Used by permission of the Riverside Church. Those who helped formulate the Membership Census Report of August 2000 were Rev. Keith Boyer, Membership Office; Rev. Susan Blain, Worship; Daniel Karslake, Stewardship and Communications; Corinne Nelson, Communications; Jane Donahue, Grants; Jill Fernandez, Human Resources; Roberta Cardwell, Information Technology; Rev. Fanny Erickson, Membership and Parish Life; Tinoa Rodgers, Media; Elizabeth Alexander, Children and Youth Ministries; Tanya Dunlap, Executive Minister's Office; and Dr. Sheila Gillams, Riverside History Project. Latisha Dautruche and Joel Dautruche calculated the statistics and produced the final report.

53. Interview with Rev. Kanyere Eaton, staff minister in charge of the Food Pantry and Thrift Store, June 29, 2000.

54. Letter to the Chinese Christian Fellowship on their thirtieth anniversary from Rev. Eugene Laubach, March 28, 1980. Mr. Heyward Wong, founder of the CCF, provided a copy of the letter from its files.

55. Interview with Mr. Heyward Wong, founder of the Chinese Christian Fellowship, July 13, 2000.

56. Ibid., letter to the Riverside Church by members of the Hispano-American Task Force of the Riverside Church, dated October 25, 1971.

57. *Carillon*, December 4, 1971.

58. Interview with Rev. Bernahu Wedneh, February 4, 2001.

59. Ibid.

60. Most of the information on Riverside's youth and young adult ministry came from an interview with Rev. Mariah Britton, June 27, 2000.

61. The terms *B-boys* and *B-girls* refer to the development of original and creative dances styles of hip-hop culture, which include "popping, locking, and breaking." The "B" comes from the break-dancing style that was popular in the 1970s and 1980s.

62. Ben Higa, "Fred Berry and Pee Wee Dance Have Got Class—Period," *Rap Pages*, May 1999, 36.

63. Pee Wee Dance, "DANCE TO THE DRUMMERS BEAT," workshop class handout, 4. Class visit by me, February 2, 2001.

64. Interview with Britton.

65. Grace Lichenstein, "The Home Run That Broke a Girl's Heart," *New York Times*. October 1, 2001, D10.

66. Interview with Mr. Ernie Lorch, July 12, 2000.

67. Interview with Britton.

68. Interview with Lorch.

69. William C. Rhoden, "Looking inside the Church for Answers," *New York Times*, March 4, 2000.

70. Interview with Lorch.

71. Rhoden, "Looking inside the Church."

72. Interview with Rev. Sally E. Norris, February 14, 2001.

73. Ibid.

74. See Alfred Schutz's concept of "multiple realities," which speaks about the ability of human beings to move to different tensions of consciousness in musical concerts, drama events, films, and the ritual enactments of religion. In *Collected Papers*, edited by Maurice Natanson (The Hague: M. Nijoff, 1962–66). Peter Berger, Thomas Luckmann, and Robert Bellah have used Schutz's analysis of multiple realities in their work on religion in modern industrial societies.

75. Program notes, "Dedication and Inaugural Recital of the Robert James Mc-Cracken Memorial Piano," Sunday, October 6, 1974, 3.

76. Kamiel Lefevere, carillonneur, and Grace H. Patton, raconteur, *The Laura Spelman Rockefeller Memorial Carillon of the Riverside Church: A Brief Story of Its History, Structure and Use* (New York: Riverside Church, 1945), 6–7.

77. Phillip E. Everett, "The Riverside Symphony Orchestra," *Church Monthly*, April 1936, 122.

78. "The First Organ," in *The Organs of Riverside* (New York: Riverside Church, 1995), 2, 3.

79. Ibid.

80. Sketch of Virgil Fox's career, "Virgil Fox (1912–1980)," in archives.

81. Livermore, "Supplementary Report," 6, 10.

82. Comments by Professor James Washington during a visit by a research team before the formation of the Riverside History Project, June 1996.

83. Interview with Dr. Timothy Smith, director of music and organist of the Riverside Church, March 14, 2002.

84. Ibid.

85. Ibid.

86. Constance L. Ball, chair, "Report on the Development of the Program of Religious Drama in the Riverside Church," March 18, 1964, 2.

87. Ibid., 3.

88. Ball, "Report," exhibit B, "What Is Meant by Religious Drama," 12.

89. Ball, "Report," exhibit B, "What Is Meant by Religious Drama," 12, quoting Joseph Duffey, "Religious Values in Reading," *United Church Herald*, April 6, 1961. I added "a play" to Duffey's comments about the religious dimensions of books.

90. Ball, "Report," exhibit B, "What Is Meant by Religious Drama," 12.

91. Emily Deeter, director of public relations, "La Famiglia," *Riverside News*, May 31, 1974, 29–30.

92. Interview with Jewel Miguel, director of the Riverside Theater, February 14, 2001.

93. Ruth St. Denis, widely acknowledged as the "mother of modern dance," and her husband Ted Shawn formed the Denishawn School in 1915, which trained some of the most influential modern dancers of the century: Martha Graham, Doris Humphrey, and Charles Weidman. See Women's Stories, http://writetools .com/women/stories/stdenis_ruth.html. In reaction to the more Catholic view of Mary in the presentation, the Riverside Guild's newsletter commented, "Though we do not accept the theological implications of the presentation, we are in harmony with its symbolic message, and its spirit of beauty and reverence." *Horizons*, January 10, 1935.

94. David K. Manion, director of the Riverside Dance Festival, in the "Riverside Dance Festival Retrospective," *Program Bulletin*, January 5, 1982. Although Riverside began experimenting with liturgical dance in 1934, a more formal dance program was not started until 1963 as part of the Program of Religious Drama. See Leslie Martin, "Dance at Riverside Church, New York City (1930–1980), unpublished paper written for New York University Department of Dance and Dance Education, 8; box 394, shelf GG1, cage 2, Dr. Eugene Laubach's papers.

95. Martin, "Dance at Riverside Church."

96. Interview with Miguel.

97. Manion, "Riverside Dance."

98. List of Dance Company performances at the Riverside Theater from 1982 to 1984, RG 17.1.

99. Brochure of the Second Annual New York Family Arts Festival: "Building Community One Family at a Time."

100. Interview with Miguel.

101. Ibid.

102. Interview with Martha Rolon, associate director of social services and social worker, June 29, 2000.

103. Interview with Rev. Kanyere Eaton, June 29, 2000.

104. Interview with Betty Davis, July 9, 2000.

105. For examples, see John N. Vaughn, *Megachurches and America's Cities: How Churches Grow* (Grand Rapids, Mich.: Baker Books, 1993); Scott L. Thumma, "Megachurches of Atlanta," in *Religions of Atlanta*, edited by Gary Laderman (Atlanta: Scholars Press, 1996); Scott L. Thumma, "The Kingdom, the Power and the Glory: The Megachurch in Modern American Society" (Ph.D. diss., Emory University, 1996); and Lawrence H. Mamiya, "A Social History of the Bethel African Methodist Episcopal Church ion Baltimore: The House of God and the Struggle for Freedom," in *American Congregations*, vol. 1, edited by James P. Wind and James W. Lewis (Chicago: University of Chicago Press, 1994).

106. Interview with Corinne Nelson, director of communications and chair of the All Staff Committee, March 14, 2002.

107. See HayGroup, "Hay Study Review of Compensation and Benefits at the Riverside Church by the HayGroup," report to the Personnel and Salary Committee, April 10, 2000.

108. Interview with Nelson.

109. See Emile Durkheim, *The Elementary Forms of the Religious Life*, translated by Carol Cosman and abridged with an introduction and notes by Mark S. Cladis (New York: Oxford University Press, 2001).

110. "Report on the Think Tank on Urban Ministry," meeting at Grey Dunes, Long Island on Friday, March 18, to Sunday, March 20, 1972, 4; RC archives, Metropolitan Mission Study, 1972, GG 2, RG 4, box 395.

111. Lauren Rubin, "A Landmarking Battle of Gothic Proportions," *The Westsider*, November 1996.

112. See flyer from Friends and Members of Riverside Church to "Riversiders, New Yorkers, and Citizens of the World," n.d. Some of the members of "Friends" are also from "Riversiders for Riverside."

113. See draft 4, "Jubilee Five-Year Plan for the New Millennium," April 16, 2000.

114. *Carillon*, summer 2001, 1.

About the Contributors

John Wesley Cook is a professor emeritus at Yale University and a past president of the Henry Luce Foundation. His Ph.D. from Yale University was in religion and the arts, with a dissertation on Gothic architecture, especially that in Germany. He has published books, articles, and videotapes about Christianity and the arts. His major interest is in the material culture of Christianity and how it has functioned theologically.

James Hudnut-Beumler is the Anne Potter Wilson Distinguished Professor of American Religious History and dean of Vanderbilt University's divinity school. He received his Ph.D. degree in religion from Princeton University. He is the author of *Looking for God in the Suburbs: The Religion of the American Dream and Its Critics, 1945-1965* and *Generous Saints: Congregations Rethinking Money and Ethics.*

Lawrence H. Mamiya, Paschall-Davis Professor of Religion and Africana Studies at Vassar College, received his Ph.D. degree in the sociology of religion and social ethics from Columbia University. He is the coauthor with C. Eric Lincoln of *The Black Church in the African American Experience* and "Faith Based Institutions and Family Services in African American Muslim Masjids and Black Churches," *Journey Inward, Journey Outward.* He also received a Distinguished Book Award from the Society for the Scientific Study of Religion and a major research grant for the study of the black churches and African American Muslim congregations.

Martin E. Marty is the Fairfax M. Cone Distinguished Service Professor Emeritus at the University of Chicago.

Peter J. Paris, Elmer G. Homrighausen Professor of Christian Social Ethics at Princeton Theological Seminary, received his Ph.D. degree in ethics and society from the University of Chicago. He is the author of *The Social Teaching of the Black Churches* and *The Spirituality of African Peoples: The Search for a Common Moral Discourse*. He has been elected president of the American Academy of Religion, the Society of Christian Ethics, and the Society for the Study of Black Religion. He is currently directing a multiyear Pan-Africa Seminar on Religion and Poverty among African Peoples on the Continent and in the Diaspora.

Leonora Tubbs Tisdale, a free-lance author, preacher, and teacher, is a parish associate at the Presbyterian Church in Basking Ridge, New Jersey, and the former Elizabeth M. Engle Associate Professor of Preaching and Worship at Princeton Theological Seminary from which she also received her Ph.D. degree. She is the author of *Preaching as Local theology and Folk Art* and coeditor, with Brian K. Blount, of *Making Room at the Table: An Invitation to Multicultural Worship*. She is currently the vice-president of the Academy of Homiletics.

Judith Weisenfeld, an associate professor of religion at Vassar College, received her Ph.D. degree in religion from Princeton University. She is the author of *African-American Women and Christian Activism: New York's Black YWCA, 1905–1945* and the editor, with Richard Newman, of *This Far by Faith: Readings in African American Women's Religious Biography*. She has been a visiting fellow at the Institute for the Advanced Study of Religion at Yale University and the recipient of a summer stipend from the National Endowment for the Humanities.

Index

African Americans, growing presence of, 37, 289, 339n. 36
Armitage, Dr. Thomas, 143

Ball, Constance, 325
Benedict, Dr. George, 142
Benevolence Committee, 187, 190–191, 194–197, 207–208; reports of, 190, 231n. 26, 232nn. 38, 39. *See also* Jubilee Fund
Black Christian Caucus, 205, 256–261
Black Manifesto, 88–89, 208, 258–261
Britten, Rev. Mariah, 310–311, 314
Britten, Ted, first black usher, 38
Business and Professional Women's Group, 24–26, 192–193, 327; sixtieth anniversary celebration of, 232n. 41; Mary L. Stockwell, 24–25

Campbell, Ernest T.: early years, 84–88; James Forman issue, 88–89; governance issues, 45–46; installation of, 84; mission of, 34, 43; preaching method of, 91–94; worship during his years, 93–94
Carder, Eugene, 163
Chartres Cathedral, 140, 147, 158–159
Chinese Christian Fellowship (CCF), 306–307
Christian Century: on Fosdick's evangelical liberalism, 61; on McCracken, 179–180; on opening of Riverside, 19, 20–21; on Riverside and the city, 184–185
Coffin, William Sloane Jr., 34, 43; "Alex's Death" sermon, 103–104; disarmament program, 102; early life, 97–98; on ho-

mosexuality, 102; "On Homosexuality" sermon, 39; opposed by the men's Bible class, 103; preaching of, 99–106; sermons against hypocrisy, 53n. 30; theology of, 99; view of churches, 180; view of protest, 181; view of spirituality, 182; visits U.S. hostages in Iran, 100–101; worship during his years, 106–107
Collegium, in the 1960s, 44–45
Congregation(s), 279–281, 289–290
Cotto, Reverend Pablo, 45, 202–204
Cotto, Reverend Raphael, 201–202, 308

Davis, Betty, 279
Driver, Tom, 324
Dyson, Reverend David W., 286–287, 339n. 25

Ebony Ecumenical Ensemble, 107, 323
Einstein, Albert, 154–155, 306
Eisenhower, President Dwight, lays cornerstone for Interchurch Center, 130n. 48
Erickson, Reverend Fanny, 305
Ethiopian Orthodox Tewahedo Church of Our Saviour, 290, 308–310

Fagan, Gertrude, 325
Fifth Avenue Baptist Church, 143
Forbes, James A, Jr.: anti-apartheid activity of, 113; anti-poverty preaching of, 114; dispute with David Dyson, 50; early life of, 109–111; early years at Riverside, 282–289; goals for diversity, 238n. 144; Good Neighbor Week, 226;